Greek and Macedonian
Land Battles of the
4th Century B.C.

ALSO BY FRED EUGENE RAY, JR.

*Land Battles in 5th Century B.C. Greece:
A History and Analysis of 173 Engagements*
(McFarland, 2009; paperback 2011)

Greek and Macedonian Land Battles of the 4th Century B.C.

A History and Analysis of 187 Engagements

FRED EUGENE RAY, JR.

McFarland & Company, Inc., Publishers
Jefferson, North Carolina, and London

LIBRARY OF CONGRESS CATALOGUING-IN-PUBLICATION DATA

Ray, Fred Eugene, 1949–
Greek and Macedonian land battles of the 4th century B.C. :
a history and analysis of 187 engagements / Fred Eugene Ray, Jr.
p.   cm.
Includes bibliographical references and index.

ISBN 978-0-7864-6973-4
softcover : acid free paper ∞

1. Military art and science — Greece — History — To 500.
2. Military art and science — Macedonia.
3. Greece — History, Military — To 146 B.C.
4. Macedonia — History, Military.   5. Military history, Ancient.
6. Battles — History.   I. Title.
U33.R394 2012   355.4'8093809014 — dc23   2012033872

BRITISH LIBRARY CATALOGUING DATA ARE AVAILABLE

© 2012 Fred Eugene Ray, Jr. All rights reserved

*No part of this book may be reproduced or transmitted in any form
or by any means, electronic or mechanical, including photocopying
or recording, or by any information storage and retrieval system,
without permission in writing from the publisher.*

On the cover: Greek marble relief, ca. 330 B.C.,
depicting a soldier in combat (Ny Carlsberg Glyptotek,
Copenhagen, Denmark)

Manufactured in the United States of America

*McFarland & Company, Inc., Publishers
Box 611, Jefferson, North Carolina 28640
www.mcfarlandpub.com*

To my wife, Marleen, and
my father and mother, Fred and Laura Ray—
thanks for everything!

Table of Contents

Preface   1

Introduction   3

I. Sparta Ascendant
Overseas Battles and the Corinthian War (400–387 B.C.)   5

II. Trained in War
*Battles Around the Mediterranean;
Chalcidian, Boeotian and Spartan Wars (386–360 B.C.)*   38

III. Finding a Master
*Rise of Macedonia; Sacred, Persian and Sicilian Wars;
Conquest of Greece (359–336 B.C.)*   86

IV. Action and Glory
Battles in the Era of Alexander the Great (335–324 B.C.)   138

V. Many Great Combats
Battles of the Successors (323–301 B.C.)   174

Conclusions   210

Appendices: Pitched Battles 400–301 B.C.

1: Combat Factors   213

2: Decisive Factors   217

3: Heavy Infantry Losses and Point/Cause of Formation Failure   221

Bibliography   227

Index   233

Preface

Longtime interest in ancient Greek military affairs led me a few years ago to write a book on land engagements in which I explored both probability and the available literature toward trying to determine what actually happened on all of the significant battlegrounds of classical Greece. For practical reasons, that work covered only the 5th century B.C., a limitation that let me incorporate the earliest reliable descriptions of Grecian pitched actions while keeping the time frame and associated volume of data to a manageable level. Needless to say, it was an exercise that only whetted my appetite for taking an even wider look at the topic. This current volume is my attempt to satisfy that hunger by delving into the next century using a similar approach. Once more, the aim is to try and separate myth from reality toward gaining a better grasp upon past ways of war that influence how we still look at mortal combat today.

The technique here uses information drawn from ancient accounts along with suitable analogs to produce descriptions of what most likely happened on the subject battlefields. Following multiple threads of evidence in their historical context, this involves correlating and reconciling every datum (some quite peripheral in nature) and applying logical projections where needed to fill gaps and resolve conflicts in the surviving records. Where major alternatives exist, I've tried to list them; nevertheless, a preferred version is presented whenever possible. This reflects my belief that multiple projections are no more likely to have the exact same probability than bags of salt to have precisely the same number of grains. There should always be a "most likely" scenario based on the evidence at hand. Of course, we must never forget that fresh information at a later date can profoundly alter judgments on what is truly more probable. As a result, anyone following this path has to be willing to stick his neck out on some close calls, yet equally ready to revise those interpretations in light of new data.

Attempting a book like this requires one to stand on the broad shoulders of many talented historians who have gone before, both ancient and modern. Vital classical sources for 4th century B.C. warfare include Xenophon, Diodorus of Sicily, Plutarch, Frontinus, Polyaenus and Arrian; the surviving works of these men along with those of a goodly number of lesser contributors have been my constant companions throughout the writing process. Nor have modern authors been any less helpful. Here, I can name Hans Delbruck, J.F.C. Fuller, W.K. Pritchett, Victor Davis Hanson, Nicholas Sekunda and Nick Sabin among the more influential. And there's another set of scholars that I'd like to acknowledge who've kindly traded ideas with me from around the world through the medium of cyberspace. These include Paul McDonnell-Staff, Michael Park, Paul Bardunias and Dan Powers — honorable gentlemen all that have tried to keep me from folly on a variety of subjects in recent years, with resulting failures being mine and not theirs. References to all of the foregoing sources appear parenthetically enclosed within the text (MLA format), as do any footnote comments.

The reconstructions that follow generally appear in chronological sequence; however, a few series of events fall into natural geographic groupings and are so collected to create some minor overlaps in time order. Where battles are mentioned during discussions of significantly earlier or later actions, I've attached their dates to allow easier referral to the principle descriptions (all dates in the text are B.C. unless otherwise noted). As always, transliteration of the Greek alphabet poses a problem and I've followed the course of using Latinized or English equivalents wherever these are likely to be more familiar to the modern reader. Similarly, where Greek or other foreign terms make their initial appearance, they are always in italics with an English translation. Units of measure (distance, area, weight) are uniformly expressed in the metric system as the primary reference. The maps and battle diagrams included here were drafted by Joan Huckaby, whose skills and patience have made something eminently presentable out of my crude originals.

Introduction

Warfare in 4th century B.C. Greece has long held great fascination for the military enthusiast and general public alike. This is due to that period's intriguing mixture of famous battles and storied commanders. Capturing imaginations from ancient days to the present, these have inspired a host of histories, biographies and popular fictions that have turned them into the stuff of legend. As a result, even the most sober tactical analyses can be quite reverential regarding the key engagements of this time. Likewise, noted generals of the age like Xenophon and Iphicrates of Athens, Epaminondas of Thebes and the father-son team of Philip II and Alexander the Great of Macedonia are frequently made out to have been veritable gods of war. We should recognize, however, that all this runs the risk of distorting the real contributions of these events and men to the fighting arts. So lofty are their reputations that everything that went before can seem simplistic or obsolete. But is this truly the case?

I've attempted to answer the foregoing question by reconstructing all of the 4th century's significant land engagements. Putting these into historical perspective allows at least a hazy glimpse into what actually took place on battlegrounds of the day. Of course, the spottily preserved and oft contradictory nature of our surviving records means that this is an undertaking unavoidably rich in conjecture. The results must therefore be treated with a sensible level of reserve. All the same, when carried out conscientiously and within reasonable bounds, this is an exercise that can reveal a great deal about otherwise unknowable probabilities regarding the true character of mortal combat in the subject era.

A major revelation along these lines concerns the introduction of tactical improvements. Col. Thomas Hammes (2004) has examined patterns common to modern warfare and noted that new forms of fighting never seem to arrive as fully developed instruments. Instead, he sees a more gradual process of evolution. This spans decades, with fresh approaches growing out of (and existing alongside) still vital methodologies of old. Data from the 4th century appear to strongly support this view. Progression of the Grecian military arts at that time was a cumulative affair, composed of many step-like advances rather than a few revolutionary leaps.

Other key findings concern the role played by the aforementioned iconic commanders. Greek warfare in the 5th century had been a tale of militiamen struggling to cope on battlefields where their equally amateur generals fought in the ranks just like any other soldier. Over the next 100 years, this would change dramatically. Professional troops of various stripes increased in importance and their leaders tended to become full-time warlords that dominated by devising different ways to wage their conflicts. Still, it's clear that even the most lauded among these military innovators lifted and adapted their signature ideas at least in part from previous routines. Of course, we should never undervalue the creativity, industry and daring that this required. It took a quick intellect and hard work to appreciate and adopt or alter a novel technique, and also a good deal of courage to then apply it in the field, where the cost of being wrong would be measured in blood. Nonetheless, we still need to honor the historical roots that seem to nourish even the greatest of military geniuses. Gods of war these men may have been, yet if so, they were surely mortal gods — products not only of their own abilities and experience, but of those of their predecessors as well.

Finally, one of the more intriguing insights gained from reconstructing 4th century combats is that some celebrated campaign and battlefield successes attributed to the use of groundbreaking tactics were, in fact, very closely run affairs. Their outcomes could have gone either way and were often every bit as subject to the whims of choice and chance as to any tactical maneuver. Recognition of this reality fosters an enhanced appreciation for the phrase "fortunes of war."

I. Sparta Ascendant

Overseas Battles and the Corinthian War (400–387 B.C.)

> "Although the Spartans during this [Corinthian] war had been rather evenly matched with their opponents, they nevertheless gained a much more eminent position from this so-called Peace of Antalcidas."
>
> *Xenophon (Hellenica 5.1.36)*

The Grecian domain of classical times was a collection of some 1,000 city-states or *poleis* (*polis* singular) whose borders stretched around the Mediterranean basin, reaching east-west from Asia Minor to the shores of modern France and north-south from today's Ukraine to the coast of North Africa. At the center of this politically divided but culturally cohesive realm sat mainland Greece at the southeastern tip of Europe. It was from here that the Greeks had sailed and marched out to expand across the region and it was here where most of their more powerful states and most revered shrines still stood at the dawn of the 4th century B.C. But Greece at this time was a badly wounded land, one yet recovering from the longest and most devastating conflict in its history. The leading poleis of Sparta and Athens had spent most of the last third of the 5th century in a violent struggle for culture-wide dominance known as the Peloponnesian War. Waged all across the Grecian world, this grand fight had only ended with the exhaustion and surrender of Athens in 404. The legacy of the war was still very much in evidence as the new century opened, not only around its original epicenter on the European mainland, but on fresh battlegrounds overseas as well.

A Grecian War in Africa

One place where fallout from the great conflict between Sparta and Athens had significant impact was in the Peloponnesian Peninsula of southwestern Greece. This was the site of Lacedaemon (Laconia), home to the war's victors, the Spartans. Sparta had used its powerful army to intimidate the surrounding peoples into a series of bilateral treaties that created a military alliance that the ancients called "the Lacedaemonians and their friends," but is better known today as the Peloponnesian League. This arrangement was vital to Sparta in providing the manpower needed to remain a leading state. Spartan citizens were few in number even by the modest population standards of the day, the result of a strict social system that kept their nation under control of a very small body of elite warriors led by two general-kings. The *spartiatoi* or spartiates in this uppermost class spent their lives from childhood to old age in pursuit of military excellence. Taking the field in crimson tunics and gleaming, bronze armor, they marched into combat at a slow, menacing pace to the sound of pipes, carrying all before them to win fame as the greatest foot soldiers of their age. Yet both numbers and auxiliary arms were valuable in war as well. And it was for these that the Peloponnesian League was crucial to Sparta, providing additional spearmen as well as ships and cavalry. The Spartans therefore put a priority on shoring up cracks in their regional dominance created during the long struggle with Athens. This included removing a long-standing local threat — the Messenians.

At the base of Spartan society were serfs called helots (*helotoi*). These tilled the land in support of the spartiate caste (which held no other occupation save that of warrior). Distinct from the state's working freemen (the *perioikoi* or perioeci), helots were little better than slaves. They not only had to yield much of the fruits of their labor to the spartiates, but were subject to legal murder should those social betters ever want to put them in their place. Known as Messenians, both the perioeci and helots had once been free inhabitants of Laconia. The Spartans had arrived to conquer them in the 8th century as part of a mass migration into the Peloponnese of "Doric" peoples (Dorians, after their legendary homeland of Doris in central Greece). Some Messenians fled westward to join kin in the neighboring region bearing their people's name, Messenia. This land was eventually absorbed by the Spartans as well, though its inhabitants escaped slavery to become perioeci.

In the 460s many helots took advantage of a devastating earthquake to escape Laconia and bring Messenia into revolt against Sparta. Unable to drive the rebels out by force of arms, the Spartans agreed to a truce sometime 461–455. Athens had then intervened to settle the insurgents on the north shore of the Corinthian Gulf at Naupactus and on the island of Cephallenia off the northwestern Greek coast. These new poleis had been staunch allies of the Athenians during the Peloponnesian War and their very existence was a symbol of defiance to Spartan rule that might well inspire others, both subjects and vital League allies, to dream of similar independence; thus, the Spartans came down hard once Athens had been defeated. They evicted the Messenians from Naupactus and Cephallenia at spear-point and drove them out of Greece. Some of these outcasts landed at the Greek colony of Cyrene in North Africa, where a civil war was brewing that gave them an opportunity to fight for a new home.

Cyrene I (400 B.C.)

Cyrene lay due south of Greece on a large promontory west of Egypt. This area was rich in farming and grazing land and its Greek colonists had come to hold both the coastal plain and adjacent interior, their polis being at the center of several satellite settlements and lending its name to the entire region of Cyrenaica. Originally led by kings, Cyrene adopted a republican form of government c. 440, but wealthy elites continued to hold sway over the state. A Cyrenean named Ariston had recently led an uprising to seize power on behalf of the lower classes. The new rulers put some 500 of the polis' leading citizens to death and drove many others into exile. It was into this tense situation that the Messenians sailed in the spring of 400, coming ashore just east of Cyrene at its port of Apollonia. Making common cause with the exiles, the Messenians took up arms against the city.

The Cyrenean civil dispute was settled on the battlefield as exile and polis armies fought it out in what must have been a major action with several thousand men on each side. Though professional soldiers (mercenaries and state-supported citizens known as *epilektoi*) had become increasingly common during the 5th century, Cyrene, like most Greek states at this time, still relied primarily upon amateur militia for the core force of heavy infantry in its army. These soldiers, known as hoplites (*hoplitai*, *hoplites* singular), were the premier fighting men of the Greek world.

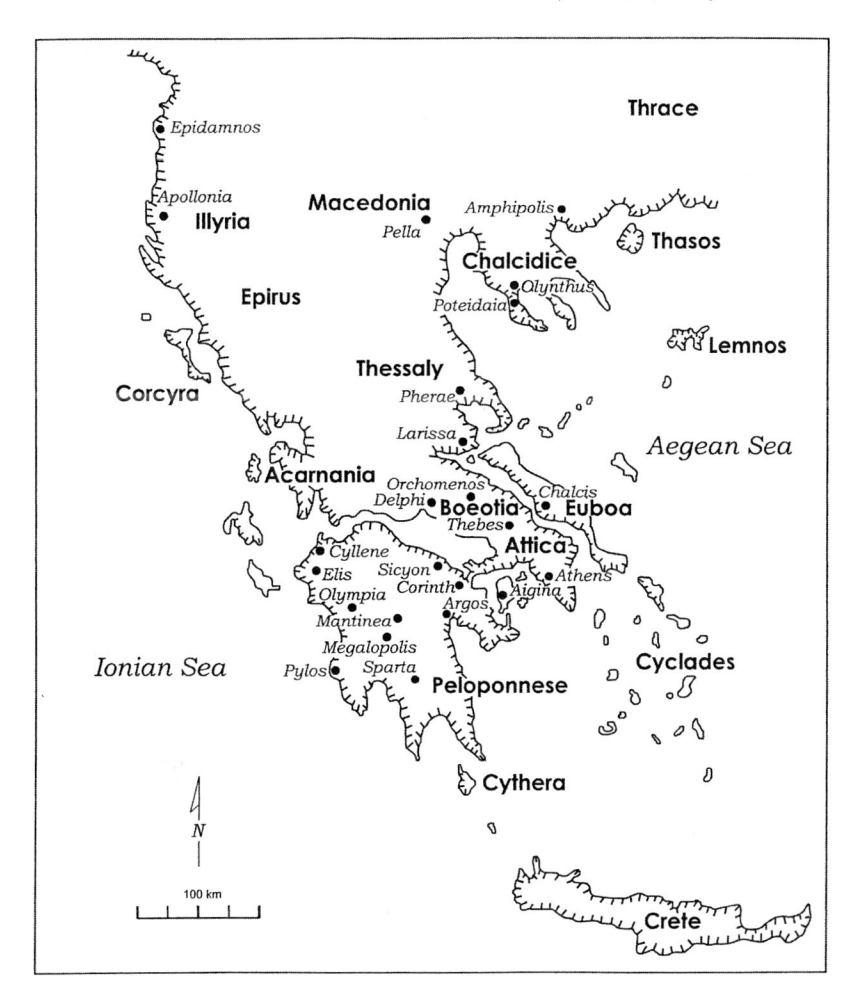

CLASSICAL GREECE

The hoplite's name derived from the Greek word for arms (*hopla, hoplon* singular) and he carried a thrusting spear or dory (*doru* or *enchos*) in the right hand as his main weapon. This was generally about 2.0–2.5m long with steel head and bronze or steel butt spike (*sauroter* or *styrax*). The shaft of the dory was of ash or some other light, strong wood with a grip of leather wrapped around the balance point, which sat about one third up from the butt due to both the weight of the sauroter and forward tapering. A hoplite would rest the dory on his shoulder while marching and carried it upright when awaiting contact with the enemy that it might provide some small protection from falling missiles. Lined up in stacked rows for battle, hoplites would lower their spear for *doratismos* (spear fighting). Most of the time, this involved use of an overhand grip that allowed more powerful strikes, though underhanded thrusting saw occasional use as well. In this way, the first two (less likely three) rows of spearmen could all reach the leading line of enemies standing opposite. The hoplite's most common secondary weapon was actually the back half of this same spear. Fitted with its sharp spike, the rear end of the dory could be jabbed down to either bury it and free the hand or finish off a fallen foe. However, spears often broke in front of the grip during a fight, leaving its owner with only the butt end. They could then reverse and use this stub as a shorter spear with the sauroter serving as its head. Should a hoplite lose this improvised pole-arm as well, he could grab for the sidearm hanging on his left hip.

This was usually one of two types, either a double-edged, straight sword (*xiphos*) or a downward curving saber (*machaira* or *kopis*) with cutting edge confined to its underside. The former was better for slashing around the side of an opposing shield and the latter more effective for striking down over the shield's top (its dull backside preventing inadvertent damage to comrades ranked behind).

Defensive gear for hoplites included a bronze helmet. This *kranos* was often high-crested (making its wearer appear taller and more menacing) with a nose-guarded variety (called "Corinthian") having slender slits for the eyes being most popular. There was also torso armor (*thorax*, generally of stiffened linen or leather in this era) with shoulder pieces (*epomides*) and kilt-like strips of material at the bottom (*pteruges*) that warded the loins. Hoplites also wore snap-on bronze greaves (*knemides*) on their shins. But the most important and distinctive piece of the Greek spearman's protective equipment was his large shield or *aspis* (*aspides* plural). This was made of wood sheathed on the forward surface (at least around the rim) by a thin layer (less than 0.5mm thick) of bronze. Other elements of his arms and armor (*panoplia* or panoply) might be discarded to save weight or expense, but the spear and aspis were essential. The aspis was heavy (nearly 7kg), round and about 1m across, covering from chin to knee with a concave shape that provided breathing space for the chest. This last prevented asphyxiation when a hoplite was crushed against the man ahead in file during concerted pushing attacks (*othismos*) that often characterized hoplite warfare (see Bardunias [2011, 63–65] for an excellent discussion of this process). Thickened, metal-reinforced rims on the shield enhanced its vital, domed shape and also helped prevent splitting from blows or pressure during combat. An aspis was held along the left forearm with a loop (*porpax*) at center that fit just below the elbow and a handgrip (*antilabe*) at the shield-edge. It thus covered the holder's left side while extending out to protect the right side of the man next in line.

Hoplites had light-armed support in the form of foot skirmishers and horsemen. These were all missile troops whose primary role during combat was to defend the flanks of their hoplite formation as it determined the battle's outcome. Light infantry lacked armor and was dominated by men using javelins (*palta* or *akontia*). In the 4th century, such fighters also carried a small shield (*pelte*) from which they were known as *peltastai* (peltasts). These javelineers could increase the accuracy and range of their weapons using a thong wrapped around the shaft which was unfurled during the throw to impart rifling-like spin. A man's last javelin was usually retained for close-in combat. Lesser numbers of foot skirmishers used longer ranging tools. These included archers (*toxotai*, using the bow or *toxon*) and slingers (*sphendonetai*, with the "shepherd's" sling).

Greek horsemen (*hippeis*) rode their small, shoeless mounts without stirrups. They seldom had shields and usually fought with javelins (though Athens had some mounted archers as well). Here again, a last javelin could serve as a short lance should hand-to-hand fighting become necessary. Riders formed compact rectangular, triangular and diamond shaped arrays and maneuvered at modest speed to better keep good order. Chariot-mounted horsemen were extinct in Greece, but still survived among the Greeks of Cyrene (as well as on the isle of Cyprus). Cyrenean chariots were similar to those used elsewhere in North Africa (by the Carthaginians and Libyans [Head 1982, 179–180]), featuring four horses and three passengers (Diodorus 22.40.41). The latter consisted of one driver and two fighting men armed with javelins. Chariots usually fought spaced out in a line and were accompanied by small teams of light infantry out-runners.

The contending armies came up against each other on the plain outside of Cyrene. Their manpower is highly speculative, but we can derive estimates from the lone number in our sources: 3,000 men for the Messenian contingent (Diodorus 14.33.3). These might have been some 2,400 hoplites and 600 javelinmen (assuming a ratio in line with prevailing trends in southern Greece, the original Messenian homeland). As for the exiles, they must have been at least equal in number. This suggests a combined rebel force of around 5,000 spearmen and 1,500 in light infantry. Mounted troops in this land famous for its horse breeding (Hornblower and Spawforth 1996, 421) would have been abundant by period standards. We might then propose 500 or so local cavalrymen with 50 chariots. This gives 650 horsemen in all, equal to about one for every four hoplites among the exiles and consistent with estimates for other horse-rich musters in this era. Granted that the city folk willingly offered open battle, it's likely that they fielded a fair match in heavy infantry. Yet they should have been stronger in mounted resources, since the Messenians had brought no cavalry on their voyage. Thus, even if the rebels had a larger number of aristocratic riders, we might still project that the city army probably held a 50 percent or better advantage in the size of its cavalry and chariot corps.

Both sides would have arrayed in some version of the ubiquitous main battle formation of classical Greece known as the "phalanx." This array is best distinguished as the "Doric phalanx" (after those old invaders into the Peloponnese, who are credited with its invention) to distinguish it from the "Macedonian phalanx" (a variant to which it would give rise in the mid-4th century). This was a linear body of hoplites ordered by rank and file, with ranks commonly ranging from hundreds to over 1,000 men in width. Files normally had a count of eight men, but could increase to provide greater combat capability (improving othismos, boosting confidence and crowding the way for anyone who might want to retreat from the front) or fit a narrow battlefield. Files could also be reduced. This sacrificed durability to provide a broader formation when needed, though files of less than six men were difficult to maneuver for all but the most professional troops (Goldsworthy 1996, 196–197). It was also hard to keep good order when traversing broken ground, thus phalanxes generally kept to the flattest terrain available. Spearmen in the phalanx stood with shields nearly overlapping, thus presenting a front of 1m per man (the width of his aspis). Not a very agile formation given its need for such tight spacing, the phalanx was at hazard at the back and on either end (especially the right, which was the hoplites' "spear" side where their file had no protection from shields held on the left arm). An attack on these areas almost always caused the array's members to break apart and trigger defeat. It was therefore standard procedure to screen the flanks with light infantry and cavalry to secure against a lateral strike or the enemy folding around the end of the line (an "envelopment") to attack from the rear as well.

Based on the foregoing speculation on army sizes, the phalanxes at Cyrene would probably have deployed eight men deep (or at "eight shields" to use the common terminology of the day). This created opposing lines over a stretch of around 625m. For the rebels, the local exiles undoubtedly stood on the right side (wing) of their formation, this having the unshielded flank and thus being the more dangerous post of honor for those fighting on home soil. The Messenians then took up the left wing of the phalanx. Initial deployment occurred as foot skirmishers dueled back and forth between the armies, buying time for the hoplites to observe the opposition's dispositions and adjust. Here it was important to approximately match the enemy's length of formation so as to avoid an overlap that might invite envelopment. If the assessment above of relatively even hoplite strengths for this action is correct, there would have been no need to rearrange the heavy formations at Cyrene. Both armies therefore simply called back their skirmishers, divided them to join the mounted troops on either flank and prepared to charge.

On signal by horn (*salpinx*), both phalanxes swept forward at a slow pace, men giving distinctive battle-cries to raise their spirits and singing rhythmic chants (a traditional war poem or *paean*) to stay in step and maintain good order as the fronts closed on each other. Finally, at no more than a few tens of meters separation, both sides picked up the pace a bit, raising dust from the dry earth as their front-fighters came together and began a duel of spears. With a dreadful crash of steel points striking shields, some yelled in fury and others screamed in pain as a cacophony of sound enclosed and deafened everyone along the line of battle. And given the swirling dust and restricted view from the narrow slits of a Corinthian helmet, sight was nearly as limited as hearing for those struggling to kill and stay alive, with sweat from the African heat and desperate effort streaming down to burn the eyes and further obscure their vision. And then there was the smell. Dust and sweat, of course, but also the products of bladders and bowels inevitably reacting to overwhelming waves of excitement and mortal fear. As the fight raged on, there was also the sickly sweet, metallic odor of blood as that precious fluid joined the other dreadful lubricants of war to slick the ground and make footing difficult during the violent give and take of combat.

Thrusting and stabbing with spear or broken shaft or swinging sword or saber, the frontfighters eventually closed shield-on-shield. Each phalanx then shoved with all its concerted might toward forcing the foe backwards. It would be crucial if even a few steps could be gained, because once a formation began building momentum and driving forward, its opponents would begin to panic. Men leading the files were trapped in place; caught in a claustrophobic press between friends shoving into their back and the enemy's force coming from ahead, they could only face forward and try amid the terrible crush to keep chest free and breathing within the hollow bowl of their aspis. Driven backwards, the fear of those losing ground at the front eventually infected their comrades in the rear. There at the phalanx's trailing edge, the troops putting their shoulders into the effort to drive ahead actually had the option to escape. If a strong sense of defeat ever got to them, the entire formation would unravel from the tail up as one rank after another peeled away to take off in a race for safety. At Cyrene, it was the exiles and Messenians who would fall prey to this disastrous sequence of defeat.

We have no account of just how the engagement turned, whether superior numbers of enemy riders chased off a flank screen to envelop one end of the line or if collapse was due to pressure from spearmen along the front. Whatever the case, some rebel rear-rankers finally decided to run for it and started a chain reaction that tore their phalanx apart. Diodorus' report on casualties (15.34.5) suggests that the decisive failure might have come among the exiles. While they suffered heavy losses, the majority got clear. The Messenians, on the other hand, were killed "almost to a man." This is most consistent with the exiles fleeing, either yielding to overwhelming force or simply losing heart. In fact, this last seems the more likely prospect given that the winners also suffered serious losses. The intense physical demands of phalanx battle usually made for a short fight (though mutual pauses along the front might stretch things out some) and heavy casualties were normally confined to the losers, mounting as they turned to run and were cut down from behind. Steep losses among the winners are therefore indicative of an uncommonly long and ferocious melee that shed a lot of blood on both sides before somebody gave way. This implies that some of the exiles may have lost their nerve during an especially long fight and became the first to run. At any rate, the ensuing rout probably saw the Messenians clinging too long to their post. Their foes were thus able to surrounded them (carrying out a "double envelopment" in military terms), press in from all sides and, rejecting any attempts at surrender, complete a massacre. The Cyrenean factions thereafter negotiated a peaceful reunion. It would be nice to think that the surviving families of the slaughtered Messenians might have benefited from this settlement, but the record is mute.

The Ten Thousand

Cyrene wasn't the only place outside Greece to see that land's warriors in action after the Peloponnesian War. While the Messenians were meeting their doom on the shore of Africa, a large body of Greek mercenaries was fighting its way along the coast of the Euxine (Black) Sea. Many such soldiers for hire had been idled by the cessation of combat in Europe and a host of them had taken service with the Persian prince Cyrus. They had followed him into the heart of the vast empire of his brother Artaxerxes II, Great King of Persia, on a quest to usurp the throne for their young paymaster. These Greeks, around 14,000 strong with over 10,000 hoplites, had taken their share of the field during a great battle in 401 at Cunaxa near Babylon. There, they had carried all before them on their wing without losing a single man, only to have Cyrus fall elsewhere that day and bring their expedition to ruin. An act of Persian treachery then claimed most of the Greeks' generals. Keeping their heads, the mercenaries elected new commanders and set out for home on a long march (*anabasis*) through hostile country. The epic story of their journey has come down to us today through the memoir of one of its leaders (and later historian), Xenophon of Athens.

The mercenary army dusted off Persian pursuit and pushed aside hostile natives to make a brutal winter crossing of the mountains between the valley of the Euphrates River and the Black Sea. In the late spring of 400, it was moving at last just below the coast in the land of the Colchians, who massed in line of battle on the side of a large mountain and across the road forward. Xenophon stood before his comrades and said: "Soldiers, these men yonder whom you see are the only ones who still stand in the way ... if we possibly can, we must simply eat these fellows raw" (*Anabasis* 4.8.14).

Colchis and Metropolis (400 B.C.)

The arduous winter trek had combined with desultory fighting along the way to take a heavy toll on the Greeks who had set out after Cunaxa. They currently numbered under 10,000, including around 8,000 hoplites and 1,800 peltasts, slingers, archers and horsemen (Xenophon *Anabasis* 4.8.15–19). On the other side, the number of Colchians is unknown, but it was no doubt in the thousands to give those tribesmen enough confidence to risk battle with a foe whose strength they must have scouted. The Colchians, like other barbarians in their region (Nelson 1975, 62–63), were shock fighters. They wore metal helmets and, possibly, some body armor, carrying shields of medium to large size and thrusting spears similar in proportion to those of the Greeks. They may also have had a few javelin-armed foot skirmishers.

The mercenaries at first matched the opposing line by setting up in a phalanx with files of four (such as they had used at Cunaxa); however, they quickly grew concerned that this thin array might be penetrated. They therefore reformed upon the advice of Xenophon into 80 columns, each having a single 100-man company (*lochos*, *lochoi* plural) of hoplites and separated by 50m so as to keep the former formation width. (Note that the term "lochos" also applied to larger units [battalions] that commonly had 300–600 men.) Any attack into the gaps between columns was to be met by the companies turning back into line to support each other. The spearmen could now advance with less fear of disarray (order being much easier to keep over uneven ground with deep files) and strike with greater depth for security and othismos while still covering the same broad front. As for the light infantry, it took station in three groups of 600 men apiece, with one team skirmishing in front and the others along the sides.

Once redressed, the Greeks began to move upslope toward their foes at a deliberate pace. Their senior general, the Spartan Cheirisophus (who had commanded the army's vanguard during the march), led the companies on the right wing and Xenophon (who had commanded the rearguard on the road) led those on the left. The barbarians could clearly see that they were going to be flanked not only by the enemy's skirmishers but by their hoplites on each wing as well; they responded by attacking outboard on both ends. This rendered their center virtually unmanned. The peltasts leading in front of the mercenaries gave cry and charged into this opening as the hoplites in the center followed to split the Colchians in two. Its formation now hopelessly compromised, the barbarian horde cut and ran. The Greeks thus claimed the field and reached the sea at the Grecian city of Trapezus within two days.

The mercenaries sent Cheirisophus off by ship to seek transport home and settled in to wait. They supported themselves by raiding into Colchis and got aid from the local Greeks in return for helping them make war on nearby enemies. But as time wore on, the foraging became less fruitful and met growing resistance. The army finally decided to move on to more promising territory and, after sending off its sick and aged aboard a few small vessels available at Trapezus, it headed west along the coast. A count at this point tallied some 8,600 men (Xenophon *Anabasis* 5.3.3), apparently 7,000–7,600 hoplites and 1,000–1600 light infantry and horsemen. The mercenaries reached the Greek city of Cerasus after three days and rested briefly. They then entered the land of the Mossynoecians, another of the tribal folks in the region. These were fierce fighters armed with long (nearly 3m) thrusting spears with round counterweights on the butt. They had leather helmets with a tufted crest and carried wicker shields covered in white, shaggy ox-hide in the shape of a leaf of ivy (having three lobes at the top). The Mossynoecians wore no armor, but had thick tunics of linen and used throwing spears with hand-axes as secondary weapons. The first tribe encountered proved unfriendly, refusing safe passage through their land. Allying with a competing Mossynoecian band, the mercenaries set up before the wooden-towered coastal city of their foes, which sat on high ground and was called Metropolis.

The first attempt on the fortress failed. This happened when the allied tribesmen, who had deployed in front of the phalanx, charged prematurely and pulled some peltasts along. The city's defenders drove off this weak attack, killing "a considerable number of the barbarians and some

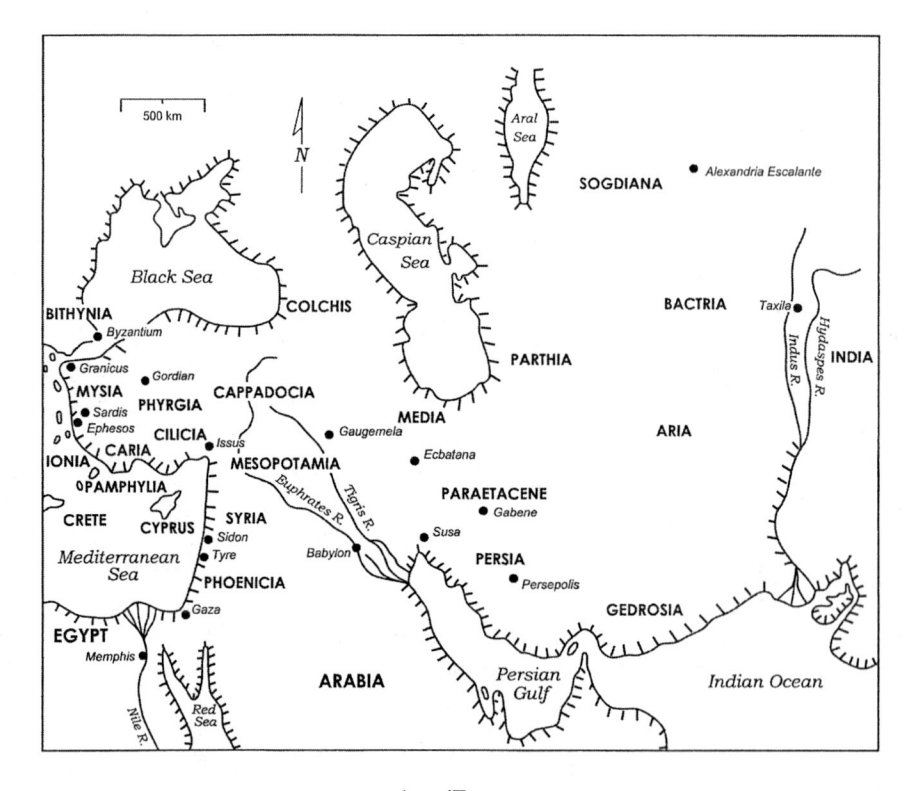

ASIA/EGYPT

of the Greeks who had gone up the hill with them" (Xenophon *Anabasis* 5.4.16). Falling back when the hoplites then advanced, the Metropolitans cut off heads and brandished them to taunt their enemies below. The mercenaries were angry, but with their allies in disarray they elected to withdraw. The next morning, however, they again formed in front of town, this time putting the excitable locals on the left flank under close supervision. They next sent their peltasts forward grouped into companies with bowmen between each unit. These skirmished at the fore as the hoplites slowly advanced, their array no doubt eight shields deep with Xenophon (now brevet commander in Cheirisophus' absence) on the right wing.

The Metropolitans sallied several thousand strong against the peltasts and bowmen, yet gave way when these retired and the hoplites came forward. Then, as the phalanx neared town, the barbarians reversed once more, turning to hurl their small spears as they closed into shock combat with shield and heavy lance. This was just the sort of action for which the phalanx was designed and its hoplites pushed and speared relentlessly ahead, driving their tribal foes back all along the front until the barbarians' courage failed and they broke from the fight. The Metropolitans abandoned the city as the Greeks and their allies took the walls. Burning the local chieftain and his commanders alive when they tried to make a stand in one of the wooden towers, the victors sacked Metropolis before marching on to the polis of Cotyora.

The mercenaries had a long stay in Cotyora, where they found ships to sail farther west along the Black Sea strand and reach the port of Sinope. Cheirisophus finally rejoined them there. But instead of a fleet to take them home, the Spartan brought the offer of another contract, this one to serve Sparta, which was gathering an army at Byzantium to make war on Persia. The mercenaries now agreed to reaffirm Cheirisophus as their commander and broke into contingents that would proceed separately to Calpe Harbor in Thrace for a meeting with Spartan representatives (Xenophon *Anabasis* 6.2.16). The Arcadians and Achaeans from the northern Peloponnese formed the largest group with more than 4,000 hoplites under a team of ten captains. Next came the men from the southern Peloponnese, who were 1,400 spearmen with 700 Thracian peltasts. These followed Cheirisophus and had another Spartan, Neon, leading the contingent from his own polis (perhaps 700 spearmen remaining from an original complement of 1,000). The third group had men from outside the Peloponnese: 1,700 hoplites, 300 peltasts and 40 horsemen with Xenophon in command. The Arcadians and Achaeans immediately sailed out as the Spartan-led party marched away toward Thrace; then, after a small delay, Xenophon and his men took ship as well.

Calpe Harbor I, II, and III (400 B.C.)

The Arcadian/Achaean division landed in darkness at Calpe Harbor, a sharp promontory about midway along the Thracian coast in Bithynian territory. Fixing a hill inland as a rallying point the next morning, the mercenaries divided into their 400-man companies to spread out and raid the countryside (most of the units set out alone, but there were a couple of double-company teams). The Thracians were able to gather for a counterstrike and caught two of the single-company raiding parties as they were withdrawing for the day with their booty. First hit was a team of Arcadians under Smicres. With Bithynian peltasts swarming all about, these hoplites tried to keep a tight formation and make a fighting withdrawal; however, their harried retreat met with disaster when trying to cross a ravine. The enemy pounced on the heavy spearmen as their formation fell apart, forcing them to fight as individuals. The much more agile javelineers then wiped out Smicres and his hoplites to the last man. The Bithynians shortly thereafter caught a second company on the move. This group of Greeks fared little better than the first, its commander managing to escape alive with only seven of his men. The other eight companies made it back intact to set up a perimeter on the appointed hill, where a siege began the next day as the Thracians circled with a growing mass of horsemen and peltasts. The spearmen had no light infantry or cavalry of their own and were helpless to strike back as the enraged tribesmen launched one assault after another, throwing their missiles from a safe distance and then retiring without fear of pursuit. The barbarians soon cut off the water supply, which gave the Greeks no choice other than to seek a truce; and when negotiations hit a snag, things were beginning to look desperate. Just then, help arrived.

Xenophon and his men had landed on the eastern border of Bithynia and set out from there on foot. They were just now approaching, and the sudden appearance of this new Greek fighting force in the area took the besiegers by surprise. Dispersing during the night, the tribesmen allowed the trapped hoplites to escape to Calpe Harbor where they joined Cheirisophus and his men, who had just arrived. Xenophon's column reached the harbor shortly thereafter; however, any hope of reconstituting the army's old organization came to a quick end when Cheirisophus died after taking some medicine for a fever. This left Neon in command of the southern Peloponnesian division and he wasn't on good terms with Xenophon.

The Greeks sat down to await arrival of Cleander, the Spartan *harnmost* (governor) of Byzantium, to discuss terms of employment. In the meantime, rations were running low, so Neon took it upon himself to secure supplies and went out to forage with his division of 2,100 men. This went terribly wrong when he was attacked by horsemen (perhaps a regiment of 600–800 javelin-armed riders). These troopers had been sent by Pharnabazus, the Persian in charge of Phyrgia in Asia Minor, who had come to the aid of the Bithynians in hope of preempting a Grecian invasion of his own land. Joined quickly by Thracian cavalry and peltasts, the Persians killed at least 500 of Neon's men without the need for a set battle, since the victims had been widely scattered in the process of scavenging. The remaining Greeks dug in on high ground until Xenophon came to rescue them with a mixed command composed of all the younger, speedier soldiers from Calpe. Falling back to the harbor camp, the mercenaries suffered attacks on their outposts throughout the night before relocating the next day to a better site, which they then fortified.

Pharnabazus' infantry, possibly a 6,000-man division of mixed arms (some with shield and spear and others with bows) thereafter joined his horsemen and their Bithynian allies to threaten the Greeks. Xenophon sortied to meet this challenge, leading out all of the mercenaries under the age of 45 and leaving the rest behind to guard the new camp. He had perhaps 4,500 spearmen (if the younger men were some 75 percent of the remaining 5,900–5,950 hoplites) and maybe 600 foot skirmishers plus 30 horsemen (again at 75 percent of those surviving). Finding the enemy holding fast on high ground, Xenophon set up his phalanx (likely eight shields deep over a front of better than 550m) with his light-armed troops off the flanks and the few horsemen on hand sitting far right. The Greeks advanced to the attack, but their peltasts charged without orders and were routed by the opposing cavalry and Bithynian javelinmen. Despite this setback, the hoplites continued to sing their paean and close, easily shedding aside a shower of missiles with shield and armor. And when they got near and lowered their spears along the front with a shout, their foes lost heart and ran away. Xenophon's cavalry chased the enemy left wingers and slew a large number. Less rapidly pursued, those on the opposition right managed to reach a hill and take a defensive stance; however, when the phalanx moved against this position in turn, the barbarians again fled.

Having regrouped, it was the Greek peltasts who now gave chase, though they didn't kill many due to cover from the Persian cavalrymen, these having kept well-ordered despite all hell breaking loose around them. The Persians were soon joined by Bithynian riders and took post on a rise to menace the phalanx, which had at last become somewhat disordered in pursuit. But rapidly redressing ranks, the mercenary spearmen resumed their advance and for the third time that day saw opponents refuse to stand and fight. The enemy horsemen fled down the back slope in haste, leaving Xenophon and his men to set up a trophy and return to camp. After this humiliating beating, the Thracians and their friends prudently avoided further combat.

Cleander arrived at last and proved a haughty bully; still, the mercenaries eventually agreed to relocate to the Asian side of the Bosporus opposite the Spartan base at Byzantium. At this point, greed intervened. Sparta's admiral in the region, Anaxibius, took a bribe from Pharnabazus to get the hireling army away from the Persian's satrapy by offering a job in Europe. Anaxibius reneged on this deal once he'd gotten the mercenaries to move back across the Bosporus; however, they wound up finding employment all the same, joining Seuthes, warlord of Odrysian Thrace. They would work toward winning Seuthes a kingship before finally accepting transfer into Spartan service in 399 to again deploy against Persia.

Sparta's War on Persia

The attempt by Cyrus on the Persian throne that had ended with his death at Cunaxa originated out of the district on the western edge of the Persian Empire where the young man had been governor (*satrap*, his province being a Persian political unit called a *satrapy*). The coastal portion of this area was composed of a number of Greek colonies that dated back in some cases to before 1,000 B.C. These had in recent times fallen to the Lydians immediately to their northeast and then to Persia upon its conquest of Lydia. The Greeks here, known collectively as "Ionians" for the predominance of the Ionian dialect of Greek among them (their region hence being commonly called "Ionia"), had risen up against Persia in 499 only to be defeated. And while Greek successes following the failed Persian invasion of Europe in 480–479 had let them break free for a time, the Great King had once again taken over in the course of helping Sparta win the Peloponnesian War.

So things sat at the beginning of the 4th century. That's when the Spartans, full of hubris after their triumph over Athens and successful consolidation of power on the Greek mainland, began to reconsider their relationship with Persia. There was, after all, a good deal of profit to be had from claiming Ionia and plundering the wealth of its Persian masters. Their first step had been to support the coup of Cyrus. When this went badly, the dead prince's replacement as satrap, Tissaphernes, arrived in Ionia to demand submission from its Greek poleis. These had been well disposed toward Cyrus and were of no mind to have a less acceptable fellow running their affairs. Their solution was to seek aid from Sparta that they might again tear away from Persia. The Spartans took advantage of this to send out their own man Thibron as Ionian governor, providing him with 1,000 freed helots armed as hoplites along with 4,000 other spearmen drawn from their Peloponnesian allies and 300 horsemen provided upon request from Athens. Gathering more troops from the Ionians, Thibron prepared to contest the Great King's forces for control of Asia Minor.

Bithynia (399/98 B.C.) and Cyllene (398 B.C.)

Thibron opened his campaign against the Persians with caution. Wary of their cavalry, he refused to lead his army out onto the plains where the superiority of his phalanx in close-in (shock) fighting along the front would be offset by its lack of speed and vulnerability at sides and rear to encircling horsemen and light infantry. The Spartan thus kept to the defensive at first; however, after the arrival of Xenophon and the mercenaries that had served with Cyrus (the "Cyreans" as they came to be known) he grew bolder, benefiting from their past experience against mounted foes. He was thereafter able to capture a number of cities by surrender or storm before taking station at the major Grecian port of Ephesos along the central Ionian coast. There, he was readying an invasion of Caria, the mixed barbarian–Greek province to the south, when Dercyllidas arrived as his replacement.

Dercyllidas took stock of the situation and saw that the two Persian satraps he faced weren't on friendly terms with each other. He therefore arranged a ceasefire with Tissaphernes, whose satrapy covered all of the former Lydian territories including Ionia. This let him concentrate against Pharnabazus, whose province of Phrygia lay to the north and east. Moving up the coast, Dercyllidas seized the cities there and then headed inland to gain surrenders from all the other towns in Aeolia, which sat just west of Pharnabazus' realm. The Spartan went on to capture more sites and add their mercenary defenders to his own army until he had some 8,000 hired men under arms (Xenophon *Hellenica* 3.1.28). Dercyllidas now had a strong base for moving against Pharnabazus and the satrap chose wisely to come to terms for the winter. Dercyllidas therefore withdrew to take up quarters in Bithynian Thrace.

When the Greeks arrived in Bithynia, they began raiding for supplies. To help in this, Xenophon's old employer Seuthes sent a contingent of his Odrysians numbering 200 horsemen and 300 peltasts. Dercyllidas gave these allies 200 hoplites to provide a heavy guard for their camp and they headed out to gather more spoils. However, with the light-armed men out on the hunt, the hoplites suffered a dawn attack from local Thracian riders and javelinmen. The Greek spearmen took a number of casualties from missiles before charging from their palisade in formation. This proved a futile effort, since the much fleeter tribesmen were easily able to escape slow-moving hoplites, who were not only burdened with armor but also had to stay in close order. The Thracians showered their foes with javelins from one side and then the other as they skipped back from every rush the spearmen tried to make. In the end, "the Greeks were shot down like cattle shut up in a pen" (Xenophon *Hellenica* 3.2.4), with just 15 escaping slaughter by slipping off amid the chaotic fight. By the time that Dercyllidas was able to send help, his relief force found only the bodies of the dead stripped bare where they had fallen. More alert from then on, the Greeks and their tribal allies were able to avoid repeating this debacle and got through the rest of the winter without further loss.

Dercyllidas returned to Asia in the spring, marching to Lampsacus at the lower entrance to the Hellespont. But there was to be no action on Persian soil this season, as Pharnabazus signed onto yet another temporary ceasefire. The Spartan commander was thus free to attend to matters elsewhere and elected to turn westward for a while that he might aid fellow Greeks complaining about Thracian attacks in the Chersonese (the long, narrow peninsula forming the European side of the Hellespont). Returning from this brief diversion, he spent the rest of the year consolidating his gains.

Dercyllidas received orders for 397 from the Spartan leadership that he was to end his truce with Tissaphernes and move to take Caria. Meanwhile, Pharnabazus had reconciled with his fellow satrap and they now joined to march against the Spartans, planning to cross the Meander River northward into Ionia. Dercyllidas led his army down into Ionia and met the Persian forces aligned in battle formation across the road somewhere on the plain above the Meander. The satraps had a combat array that included maybe 4,000 Greek spearmen on the left wing. (These included 1,000-man mercenary bodyguards for the satraps and 2,000 or so militiamen from the Aegean coast of Caria, the latter providing around 25 percent of the full national levy [Ray 2009, 41].) There were barbarian Carians on the right wing (hoplites with white, leather-covered shields), possibly 6,000 strong per the remaining 75 percent of Carian manpower. Persian infantry held the center. Each satrap probably had a garrison division (*baivarabam*) of imperial footmen at a nominal strength of 10,000 men, thus Diodorus' claim of a 20,000-man total (14.39.5). However, only 30–60 percent parade strength was common for such standing units (Sekunda and Chew, 1992, 5–6); therefore, there were likely only 6,000–12,000 Persian foot soldiers actually present.

Pharnabazus rode with maybe half the cavalry on the left. He might have had as few as 750 or as many as 3,000 riders, depending on whether the total mounted force was five 1,000-man companies (*hazaraba* at 30–60 percent nominal manpower per a common ratio of one rider per four line infantrymen) or ten such companies as suggested by Diodorus in citing 10,000 riders. Tissaphernes led his own horsemen at the same strength on the right. Both mounted bodies no doubt had supporting light footmen that might have matched the cavalry in number. These would have been Phrygian peltasts for Pharnabazus and most likely similarly armed Carians for Tissaphernes. Deployed at eight shields deep for the Greeks and a depth of ten men for the Persians (using their smallest organizational unit, the ten-man *dathabam*, for each file) as well as the Carians, the heavy, shield-bearing troops would have spanned a 2,000m front.

Dercyllidas ordered his men to array in phalanx eight shields deep (Xenophon *Hellenica* 3.2.16), splitting the light footmen off each flank along with what few horsemen were available. There could have been 14,000 hoplites at most. This honors a heavy corps that would have included the 5,000 spearmen brought from Europe, 7,000 mercenaries (Cyreans and recent additions less about 1,000 to account for both garrisons left behind and casualties in Bithynia) and perhaps 2,000 from Ionia (Cartledge 1987, 210). (Note that Diodorus put the Greeks at no more than 7,000 men, an underestimate that would seem most likely to have taken into account only the non-mercenary hoplites.) This would have let him set up his phalanx across a 1,750m span—short, but at least approaching the opposition's breadth of array. However, the local amateurs (probably in the formation center where Greek generals usually stuck those considered least reliable lest they endanger their more vulnerable flanks) lacked the stomach for a fight, some deserting and the rest openly showing signs of fear.

As it turned out, a key figure on the other side had no greater desire to tangle; for though Pharnabazus was keen for action, Tissaphernes was not. That general had led the Persian left when it faced hoplites at Cunaxa, including the Cyreans now standing resolutely on the other side of the field. He'd watched his Asian infantry there simply melt away before a Greek charge and was now of no mood to hazard another round with odds anything near to even. As for Dercyllidas, he seems to have had his own reservations. Famed for painstaking preparation and having been surprised by the enemy blocking his march, his resulting hasty deployment must have been disconcerting. Moreover, he was sitting on an open plain with a much inferior mounted arm. Ultimately, such mutual discomfort led to a peace agreement being negotiated on the spot that avoided battle by declaring Ionia free from both Persian *and* Spartan rule.

While Dercyllidas was prosecuting the campaign against Persia, his fellow Spartans were engaged in a conflict of their own against Elis. That polis on the northwestern coast of the Peloponnese controlled Olympia and had barred Sparta from the Pan-Hellenic games held regularly at the sacred site. The Eleans had also made alliances of which the Spartans did not approve. Sparta retaliated in 399 by demanding that Elis relinquish some of its outlying territories and, when this was refused, declared war. Agis, one of the Spartan kings, led out the national host, but turned back after an earthquake. However, another force set out for Elis under Agis later in the year, this one including some allied troops from the Peloponnese and Athens.

Agis ravaged the countryside, but chose to spare the un-walled capital city of Elis, moving instead toward Cyllene on the northwest Elean coast. A civil war now broke out there between members of the wealthy, oligarchic party, who wished to yield to the approaching Spartans, and those in the popular faction opposed to this. The result was a pitched battle that perhaps involved

500–1,000 spearmen with appropriate light support. The popular group probably held a small edge in hoplites and a larger one in light footmen, while its more aristocratic opponents would have had most of the horsemen present. We've no detailed account of the action, yet know the oligarchs took a beating that most likely reflected the manpower differences in what must have been an infantry-dominated scrap. The winners then set out to defend the city walls as the losers escaped to Agis. Not interested in being tied down with a siege, the Spartan king marched home to disband his army, leaving a garrison behind in Elean territory that included those fled from Cyllene. This outpost force proceeded to spoil Elis throughout the rest of the year and into the next, causing the Eleans to finally capitulate and sign a peace with Sparta on the latter's terms.

Pactolos River, Sardis and Dascyleium (395 B.C.)

The campaign against Elis would prove Agis' last as he passed away shortly thereafter. His brother, Agesilaos II, emerged from the succession dispute that followed to become king in 396. His first crisis would arise when word came from Asia that Tissaphernes was preparing a fleet whose destination was unknown. Lysander, a hero from the last stages of the conflict with Athens, advanced the idea that this armament was aimed at Sparta and it was decided to renew the war against Persia. Agesilaos took command and sailed out with 1,000 helot hoplites, 6,000 allied Peloponnesian spearmen and supplies for six months in the field. Gathering reinforcements in Asia (both Ionians and mercenaries, including Xenophon and the Cyreans) to the strength of 4,000 hoplites and 400 horsemen (Diodorus 14.79.2), he set up base at Ephesos. Tissaphernes stalled by discussing a truce even as he asked the Great King for more troops.

Tissaphernes had sent his cavalry up to the Ionian border along the Meander plain (flat country well suited to mounted operations) while keeping his infantry back in the Carian hills. But Agesilaos, though he had made preparations suggesting an imminent march on Caria, now set off toward Phrygia and was able to prosecute a profitable campaign of plunder with very little resistance. There was, however, a mounted skirmish near the town of Dascyleium in which a body of his Greek cavalry took a beating from Persian horsemen. This was a minor action to be sure, but one that made a strong impression on the savvy Spartan tactician. Agesilaos now judged that an improved mounted force would be needed on the broad Asian flats. When he returned to Ephesos that fall, he therefore went about gathering more cavalry from the wealthier of his local allies. He did this by allowing them to fulfill their personal levy obligation by substituting a competent man and horse in its stead.

Agesilaos marched out from Ephesos the next spring, making for the Lydian city of Sardis, capital for the Persian satrapy that included Ionia. This once more frustrated Tissaphernes' defenses, which had set up as before with infantry in the Carian rough and cavalry on post above in the valley of the Meander. The satrap was under great pressure to answer the Spartan's maneuver this time and he headed north to counter with a large army. (Diodorus puts Persian forces at 10,000 horsemen and 50,000 foot soldiers, probably reflecting nominal manpower of the units involved. If these were five divisions of foot plus ten companies of cavalry at a more reasonable 60 percent of establishment strength, then we're talking about some 30,000 footmen and 6,000 riders. And given at least one infantry division being light-armed skirmishers, this would yield 24,000 line fighters at a likely 4 to 1 ratio with their horsemen.)

Tissaphernes reached Sardis and sent out his cavalry to scout the approaching Greeks. The horsemen set up a forward base south of the city on the east side of the Pactolos River and then crossed to attack men engaged in plundering the countryside. After a good many of these had been killed, Agesilaos' newly upgraded mounted division came to the rescue and the Persians drew back to form a line of battle, standing before the Pactolos with their camp beyond. Agesilaos had arrived with his infantry by now and, when he saw no enemy footmen, sent out an advance wave of his cavalry, followed in order by peltasts at double speed and then the younger, swifter hoplites. He came marching behind these with the rest of his spearmen in phalanx. The Persians engaged the horsemen, but once the javelineers and hoplites arrived and the full phalanx with lowered spears began to close, they broke into flight. The Greeks gave chase and killed several at the back of the galloping mob as it crossed the river. With the rest of the beaten riders on the run, Agesilaus' men plundered their encampment.

This setback spurred Tissaphernes to march out of Sardis and take the field in full force. Outnumbered and unwilling to engage his more mobile foe on open ground, Agesilaos retreated in column with the Persians following to harry his rear guard. The Spartan king saw an ambush opportunity in this. He sent his cavalry commander Xenocles ahead with 1,400 men from the vanguard (likely 400 horsemen and 1,000 peltasts) to hide at a heavily forested site that had been scouted along the route. The next day, Agesilaos led his army past this spot just at dawn with Tissaphernes' column tailing close in his wake. Once on suitable ground beyond, the Greeks suddenly spun about and presented the startled Asians with a spear-brisling phalanx ready for battle. Frontage for Agesilaos' 11,000-man hoplite array could have been over 2.5km had it deployed only four shields deep as would seem probable.

The Persians are unlikely to have had time for any fine adjustments to their own formation. They thus probably spread out in standard order ten men deep with a span much like that on the other side if the foregoing guesswork on their having around 24,000 line infantry is correct. With barely enough time to scramble into fighting order, the Great King's men must have met the ensuing Greek advance with considerable uncertainty as a "sharp battle" (Diodorus) commenced. But no sooner had this action gotten well underway than Xenocles and his ambush party came up on signal to hit the Persian rear. Caught front and back, the imperials fell apart, with Tissaphernes and his troops running for their lives. Agesilaos' men gave hard chase and killed 6,000 while capturing a large number as well per Diodorus. The fatalities (20 percent of 30,000 foot soldiers) are about what one would expect from a thorough pursuit. (Note that there is a great deal of controversy as to whether this engagement and the previous one at Pactolos River are actually duplicate reports on the same action by Xenophon [*Hellenica* 3.4.21–24] and Diodorus [14.80.2–5]. Plutarch [Vol. II *Agesilaos*, 46] has an account more like Xenophon's while that of the Oxyrhynchus Historian [6.4–6] leans toward Diodorus. Given the marked differences in particulars in the two descriptions and Diodorus' clear implication that there was more than one encounter at this time [14.80.6] despite his giving details on only one, the foregoing scenario of separate battles is considered the more likely case.)

There was major fallout from the Persian defeat at Sardis. King Artaxerxes II sent out Tithraustes to execute and replace Tissaphernes. The new Persian commander then tried to arrange a truce with Agesilaos, putting the blame for all past problems between the Empire and Sparta upon his predecessor's severed head in hopes that a reconciliation could be reached. However, once it became obvious that Agesilaos was not to be dissuaded from continuing his campaign, Tithraustes took another tack. Sending money into Greece, he now sought to induce several poleis to bedevil Sparta. If the Spartans couldn't be driven from Asia, maybe they would draw off to deal with trouble at home.

Agesilaos had by fall moved into Phrygia to lay it waste and close on Dascyleium, where Pharnabazus was headquartered. Here, the Spartan had a small reverse. Some of his men were scouring about in search of supplies when Pharnabazus caught one of the raiding parties with a force of 400 horsemen supported by two chariots fitted with scythes that extended on each side from the axle. The 700-man Greek contingent quickly prepared to face a mounted attack by drawing together into a tight body. This was a mixed-arms formation, most likely a square that had the hoplites on the outside and light-armed men in the middle. Such an arrangement would let the well-armored spearmen use their aspides to fend off enemy missiles all around while their protected skirmisher comrades at center hurled javelins at any approaching horsemen. (The Greeks' darts could hit home before the riders even got into range to use their own weapons, since they couldn't hurl a javelin nearly as far sitting on a saddle.) But Pharnabazus negated this otherwise sound scheme by charging with the chariots in front of his cavalry. Seeing these fearsome engines closing fast, the Greeks lost nerve and scattered rather than meet their spinning blades. The Persian horsemen then rode among their fleeing foes to lance and slash down a hundred as the rest ran away. Bad as it was, this slaughter would have been even worse but for the arrival of Agesilaos with a large contingent of hoplites that had by chance been nearby. Pharnabazus and his riders prudently withdrew in the face of these reinforcements, content with the damage already dealt.

Shortly thereafter, a meeting between Agesilaos and Pharnabazus produced yet another truce and the Spartan withdrew that he might prepare a march on Tithraustes to the south. But this campaign never got going, as word now arrived from Sparta that Persia's meddling back in Greece was finally paying off in combination with the sorts of inter-polis disputes and rivalries that were always present even during the best of times in that highly fragmented land. The Spartans were on the verge of going to war with a coalition of Greek states and needed both their warrior king and his army to return and defend the homeland. Agesilaos forthwith appointed Euxenus as governor for Ionia and, leaving him with a garrison of 4,000 men, set off with whatever other troops he could take on the long trip back to Sparta.

The Corinthian War I

It was a triangle of tensions between Greece's leading city-states of Sparta, Thebes and Athens that set off what would come to be known as the Corinthian War. The Thebans, perhaps inspired at least in part by money flowing from Persia, had influenced the Opuntian Locrians on their west to expand upon a land dispute they were having on their southern border with neighboring Phocis, which was an ally of Sparta. The Locrians levied cash payments from the contested area and triggered a Phocian invasion in retaliation. Locris then asked for help from Thebes and the Thebans launched a counter-invasion against Phocis, ravaging the country before pulling back to Boeotia. Phocis immediately called for and got a pledge of aid from the Spartans. The final major player in this three-cornered game entered at this point as Athens, fearful of Spartan intentions outside of the Peloponnese, formed an alliance with the Thebans.

Haliartus and Naryx (395 B.C.)

The Spartans had sent Lysander to Phocis to gather a force from local supporters. This he did, collecting Phocian hoplites (perhaps 1,000) and cavalry (a few hundred at least). He also got spearmen (up to 1,000) from the Spartan colony at Heraclea (to the northeast at the base of the pass of Thermopylae) and Malis (farther north in Thessaly), the latter likely contributing skirmishers as well. To these he added a possible 500–1,000 in light infantry from Aenis in the Thessalian highlands. He marched into Boeotia with these men and camped in the vicinity of Haliartus, a town on the south side of ancient Lake Copais about midway between the poleis of Thebes to the east and Orchomenos to the west. Lysander was under orders to wait there for Pausanius, Agesilaos' partner king, who would shortly be marching out with the rest of the polis army and a full levy from the Peloponnesian allies. While he waited, the Spartan general took advantage of long-standing enmity between Thebes and Orchomenos to add the latter's 2,000 hoplites and 200 horsemen (plus perhaps 700 foot skirmishers) to his expedition.

When Pausanius didn't arrive on schedule, Lysander decided to go on the offensive by himself. He led his allied force of around 4,000 hoplites, 1,500 light footmen and 700 cavalry close to the walls of Haliartus and urged those inside to join Orchomenos in revolt. As it turned out, the place was possessed of a Theban garrison and refused. The Thebans, meanwhile, arrived in force and a battle ensued. Xenophon's account (*Hellenica* 3.5.18–21) is uncertain whether Lysander was even able to deploy, and neither Diodorus (14.81.1–3) nor Nepos (6.3.4) gives details to resolve the issue. In fact, light fatalities among those beaten (comparable to those of the victors at around 200) seem more in tune with a surprise attack in which Lysander's men took off before the enemy got close, leaving him and a few Spartan companions to be taken down by the Theban advance. Lysander thus died beneath the walls of Haliartus while most of those lost among his army fell in flight beyond the battlefield. However, once on nearby high, broken terrain, skirmishers in the fleeing crowd turned and let loose a hail of javelins. This killed several men leading the pursuit and encouraged others among those beaten to roll down stones and otherwise fight back. Their resistance cost the Thebans the aforementioned 200 or so dead before they gave up the chase. In fact, at day's end, there was considerable despondency on the winning side at having fared no better in the casualty department than the losers.

Theban spirits picked up the next morning when it became clear the Phocians and others that had come with the fallen Lysander were leaving. But this satisfaction proved short-lived when Pausanius finally showed up at Haliartus only a day later. The Spartan king had 6,000 hoplites in tow (Diodorus 14.81.1), likely including a couple of much feared Spartan regiments (*morai*, *mora* singular) of some 1,000 men each (see "Manpower" discussion Chapter II under Leuctra in 371) along with 4,000 Peloponnesians. The outnumbered Thebans weren't eager to fight, nor were the Spartans due to the fact that they didn't have as many hoplites as originally planned (with the loss of Lysander's division and Corinth's refusal to honor its alliance obligations) and had very few horsemen of any sort (the Phocian cavalry on which they had counted having fled). As a result, a pact was negotiated that ended what Diodorus called the "Boeotian" War, but is better characterized as the opening round of the Corinthian War.

The summer of 395 saw Thebes and Athens join with the Spartans' long-time foe Argos and their increasingly hostile nominal ally Corinth to form a grand alliance. Setting up a council at Corinth to direct joint activities, one of the allies' first acts was to send 2,000 Boeotian and Argive hoplites north into Thessaly to aid Medius, dictator of Larissa, in a war against his fellow tyrant, Lycophron of Pherae. Inland Larissa and coastal Pherae were rivals of old for leadership of Thessaly and the latter was allied with the Spartans. These troops helped Medius seize Pherae and then departed on their own to capture the Spartan outpost at Heraclea to the south.

Leaving the Argives to garrison Heraclea, the allied commander, Ismenias, took his Boeotians as well as recruits from the region thereabout and moved on Phocis. He had a little less than 6,000 men in all (Diodorus 14.82.7–10). A possible breakdown of these might be 1,000 Boeotian hoplites, 2,000 northern allied spearmen and nearly 3,000 light footmen and horsemen combined, with the latter including 100 riders from Boeotia. The Phocians, led by Sparta's Aleisthenes, came against Ismenias after he camped on their northern border at Naryx in Opuntian Locris. We have no figure for Phocian manpower, but by calling in allies like the Malians there might have been some 2,000 hoplites, 1,000 foot skirmishers and 400–500 horsemen. The ensuing battle was "sharp and protracted" per Diodorus, claiming high casualties on both sides before turning at last in Ismenias' favor. This most likely came on the superior quality of his famously fit Boeotian spearmen. These hardy fighters might have turned one enemy wing (the left?) against hoplites of lesser stamina (possibly the Malians). The ensuing pursuit essentially doubled the losers' death toll to nearly 1,000 men. Still, Ismenias had also paid a high price, the long, hard action having claimed around 500 men on his side as well. The Spartans now saw their united foes collect troops at Corinth, prompting them to recall Agesilaos and prepare for a fight.

Nemea River (394 B.C.)

Agesilaos began his journey back to Greece in the spring of 394, but events in the Peloponnese weren't waiting. With a large allied force already gathering against them, the Spartans called up their muster and those of their allies to create a powerful army. They had some 18,500 hoplites, 300 expert bowmen from the island of Crete and 400 slingers plus 700 horsemen (Xenophon [*Hellenica* 4.2.16], though Diodorus [15.83.1] says only 500 riders). There must have been non–Spartan javelinmen present as well, perhaps 3,500 to bring the infantry into line with Diodorus' sum of 23,000. The Spartans had 6,000 of their own hoplites, either all six morai or (if a mora documented shortly thereafter at Orchomenos had been posted after the engagement at Haliartus the year before) five morai and 1,000 freed helots. Their allied spearmen included almost 3,000 from Elis and elsewhere in the northwestern Peloponnese, another 3,000 from the southeast and 1,500 from Sicyon. There were also around 5,000 Arcadian and Achaean hoplites. (These last were not described in detail by Xenophon. See a good review of this issue in Sabin [2007, 111].) The Spartans' army moved to approach Corinth from the west along the coast of the Corinthian Gulf, having shifted to this more open path after harassment from enemy peltasts and archers in the hills inland. It set up camp in the territory of Sicyon just short of the Nemea River, which marked the Corinthian border. The enemy host, meanwhile, had also come up and went into camp across a river (perhaps the Nemea, but possibly the Rachiani farther east).

The allied army was considerably larger than that of Sparta in all categories. Its hoplites totaled around 24,000, including 6,000 from Athens, 5,000 from Boeotia (sans the Orchomenians), 3,000 from Corinth and another 3,000 from all across the large island of Euboa just off the eastern coast of Greece. Xenophon also reported 7,000 spearmen from Argos (though he appears to have been somewhat less certain of this and it does seem high, perhaps representing more than just Argives). Mounted forces included 800 Boeotians, 600 Athenians, 100 Euboans and 50 Opuntian Locrians. Light infantry came not only from the foregoing poleis (especially those also providing cavalry) but also from Ozolian Locris (below Phocis), Malis and Acarnania (in northwestern Greece). In all, the foot skirmishers might have reached 7,000–8,000. (Note that Diodorus gave alternative figures for the allies. However, these lack detail and seem less reliable, indicating a much smaller force of 15,000 infantry and 500 cavalry.)

The allies crossed the Nemea and both armies set up for a fight on the coastal plain. What followed would prove to be the largest battle of the Corinthian War. The allies spent some time discussing depth of array, wanting to take advantage of their superior heavy manpower with longer files at 16 shields over a 1,500m front, but concerned about getting too deep lest the enemy overlap and roll around the end of an overly shortened line. This was a definite risk should their foes file at under twelve men (as deep as they could go and still equal the allied width). A major concern here was the Boeotian contingent, among which stood the Thebans who had a history of lining up at extreme depths. Originally assigned to the left wing, where the Spartans would undoubtedly stand in the opposing post of honor, there was concern that they would mass too deeply against those elite foes and jeopardize the rest of the phalanx. They thus were switched to the right wing against the Sicyonians etc. with the Athenians taking their place on the left. As it turned out, once the phalanxes began to close, fear about the enemy's depth was alleviated (it was twelve as expected), but the Thebans did misbehave, stacking much deeper than 16 (perhaps 25) and veering markedly rightward as they closed. The latter looked to outflank the opposition left; however, it forced the rest of the allies to move that way as well. This put the Athenians at risk of envelopment from the Spartans, who were also drifting right.

As the fronts came together, the unauthorized Boeotian stacking and rightward swing did its inevitable work. The Spartans had taken advantage to extend their wing outside the terminus of the enemy's line and now pushed aside any light-armed screen on that end to wrap around the Athenians there. At the same time, the Boeotians enveloped on their flank to send the enemy into flight as far down as the Tegeans, who stood beside the Spartans and faced a portion of the Argive array. The only Spartan allies that held their ground for long were the men from Pellene, who kept fighting equally determined Boeotians from Thespiae. However, even as most of their allies ran, the Spartans themselves were taking down many of the opposing spearmen from Athens. They chased the rest off and advanced to pivot in formation. (Their front rank facing right into column and following its lead man to turn left at his original post and move

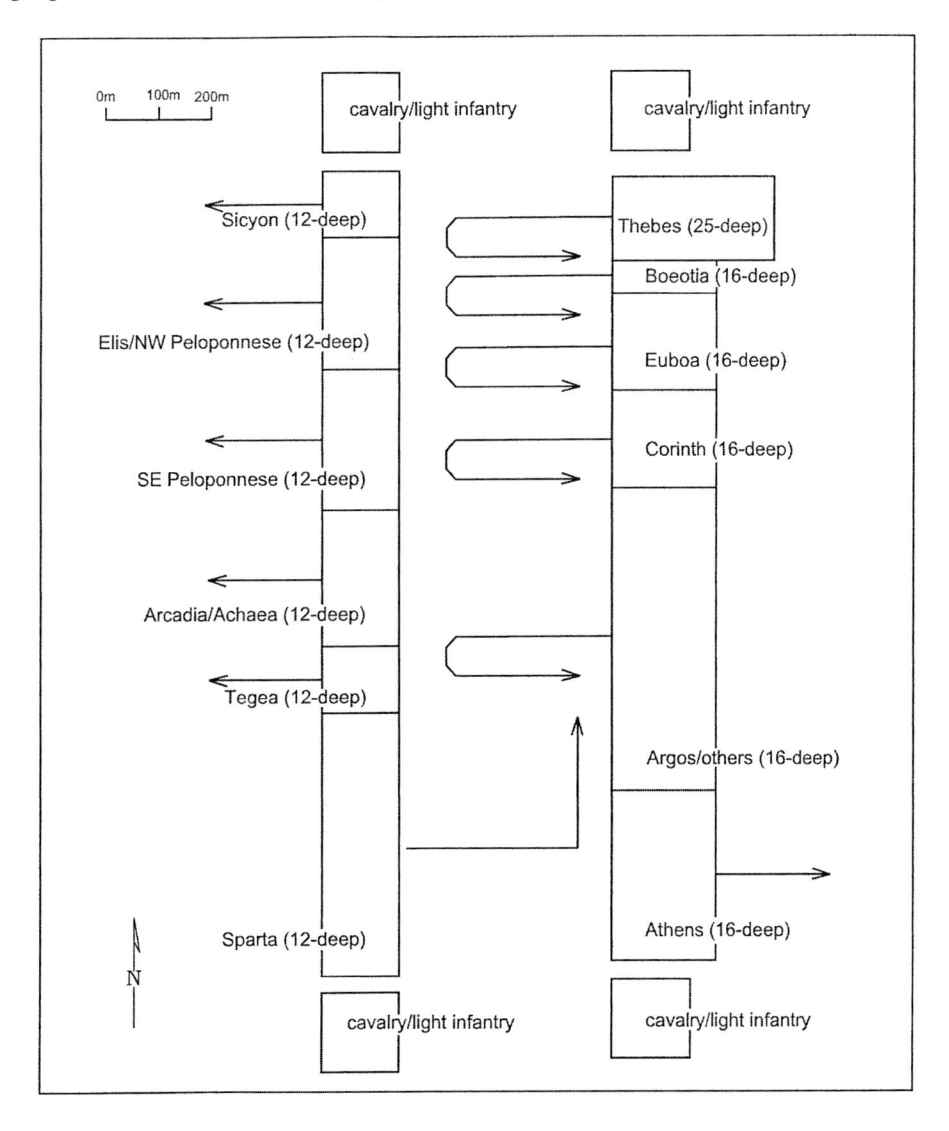

BATTLE OF NEMEA RIVER (394 B.C.) (BOXES REPRESENTING FORCES ARE EXAGGERATED TO SHOW RELATIVE SIZES.)

up until all could spin left and face toward the enemy flank. Each subsequent row in turn then did the same thing, lining up behind the one ahead until the entire formation had rotated 90 degrees to its original orientation.) Dressing ranks, the Spartan phalanx then swept laterally across the field. It first met the Argives as they returned in poor order from their brief chase. Letting the leading ranks pass, the Spartans charged into the rest, taking them on their unshielded right to slaughter many and scatter everyone else. The Spartans kept on going after that, steadily progressing down the enemy line to launch similarly devastating flank attacks on the Corinthians, the Thespians and other Boeotians and, finally, the Thebans, cutting up each contingent either where it stood (Thespians?) or as it straggled back from pursuit. The allies thus met costly defeat in detail mere minutes after seeming victorious across most of the field. They lost 2,800 men (nearly 12 percent of their hoplites) per Diodorus, while the enemy paid only 1,100 (6 percent), including a mere eight Spartans. (A report of 10,000 allied dead that Xenophon [*Agesilaos* 7.5] said was sent out from this battle clearly must have been extremely overblown.) It was a stunning reverse against an outmanned foe, reinforcing the impression of Spartan invincibility even as it shattered allied confidence.

Coronea II (394 B.C.)

Agesilaos had by now entered northernmost Greece to learn of the Spartan victory at Nemea River. He proceeded down into Thessaly along the northwestern Greek coastline where he met some resistance from Boeotia's allies in that region, who were renowned equestrians. Forced to fend off cavalry attacks against his rear, he took to marching in a hollow square with his hoplites on the outside and trailing a guard of horsemen. This led to a cavalry action near Mount Narthacium in which the enemy riders, unwilling to engage his smaller mounted force supported by hoplites, were caught and defeated by an unexpected charge of his horsemen. Having thus battered the Thessalians off his tail, he was able to move into Boeotia without difficulty, where his men carried a couple of skirmishes along the route of march. But more serious opposition soon arose as Agesilaos met a large allied force near Coronea in west-central Boeotia at the southwestern corner of Lake Copais.

The contending armies spread out in battle order across the plain below Coronea. Agesilaos had some Spartan troops with him, since a mora had arrived from the national army that had fought at Nemea River along with a personal bodyguard for him of 50 volunteers from Sparta (Plutarch Vol. II *Agesilaos*, 51–52). Also, a lochos (battalion) that had been half of a mora garrisoning Orchomenos came over, bringing with it that nearby allied polis' troops. This gave him around 1,500 Spartan and up to 2,000 Orchomenian hoplites. Among the men he'd brought from Asia were his helot spearmen (somewhat less than their original 1,000 by now) plus the mercenary and Ionian hoplites gathered there (4,000 per Diodorus [14.79.2]). He'd also added troops from uppermost Asia Minor and the Hellespontine region, including perhaps another 2,000–3,000 heavy infantrymen. Phocians (and possibly Malians) had joined him upon entering Boeotia, bringing maybe 1,000 hoplites along, and he had attached spearmen from Greek poleis in the Thraceward region during his march, these last a possible 3,000 in all. Though highly speculative, this suggests that the Spartan king had some 15,000 hoplites. He had started with 400 horsemen when he entered Ionia and had boosted his cavalry there and likely since (adding riders from the northern Greek cities and Phocis); thus, his mounted corps could have come to 1,000 men. Xenophon's account (*Hellenica* 4.3.15–21) claims that the Spartan force was superior to the other side in light infantry, suggesting that its skirmishers might have numbered 6,000 or more. Agesilaos set up a phalanx that was likely eight shields deep, splitting cavalry and light footmen off either wing. The king and his Spartans took post on the far right of the heavy array with the mercenaries and then the helots next in line followed by the Asian contingents and then the other allies. The Boeotians from Orchomenos held the extreme left.

Numbers for the allied army are also uncertain, but Xenophon said that "the opposing lines of battle were exactly matched in strength and the number of cavalry on both sides was about the same" (*Agesilaus* 2.9). If so, the hoplites probably included 4,000–5,000 Boeotians, 2,000–4,000 Athenians, 2,000–4,000 Argives, 1,000–2,000 Corinthians, 1,000–2,000 Euboans and 1,000–2,000 combined from elsewhere including Opuntian Locris. The cavalry's 1,000 or so troopers would mostly have been Boeotians and Athenians. This left the light infantry as the only inferior allied arm, likely counting only some 4,000–5,000 men. The allies must have designed their phalanx to match that of Agesilaos at eight shields deep over a front of nearly 1,900m. Thebans held the right end of this formation with the other Boeotians next to them and the remaining contingents spread leftward along the line down to the Argives against the opposite flank.

The battle arrays marched on each other slowly and in silence at first; however, as they drew close together, the Thebans gave a shout and sped to the fore followed by a similar rush among the mercenaries and the other troops from Asia on the Spartan side. Probably already badly demoralized by their recent thrashing at Nemea River, the men from Argos broke before the Spartans even got to spear-length, tossing shields to run for the nearby slopes of Mount Helicon. And their panic took most of the rest of their army with them as Agesilaos' phalanx swept the field with minimal effort. The exception to this swift victory was on the allied right, farthest from the king's position; here, the Thebans had pushed through an Orchomenian contingent that seems to have been as spooked by its past defeat against Thebes (at Haliartus) as the Argives had been by theirs against Sparta. Maybe thinking that their companions were equally successful, the Thebans continued on through to the enemy baggage train.

Agesilaos acted swiftly upon learning that the Thebans were victorious and to his rear. However, rather than following the tactics that had worked so well at Nemea River and seeking to make a flank attack, he turned his phalanx a full 180 degrees to face his returning foes head-on. (Rotating left into column, the formation advanced to the other end of the field, turned back into phalanx and then countermarched to reverse its original facing, the men in the rearmost rank holding position as their files moved around to redress in front of them [Asclepiodotus 10.14].) He thus blocked the Theban route of escape with his "main body" (Xenophon *Agesilaos* 2.11), this likely being the Spartans and mercenaries (some 3,500 spearmen), the rest of his army having scattered in pursuit. Probably at about even strength with Agesilaos, the Thebans formed up and closed front-to-front for a second round. And this time there was no quick giving way on either side; instead, it was an extended and brutal action in which "setting shields against shields, they shoved, fought, killed and were killed" per Xenophon (*Hellenica*), who was a participant. The Thebans were eventually able to punch a hole through the enemy line, cutting a narrow path along which some of them escaped as their weary foes drew back on either side. Agesilaos' men soon recovered and turned to chase the Thebans. They killed many of the fleeing men, but most got away, 80 finding sanctuary in a temple while the majority joined their beaten allies on Mount Helicon.

At day's end, the Spartans held a field that Xenophon described in some detail: "the earth stained with blood, friend and foe lying dead side by side, shields smashed to pieces, spears snapped in two, daggers bared of their sheaths, some on the ground, some embedded in the bodies, some yet gripped by the hand" (*Agesilaos* 2.14). The allies sent down from Helicon the next day to get a truce from Agesilaos (who'd been badly wounded late in the fight), which he granted so that they might recover their dead. Nepos (17.4.5) cited 10,000 allies slain, but that is surely an impossible figure and likely an echo of the inflated claim Xenophon reported for

Nemea River. It's more probable that the Thebans lost 500–1,000 spearmen (15–25 percent) and their allies another 1,000–2,000, while Agesilaus' cost was below 600.

Agesilaos sailed home to recuperate while Gylis, who had led the mora that came up from Corinth, took command of the army. He would march into Phocis and lose some troops skirmishing with Locrian missilemen. Seemingly a mere side note, this action is worthy of attention because it marked the sort of minor clash that now came to dominate the war. Badly beaten in two large-scale outings against the Spartans, the allies weren't willing to chance a third. The fighting on land would henceforth be confined to smaller engagements, primarily in the vicinity of the allied base at Corinth, thus giving the conflict the name it carries today. Meanwhile, the larger, strategic struggle would play out for the most part at sea over the next several years.

Sicily and Italy

Colonists stepping westward from the Greek home cities had founded poleis in the 8th century across both southern Italy and its large, satellite island of Sicily. On the latter, they had come into competition for the land not only with earlier tribal inhabitants (the Elymians, Sicans and Siculi), but also with "Punic" settlers from Phoenicia. The tribesmen had largely taken to the less desirable interior by the early 5th century, and that's when warfare broke out in earnest between the newcomers. The Greeks worked the soil and had built cities at the best sites from the broad eastern side nearest Greece along a majority of Sicily's roughly triangular shoreline. The Phoenicians were largely merchants and held trading centers in the western tip of the island closest to their powerful colony at Carthage on the North African coast. As frictions arose, the Carthaginians had mounted campaigns against the Greeks on Sicily. Outcomes for their efforts ran from disastrous to moderately successful. The last of these conflicts in 406–405 had led to the overthrow of democracy in the leading Grecian city of Syracuse on the island's southeastern shore. A young aristocrat there, Dionysius I (to be dubbed "the Great"), set up a tyranny and negotiated to keep his polis and Carthage at peace going into the new century. But in the days when Agesilaos was campaigning in Ionia and tensions on the Greek mainland were moving it toward the long grind of the Corinthian War, Dionysius was casting a covetous eye upon Carthaginian land in western Sicily and plotting to add to his domain by force of arms. This would kick off the tyrant's "Second Carthaginian War" (that of the late 5th century being the first).

Messana II and Taruomenium (394 B.C.) and Abacaene (393 B.C.)

Dionysius sent an ultimatum to Carthage in the spring of 397. This unreasonably demanded that all Greek settlements remaining under its control be freed. He then marched against Motya, which was the leading Punic city on Sicily. Motya sat on a small, rounded island off the west coast, connected by a long causeway to the mainland. Dionysius came against this place with a possible 40,000 infantry and 3,000 horsemen (Caven [1990, 100], the figure for footmen disputing Diodorus' unlikely claim of 80,000 [14.47.7]). These included both a large number of local tribesmen and a probable 10,000 or so Greek mercenaries. Beating back a Carthaginian seaborne relief force by using bolt-throwing mechanical bows (a Syracusan invention dating to the turn of the century per Diodorus [14.42.1]), Dionysius was able to capture Motya before the end of the summer. However, the Carthaginians landed a large army in 396 and, after the tyrant lost a major sea battle, he retired to Syracuse to face a siege. The following campaign season saw small skirmishes on land and a modest Greek naval victory in the Great Harbor of

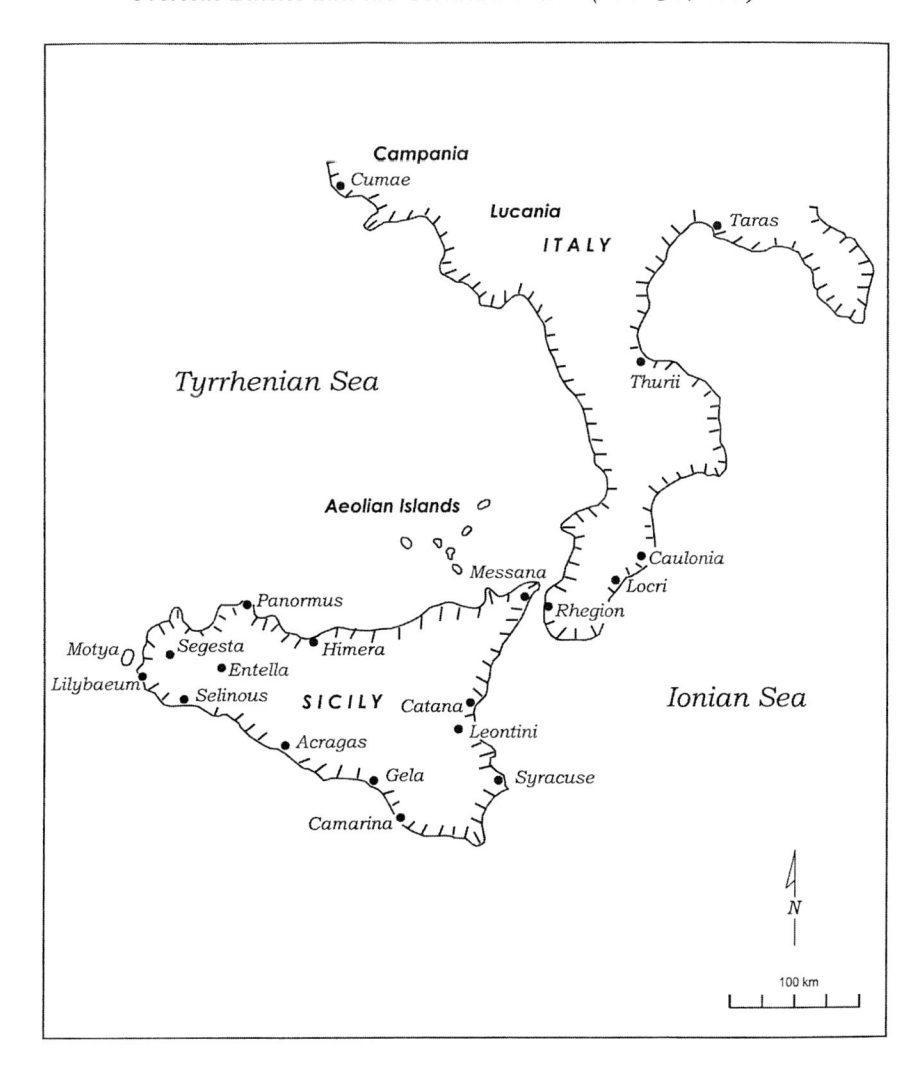

THE GREEK WEST — SOUTHERN ITALY/SICILY

Syracuse on the south side of the city. However, the main event that year didn't take place in combat, but rather in the Carthaginian camp where a plague broke out. Weakened by disease, the Punic fleet and encampment came under damaging attacks by Dionysius' forces and the Carthaginian commander, Himilco, eventually agreed to pay an indemnity and withdraw his citizen soldiers (perhaps 3,000–6,000 men whom he evacuated on 40 ships). This callously abandoned the rest of his army to be captured and enslaved by the Greeks. (The lone exception was a Spanish mercenary unit. This put up strong resistance and was taken into service at Syracuse.)

The operations of 397–395 had not gained either side its strategic goal (taking western Sicily for the tyrant and permanently crushing that Syracusan threat for Carthage). This guaranteed that the war would continue. There was, however, some delay. Carthage had to first deal with a revolt among its Libyan subjects, who had lost a large contingent among the men betrayed and left behind at Syracuse. This uprising couldn't be brought under control until the end of 394. Meanwhile, Dionysius had distractions as well. His finances were hard pressed and he found it difficult to pay the mercenaries and honor stipends owed to his citizen hoplites. As a result, he had to scramble to avoid a rebellion of his own. Dionysius solved the problem by giving land to the hired men. And among the communities he set up, ceded or resettled at this time was Messana, which sat on the northeastern corner of Sicily along the strait that separated the island from Italy. Across the way, the Greek colony of Rhegion commanded the Italian side of this narrow channel.

The Rhegians had taken in a good number of Dionysius' exiled foes and were concerned that their city might soon become a target for the tyrant's ambitions. They therefore decided to preempt an attack by crossing over and taking out his outpost at Messana to control both sides of the strait. As Rhegian forces prepared an investment, the new Messanian settlers sallied to fight on open ground. Based on its population of the recent past (Diodorus 14.78.5), Messana could likely field around 4,000–5,000 hoplites with 1,000–1,500 foot skirmishers. As for the Rhegians, previous deployments suggest that they might have sent at least 3,000 spearmen of their own (Ray 2010, 26). To these we can then add 1,000–2,000 Syracusan exiles, the present invasion force being led by just such an outcast named Heloris. With hoplite manpower thus closely balanced, the Messanians scored a solid victory in the ensuing battle, slaying 500 of the enemy (Diodorus 14.87.2). Such hefty casualties at 10–12.5 percent on the losing side suggest either a thorough pursuit or the envelopment of a wing. Messanian losses would have been much lower, probably less than 5 percent.

Dionysius wanted to repay the Rhegian attack. First, however, he felt it best to better secure the strait-crossing that would be in his rear by eliminating the nearby hostile Siculi hilltop stronghold of Taruomenium. But when he and his army of perhaps 10,000 mercenaries (with 7,000–8,000 hoplites) managed to break into the city, they found themselves in serious trouble against its skirmisher-equipped defenders despite outnumbering them by maybe as much as 3 to 1. The barbarians formed into a body and blocked the town's narrow passages. Unable to deploy at any width, the tyrant's superior manpower proved of little value. At the same time, the heavier equipment of his spearmen was offset by hordes of enemy missilemen firing down from the rooftops and other high ground to devastating effect. The barbarians ultimately pushed their Greek foes out of the city and inflicted serious losses (600 men per Diodorus [14.88.4]). So bloodied, Dionysius decided to put his plans for Rhegion on hold.

Messana would again become a flashpoint the next year when the Carthaginians, not yet fully recovered from the uprising at home, used resources already on Sicily to launch an attack there. Magon, who commanded all Punic forces on the island, led his men around to ravage the countryside. However, he then withdrew upon the approach of Dionysius, falling back on the allied city of Abacaene. The Carthaginians rallied there and offered the Greeks a pitched battle. Our lone source (Dionysius 14.90.3–4) gives no strengths for the contending armies, but we can assume from the mutual agreement to accept engagement that they were comparable. Complements of around 10,000 might have been present on either side, each fielding perhaps 8,000 or so in heavy infantry. This represents an effort on the tyrant's part that used only his mercenary contingent. Magon's force would have been a combination of levies drawn from garrison troops (hoplite-type soldiers from North Africa and Italy and perhaps some armored spearmen with shields from Spain) and allied Siculi light infantry and cavalry. Once combat opened, the more uniformly armed, professional hoplites of the dictator seem to have carried the day, killing 800 of Magon's men (8 percent of his line infantry) and chasing the rest into Abacaene. Dionysius withdrew with his army intact (having undoubtedly suffered only a couple of percent loss) and took ship to finally strike Rhegion. Though he was unable to take that city, he did pillage the area and forced the Rhegians into a truce that let him return home with his booty.

The Second Carthaginian War of Dionysius would end in anti-climactic fashion in 392. That's when Magon, having been heavily reinforced from Carthage, faced off against the Syracusan and his full resources in central Sicily outside Agyrium. This was the capital of a powerful Siculi community that had not allied with Carthage. The tyrant was unwilling to risk a battle and Diodorus claimed (14.95.1–3) that his 20,000-man army was outnumbered by 4 to 1. However, the historian's figure for the force from Carthage is undoubtedly much inflated. Based on earlier expeditions, it's more apt that Magon held no more than a 50 percent advantage in overall numbers that was then reduced when the Agyrinaeans joined Dionysius. Another indication that the odds weren't so lopsided is that the Syracusans thought a favorable battlefield solution was quite feasible. When Dionysius chose to starve the enemy out of Sicily, his inpatient citizen levy went home. This took at least 5,000 hoplites out of the field; all the same, the tyrant persisted in his strategy with total success. Magon grew so short on food that he was willing to negotiate a peace treaty and leave without a fight. Dionysius actually got very good terms. These not only kept his current realm intact, but added to it most of the Siculi that had been Punic allies.

Laus and Elleporus Rivers (389 B.C.)

Once more at peace with Carthage, Dionysius turned his attention from western Sicily to focus efforts on southern Italy. The Grecian poleis there had by this time formed an "Italian League" to defend against him. Accepting this challenge, he launched a campaign across the channel in 390, leading an army of 20,000 foot soldiers (likely 15,000 hoplites and 5,000 skirmishers) and 1,000 horsemen that he ferried over in 120 ships. The tyrant landed at Locris, which lay northeast of Rhegion on the eastern coast of the "toe" of Italy, and marched inland to ravage Rhegian territory. However, when he was unable to entice the Italian Greeks into a decisive battle, he sailed home that winter. Looking for a more effective way to damage his foes above the strait, he next made an alliance with that area's Lucanian tribesmen.

The Lucanians were a hill people that had formed a powerful federation of eleven tribes, each perhaps able to field an average 4,000–6,000 fighters. Part of the Oscan tribal grouping, Lucanian warriors were individually outfitted according to their personal wealth. At the upper end were men with spear and/or javelins that carried a large, center-grip shield (*scutum*) and wore a metal helmet, a harness for the chest (with one to three small metal plates or *pectorales*) and greaves (at least one on the left leg that was put forward in fighting stance). Poorer folk would sport only a portion of this panoply according to what they could afford. For every eight to ten men who fought on foot there was usually one high-born horseman equipped in the wealthier fashion and wielding javelins but sans shield. Inspired by their alliance with Dionysius, the Lucanians descended upon the territory of Thurii, a polis that sat at the front-instep of the Italian boot along the southeast shoreline. The Thurians called for help from the Italian League and, though they apparently set out at first by themselves, soon were part of a force of 14,000 infantry and about 1,000 cavalry (Diodorus 14.101)—this probably included troops from just the closest allies as it was less than half of Italiote potential. The infantry likely broke down into 10,000 hoplites and 4,000 light-armed.

Rather than fight their foes on open ground favorable to the Greek phalanx, the Lucanians fell back into their own rugged territory. In this way, they were able to contact and gather perhaps half to two-thirds of their federated manpower and create a huge counter-force some 30,000 strong. The Italiotes, meanwhile, had followed and wound their way through narrow pathways to come out on a plain near the mouth of the river Laus, a bowl-like expanse surrounded by high hills and cliffs. This was where the Lucanians had set up an ambush, and the tribesmen suddenly came down from forest cover on the enclosing heights to attack on all sides. Taken by surprise, the Greeks tried to form up and meet the charging barbarians, but any attempt to create a defensive square seems to have fallen victim to both the speed of the assault and the lack of organization of this ad hoc collection of militia spearmen from different cities who had never drilled together. The result was a slaughter as the tribesmen shattered any nascent cohesion the hoplites might have gained, cutting them down in place or as they ran away. Diodorus claimed that 10,000 Greeks lost their lives. This might be an exaggeration honoring the total hoplite force involved; still, the death toll among those defeated must have been huge and Diodorus' 67 percent tally is certainly within the realm of possibility. Around 1,000 of the survivors did manage to reach the sea, where they were taken captive by Dionysius' brother, Leptines, who was there with some warships to support the Lucanians. The Syracusan on his own initiative arranged a ransom to be paid for the prisoners and mediated a truce between the tribesmen and the Italiote cites. This was clearly very pro–Greek of him, but quite contrary to his brother's plans and got Leptines removed from command.

Though his sibling had managed to blunt the effect somewhat, Dionysius' pact with the Lucanians had still greatly weakened his foes in Italy. He now felt safe in personally taking the field against them. The Italian League mustered its full remaining strength (maybe only 70 percent of what it had been before Laus) with 25,000 footmen and 2,000 cavalry (Diodorus 14.103.6). These gathered at Croton, the League's largest city. Heloris, the exile who'd been turned back at Messana five years earlier, took command of the Italiote forces. Once organized, he led his army out with the intent of engaging Dionysius where he was laying siege to the coastal town of Caulonia east of Rhegion. Word of this march soon reached Dionysius. Withdrawing quickly from around the city, he hurried off to confront Heloris, taking him unaware just after dawn as his army was preparing to leave a campsite along the Elleporus River. The Syracusan force included 20,000 infantry (probably 15,000 hoplites and 5,000 skirmishers) and 3,000 horsemen (Diodorus 14.103.2) and these closed to catch the enemy commander separated slightly from his main body with a select vanguard lochos of 500 men. Forming a close-knit phalanx, the tyrant's spearmen swept forward like a wave, surrounding and wiping out the exile and his small band of elites almost to a man. Dionysius' array then advanced to take care of the rest of the League army. A runner from Heloris had by now reached its campsite and the various allied contingents were rushing up from the river one at a time and in some confusion.

The scrambling Italiotes met defeat in detail as each group came on the scene, never able to properly organize an effective composite formation against their well-ordered opposition. Thus, despite having essayed a heroic effort, they finally took to their heels. Some of the beaten men scattered through the countryside, but a main body of about 10,000 managed to stay together and dig in on high ground for a last stand. Rather than waste troops on a disadvantaged uphill assault, Dionysius surrounded this waterless position and waited for his thirsty foes to give in. This they did the very next day. In a surprise to all, Dionysius treated those captured with lenience in a savvy move that dismantled the Italian League's unity against him. He then set off for Rhegion. Isolated now, the Rhegians came to terms and the tyrant returned to Caulonia. That city surrendered as well and he leveled the place, relocating its population to Syracuse. The year therefore closed with Dionysius having established sway over a good portion of the southern Italian mainland.

The Corinthian War II

Nearly two years after having won grand victories at Nemea River and Coronea II, Sparta was struggling in its twin wars against the allied coalition on one hand and Persia on the other. The former from its base at Corinth had been able to control the isthmus leading out of the

Peloponnese, curtailing broader operations and largely confining the Spartans to working close to their own local stronghold of Sicyon. What little action there was in 393 and into early 392 thus consisted of raids and skirmishes around Corinth, and these did little more than damage that polis' own property. Meanwhile, a Persian financed fleet under the Athenian Conon had been ravaging the Laconian coast. Worst yet, the latter even captured Sparta's most vulnerable homeland district, which sat off the southern shore on the island of Cythera. With no military solution in sight on either front, the Spartans began in 392 to seek a three-way negotiated peace. The discussions did not bring an end to the war, however, since the terms being pushed by Sparta's representative Antalcidas appealed neither to the coalition (as it left the Spartans dominant over Greek affairs) nor the Persians (who wanted to regain Ionia). Still, Sparta was able to convince the Persians of a future threat from Athens, leading them to end support for the allied sea effort.

Long Walls of Corinth (392 B.C.)

The allies had helped secure Corinth by constructing a walled corridor that widened from a couple of kilometers separation near the city to pass up either side of its port of Lechaion to the north on the Corinthian Gulf. There was, however, turmoil within Corinth over whether it should continue on the allied side in light of all the damage it was taking on the coalition's behalf. Political upheaval in the city led to a change of government in the spring of 392 and the union of Corinth and Argos into a single, democratic state with the blessing of Athens and the Boeotians. All this trouble had exiled a number of Corinthians and disaffected others still in town. Some of the latter now conspired to let the garrison commander at Sicyon bring his troops inside the port corridor. The Spartan Praxitas moved at night to enter through an open gate, bringing with him his own mora (around 1,000 spearmen), troops from Sicyon (maybe including a two-thirds muster of 2,000 hoplites) and 150 heavy-armed Corinthian exiles along with a few Spartan-led horsemen and maybe 500–1,000 in light infantry. Mindful of a small Theban garrison at Lechaion, Praxitas set up his men in a battle line facing Corinth with the corridor walls on either flank.

Praxitas had to move south toward town where the corridor was narrower in order to cover the entire span with so few troops. And even so, his array was too thin for conventional phalanx action, perhaps a single rank a little less than 3km wide. The Spartan therefore used a field work to stiffen his front, starting with a shallow ditch. This would discomfit the enemy front-fighters by making them battle upward, disturbing their footwork and keeping the following rank a pace or so back where they were less able to apply effective othismos and might even be out of spear reach. Behind, he placed a short barrier of some sort incorporating dirt piled up from the trench. His spearmen could lean over it to fight while being protected below from spear strikes and any pushing of opposing files. This effectively limited potential engagement to just one rank on each side toward negating any enemy advantage in manpower. His skirmishers then spread out in back of the hoplites to give covering fire over their heads.

Neither reinforcements nor enemies arrived the first day, but on the second an allied force came up from the city. This consisted of spearmen from Argos (perhaps 3,000) and Corinth (likely 2,000) plus mercenary peltasts (maybe 800 or so) under Iphicrates of Athens. The allies found the Spartans in charge of the right side of their array, fixed against the western wall, with the exiles holding a short stretch from an anchor on the east wall and the Sicyonians standing across the rest of the front. Forming into line of battle, the Argives went after the men from Sicyon, the Corinthians advanced to oppose the Spartans and the peltasts charged the outcasts. The Sicyonians were soon defeated, running away as spearmen from Argos pushed a broad hole through the barrier without further opposition. The Argives chased their beaten foes all the way to the sea where they caught and killed quite a few. The Spartan cavalry commander, seeing this unfolding tragedy, had dismounted with some volunteers and attempted to aid the fugitives using discarded Sicyonian shields, but he and most of his handful of men were quickly overwhelmed and slain.

Elsewhere on the field, it was the exiles and Spartans that prevailed. Iphicrates and his peltasts had been impotent against the well-protected outcasts on the east wing, the hoplites' lower bodies covered by the field work and upper by helmets and shields proving impervious to javelins. Likewise, there was no hope for the lighter armed men to force their way through hand-to-hand as the Argives had done, since their opponents' heavy gear was much superior in shock fighting. The javelinmen therefore beat a retreat under fire from the exiles' own backing missilemen. As for the Spartans, they had simply proven better man-for-man, outdueling and intimidating their opponents until the Corinthians lost heart and retreated when the spearmen from Sparta threatened to mount their low barrier and bring the fight to them.

While the outcast hoplites and their light infantry advanced toward the city in the wake of Iphicrates' retreat, Praxitas did indeed lead his troops over their fronting wall and ditch. He then arrayed a phalanx maybe four shields deep and 250m across facing east toward where the Argives had broken through, setting his left wing next to the abandoned field work and having the light infantry screen the other flank. This let him move forward to attack the men from Argos on their unshielded right as they returned from besting the Sicyonians, straggling back unit by unit in ragged formation through the wide breach in the defensive barrier. In truth, this was a smaller scale replay of the Argives' defeat two years earlier at Nemea River. Many on the Argive right were killed, while those on the other side crowded into a mob along the eastern wall and fled toward town. However, they soon ran into the Corinthian exiles in that direction and turned back toward the Spartans once more.

What followed was a slaughter. Some Argives were shoved together and lanced down where they stood. Others were trampled and suffocated in a hysterical crowd of their own men. The Spartans speared a few from steps in the wall as they tried to go up, while most who reached the top to jump down met pursuit and death on the far side. In the words of Xenophon: "so many fell within a short time that men accustomed to see heaps of corn, wood, or stones, beheld then heaps of dead bodies" (*Hellenica* 4.4.12). Diodorus (14.86.4) cited 1,000 dead on the day for the losers, which likely was 25–30 percent of the Argives and 5–10 percent among the Corinthians. For the winners, Sicyonian losses would have been steep as well (perhaps 400 men or 20 percent), but casualties must have been minimal among the rest.

Praxitas followed up his success in the battle of the "Long Walls" by destroying the Theban garrison at Lechaion to take the port. He would later tear holes in the corridor barriers and lead an offensive to the east against Athenian ally Megara in which he captured and garrisoned two outposts near that city. All the same, despite having gained another crushing (albeit smaller) victory that broke the blockade across the isthmus, Sparta was still no nearer to ending the war.

Lechaion and Methymna (390 B.C.)

The next year saw Agesilaos invade the Argolid to ravage the countryside without meeting any real resistance. Meanwhile, Iphicrates' peltasts chased off a guard of Mantinean hoplites below Lechaion, which allowed for a rapid repair of the gaps that had been made in the long walls. This work soon went for naught, though, as the returning Agesilaos swung by Corinth and ripped the barriers down again. Elsewhere, Iphicrates' peltasts notched another success, ambushing hoplites from Sicyon on their own soil and so terrorizing them that they developed a phobia regarding the javelineers. But while the Athenian and his men were able to range down as far as Arcadia to the north of Sparta and do well against spearmen there as well, they had their own overwhelming fear of the Spartans themselves. They would run from the dreaded Laconian hoplites, and even then sometimes came to grief when the younger spearmen proved capable of catching them from behind (Xenophon *Hellenica* 4.4.16). It was in this light that a mora of Spartans was able to freely sortie out of Lechaion to range all about Corinth. (Note that there is uncertainty as to the timing of Iphicrates' actions, some of which might have taken place in late 392 prior to Agesilaos attacking Argos.)

With the war in Europe running at low key, there was new trouble for Sparta on the Asian front. Struthus had gone into the field there for the Great King with an army that included 5,000 mercenary hoplites (Diodorus 14.99.2). However, it was the Persian's horsemen that caused the greatest harm at this time. The Spartans had sent out Thibron to deal with Struthus and he had taken that opportunity to pillage enemy territory and carry off a good deal of booty. Unfortunately, these expeditions were being carried out in a very casual and haphazard manner and Struthus' cavalry managed to catch the Spartan and some of his raiders lounging about on open ground just after breakfast. Sweeping down, the Persians killed Thibron and a number of those with him to put a sad damper on Sparta's counter-offensive in the region.

As the sporadic fighting around Corinth persisted into 390, it remained mercenaries like those led by Iphicrates that saw most of the action, with neither side seeking to involve large bodies of their citizen militias. The year did, however, see one modest but much ballyhooed engagement involving the heretofore all-conquering Spartan spearmen. This was sparked by, of all things, a religious festival back in Laconia. The people of the Spartan district of Amyclae set great store by a certain annual event that celebrated the god Apollo, and King Agesilaos elected to let his hoplites from there go home for the festivities. These men (some 400 in number) formed most of a single lochos, which was part of the mora currently on garrison duty at Lechaion. Leaving behind allied troops to hold post, the mora marched out with their cavalry to escort the Amyclaeans safely out of range of the enemy at Corinth. What was left of the Spartans (about 600 spearmen) saw their comrades off along with the horsemen and then headed back for Lechaion. This was all seen by the Athenians, who noted that the enemy regiment was not only temporarily undermanned, but also moving exposed along the coastal road with no mounted or light infantry support. Callias of Athens (who must have commanded at least 1,000 hoplites — an Athenian tribal levy or *taxis* [*taxeis* plural] roughly equivalent to a mora at Sparta) moved out with Iphicrates and his peltasts (maybe 800 strong) in the lead. Callias caught the Spartans just outside the port and set up his spearmen in phalanx at a fair distance to the south as the javelineers ran forward.

The peltasts took down several hoplites with their missiles and then retreated. The Spartans had the baggage-carriers that always accompanied them take the wounded into Lechaion and sent out their youngest soldiers to chase the attackers. Unable to catch their fleeter foes, these Spartan out-runners turned about only to be attacked on the way back by the missilemen. This set the pattern for what was to follow. Iphicrates' troops advanced time after time to hurl javelins into the Spartans, pull away, and then inflict even greater damage against any attempt at pursuit by the slower hoplites. Even when the Spartan horsemen showed up after completing their escort duty, there was no relief. This was because those inept riders did no more than keep even with their out-running infantry cohorts to suffer along with them.

As more and more of the Spartans fell, those remaining began to lose heart and finally withdrew in desperation onto a small hill close to the sea. But the missiles kept coming at them and, when the enemy phalanx began to close on their badly depleted ranks as well, they gave way at last. Some escaped with the horsemen and others swam out to friendly boats that had drawn near. Behind them, they left 250 dead, over 40 percent of their number lost without having done any damage at all to the enemy. It was a small victory over the Spartans compared to the reverses at Nemea River, Coronea and the Long Walls, which had cost the allies thousands of casualties; still, this was a great propaganda triumph that tarnished the image of Spartan invincibility.

The Athenians also scored against Sparta in Asia during 390. The island of Lesbos there off the Ionian coast had allied with the Spartans save for its leading city of Mytilene. In an effort to address this, the Athenian admiral Thrasybulus landed at that city with a 40-ship fleet from which he off-loaded its hoplite marines (*epibatai*). These numbered 400 at ten per vessel (Xenophon *Hellenica* 4.8.28). He then added spearmen from Mytilene, which might have come to 600 if a quarter had gone into exile (see Ray [2009, 160] for a discussion of manpower potential on Lesbos). Exiles from the other Lesbian cities that had fled to Mytilene joined him as well (maybe 300–400 at a quarter of the spearmen from the rest of the island) to total 1,300–1,400 hoplites in all. Light support would have been on the order of 300–500 foot skirmishers including both locals and oarsmen from the fleet. Leading this combined force from the city, Thrasybulus advanced on Methymna, which sat at the northern end of the north-south elongate island and hosted the local Spartan governor.

Therimachus of Sparta learned of Thrasybulus' approach and collected an army of his own. He could call upon a body of marines (perhaps on a par with Thrasybulus' at 400–500), the hoplites of Methymna (around 400–500 sans reserves and defectors) and some Mytilenian exiles (200 or so). This let him offer battle outside the city with a heavy-armed array that was probably only slightly smaller than that of his Athenian opponent. Sadly, we have no description of this engagement save Diodorus' claim that Thrasybulus made a "brilliant fight" (14.94.4) in which Therimachus died in action (per Xenophon) and many Methymnaeans lost their lives in a pursuit that drove the survivors back inside the city walls. Thrasybulus wouldn't long survive this victory, as he later sailed to the Asian mainland and took his fleet into the Eurymedon River to prey upon the communities along its banks. Striking back, some of the locals made a nighttime attack on the Athenians' camp that claimed Thrasybulus and several others and chased the fleet back to sea.

Acarnania and Cremaste (389 B.C.) and Tripyrgia (388)

Achaea in the north-central Peloponnese had interests across the Gulf of Corinth in Aetolia and was in conflict there with the Acarnanians, members of the anti–Spartan alliance whose land lay above the mouth of the Gulf in northwestern Greece. The Achaeans threatened in 389 to withdraw from their pact with Sparta unless it promised to attack Acarnania. The Spartans agreed and sent out Agesilaos with two morai (2,000 hoplites) and a matching contingent of allied troops along with some cavalry to join the entire Achaean levy (perhaps 2,000–3,000 spearmen). The Acarnanians withdrew to their walled cities and refused demands by the Spartan king that they pledge fealty to his polis, causing him to respond by spoiling their land. After enduring considerable economic damage, the Acarnanians finally united to attack the invading force as it camped on a mountain slope. Acarnania was a pastoral nation that had many slingers among its herdsmen and large numbers of these fired their bullets down from the upper slope as comrades threw rocks. Caught in this dangerous hail, Agesilaos and his men retreated onto the narrow plain of the valley below, where they camped beside a lake as the Acarnanians drew off at nightfall.

Agesilaos decamped the next day and began to march out, but found the enemy in possession of the surrounding mountainsides from which they hurled javelins and stones. This harassed his column to the point that further progress became impossible once it was faced with exiting through a narrow pass. And any attempt to strike back that the Spartan's hoplites and horsemen made encountered the same problem the mora at Lechaion had met, with fleeter foes able to retreat and easily keep out of reach. Assessing the terrain in this dire situation, Agesilaos saw that the slope on his left was more accessible for his riders and spearmen and decided to have a go in that direction. The king sent his cavalry up in company with his youngest and most agile hoplites as he followed behind with the rest of the spearmen in formation.

This time, the Spartan out-runners were able to catch and kill many light-armed men as they tried to scramble away; however, they had to break off pursuit once near the ridge's crest because the Acarnanians had hoplites in place there (perhaps 2,000–3,000 strong) along with the bulk of their peltasts. Agesilaos' riders retired to flank position and the younger spearmen rejoined his ranks as the escaping skirmishers passed through their own heavy array, which then closed order to meet the advancing phalanx. The Acarnanian peltasts now hurled javelins and a number of their hoplites cast their spears as well in a desperate attempt to turn back the Spartan charge. But though this deluge took down a few horses, it didn't deter the battle-savvy southern spearmen, who kept relentlessly closing. The Acarnanians, many now having disarmed themselves by exhausting their javelins or throwing away their spear, didn't wait for the deeper Spartan formation to strike and made to run off downhill in the other direction. Lunging up into the disintegrating enemy battle line, Agesilaos' front-fighters managed to kill about 300 of their foes (10–15 percent) before the rest escaped. The king then returned to his ravaging of the land before heading home in the fall, doing so thorough a job that the Acarnanians would surrender without further contest when faced with the prospect of another invasion the next summer.

Meanwhile, events were heating up in the northern Aegean. The Spartans had sent Anaxibius there with three warships, perhaps 120 Spartan hoplites as marines and enough money to hire 1,000 mercenaries to deal with the Athenian forces in the Hellespontine region. He set up at Abydos, which had the best harbor on the Asian side of the Hellespont, and began raiding nearby cities and capturing Athenian cargo vessels. Athens reacted by dispatching Iphicrates with 1,200 mercenary peltasts on eight ships that also carried 80 epibatai. Iphicrates discovered that the Spartan had marched south to Antandrus with his marines, mercenaries (probably 600–800 spearmen and 200–400 peltasts) and 200 hoplites from Abydos. He therefore landed at night to set up an ambush (Xenophon *Hellenica* 4.8.35–39). The chosen spot lay just below Abydos near Cremaste and beside the west-flowing Rhodios River that would serve as the Spartan's route home. And sure enough, Anaxibius and his men before long came down the path above the river bank, strung out along that narrow track and heedless of any danger in friendly country. Iphicrates allowed the Abydene spearmen in the van to pass down toward the stream and then sprang out to surprise the Spartans next in line. Seeing that the situation was hopeless, Anaxibius dismissed his men and turned to fight a suicidal delaying action along with a dozen local Spartan commanders who had gone with him on the Antandrus expedition. The peltasts overran this small rearguard and then chased the marines and others who had fled, dispatching many of the Spartans (maybe 20–30 percent) and about 200 of their mercenaries plus 50 of the men from Abydos as well.

Athens' Chabrias sprang a similar trap the next year (Xenophon *Hellenica* 5.1.10–13). This was on the island of Aigina in the Saronic Gulf, which lay just west off the shore of the Athenian homeland of Attica. Chabrias had brought 800 peltasts and 80 marines on ten ships of his own plus some more hoplites on vessels sent from Athens (possibly the remaining 18 triremes of 28 that had been in Athens' main harbor just to the east at Piraeus). Chabrias thus might have had up to 800 spearmen in all. Like Iphicrates, he made a night landing, coming ashore near where the Spartans were based. He set up an ambush in a hollow near the hill of Tripyrgia and had his hoplites ascend the rise next morning and make themselves known to draw out the enemy. The Spartan commander, Gorgopas, came with all his own epibatai (350–500 at around 30–40 each from twelve ships), men drawn from his ship crews (perhaps 400–500 with makeshift weapons) and some spearmen from Aegina (citizens and resident aliens, maybe 600 or so). Unaware of the hiding peltasts, he was looking to have a near 2 to 1 advantage against the enemy arrayed on Tripyrgia.

The Athenians' javelineers let the opposing van of marines go past and then rose to shower missiles on the rest of the thin enemy column. At the same time, their hoplites began to descend off Tripyrgia, attacking in formation to destroy the disorganized lead element that had been allowed beyond the ambush site. Among those who fell there were Gorgopas and eight spartiates who were with him, their deaths sending the remaining vanguard to join their entire force in flight. Those killed with Gorgopas' advance section probably amounted to 100–150 men, while the crewmen and locals present lost another 350 (around 30 percent) against what must have been negligible casualties among the victors.

The campaign season of 388 saw Sparta's King Agesipolis lead another foray by his polis' levy into Argos, but the war on land in Greece remained largely stalled as fall arrived. There was a major turning point at sea early the next year, however, as the Spartans took advantage of Athenian overconfidence after their success on Aegina to launch a strike into the harbor at Piraeus under the command of Agesilaos' brother Teleutias. It was a stunning insult to the pride and reputation of the Athenian navy. What followed was a very successful campaign by Teleutias against Attic coastal sites and commercial shipping that dealt a heavy economic blow to Athens.

It was at this point that the Persians and Spartans finally came to an understanding to end their fighting in Asia. This called for Sparta to concede Ionia in return for Artaxerxes' pledge to join the Greek states in recognizing the independence of all mainland poleis. Agreed between Antalcidas for Sparta and Artaxerxes II as Great King, this pact was known variously as the Peace of Antalcidas or the King's Peace. With Persian backing and aid from Syracuse, Antalcidas was now able to confine the Athenian fleet within the Bosporus and close the route that Athens relied upon for vital grain shipments from the Black Sea region. With the allies' naval champion thus crippled and ready to give up, Agesilaos headed a conference in Sparta during the winter of 387/86 in which all of the belligerents agreed to the terms set out in the Peace of Antalcidas to bring the long Corinthian conflict to an end.

Tactical Discussion: 400–387 B.C.

Grecian tactical practices during the early 4th century very much continued those of the recent past. The largest phalanx actions saw Spartans dominate by sweeping around (*cyclosis*) or pushing through the opposing left. A well worn method described by Thucydides at Mantinea I in 418 (5.71–73), this was a deliberate exaggeration of the natural tendency for hoplites to drift rightward during advance so as to move closer to the protection of their line-mate's shield on that side. After this maneuver, if needed, they would then reform to engage any foes still remaining on the field. Variations in the subject era included Agesilaos making his second engagement at Coronea II (394) into a frontal assault (rather than the usual flank attack) and employment of a field work at the Long Walls of Corinth (392). The former proved a costly mistake not to be repeated and the latter was unique as well due to its singular setting. Another notable trend was that ambushes were unusually common. Such surprise attacks were factors in half a dozen engagements, nearly a quarter of the total, and every one was successful. The most telling of these by a Grecian army came against the Persians at Sardis in 395. Yet this ploy had precedent in that Demosthenes of Athens had sprung a very similar trap against the Spartans at Olpae in 426/25 (Thucydides 3.107–198).

Perhaps the tactical event in this era most often seen as revolutionary was the light-armed attack that destroyed the mora at Lechaion (390). However, this too had pre-existing roots. Javelineers from Athens backed by hoplites had defeated Spartan spearmen in much the same fashion at Spaectaria back in 425 (Thucydides 4.29–37). The only truly new approach to pitched combat during this period belongs to Xenophon at Colchis (400). His use there of long, multiple columns interspersed with light infantry was a very creative solution to the challenge of fighting in difficult terrain and foreshadowed specialized formations to be employed later by Alexander the Great in some of his lesser actions against tribal foes.

Three commanders that have gained lasting fame emerged at this time: Xenophon, Agesilaos and Iphicrates. Xenophon's exploits may be a bit overstated due to our record of them coming mostly from his own accounts, which likely were at least somewhat self-serving. Still, the tactical evolution at Colchis probably wasn't proposed by his conservative Spartan co-commander; thus, this and other progressive approaches outlined in the *Anabasis* may well be his own. All the same, where we know Xenophon held sole command (in 400 at Metropolis and Calpe Harbor III), he used very conventional tactics, suggesting that he was quite traditional most of the time. And Agesilaos, a general much lauded by Xenophon, was likewise only a modest innovator. He did, however, have a large bag of "tried-and-true" tricks as shown by his adeptness at indirect approaches (leading foes to misread the true destination of his marches) and the surprise attack at Sardis. Agesilaos was at his most progressive in the employment of cavalry. Based on experiences in Asia, his development of a strong mounted arm was daring in context of the intense focus on heavy infantry in his native Sparta. And his aggressive use of riders at Acarnania (389) turned a major pending defeat into victory. As for Iphicrates, he excelled at leading peltasts, both paired with hoplites (Lechaion) and on their own (Cremaste in 389). Possessed of a highly creative and practical mind, he would go on to have a significant impact on evolution of the Grecian fighting arts.

* * *

The Spartans had overcome limitations of their insular state with regard to wealth, gross manpower and military capability beyond heavy infantry to bring the Corinthian War to a conclusion on favorable terms. But while Sparta could still claim to be Greece's leading power, with authority to enforce the conditions of the cease fire on its other signatories, the situation remained volatile. The Peace of Antalcidas was accepted only with great reluctance outside of Sparta, especially at Athens and Thebes. For the Athenians, betrayal of Ionian freedom was deeply resented, while the Thebans had seen the agreement's guarantee of autonomy for all poleis destroy their Boeotian confederacy. These issues along with a variety of individual agendas and the specters of Persia in the east and Carthage in the west all hung heavy over the Greek world as the new century continued to unfold.

II. Trained in War

Battles Around the Mediterranean; Chalcidian, Boeotian and Spartan Wars (386–360 B.C.)

[Lycurgus, the law-giver of Sparta, ordered] "that they should not make war often, or long, with the same enemy, lest that they should train and instruct them in war, by habituating them to defend themselves. And this is what Agesilaos was much blamed for, a long time after, it being thought that by his continual incursions into Boeotia, he made the Thebans a match for the Lacedaemonians."
Plutarch (Vol. I *Lycurgus*, 64)

The end of the Corinthian War offered the Greeks a great opportunity for an extended period of relative tranquility. Sadly, this was not to be. The next quarter century saw leaders that had risen to prominence defending their native lands and/or the greater cause of Grecian freedom now spawn a widespread series of deadly conflicts. Thus, Evagoras I of Salamis would strive to liberate most of Cyprus from Persia, yet lose much of what he'd gained in a bid to extend his reach onto the Asian mainland. Likewise, Dionysius I of Syracuse, whose selfish efforts had nonetheless protected Sicily from Carthage, would initiate wars of aggression in a quest to expand hegemonic control across his island and well beyond. Meanwhile, Agesilaos II of Sparta, who had gained fame in the century's opening decade as a champion of the Greek cause in Asia, would in this new era turn his nation's fabled military might toward denying liberty to fellow Greeks, waging oppressive campaigns across a swath running from the Peloponnese all the way to Chalcidice in the far north. And, finally, Pelopidas and Epaminondas of Thebes would shine in leading a crusade to rid their land of foreign domination, only to then have their passions for spreading Theban power and polices lead them into aggressive and ultimately fatal foreign ventures.

Cyprus, Italy and the Chalcidice

Even as fighting in Greece ceased with the Peace of Antalcidas at close of winter 387/86, another clash involving Greek arms had reached no more than mid-passage in what would ultimately be a decade-long run. This was the conflict between Persia and Evagoras, master of Salamis and nearly all the rest of the island of Cyprus. Evagoras' prolonged struggle against the forces of the Great King was largely a matter of long periods of preparation punctuated by city assaults, a naval action and siege, but generated at least one significant land battle.

Citium (386 B.C.)

Cyprus in the far eastern Mediterranean hosted some of the most distant outposts of Greece. These small kingdoms, many derived from settlements dating back to Mycenaean times, had come to share their island with other cities that were of Phoenician origin. Ruled first by Assyria and then Egypt, Cyprus came under nearly continuous Persian domination after 545; however, an attempt to change that subordinate status began in 411. This was when a Greek royal named Evagoras returned from exile in Cilicia to gain the crown of his native Cyprian Salamis.

An ardent advocate of Hellenic culture, Evagoras embraced a program of spreading its values throughout Cyprus in league with Athens. Critically, his policies also seem to have been visibly expansionist (Isocrates *Evagoras* 59) and raised frictions that c. 391 led to a state of war with Persia. Evagoras had built up a large military and Diodorus claimed (15.2.3–4, 3.4) that his army contained 6,000 of his own subjects (predominantly hoplites) plus an even larger number of men sent by his allies (perhaps 9,000 or more mainly Greek mercenaries). He had personal funds to hire troops directly as well, these likely including both Ionian and Carian spearmen. Evagoras might thus have collected some 20,000 fighters in all, representing maybe 16,000 heavy footmen supported by light infantry and cavalry.

Evagoras fared quite well early on in his campaigns against Persia according to both Diodorus and Isocrates (*Evagoras* 62). He was thus able to hold his own at home while capturing Tyre as well as other Phoenician cities. Indeed, his successes on the mainland proved sufficient to eventually bring the Cilician interior into revolt against the Great King. The Persians responded by gathering a large army in Cilicia in 386. The true nature of this force is clouded by an exaggerated estimate of its size by Diodorus (15.2.1); however, it might have consisted of around 30,000 line infantry (a tenth of Diodorus' claim for the entire armament) with strong supporting light elements. The heavier-armed backbone of the Persian host would probably have come from a garrison already on post in Cilicia (maybe 6,000 men at 60 percent nominal strength) plus three more baivaraba mustered from elsewhere in the empire (24,000 soldiers at 80 percent nominal). Likely on hand as well were some 3,000 horsemen (four hazaraba, each attached to a respective baivarabam of foot at 10 percent its manpower) and some local Cilicians armed with javelins. The latter might have counted about one skirmisher for each four line infantrymen to bring the entire army to around 40,000 combatants. Given significant seagoing requirements, the imperials also assembled an armada that could have had better than 300 triremes as well as numerous supply transports.

The Persians at first kept mostly to the mainland that they might guard vulnerable sites. Still, they landed an advance contingent at Citium, a Phoenician port lying just below and to the west of Evagoras' stronghold at Salamis in the eastern quarter of Cyprus. Diodorus' account then states that the Greek leader fell in with "a body of the land force near the sea" (16.4.2), which he was able to defeat. This isn't much to go on, but could well describe an action involving a single baivarabam (8,000 or so foot soldiers) along with a regiment of cavalry (800 riders) and some javelinmen. If so, the Persians were probably probing toward Salamis along the shores of modern Larnaca Bay, which spreads northeastward from the site of ancient Citium. The Greek force here is even more speculative. However, as little as half of his army would have let Evagoras match fronts by forming up his hoplites eight-deep against opposition filed at a similar depth. With the Persian right and Cypriot left holding posts tight against the coast, the spearmen of Evagoras (having arms better suited to the occasion) must have either outflanked or outfought the imperial inland wing. This would have let them roll around that end under cover from a screen of riders and light footmen. No doubt rapidly routing their foes, the Greeks probably chased them back down the strand toward the Persian base. Fatalities in this engagement could have run in the range of 1–3 percent for the victors and around 5–10 percent for the losers.

Evagoras was much encouraged by his success in this action, yet it would prove irrelevant when the Persians won a pivotal sea battle off Citium. Having reduced enemy naval assets in that fight, they now felt free to move most of their army onto Cyprus. Evagoras seems to have been reluctant to challenge so strong a force in the field and eventually found himself invested within Salamis. In the end, seeing no way forward after most of his allies had deserted (Isocrates [*Panegyricus* 141] made the no doubt hyperbolic but telling claim that he was down to only 3,000 light-armed troops at this point), Evagoras sought and came to terms in 380.

Pyrgi (384 B.C.)

On the other side of the Greek world from Cyprus, Syracuse's Dionysius had been spreading his influence into the Italian south and now reached around the Adriatic and even toward mainland Greece. The tyrant founded colonies in northern Italy and Illyria and allied in 385 with Illyrians at war with the adjacent tribal Molossians of Epirus. He supplied his new barbarian allies with 2,000 soldiers and 500 sets of heavy Greek fighting gear. The Illyrians, already being oriented toward shock action with spear and shield, gave the gifted panoplies to their best men and worked the tyrant's loaned troops into their combat array. But it seems that they now overplayed their hand. Seeking to promote Alcetas (who had been a resident exile at Dionysius' court) to the kingship of Molossia, they invaded Epirus and fought a great battle against its Greek tribesmen. Diodorus reported that 15,000 Molossians died in a sharp defeat (15.13.3). And while that claim is surely a gross amplification of their losses, the scope of the reverse was nonetheless vast enough to prompt the Spartans to intercede and intimidate the Illyrians into withdrawing.

Having failed on the northeastern front in Greece, Dionysius shifted his aim the next year. His new target was Pyrgi up the southwest Italian coast, which served as port for the Etruscan (Tyrrhenian) city of Agylle (Caere). Lying just north of Rome's harbor at Ostia, this was part of a realm known for its Carthaginian sympathies and (more importantly as a draw for the tyrant's interests) for having a temple filled with abundant riches. Keen to appropriate the reputed wealth, Dionysius gathered a seaborne strike-force for a lightening raid against the Etruscan site.

There is uncertainty about just how large a fleet sailed from Syracuse to attack Pyrgi. Diodorus (16.14.3) gave it 60 triremes while 100 ships have been cited elsewhere ("pseudo Aristotle," Caven 1990, 191), and Polyaenus (5.2.21) claimed that there were 100 triremes and horse transports combined. Diodorus would normally be the preferred authority on such an affair related to Sicily; however, his text here has survived only in abbreviated summary form. Therefore, while we've no call to doubt their accuracy, it's quite possible that his data aren't completely preserved. It seems best then to give some credence to the other sources. A reasonable proposal along these lines is that there indeed were 100 triremes, but that only 60 carried the primary infantry force. This leaves the other 40 to bring an auxiliary contingent of horsemen. The cavalry might have traveled on fast triremes, which could man a full three banks of oars and take a shipment of horses and riders instead of their maximum cargo (in line with Herodotus 6.15) of 40 or so foot soldiers. This called for substituting at a rate of one horse for five men (Rodgers 1937, 15–16). Some 200 cavalrymen and their mounts as well as a few other passengers may then have come on those 40 vessels. This would allow for a landing party of around 2,000 hoplites,

500 foot skirmishers (mainly peltasts) and 200 horsemen. Alternatively, Caven (1990, 191) has suggested 4,000 foot soldiers and 300 riders based on a 5th century analog. But though consistent with Polyaenus, this gives no heed to Diodorus' number; moreover, such a fleet would have drastically increased travel time by using underpowered horse carriers. And had speed not been a priority then there would have been no need for such a large number of ships in the first place, since 4,000 infantrymen required less than 30 equally sluggish troop transports.

Beaching in the dark, Dionysius' men struck at daybreak, penetrating stout fortifications to overpower the small guard within. The locals gathered to take back their temple. Etruscans fought in the same style as their Greek foes, using a phalanx of hoplites (Sekunda and Northwood 1995, 13) that featured bodies of light infantry (archers and men with throwing spears) and cavalry (Penrose 2005, 47–49) outboard in flank support. How large was the army that arrayed to counter the incursion at Pyrgi? In light of there being no more than very short notice for mustering, it was probably not much if any bigger than even the smallest raiding party discussed above. And whatever strength the Etruscans could field, they had collected in haste and are unlikely to have been in a confident mood. Thus, once engaged the Greeks must have used main force to awe and rapidly push through unsteady Etruscan ranks, setting off a panic that saw their foes drop shield and spear to either run or beg for mercy. Taking a good many prisoners on the spot (Diodorus 16.14.2), the Syracusans went on to waste the nearby countryside before heading home with their spoils.

Mantinean Plain (385 B.C.)

No sooner had the Peace of Antalcidas gone into effect than Sparta began throwing its weight around in the Peloponnese in violation of the pact's provisions for insuring the independence of all Greek poleis. This first took the shape of aggression against nearby Mantinea. A former ally, that city had failed to back the Spartans during the Corinthian War and would now face serious consequences.

The Spartans opened hostilities by ordering in 385 that Mantinea tear down its walls. When this was denied, the Spartan king Agesipolis called out his current allies, including the recently suborned Thebans. He marched into Mantinean territory, plundered the countryside and then closed upon the city to initiate a siege. Information about the opening stages of this investment is sparse; however, Plutarch indicated that the Mantineans sought to fend off the Spartans by sallying to fight a battle on the plain in front of their city (Vol. I *Pelopidas*, 387). The scope of this engagement is speculative, but past operations suggest that Mantinea might have been able to field up to 2,500 hoplites, including reservists who likely took the field in this dire crisis. These line troops would have been backed by a modest number of light-armed skirmishers. As for the Spartans, there were probably at least 2,000 of their own spearmen present (two 500-man lochoi of spartiates and two more of perioeci) with possibly a matching force of allies. Perhaps half of the latter came from Thebes and the rest from Tegea (Mantinea's fierce Arcadian rival).

Had Agesipolis actually held the advantage in hoplite manpower proposed here, he no doubt would have aligned his heavy infantry eight shields deep across the entire breadth of his phalanx while placing whatever light forces he had on hand outboard off either side. It seems that the king and his spartiates took their usual station on the right and set the other Lacedaemonians on the far left. (This was much like the distribution of Spartan troops at Mantinea I some 33 years earlier, when perioeci had similarly stood on the left end of the array.) The allied hoplites would then have ranked across the middle of the formation, where we know that the Theban troops took position alongside the perioeci. This left the Tegeans to fill in next to the spartiates. These dispositions mandated that the Mantineans file only half as deep along the left wing of their own formation if they were to avoid an overlap. Critically, however, they could still deploy at a much more competitive depth of six along their right wing.

The slender array forced upon Mantinea would have put its phalanx at hazard of falling into dangerous disarray had it attempted to advance. It's therefore probable that the locals held steady close in front of their city walls. This sent the Spartan formation marching across the field at its traditional slow, flute-timed pace until coming into contact and initiating a lethal contest of dueling spears and pushing shields. As it turned out, this action played out along lines seen in many other hoplite battles to produce a mixed tactical result in which the Spartan king and his crack troops overcame the outmanned Mantinean left while the locals at the same time pushed back to partially disperse the left half of the Spartans' phalanx. And as the perioeci grudgingly gave ground, some of the troops from Thebes apparently broke ranks and fled. This put those few Thebans who still held station in great peril.

Among the men endangered in the Theban ranks were two later to rise to great fame: Pelopidas and Epaminondas. The former, in fact, went down with multiple wounds and would have died save for the courageous efforts of Epaminondas, who stood over his fallen comrade as he also took serious damage from both sword and spear. In one of history's more ironic turns, both of these deadly future foes of Sparta might have been slain had their position not been reinforced by the victorious Spartans crossing from the other side of the field. Beaten outright on their left and now finally undone on the right as well, the Mantineans withdrew, leaving behind maybe a tenth of their initial number dead or dying. Agesipolis, having probably lost no more than 5 percent of his own command, followed up this tactical success with a siege.

The city of Mantinea lay in a closed "polje" (Higgins 1996, 70–71), which is a low-lying area that does not effect its ultimate drainage on the surface; instead, its streams fall into sinkholes (ponors) and the flow channels underground to the sea (into the Gulf of Argos in this instance). There were five such sinkholes surrounding the site of ancient Mantinea and the Spartans set about plugging them. (They had used the same trick in 418 to precipitate the battle of Mantinea I.) As a result, when the rains came, flood waters rose and the river that flowed directly through town washed away the Mantinean defenses. So exposed, the city surrendered in 385 and the Spartans scattered its population into the same four villages that existed prior to the union that had created Mantinea in the mid-6th or early 5th century. These small communities were without the protection of walls and had to submit allied troops to Sparta upon demand.

Olynthus I (382 B.C.) and II (381 B.C.)

It was in context of the sort of aggression unleashed on Mantinea and anyone else that dared to oppose the Spartans that the cities of Acanthus and Apollonia sent envoys to Sparta in 383. Seeking to break free of Olynthus and its Chalcidian League in the far north, they begged for assistance. The Spartans saw a chance here to justify reaching into that region and set about collecting levies from their allies to send a large army to the Chalcidice. While this was being done, they decided to dispatch a small advance force to smooth the way, putting the general Eudamidas in charge.

Eudamidas undertook the Olynthian campaign in command of 2,000 hoplites (Xenophon *Hellenica* 5.2.24). It's likely that these included 1,100 spearmen in two perioecian lochoi (one of them the 600-strong Sciritae who usually scouted in front of a Spartan army when on the march) with the rest being freed helots. This forward contingent set up a base at Potidaea, which had deserted Olynthus, and proceeded to make small-scale war upon the enemy while lending garrison detachments to other cities wishing to rebel. Phoebidas in the meantime took charge of the main army and set out to join Eudamidas, who was his brother. He camped outside Thebes in route and there took a fateful step aimed at boosting the prestige of his polis. Acting on the spur of the moment, there was no way he could have known that he'd trigger a conflict that would alter the balance of power in Greece.

Leontiades, a Spartan client of long standing and leader of an oligarchic Theban faction, came to Phoebidas with others of his ilk and offered to bind his city to the Lacedaemonians in return for help in carrying out a coup. The Spartan and a party of his hoplites followed these traitors inside the gates of Thebes and took up position within the Cadmea, the city's fortified acropolis. Leontiades and his friends then went to the Theban senate and led a takeover of the government, replacing its former democratic format with a very narrow oligarchy (*dunasteia*) that fulfilled the conspirators' pledge by bringing Thebes into full sympathy with Sparta's interests. Phoebidas' action seems to have been in clear violation not only of the recent peace accord, but of Spartan law as well. However, though Phoebidas was removed from his command and fined, Agesilaus, who was probably a kinsman (Cartledge 1987, 373), defended what he had achieved. He did this by arguing that ends justified means, therefore making any sort of deed acceptable just as long as it benefited the state. The Spartans then compounded this flagrant moral transgression by proceeding to provide a trio of officers, a few of their own troops and some allied soldiers to help garrison the Cadmea in support of Thebes' new regime. At the same time, they sent out Agesilaus' brother Teleutias to replace the cashiered Phoebidas on the Olynthian campaign.

It appears that there had been some difficulty in gathering allied troops for an adventure so far from home. Thus, Phoebidas' original command must have started out somewhat shorthanded. But with the effective conquest of Thebes to trumpet, Teleutias had no trouble inspiring his allies to meet the expedition's declared manpower targets. Among these were 10,000 hoplites (Xenophon *Hellenica* 5.2.37), which would have included those sent out earlier. The spearmen in the reinforcement that now marched north probably counted 1,000 each from eight geographic areas that in 378 would formally make up the Peloponnesian League. Per Diodorus (15.31.2), those regions were Sparta, Arcadia, Elis, Achaia, Corinth/Megara, Sicyon/Phlius/Acte, Acarnania and Phocis/Locris (with Arcadia being split into two parts and the Chalcidice added to make up a ten-district format at that time). Of these, the Phliasians may have provided cash rather than troops as we know they did later (Xenophon *Hellenica* 5.3.10). If so, mercenaries might well have filled their slot in the battle order. As for the column's Spartans, they likely included at least a few full spartiates, with the rest mostly citizens of lesser privilege. Attaching these men to the perioeci already in the field produced a double allotment that consisted of two morai of citizen spearmen. Along with the earlier helot contingent and maybe 100 horsemen, this made for a very strong Lacedaemonian presence. Teleutias also brought a Theban levy of perhaps 2,000 hoplites and 200 riders. These troops represented yet another double draft, with Sparta's newest allies apparently being eager to give "even more than what was demanded of them" (Xenophon *Hellenica* 15.2.36).

Once arrived in the Chalcidice, both mercenary peltasts and more horsemen joined the Spartan effort. Macedonia's king Amyntas III had hired the javelinmen (no doubt Thracians) and also sent 100 or so elite troopers from his own cavalry. Amyntas seems to have been motivated to give this aid in hope of then gaining Spartan help to recover land that he had ceded to the Chalcidian League in a state of weakness after a recent defeat against the Illyrians. An additional 400 horsemen came from Derdas, who was ruler of the then separate Upper Macedonian district of Elimea. He was presumably throwing his lot in with the Chalcidians' foes out of fear that he might soon himself fall victim to the same sort of bullying that the League had inflicted on Amyntas.

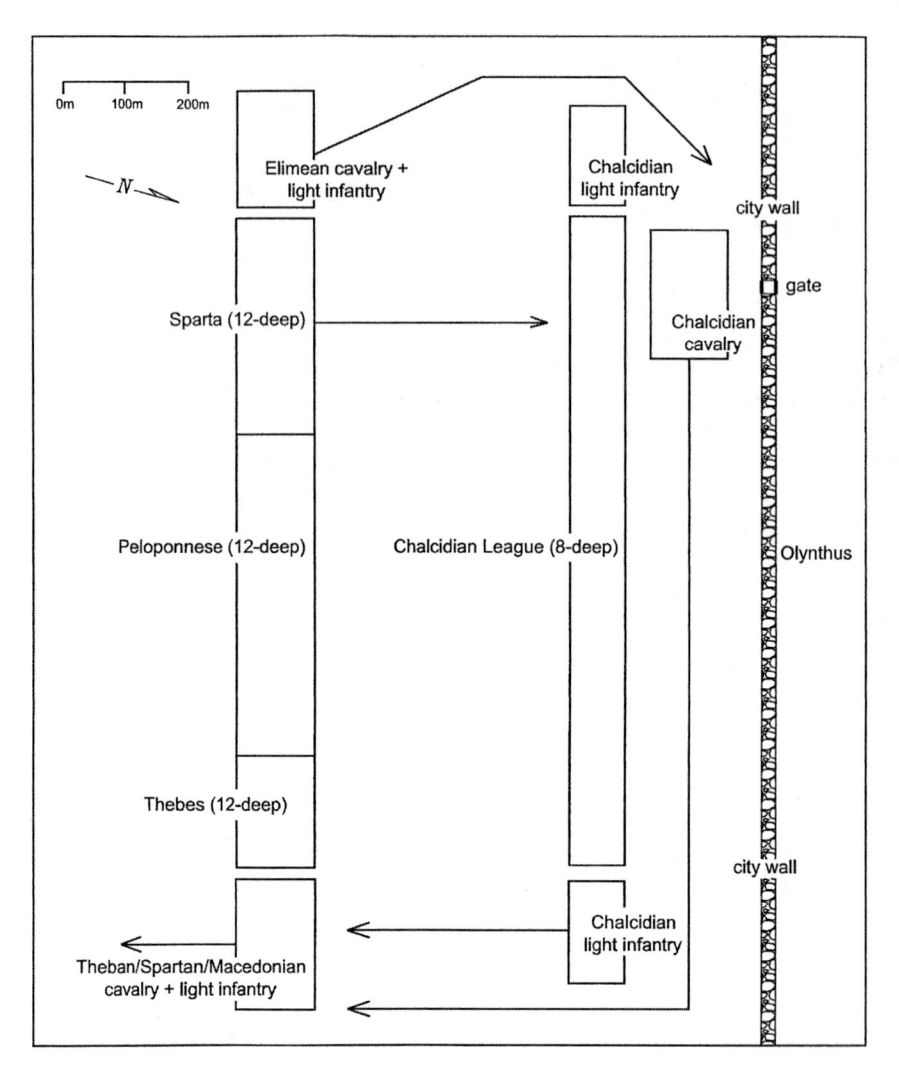

BATTLE OF OLYNTHUS I (382 B.C.) (BOXES REPRESENTING FORCES ARE EXAGGERATED TO SHOW RELATIVE SIZES.)

Teleutias approached Olynthus and put his phalanx in order, lining up with his Spartans on the left wing and arraying the allies rightward with the Thebans perhaps at the far right end. Having called in all of Eudamidas' troops (Diodorus 15.21.2), he was able to deploy some 12,000 hoplites, probably filing them twelve-deep over a 1km width. It was, of course, unusual for Spartan spearmen to ever stand solely on the left, the other wing being the traditional leadership slot. In this rare case, it seems that Teleutias took post on the left side so that his best men could hold station in front of the gate from which the enemy would have to emerge. With the heavy infantry so arranged, he then split his light forces into place on either flank. This put the Theban, Spartan and Macedonian riders with half the Thracian footmen on the right and the remaining peltasts and Derdas' cavalry on the left.

The locals issued forth and formed up into a phalanx in front of their ramparts. Their numbers for this action might have come to some 8,000 hoplites and 800 horsemen along with a couple of thousand foot skirmishers. (This honors Demosthenes' estimate of Chalcidian League strength in the later 4th century [19.230, 266] less about 20 percent, the reduction reflecting manpower lost from cities currently in rebellion.) If so, the spearmen would have had to line up eight-deep if they were to match widths with the Spartan heavy array. The light infantry moved into position off each end and then it was the cavalry's turn to set up in the rear. That's when the defenders sprang a novel maneuver that nearly won the fight at its very onset. A signal rang out and the entire Chalcidian mounted corps charged from an obscured post behind its phalanx. Led by their light footmen from the left flank and riding hard, these horsemen swept ahead to fall upon the enemy flank-guard on that side of the field. So swift an assault from a cavalry force half again their size caught Teleutias' riders unprepared and they and their skirmishers broke and fled. And as the victors turned upon the now exposed allied hoplites on that wing, those too began to give way.

All was on the verge of calamity for Teleutias when Derdas and his Elimean troopers came to the rescue. Breaking from the Spartan left edge, they took advantage of the enemy having committed all of their cavalry on the other side of the field to ride forward without opposition. They skirted the enemy's light footmen and made for the still open gate. The Chalcidian horsemen saw this and took fright, wheeling back that they might rescue their path for retreat. The Elimeans were able to kill many of these panicked riders as they galloped past to escape back into town. Meanwhile, Teleutias and his left wing had followed up on Derdas' initiative by advancing into contact with the northern phalanx. With their cavalry in flight, being exposed to a possible mounted attack at the rear and quickly getting the worst of a shock fight against a deeper and determined enemy formation led by Spartan fighters of fearsome reputation, the Chalcidian hoplites gave up as well and trailed their cavalry inside the city. Technically a victory for the Spartans in that they held the field at day's end, Diodorus' claim that the battle was "an even contest" is much closer to the truth. Likewise, the description of Xenophon (*Hellenica* 5.2.40–43), while noting significant losses among the Chalcidians' horsemen, makes the point that very few of their foot soldiers died "because the wall was near." Teleutias duly set up a trophy, yet still had to use great caution as he pulled away from the battle site, finding it necessary to cut down trees and strew them in his wake as a precaution against mounted pursuit. He dismissed his Macedonian and Elimean allies as fall approached, but ended up suffering from galling Chalcidian raids throughout the winter months.

The next spring, Derdas rejoined the war with his horsemen and inflicted another reverse on the enemy during a cavalry action in which he surprised and routed a 600-horse contingent of raiders. This kept the Chalcidians close to Olynthus, where Teleutias again closed against them with his army that summer. This time, the defenders sent out their riders to harass him as he approached a nearby river and he countered with some of his peltasts, whose appearance caused the horsemen to draw back across the stream. The javelinmen saw this and pursued into the water only to have their quarry wheel about and attack. The Chalcidians dealt the peltasts a costly defeat, killing 100 including their leader. This so enraged Teleutias that he sent his cavalry and remaining peltasts after the offending horsemen while he followed close behind with his hoplites. The Chalcidians fled into Olynthus as the furious Spartan commander chased them near the periphery of the city. He then assembled his phalanx to offer a rematch of last year's battle. But in the heat of anger, he was guilty of a grave tactical error, having deployed within range of skirmishers on the wall above. These now showered missiles onto his men so densely that they had to pull back out of reach in some disorder. And at that vulnerable moment, the Chalcidians struck.

Lead by their cavalry and peltasts, the defenders' hoplites emerged from the nearest gate to quickly form up and rush the Spartan phalanx. Teleutias and his troops were in confusion, caught with ranks jumbled in retreat and distracted by darting attacks from the Chalcidians' riders and foot skirmishers. This left them poorly prepared and their front crumpled before the northerners' well-ordered charge. The Spartan general then fell fighting in the ensuing melee.

Once Teleutias had been killed, his countrymen on that wing (probably once more the left) abandoned what had already proven an unequal combat and the rest of their phalanx fell apart to send men fleeing in all directions. The Chalcidians pursued in earnest, killing so many foemen that Xenophon's account of the battle (*Hellenica* 5.2.2–3.6) claims their victims made up "the most serviceable part of the army." Likely listing only Spartan spearmen, Diodorus cited more than 1,200 slain (15.21.2), a good +40 percent of those present. The victors' losses must have been slight in contrast at well less than 5 percent.

The Spartans reacted to this disaster by sending out a new army that they mustered by calling upon volunteers from all classes within their own state in addition to fresh levies drawn from the allies. This host rushed northward under the king Agesipolis, attaching horsemen from Thessaly on the way. Macedonia and Elimea again contributed reinforcements when the Spartans arrived on the ground. So strengthened, Agesipolis descended on Olynthus and, when the inhabitants wouldn't engage, took it out on their croplands. The Spartan monarch would die of a fever that summer, but his replacement as general, Polybiades, went on to see the campaign through, continuing to besiege the Olynthians until they surrendered in 379.

The Third and Fourth Carthaginian Wars of Dionysius

In the west at this time, Dionysius had used the wealth gained from Pyrgi to hire even more mercenaries. This was part of preparations for waging yet another war with Carthage toward adding western Sicily to his realm. The Syracusan kicked off this conflict by supporting successful revolts of several cities in Carthaginian Sicily and then ignoring Punic pleas for their return. Seeing common cause, Carthage launched the Third Carthaginian War against Dionysius by allying with Italian Greeks. It was a move that opened two fronts against the tyrant, allowing action against his interests in Italy while freeing Punic forces to hit at Sicily. Fortunately for Dionysius, the fighting ended up progressing in two phases that he was able to address separately. The first sequence played out in Italy, where the Syracusan was successful in taking Greek sites while preserving his own strongholds over the period 383–380. Diodorus described this interval's action as consisting of scattered skirmishes between small contingents "in which nothing of consequence was achieved" (15.15.3). Only later did the Carthaginians land a significant army on Sicily to activate that second theatre.

Cabala (377 B.C.) and Cronium (376 B.C.)

Carthage suffered a series of calamities 379–378. These included a plague along with a pair of rebellions (in Libya and Sardinia) that sought to exploit the disease's weakening of Punic strength. As a result, it wasn't until 377 that all was back in order for a strike on Sicily. Magon received command of the expedition, but our sources don't record the size of his armament. Caven has reasonably suggested (1990, 196) that Carthage's recent problems likely resulted in a somewhat smaller effort than had been mounted in 397. Magon also probably had fewer of the rebellious Libyans aboard. This would have forced him to rely more heavily than in the past upon manpower called up from his city's native population. We might therefore propose that he undertook this campaign with something on the order of 25,000 fighting men. Perhaps 15,000 of his infantry were heavy-armed, representing approximately 60 percent of the army's total manpower and equaling Diodorus' minimum for Africans later killed and captured in battle (15.15.3). Most of these troops of the line must have been full citizens and Liby-Phoenician perioeci. There also probably would have been 6,000–9,000 light-armed footmen involved, including troops drawn from garrisons already in place on the island. Finally, we can reasonably assume that the Carthaginians had substantial cavalry support, possibly to the tune of 1,000–3,000 riders.

Magon advanced in late summer, perhaps marching via an inland path. (Polyaenus [6.16.1] implied that their route led to a battle site at some distance from the coast.) Dionysius met them at an otherwise unknown location called Cabala, which may have lain in eastern or central Sicily (Champion 2010, 214). The Greek leader had come back from Italy after having stabilized affairs there for the moment only to then gather all available troops in order to deal with this new threat. Given ongoing commitments on the mainland and his separation from any potential allies in western Sicily due to Magon's position, it's likely that the tyrant fielded an army of mercenaries and Syracusans much like the one for his last bout against Carthage in 392. If so, he would have had about 20,000 fighting men, including around 15,000 hoplites. Light footmen might have been 3,500 to 4,000 strong (around 20 percent of the infantry force) while there could have been 1,500 horsemen at one per ten hoplites.

There is no account of what took place on the field at Cabala. All the same, our surviving claim for severe Carthaginian losses there, even if exaggerated, points to quite a strenuous engagement, one in which Caven proposes that Dionysius might well have taken serious casualties as well (1990, 198). Based on the foregoing projections, the Punic force would seem apt to have been much deeper in light-armed men; however, it might have no more than equaled Greek numbers in heavy infantry. Granting that hoplites were the meat of Dionysius' army, it was probably these hardy spearmen who provided the key to victory in a long and vicious fight that severely sapped the strength of both sides. Again, we have no specifics, but it's highly probable that the Greeks held their own in light-armed skirmishing off the edges. This then allowed them to flank at least one end of the opposing heavy array and spark a rout. Such a turn of events best explains their ability to cut off the number of troops said to have given up at the same time they took down many more in pursuit.

Magon was killed in the battle and the bulk of his men fled the field. Making good their immediate escape, they sought refuge in a stout defensive position on nearby high ground. Dionysius regrouped his victorious troops and followed to surround the Carthaginians. Despite Diodorus' claim of hefty losses among the defeated Africans, they clearly remained potent. Dionysius thus elected to negotiate their surrender rather than risk another potentially costly fight against desperate men that no longer seemed to pose a strategic threat. He granted a truce (Diodorus 15.16.1–2; Polyaenus 6.16.1) and stood down to give his foes time to consider terms. The Carthaginians took advantage of this temporary respite to recover their dead. However, they then exploited the situation by making an escape when the Greeks had relaxed their guard. Reaching the coast ahead of any chase, they reunited with their fleet and proceeded to safely retire into secure winter quarters at Panormus.

Magon's son Himilco took command of the Punic expedition before the following campaign season. Replacing his father's losses, he next put his troops through an intense and highly effective training program. This allowed him to take the field in late summer and menace Syracuse with an army that was not only at least as large as that of the preceding year, but also rather more capable. Dionysius answered by heading back into action with a force likewise very similar in strength to the one that had fought at Cabala. (We might here consider Diodorus' report on the tyrant's casualties as being more in line with a tradition on his heavy infantry total. The historian's "more than 14,000" matches very closely with probable size of the previous engagement's hoplite contingent less about 5 percent losses.) Bursting with confidence on the basis of their year-earlier success, the Greeks met Himilco's host somewhere near Panormus at a site called Cronium, where both armies set up camps. Cronium appears to have been a barbarian enclave (maybe Sican) allied to Carthage and either already besieged or under threat of siege from Syracusan forces (Polyaenus 5.10.5).

Dionysius set his troops up in phalanx with the light-armed outboard. Taking command of one wing (most likely the right) in company with a select team of his best hoplites, he gave the other wing to his brother, Leptines. Dionysius then closed against the similarly arrayed Africans, his formation entering into a hard fight which saw the tyrant and his picked men eventually begin to push ahead along their part of the line. However, things were not going so well elsewhere. Despite a heroic personal effort, Leptines fell in the fight, with his death in the middle of so closely contested a struggle sending those around him into a profound panic. As unreasoning alarm spread like wildfire through the Greek ranks, the spearmen on that wing gave way. This collapse on his far side exposed Dionysius' inner flank and forced him to abandon all progress to that point and run from the field as well. While Dionysius managed to get clear, thousands of his men were less fortunate, being cut down in flight such that "the whole region close at hand was heaped with dead" (Diodorus 15.17.4).

The tyrant and his surviving troops took up a fortified position in their camp near Cronium. They spent a tense night in anticipation of a follow-up attack in the morning. The next day, however, Himilco seems to have judged an assault upon his beaten but still capable foes to be a rash and unprofitable prospect. The Punic general therefore decided to retire on Panormus and negotiate an end to the conflict from there. This led to Dionysius obtaining what appear to have been quite generous terms. He had to cede some modest territory and pay an indemnity, yet gained a withdrawal of the Carthaginian invasion force that preserved his dictatorship.

Dionysius would spar once more with his old African foes in 368 to set off his Fourth Punic War. Largely a campaign of maneuver paced around a couple of naval actions, this lesser affair closed on a sour note for the Syracusan ruler with loss of a fleet to surprise attack. Thus weakened, he agreed to a halt in the conflict, signing an armistice at the end of the campaign season of 367. Nonetheless, it's very likely that he intended to again take the field the next year, but fate would intervene to short-circuit any renewal of hostilities when the aged tyrant took ill and died that spring. His empire now passed to his son, Dionysius II, a rather less capable man.

The Boeotian War

After three years of its rule, the people of Thebes had grown restive under their new, pro–Spartan government. Leadership of the fast growing opposition to this regime rested in two sites. One group consisted of men who had stayed in the city, including that heroic survivor of the Mantinean plain, Epaminondas. A scholarly man, he had been playing a sage role in inspiring his polis' youth to remain fit, hoping that they would some day be able to successfully battle the Spartans for the independence of their land. At the same time, there was a hard-core team of pro-democratic exiles residing in Athens as well. Pelopidas, the man Epaminondas had saved from death at Mantinea and his close friend ever since, was a prominent young firebrand among these. The two resistance factions were in close touch and combined their efforts in the winter of 379/78 to mount a counter-coup that sparked what is known as the Boeotian War.

Plataea-Thebes Road (379 B.C.) and Cithaeron Pass (378 B.C.)

The conspirators from Athens returned to Boeotia near year's end 379 and waited outside of Thebes as Pelopidas and a handful of others stole back into the city disguised as country folk.

These young men that night exchanged their costumes for those of women and gained entry to the homes of key members of the oligarchic faction ruling the city, attacking and killing them. Having thus cut the head from the oligarchy's leadership, Pelopidas and his mates next joined with their friends in town and set about rousing the population, arming men with whatever weapons they could find toward taking back their freedom by force. Meanwhile, the 1,500-man garrison in the Cadmea, which was composed of both local and foreign troops with two Spartan officers (the third being out of the city), had been alerted by the commotion in the streets. The Spartans kept their command quietly in place, deciding against taking immediate action with their modest strength in the face of what appeared to be a widespread uprising. They instead sent out couriers to summon help from friendly Boeotian forces at Plataea and Thespiae. The remaining plotters from Athens came into Thebes at sunrise and an assembly of the people promptly put the resistance in charge of the city. Pelopidas, having taken the position of military lead, then began marshaling fighters in preparation for surrounding the Cadmea for an assault.

The Athenians stepped unofficially into the fray at this point. It seems that two generals linked to the Theban resistance had moved troops into positions along the Attic border (Xenophon *Hellenica* 5.4.9). These were to stand by, ready to quickly come up in support of the conspiracy if needed. Composed most likely of a couple of hundred hoplite volunteers and maybe 800 or so mercenary peltasts under Chabrias (Munn 1993, 137, 214–215), these men mobilized upon arrival of a body of rebel cavalry from Thebes and set out northward to join the fight. Meanwhile, the horsemen (perhaps 400–500 strong) turned west in order to oppose a contingent coming up from Plataea to address the uprising. Probably with Lysanoridas (the third Spartan commander from the Cadmea) in charge and numbering maybe 400–600 hoplites with a few light-armed attendants (likely 100–150 at 20 percent of the total force), the Plataeans would have been strung out a few abreast in marching order along the road to Thebes.

The Theban riders descended without warning on the men from Plataea, launching their javelins in a series of charge and retreat attacks as their slower, heavy-armed foes rallied into a fighting formation under inadequate cover from the few amateur missilemen in their ranks. By the time that the spearmen had achieved any sort of order, Thebes' riders had killed more than 20 of them (Xenophon *Hellenica* 5.4.10) and must have wounded a good many more. This let the cavalry return at full speed to the city. The bloodied and badly shaken Plataeans, on the other hand, were in all likelihood expecting further mounted attacks and turned back. In contrast to this loss of reinforcements for the Cadmea's defenders, the rebel cause soon gained more troops from Athens and on an official basis this time. The volunteer generals that had led the initial Athenian support for Thebes must have reported back to the authorities at home that that all was going well. This motivated the Athenians to pile on. They elected to send out the general Demophon to aid the rebellion with 5,000 hoplites and 500 horsemen (Diodorus 15.26.2).

Between local men (3,000–4,000), other Boeotians rallying to Thebes' cause (maybe another 2,000–3,000) and the Athenians (5,200 or so), there were now 12,000 hoplites arrayed against the Cadmea (Diodorus 15.26.4). There were also 2,000 in cavalry among the rebels along with a possible 3,000 light missilemen (these representing around 25 percent of the total Boeotian complement plus Chabrias' mercenaries). The citadel's defenders were able to stave off several attempts on their position over the next couple of weeks, dealing out a fair share of casualties to the attackers. Still, seeing so vast and unfavorable a disparity in manpower as well as the determination of their foes and their own dwindling supplies, the garrison's troops lost heart. Including even the few Spartans present, these over-rode objections from their officers and voted to surrender the site. Negotiations then produced an agreement that would let the garrison keep its arms and leave Thebes unopposed.

The Spartans responded to the uprising by assigning their king Cleombrotus to muster an army and retake Thebes. Gathering allied levies, he was able to field a large force of perhaps 19,000 spearmen with around 4,000 light-armed supporters and marched out in early 378. Cleombrotus was able to avoid a blockade from Chabrias and his javelinmen (who were now on post at Eleutherae) by taking the direct route across Mount Cithaeron toward Plataea, moving up this path with a contingent of his own peltasts in the lead. At the top of the pass, the javelineers encountered a party of some 150 Thebans, former prisoners of the ousted oligarchic regime who had taken on the task of blocking this entry into their homeland. Perhaps a mixture of hoplites with a few foot skirmishers, this small force might well have been adequate with proper preparation to temporally seal the narrow pass against a modest assault. Sadly for the Thebans, they were not only facing long odds, but had been caught by surprise as well. Having recently watched the garrison depart with its tail between its legs, these men no doubt didn't expect to see an enemy offensive until spring opened the next traditional campaigning period. Instead, the peltasts at maybe 800 strong took them unaware, charging forward time and again to hurl their slender darts to lethal effect. Eventually, the attackers overwhelmed their outmanned foes' hastily deployed stance, wiping them out to nearly the last man and driving off those few who survived. With the pass now clear, Cleombrotus crested the mountain to descend into Plataea.

The Spartan king relocated from Plataea to Thespiae and then advanced on the village of Cynoscephalae, setting up camp there only a few kilometers from Thebes itself. He stayed at that site for just over two weeks, probably parlaying with the Thebans in hopes of finding a mutually amenable solution to the crisis. With the rebels remaining intractable and winter conditions dimming prospects for effective military operations, Cleombrotus fell back once more upon Thespiae. There, he proceeded to install a garrison under Sphodrias. He gave this Spartan general a third from each of the allied contingents (possibly 5,000 spearmen along with 1,000 skirmishers). He also ceded all that was left of his campaign funds to be used in the hiring of mercenaries. The king then marched back to the Peloponnese where he discharged what remained of his allies. Fearful of the vengeance of a now aroused Sparta, the Athenians scrambled to repudiate their pact with Thebes, placing on trial the generals that had first involved them with the uprising. However, this contrite attitude would soon evaporate in the wake of a major Spartan strategic gaffe.

Sphodrias came up with a plan to counter the Theban overthrow by means of an operation against the main Athenian harbor at Piraeus. Marching with a large army from Thespiae under cover of darkness, he made for Piraeus with the intention of capturing the recently walled but still ungated port that morning. What followed can only be described as a complete foul-up. Not only was the invasion force seen on the move and reported to Athens during the night, but sunrise found it still a good 20km from its target. Now fully on the alert, the Athenians deployed to protect both their city and its harbor, leaving Sphodrias little choice but to turn around and skulk back to Boeotia. The fallout from this fiasco saw the mood in Athens swing entirely around to produce a fresh alliance with Thebes and put the city on the path to war with Sparta. The Athenians had by that summer gone so far as to form what has been called the Second Athenian League as a rebirth of sorts of the old anti–Persian Delian League of the 5th century. Only this new organization was dedicated to opposing Spartan rather than barbarian ambitions. Swallowing all these reversals, the Spartans remained defiant and refused even to convict Sphodrias despite his clear intent to violate the Peace of Antalcidas. If Athens wanted to fight, then a fight it would get.

Thespiae (378 B.C.)

In early spring 378, both the Thebans and Athenians began building massive field works toward helping fend off the attacks they anticipated would surely come that summer from Sparta and its allies. For Athens, this took the form of a barrier wall across the gap between the southern side of Mount Parnes and the northern end of the southeast-northwest trending Aigaleos ridge system that otherwise separated Attica from the Megarid and Isthmus of Corinth (and hence from the Peloponnese and Sparta). Called the "Dema Wall" (Munn 1993) after that opening's modern Greek name (*To Dema* or "The Link"), this barrier was crafted from local limestone and came complete with fighting platforms, sally ports, gates and watch towers. It was designed to accommodate a defensive corps some 5,000 strong, which was equal to about half the size of the Athenian army at this time. These troops were to consist predominantly of peltasts (and those mostly mercenaries), but with a strong component of hoplites as well as at least a few horsemen. Athens' current commanding general, Chabrias, was probably the inspiration behind the wall's design. He had been involved in the creation of barrier defenses when serving Persia in Egypt. He also likely had a hand in creating the defensive works that went up at this same time near Thebes. These were very different in composition and expanse from the Dema Wall, consisting of a 20km-long stockade system of ditches, earthen mounds and stakes that combined to enclose the most exposed expanse of the city's territory.

With these constructions in place, their defenders awaited the coming of the summer campaign season and its expected enemy offensive. And as anticipated, Sparta's King Agesilaos duly led out a powerful invasion force. It seems that sturdy old warrior had replaced Cleombrotus despite having reached his 60th year, an age normally marking retirement from even reserve military duty. But eager to put what they saw as their most successful general into the fray, both Spartans and allies alike had insisted that the older monarch take charge of this campaign. His host boasted 18,000 foot soldiers (Diodorus 15.32.1), probably including 4,000 Spartan and 10,000 allied hoplites. The Spartans maybe represented five morai at 80 percent establishment strength. (However, Diodorus, possibly confusing morai with lochoi, assigns just 500 men to each of these units, thus indicating only 2,500 Spartans.) In addition, there were some 2,800 allied light infantry, 1,200 mercenary peltasts and 1,500 horsemen.

Perhaps dissuaded by the Athenians' barrier wall, but more likely focused all along on striking at what he must have perceived as his primary objective, Agesilaos headed for Cithaeron and Boeotia beyond. He had sent the hired peltasts ahead to secure his target pass and his column made a rapid transit to set up camp at Thespiae. Agesilaos joined up here with the contingent already in place. This latter force might have numbered as many as 10,000 infantry per the complement that had embarked on the year-earlier Piraeus misadventure (Diodorus 15.29.6). A likely breakdown for these troops includes some 6,500 allied spearmen (5,000 Peloponnesian and 1,500 from Thespiae, Plataea and elsewhere in Boeotia). There also would have been around 1,500 allied skirmishers plus a modest cavalry force (maybe 500 riders, including a few refugee Theban aristocrats) and 2,000 or so professional peltasts. These last were Sphodrias' hires from the year before. Agesilaos marched this force across the Theban frontier near Cynoscephalae. Here, he came up against significant challenges from not only the recently erected stockade, but a reformed Boeotian League army as well.

During the winter, the Thebans had led a reorganization of the surrounding poleis that were free of Spartan control. This included restoration of the former seven-district federal government in which proportional representation of Thebes' large population gave it the power and responsibility of four districts (Hanson 1999, 28–29). There was, however, a major difference between the present union and Boeotian democracies of the past: broad, Athenian-style suffrage. By giving an equal vote to every male citizen in the region, the Thebans had uplifted men all across Boeotia, encouraging them to come forward as never before to defend their land. And at least at Thebes itself, such an improved attitude found expression in an elevated level of physical training and military organization. Talented and dedicated men like Pelopidas, Epaminondas and Gorgidas pioneered this effort. A notable step was Gorgidas' creation of an elite fighting unit called the Sacred Band (*Hieros Lochos*). Modeled after an earlier picked unit at Thebes of the same size (the "Charioteers" of 5th century fame), this comprised 300 select hoplites (said to be 150 pairs of lovers) that served at state expense in the phalanx's leading rank (sometimes possibly dispersed throughout [Balfour 2010, 45]). With the Sacred Band at their thrusting edge and powered by row after row of muscular spearmen, the Thebans would become a powerful driving force within Boeotian battle formations.

Thus, it was a reinvigorated foe that Agesilaos faced across the earthen and stake barrier outside of Thebes. Ranging up and down the stockade's length, the Spartan spoiled the land at various points on his side of the divide. Yet he found no way to cross and get at the richer fields beyond. This was because every time that the Spartan shifted his location the Boeotians did the same, always keeping across from him with the barrier providing them a daunting defensive position. Still, Agesilaos did finally manage to breach the stockade. He did this through the simple ploy of setting out unusually early in the morning before the Boeotians could take post against him. Yet though he was now able to attack the Thebans' fields right up to their city walls, he failed to gain the open battle that he wanted. This was due to his foes declining to fight on his terms while he likewise refused on theirs. A famous example of this mutual reluctance to engage at a disadvantage has come down to us via the works of Diodorus (15.32.5–6), Polyaenus (2.1.2) and Nepos (12.1.2).

At some point, the Boeotians set up in battle order along the crest of an elongated hill that lay a few kilometers outside of the city. The Theban hoplites (maybe 4,000) must have taken the far right with their Sacred Band debuting at the fore. The other Boeotian spearmen (perhaps 3,000) would then have held the middle, leaving the left wing to their Athenian allies. The latter had come with 5,000 foot soldiers (probably 4,000 hoplites and 1,000 hired peltasts) and 200 horsemen under Chabrias. It's notable that Chabrias' hoplites seem to have included some mercenaries. Munn (1993, 214) has estimated these hirelings at 500 and reasonably proposes that they formed the entire front rank of an Athenian array standing eight shields deep. On the plain below the Boeotian position, Agesilaos arranged his own phalanx, holding a significant edge in heavy-armed manpower with better than 20,000 spearmen. If he could entice his foes onto level ground then he would be able to overlap a flank (filed at least twelve shields deep against only eight over a 1,700m width versus only 1,500m). Sending his skirmishers forward, the Spartan therefore sought to goad his foes into an unwise charge down the hill. But the Boeotians and Athenians stood their ground and easily beat back this assault, using their elevation to excellent advantage. Taking a different tack, Agesilaos now had his entire phalanx advance at the sort of deliberate pace for which the Lacedaemonians were famed and feared. This was a threatening display of cool, murderous resolve that had in times past broken more than one enemy formation before the Spartans even got within spear-reach. On this occasion, however, the opposition showed nerves of steel. Rather than be intimidated, Chabrias displayed both his men's confidence and well-drilled discipline by having his leading row of veteran professionals lower their shields to rest against their knees while raising their spears alongside in near perfect unison. When Gorgidas and his Sacred Band across the right third of the Boeotian front led their amateur fellows along the rest of the phalanx in copying this adroit maneuver, Agesilaos brought his formation to a halt.

The king realized at this juncture that there was little likelihood that an assault up the slope would succeed, regardless of his hefty numerical edge. The only real hope was for his opponents to break ranks and run in fear, as the Acarnanians had done when he charged them uphill back in 389; and, given his foe's obvious élan, that just wasn't going to happen here. Thus, after offering once more to make a fight of it on level ground and being refused, Agesilaos withdrew. Ultimately unable to properly set the stage for destroying the Boeotian phalanx, he would retire upon Thespiae. Then, after fortifying that site and likely rotating in half the allied troops he'd brought from the Peloponnese to replace those previously left there, he put the Cadmea's conqueror, Phoebidas, in charge of the place and headed home. Fighting would go on after the main Spartan army left, however, as both sides made hit-and-run raids on each other's territory. These resulted in at least one important action.

The Boeotians marched on Thespiae near summer's end and overran an outpost, killing 200 of its defenders. Phoebidas sallied in response, perhaps hoping in his knowledge of the enemy's considerable strength that he could entice them into the decisive battle on favorable ground that his kings had failed to bring about to date. In any event, his vanguard of mercenary peltasts caught the raiders pulling back toward Thebes and a sharp action ensued. This engagement is variously described in our sources. Xenophon's account (*Hellenica* 5.4.42–46) makes it a minor skirmish, while Diodorus outlined an engagement of much greater scope (15.33.4–6). In light of the severe Spartan response afterwards plus the mutually reported size of the Boeotian force and unlikely placement of Phoebidas among his skirmishes (rather than with the hoplites) by Xenophon, much of the account of Diodorus is to be preferred. All the same, Xenophon's version does supply useful details. Reported casualties make it probable that Phoebidas engaged with nearly his entire hoplite contingent. This might have amounted to some 5,000 spearmen, including all the locals with the rest being Peloponnesian. At the same time, the statement by Xenophon that the Boeotians came "with their entire force" and by Diodorus that the Spartan commander "fell rashly upon the retreating Thebans" (indicating that he was significantly outnumbered, i.e. by a third or more) allow for a good estimate of Boeotian manpower. This was a full levy of around 7,000 spearmen, better than 2,000 peltasts and 600–700 horsemen.

Phoebidas went from pursuer to being the one on the run when his peltasts fell back under pressure from the enemy cavalry. The Spartan quickly set up his phalanx to engage his foe's heavy array, which was now turning to attack. In the fight that followed, Phoebidas went down after "receiving many wounds in front" (Diodorus). This implies that the Theban left might have used deeper manpower to push through his traditional leader's position on the right. Whether this is our first example of a radically overloaded Theban array on that wing (something that would later come to characterize Epaminondas' tactical style) is not documented, though it's certainly possible. Alternatively, Xenophon's description of Thespian spearmen giving way with little or no resistance would place the decisive failure on their side of the line. This was probably on the Spartan left. If so, then Phoebidas and those about him had been enveloped in the course of a collapse rolling up from the other end of their formation. At any rate, the Spartan-allied force was badly mauled. Despite pursuit being limited by fall of night, it suffered over 500 reported fatalities — better than 10 percent if these were only losses among the hoplites as seems likely.

Sparta replaced the fallen Phoebidas that winter with a new commander, who arrived with a mora of spearmen via ship across the Corinthian Gulf. The move to reinforce with citizen hoplites as well as their method of travel show that things were not going well. Dispatch of a full mora accords with a need to compensate for a large number of dead and wounded from the battle at Thespiae. It also implies that morale among the allies in Boeotia was slipping as a result of that setback and needed a boost from the presence of actual Spartans. As for choosing sea transport over an overland march, this suggests that there was trouble in the pass to Plataea. The Boeotians, emboldened by their victory, might have been contesting its control. Pressure was thus mounting for the Spartans to achieve greater success in the next campaign season toward reversing a rapidly declining situation.

Graos Stethos (377 B.C.)

Agesilaos ordered his Boeotian garrison to advance the next spring and hold the Cithaeron pass, where he joined it to unite his forces and create an army equal in strength to the one he had employed a year earlier. He then descended on Plataea and gave every indication that he intended to next move on to Thespiae. This caused the Boeotians to muster between Thespiae and Thebes that they might meet any threat against the latter from along their western front. Instead, the king suddenly led his troops on a forced march in the opposite direction. Looping around, he took his foes by surprise to quickly breach the outlying barrier system that had so vexed him earlier and close on the city from the south. Agesilaos now raided previously untouched Boeotian land on the east while advancing to the friendly polis of Tanagra, where he installed Panthoedas with a large garrison and then swung back in the direction of Thebes.

Agesilaos found on the return march that the Boeotians had united to set up for battle along his route. They occupied a long hill called Graos Stethos (aka "The Old Woman's Breast"), which sat in front of the barrier works to the east of the city. Again refusing to engage at a disadvantage against opposition holding high ground, the king bypassed this upland and made for Thebes. His foes saw this and, fearful lest they be cut off from home, hurried down to make a run for town. This gave at least two fortuitously positioned Spartan morai (one containing the Sciritae lochos) an opportunity to attack. Some of the retreating men got up another small hill that sat along their path within sight of the city and hurled javelins into this Spartan charge, but they and their comrades on the flat were soon put to flight. The Sciritae and some of Agesilaos' horsemen, who had led the way in taking the hill, now themselves exploited its elevation to shower missiles down on the last of the enemy rushing past. However, once the Boeotians had reached their nearby city wall, they spun about to threaten a counterattack and the Sciritae and mounted men withdrew without a fight.

Agesilaos camped for the night and started for Thespiae the next day. As he left, mercenary peltasts in Theban employ began harassing the back of his column with trailing support from Chabrias and a contingent of Athenian hoplites. Olynthian cavalry serving Sparta in this campaign turned on the javelinmen, who had become too far separated from their heavy infantry. The horsemen chased these peltasts up a slope and killed many while scattering the rest. With his rear elements thus clear to move, the king marched on to his base at Thespiae. He helped secure that site by settling a local political dispute and then headed back over Cithaeron, disbanding what an anecdote from Polyaenus (2.1.20) suggests was a seriously dispirited army. He'd managed some successful maneuvers this time out, yet in the end, another campaign season had passed with Thebes remaining as free as ever.

Tanagra III (376 B.C.)

Agesilaos was unable to take the field in the spring of 376 due to an attack of phlebitis. Cleombrotus took his place in command, but could not lead an army into Boeotia as the enemy had taken control of the pass to Plataea that winter. Stuck south of the mountain, Cleombrotus had to dismiss his levies and abandon the campaign. With their foes now blocking entry for reinforcements from the Peloponnese, the Spartans were dependent on the forces already in place at Thespiae and Tanagra for any operational potential in Boeotia. But these garrisons remained mostly on the defensive since they were well separated and lacked sufficient manpower for chancing a major action individually. It was therefore the Boeotians that would take the initiative as the summer wore on, launching a campaign against Tanagra, which was probably the slightly weaker of the two Spartan outposts.

By analog with the attempt made against Thespiae in 378, the effort on Tanagra must have involved the entire Boeotian levy. This would mean some 7,000 hoplites, around 2,000 light infantrymen and maybe 700 horsemen. The city's defenders responded by sallying in an attempt to head off a siege, fielding maybe 4,000 spearmen. This reflects that no more than a third of the militiamen that constituted Sparta's Peloponnesian levy could have been stationed long-term in Boeotia, thus the troops left at Tanagra in 378 must have been but a portion of the allies previously posted to Thespiae. Given the presence of a citizen mora at or near the latter since the winter of 378/77, this gave a pool of 6,000 spearmen to now divide between western and eastern outposts. We know that the Spartan mora continued to operate in the west (see Tegyra below), therefore 3,000 allied hoplites probably made up Tanagra's allotment. Additionally, the garrison could call upon 1,000 Tanagran spearmen in line with that city's past Boeotian League allotments. Light infantry in proportion might have come to around 1,000 at 20 percent of the Peloponnesian contingent and 25 percent of the Boeotians. If Agesilaos had assigned around half of the allied horsemen at Thespiae as well, then these would have joined some 100 Tanagrans for a total cavalry force 200–500 strong.

Details on the ensuing battle are sadly lacking. We only know from Plutarch (Vol. I *Pelopidas*, 394) that Panthoedas and a sizeable array went down to a defeat that cost the Spartan his life. It's most likely that the Boeotians managed to use their significant advantage in numbers to gain a substantial victory, probably turning the Tanagran right wing if the death of Panthoedas is any indication. As in the Boeotian success at Thespiae two years earlier, it's at least possible that an overloaded left wing of Thebans might have played a key role in achieving this envelopment, but we have no definitive proof. Along with the opposing general, the victors must have eliminated a fair number of enemy troops (perhaps 10–15 percent) and a weakened Tanagra would fall by no later than the following spring (Munn 1993, 172).

Seaborne action added an entirely new element to the Boeotian conflict in 376. Frustrated to date in their ground campaigns, Sparta turned offshore that summer to launch a naval blockade. The Spartans made piratical raids against Athens' shipping and shoreline from Aigina as well as the islands of Ceos and Andros in the Cyclades off the southeast Attic shore. But this strategy came to naught when Chabrias led a fleet to victory over Spartan forces near the Cyclades island of Naxos. Sparta was therefore left reeling at the end of the year, having suffered reverses on both land and sea.

Tegyra (375 B.C.)

Spartan sea power suffered further in early 375 with another Athenian naval success coming off the northwestern Greek coast near Alyzeia in Acarnania. Still, when the Thebans began to show greater confidence by ranging outside of Boeotia to threaten Sparta's ally Phocis, enough ships were mustered to transport Cleombrotus across the Corinthian Gulf with four of the Spartans' morai and a full two-thirds muster of their Peloponnesian allies. The Boeotians retired in the face of this daunting force, trailing guards in their wake as they pulled through the passes lest they be pursued. But elsewhere a battle did take place that spring.

Pelopidas had approached the western Boeotian town of Orchomenos with a lochos of 500 picked hoplites (Diodorus 15.37.1) including the entire Sacred Band (Plutarch Vol. I *Pelopidas*, 394–395). (Note that Plutarch clashes here with Diodorus in claiming that *only* the Sacred Band was on hand; however, the latter's figure seems rather the more acceptable in light of probable identity and balance of the forces involved as noted below.) A modest body of horsemen rode with these heavy troops, undoubtedly in the company of some light infantry. The Theban's mission was to scout Orchomenos, which was host for a mora (two lochoi) of 1,000 Spartan hoplites. (Note that there is much dispute regarding the strengths of Spartan units [see the discussion "Manpower" regarding Leuctra in 371 B.C] as well as the types actually present at Tegyra. Plutarch indicates two morai here, but Diodorus said that the Thebans faced "twice their number," which supports a single mora of around 1,000 men as being the correct identification.) These troops most likely were the latest replacements for the citizen regiment that sailed over with Phoebidas' successor in 378/77. Acting on information that this contingent was rotating out and crossing into nearby Locris (where it would march to the coast and board for home), Pelopidas came up with a plan to capture Orchomenos before its replacement could arrive.

Sound as this plan might have been, it soon fell apart as news came that the relieving mora was already in the vicinity. It had apparently come across from the Peloponnese well prior to its counterpart's departure and thus had only just missed being able to make the transfer of assignments on the spot in Orchomenos. Caught out by this unforeseen development, the Thebans made to withdraw, moving in a circuitous manner to the north toward the town of Tegyra due to terrain restrictions imposed by marshland thereabout (the site being along the edge of ancient Lake Copais — see Pritchett [1982] for a discussion of the topography). However, this route put the fleeing men on a collision course with the rapidly approaching mora, which was emerging from the pass leading to Locris. The Spartans proceeded to block the Thebans' path. Acting with resolve, Pelopidas sent his horsemen out to skirmish as he covered behind them and readied his foot soldiers for a desperate fight.

The Spartans spanned a passage that, though flat, featured impassable terrain on either side (the lake environs in one direction and broken and/or swampy ground in the other). This allowed them to anchor both ends of their array as a hedge against the opposing cavalry. It's not clear what depth of file was required to permit this, but subsequent events suggest that it might have been thinner than the usual eight men, possibly only six. Of course, this had potential to yield offensive advantage as well, since a longer line meant that the Spartans would overlap on at least one flank, even should the Thebans stack at four shields, which was the minimum depth for orderly maneuvering. But it was not the intention of Pelopidas to try and match his enemy's width. Instead, he arranged his spearmen very deeply (maybe fronting over a mere 20m with 25-man files per Theban density at Delium in 424) with the attacking horsemen serving to mask his formation's true form and exact position. (This would have called for Thebes' riders to spread out broadly in a very thin array across the entire front rather than compactly off the flanks as was normal practice. This seems to be the first time such a tack is described for Greek horsemen in a hoplite battle, though such wide dispersion must have been common in solely mounted actions.) When the cavalry then finally fell away and his overconfident foes began to advance, the Theban led his men forward at speed. They charged into what appears to be the right wing of the Spartan phalanx. Powerfully driven by othismos from extensive after-ranks, Pelopidas' front-fighters swiftly speared and pushed their way through a perhaps somewhat thin opposing formation, killing many of the enemy in the process (including both lochos commanders). The Thebans then wheeled on the opposition's exposed flank and backside to panic and scatter the remaining Spartans within minutes at most.

Fearful that the mora that had just left for Locris might have turned about or that help would come for the Spartans from local troops at Orchomenos, the Thebans made only a very short pursuit. Returning to the battle site, they spoiled the enemy dead (perhaps as many as a hundred spearmen) and erected a trophy to mark the victory before continuing on their way home. The account of Plutarch (and to a lesser extent the shorter one of Diodorus) makes much of this event, claiming that it was the first loss that the Spartans had taken in open combat against an opponent inferior in numbers (or even at equal strength). Actually, it's possible that Tegyra really marked no more than a variation on tactics employed by the Thebans over the last

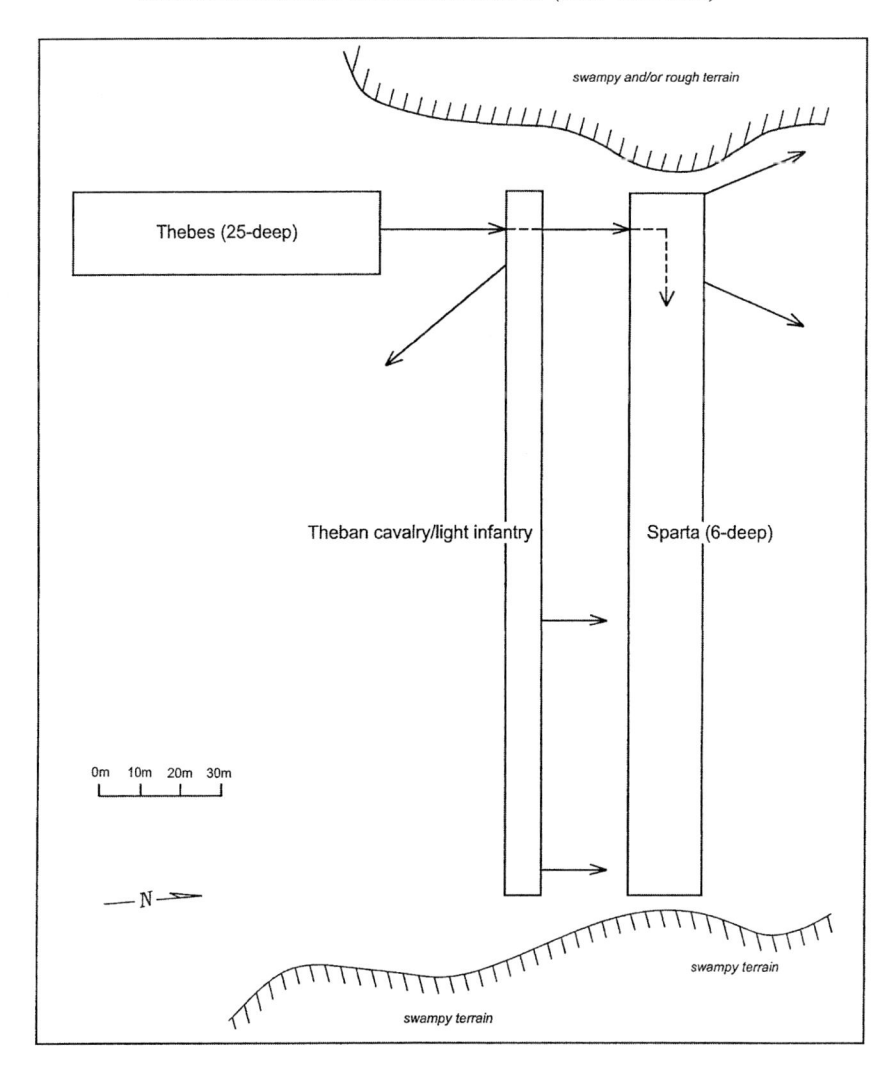

BATTLE OF TEGYRA (375 B.C.) (BOXES REPRESENTING FORCES ARE EXAGGERATED TO SHOW RELATIVE SIZES.)

three years: deeply filing their left wing to overpower the opposing right, thus taking out the enemy's best troops plus their leader(s). If so, then the only difference from the previous engagements was that there was no center or left wing in the Theban array this time, these having been rendered unnecessary by rapid victory on the right preempting the unengaged remaining opposition from even coming into play. This certainly seems to point the way for Epaminondas' sheltering of those same elements from the fight at Leuctra four years later. As such, Plutarch's comment that the triumph of Pelopidas here was "a prelude to Leuctra" is probably more appropriate than even he might have known. Regardless, Tegyra was a great morale booster for the Thebans and would prove the last land action of note before the Boeotian War came to an end.

Athens was growing concerned about how powerful the Thebans were becoming. They were currently allies, but had been bitter rivals in the past and would very likely be again at some point in the future. The Athenians were also at financial risk, not only due to the expense of maintaining their fleet on a wartime footing, but also from the cost of hiring large numbers of mercenary peltasts for the campaigns in Boeotia as well as to man the extensive defensive works along their western border. As a result, they took the initiative to send representatives to

Sparta and arrange a peace treaty. This was a bilateral pact between the Spartans and Athens, with the latter having to drag its Theban allies along as reluctant participants. Thus, though the agreement put a formal end to the current war, tensions between the signatories remained high as a foretaste of even more deadly conflicts to come.

The Peloponnese, Egypt and Corcyra

Southern Greece was in political turmoil during the mid-370s. At least some of the uproar stemmed from the rise of democratic movements in the decade after the Corinthian War, which had bred disputes between democrats and oligarchs, leading to a number of confrontations and acts of violence. Within the Persian Empire, meanwhile, the Great King was preparing a grand campaign to reclaim his long lost province of Egypt. And, finally, still simmering enmity between Athens and Sparta was boiling up among the islands of western Greece, threatening to kick off yet another round of fighting between those old rivals.

Phlius (374 B.C.)

All the political unrest in the Peloponnese led to at least one significant land action. This happened when exiles from Phlius took control of a local stronghold and collected "a considerable number of mercenaries" (Diodorus 15.40.5) with the aim of ousting the popular party ruling their polis. In the battle that followed, these outcasts claimed victory and killed some 300 on the other side. This isn't much to go on; however, such casualties suggest (assuming they were spearmen at no more than 15 percent of the total) that the bested army might have been 2,000 strong in heavy infantry. Typical support for a hoplite contingent of this size would then have been on the order of 500 light footmen and 100 in cavalry. The victors might not have had any greater manpower and more likely fielded a somewhat smaller force. Had this been the case, it must have been the professional soldiers in their ranks that were decisive, intimidating and routing an opposing array of less capable amateurs. But the exiles had little time to enjoy their success. Their own hirelings delivered them to the people and 600 were captured and executed as the rest fled to Argos.

Iphicrates' Egyptian Reforms and the Mendesian Mouth of the Nile (373 B.C.)

The Persians had sought help from Athens in the early to mid 370s to obtain a commander for the Greek legion that they were assembling for their campaign into Egypt. Long a source of such mercenary captains, the Athenians sent out Iphicrates, who had led their own hired troops so well in the Corinthian conflict. However, when that general arrived at the Persian staging area in Phoenicia, he ran into a problem. He had inherited some 12,000 (Nepos 11.2.4) to 20,000 (Diodorus 15.41.1) hired men whose ranks included too high a ratio of light to heavy infantry. Judging that he had significantly fewer hoplites than needed, he came up with a creative solution using the troops already in camp, expanding his heavy corps by rearming Greek skirmishers (Sekunda and Chow 1992, 26–27).

Perhaps drawing elements from past experiences in Thrace (Best 1969, 141–142), Iphicrates outfitted these men for shock fighting with small (0.6m across) round and rimless shields and an elongated spear or pike. The new shields initially seem to have been held in the left hand while wielding the pike in the right; however, at some point (likely after Iphicrates' time in

Persian service) these were slung across the shoulder or fixed on the left forearm to allow an option for holding the pikes to better effect with both hands. Per Diodorus (15.44.1–4), these lances were half again the length of a normal dory, putting them at around 3.7m. (Nepos [11.1.3] suggested they were twice the length of a dory. This was probably a confused reading of Ephorus' comments about doubling the length of swords, with Diodorus' paraphrasing from the same source likely being more accurate.) Other up-grades included an open-faced helmet (perhaps of the "Phrygian" style, with a coned, forward-leaning peak per the soft caps of northern Anatolia) and high leather boots called *iphicratides* (Iphicrates, the son of a shoemaker, having come up with their design).

We don't know what these new-style fighters were called, but modern writers have identified them variously as "Iphicratean peltasts" (from their small shields) or "Iphicratean hoplites" (based on use of a thrusting weapon). In fact, they fall between those two traditional categories, but are closer to hoplites in being shock troops. Yet, even so, these were certainly "hoplites on the cheap" and less shock-capable than traditional spearmen. They are probably best thought of as prototypes for the later pike-bearing troops that emerged in Macedonia under its renowned king and military mastermind Philip II. Like those soldiers, these "Iphicratean pikemen" lacked a large, concave shield and thus were incapable of a pushing attack (othismos). At the same time, plying their weapons underhand meant that only the leading rank could strike at enemy front-fighters, more forceful overhead blows weren't possible and targeting was confined to a foe's lower body. All this made for anemic offensive capability. Nonetheless, by projecting a barrier of overlapping pike points from at least the first three ranks, such troops could still perform the defensive role critical to a phalanx's center and off-wing. Iphicrates seems to have fully understood the specialized function of each section of his chosen formation and adapted his resources to match. The Athenian was to lose his position without having tested these new-style soldiers against a live opponent, though he seems to have been able to accurately assess their potential over the course of a year or so of intense drills prior to his departure.

Working under the satrap Pharnabazus, Iphicrates had found the tempo of Persian warfare frustratingly slow, doubtless a reflection of the out-sized scope that the empire's efforts always seem to have attained. After all, the massing of huge conscript armies took time, as did stockpiling the enormous quantity of supplies necessary to maintain those armies and move them over long distances. All the same, sufficient preparation had taken place by early spring 373 for the imperial host to march out at last, traveling along the coast to Egypt with a large fleet for logistical support.

Nectanebos, Pharaoh of Egypt, had made ready to oppose Persia's incursion with fortifications at each of the Nile River's seven mouths. The easternmost of these was the strongest and, though it sat first along its line of advance, the Persian command team decided to avoid it. They chose instead to mount an amphibious operation against another outlet of the Nile (the Mendesian Mouth) that had weaker arrangements and a suitable landing beach. Pharnabazus and Iphicrates came ashore with 3,000 men (Diodorus 15.42.4–5), probably all infantrymen made up from the Greek mercenary legion. On this basis, it's likely that the imperials hit the beach with 2,000–2,500 hoplites and 500–1,000 peltasts. The Egyptians responded by making a sally with 3,000 men of their own, a mix of foot soldiers (mostly heavy-armed shield-bearers) and cavalry, the latter perhaps numbering no more than 300 (10 percent of the total). With such a close match in manpower, the battle was hotly contested in the beginning (a "sharp" action per Diodorus). But when a horde of marines and light-armed rowers from the fleet joined the fray, the Egyptians were quickly overwhelmed on their flanks, doubly enveloped and badly beaten. Killing many (probably 30 percent or more) and capturing others, Iphicrates' men chased those that managed to escape, following them all the way inside their walls (a gate remaining open amid the confusion). The Greeks captured the fortress and razed it to the ground.

The Egyptian campaign had thus gotten off to a rousing start. However, it was soon to unravel in a fit of bickering among its leaders. After Pharnabazus refused to give Iphicrates latitude to operate as he pleased, arguments broke out and distrust grew. Meanwhile, lack of swift action on the invaders' part allowed the Egyptians to recover, improving their defenses to repulse attack after attack and strike back to deal the Persians considerable harm. Then the Nile began to rise, flooding the land and making operations extremely difficult. The Persians finally decided to withdraw. Having argued heatedly with Pharnabazus one more time on the way home, Iphicrates began to suspect that he might be arrested; he therefore escaped the Persian camp by night to sail back to Greece. His fears were confirmed shortly thereafter when representatives of Artaxerxes arrived at Athens to accuse him of having brought about the failure of the Egyptian expedition. But the Athenians resolutely defended Iphicrates against this charge, having already appointed him to take over their own fleet.

Corcyra Cemetery (373 B.C.)

Sparta and Athens began to spar once more shortly after the peace treaty for the Boeotian War went into effect. The focus this time was in the islands skirting the western shores of Greece. There, the Spartans supported a bid to overthrow the democratic government on Corcyra off the far northwest coast, ultimately sending their general Mnasippis there with a large force. He set out with 60–65 vessels under his command, the lower figure per Xenophon (*Hellenica* 6.2.3) and the higher from Diodorus (15.47.1). These were most likely standard triremes, which could carry 2,400–2,600 troops at a maximum load of 40 passengers and marines per ship above the normal crew complement. The allies having supplied money instead of men for the campaign, these troops included 1,500 mercenaries (likely 1,000 hoplites and 500 peltasts). This left room aboard for around 1,000 Spartans. The exact nature of these latter isn't recorded (Xenophon *Hellenica* 6.2.5), but they were probably a mix of classes with a majority being perioeci.

Mnasippis came ashore to raid outlying farmland and, having driven a contingent of troops off a nearby hill, put the city of Corcyra under siege. This prompted the Corcyrans to seek help from Athens. The Athenians responded by first sneaking Ctesicles with 600 mercenary peltasts (per Xenophon, only 500 according to Diodorus) onto the island by night to reinforce the city garrison. The newly returned Iphicrates then set sail for Corcyra with 70 ships in late 373. Meanwhile, on the island, an overconfident Mnasippis had discharged some of his hired men and angered the rest with no pay and poor provisioning. Ctesicles, seeing his opposition scattered and inattentive along the siege lines as a result, sent out his javelinmen and a few hoplites to kill 200 peltasts (Diodorus) and capture others to take out fully half of Mnasippis' hireling skirmishers in one fell swoop. Enraged, the Spartan called out his corps of spearmen to retaliate, though the disgruntled mercenary contingent took to the field only reluctantly and without much enthusiasm.

Mnasippis stood with his countrymen on the right wing as he formed up his phalanx eight shields deep. Perhaps counting only 1,500 spearmen now, his formation would have fronted over less than 200m. This array advanced slowly on the enemy troops outside the ramparts and flushed them toward town. However, once these retreating men gained a cemetery close beneath the city wall, they turned to cover behind the tombs and hurl spears and javelins at their pursuers. Meanwhile, Ctesicles led out the Corcyran army and began arranging it in battle order. Based on past musters on the island, his phalanx might have contained at least 2,000 spearmen. Seeing the enemy lining up at depth, the hirelings with Mnasippis sought to increase the length of their own files by folding ranks. This maneuver is known as the *anastrophe* or "wheeling-back" (Lazenby 1989, 65–69). It called for troops standing on the left side of the mercenary array to make an about-face and walk rearward, then spin left and move in back of their right-side ranks until reaching the far end, where they would halt and face forward once more. Properly carried out, this doubled depth by shifting half the original files behind those that had remained in place on the other side of the formation. Though complex, this move was well within the capability of these well-drilled professionals; still, it was a dangerous thing to do with the enemy so close. And it backfired horribly in this instance. The Corcyrans mistook the planned evolution for a retreat and rushed to attack before the mercenaries could finish.

The islanders' charge rapidly began to rout their now badly disordered foes and there was nothing that Mnasippis could do about it from the other wing, where the enemy had moved up to engage him frontally. The Spartan's phalanx collapsed from the left, leaving him and a small band holding their ground to be surrounded and slaughtered. The rest of his phalanx fled beneath a hot pursuit until reaching their camp, where they rallied under Hypermenes (Mnasippis' second-in-command) and held their walls. But as Iphicrates drew nearer, the surviving Spartans and mercenaries elect to board their ships and leave. Iphicrates went on to carry out other operations in the region, including the capture of some ships from Syracuse (a Spartan ally) from which he gathered booty, including items meant for the shrine at Delphi. It was now clear that Athens was back at war in earnest, no longer concerned with a single campaign, but rather willing to put any and all of Sparta's interests and allies at hazard.

Leuctra (371 B.C.)

Sparta and Athens initially concentrated on each other during the renewed fighting, leaving Thebes free to continue consolidating its position in central Greece. And the Thebans became increasingly aggressive, menacing Phocis, tearing down the fortifications at Thespiae and driving the Plataeans into refuge at Athens. The latter, especially, raised an alarm among the Athenians, who had a long history of friendly relations with Plataea stretching back into the 6th century. Seeking common cause against Thebes, Athens thus took the lead in bringing about a peace that would allow both it and Sparta to turn their efforts against this rising threat in the north. The result was a pact that sought to reinstate the lapsed tenets of the Peace of Antalcidas that had ended the Corinthian War. This called for disbanding military forces now afield and guaranteeing independence for all Greek states. Serious trouble then arose when Thebes objected to insistence by Sparta's king Agesilaos that having signed as "Thebans" rather than "Boeotians" meant its confederation must again be dissolved in order to grant autonomy to the member poleis. And when Thebes finally spurned the treaty on this point, it was tantamount to declaring war.

At this time, Cleombrotus was in Phocis with a modest allied army protecting that land from Theban threats. Rather than retiring to release his forces per the peace accord, he set out first to deal with Thebes. Additional troops had arrived from Sparta (Diodorus 15.54.6), probably bringing instructions on how to deal with the quickly developing crisis. The king's army now numbered 1,000 horsemen and 10,000 foot soldiers (Plutarch Vol. II *Pelopidas*, 397) with the latter likely 8,000 hoplites and 2,000 light footmen. The Spartans themselves made up perhaps half of the spearmen on hand at 4,000 strong, most of these having arrived with the reinforcement.

Cleombrotus camped below the passage to Coronea and sent an order to Thebes that it disband its army in accord with the peace agreement. When the Thebans refused to dismiss their men, he then prepared to invade and force them to do so. The most direct paths were now blocked (Diodorus 15.52.7–53.1), so Cleombrotus swung back into Phocis and marched down the mountainous coastal route, wiping out a small Theban force under Chaereas that had moved to block a pass along his path (Pausanius 9.13.3). He then entered Boeotia via Thisbae (see Pritchett [1965] for a discussion of the relevant topography). He moved from there to take Creusis on the Corinthian Gulf, seizing some Theban triremes before setting off up the road toward the old Spartan base at Thespiae. He stopped within Thespian territory and set up for the night on high ground at Leuctra. Meanwhile, Epaminondas, who led the Theban army, had been in place before Coronea when he heard that Cleombrotus had outflanked him. Moving to intercept, the Theban and his men covered the 30km to Leuctra and arranged their own camp on a hill near the Spartan position. Epaminondas had around 6,000 hoplites (Diodorus 15.52.3), who would have had support from perhaps 1,500 in light infantry and 600 riders. This was a full deployment of the available Boeotian forces, which had suffered some minor losses due to withdrawal of a few contingents loath to join in the war.

The opposing hosts set up across the small plain of Leuctra the next day with both commanders seemingly eager to engage. Cleombrotus desired to enhance a reputation tarnished by his having dismissed two earlier armies after failing to bring the Thebans to action. As for Epaminondas, he was in fear for the safety of his homeland and wanted to shelter it from the

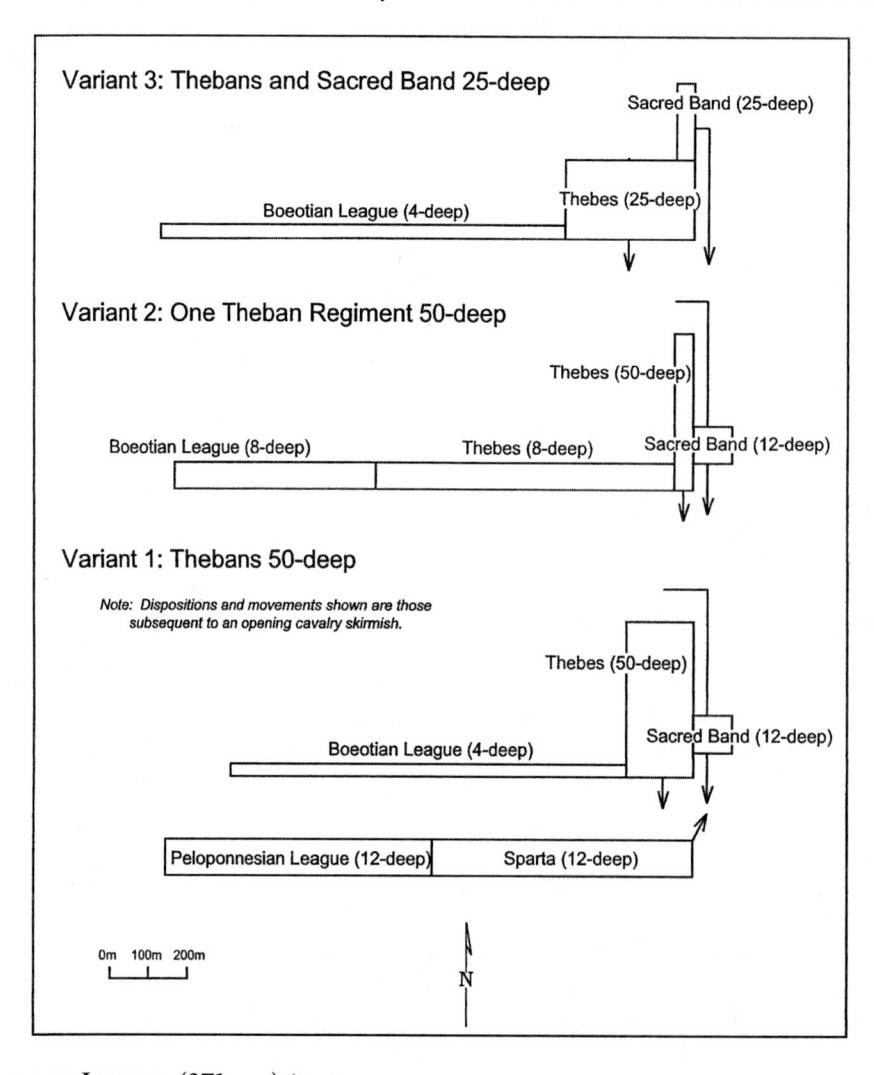

BATTLE OF LEUCRTA (371 B.C.) (BOXES REPRESENTING FORCES ARE EXAGGERATED TO SHOW RELATIVE SIZES.)

Spartans' wrath. As the phalanxes arrayed, the mounted forces from either side charged to skirmish across the ground between. Cleombrotus took advantage of his significant edge in hoplite strength to file twelve shields deep (Xenophon *Hellenica* 6.4.2) with his Spartans holding the entire right wing. This gave him a front of just over 650m. While this deployment was very traditional, that of his opponent was to prove far from the same.

Epaminondas, perhaps expanding upon precedents set in several previous Theban engagements, loaded up the left extreme of his phalanx at an astounding depth of 50 shields per Xenophon. There are several ways he could have arranged his formation that would have accommodated this singular concentration of manpower on one side while still roughly matching his enemy's line length. One variant was to use nearly all of his Theban spearmen in the deeper element and have the remaining troops stand in minimal files of four. A second variant was to thickly align no more than a single Theban regiment of 1,000 hoplites and set up the remainder of his phalanx with eight-man files. The former most closely matches Xenophon's description and has the virtue of not wasting manpower that (as events would show) Epaminondas never really intended to put into combat. The second is possibly more in tune with what Pelopidas had done at Tegyra, deploying across a 20m front with a depth advantage of maybe just a little over 4 to 1. Either way, the Theban had readied an innovative formation that he might launch a swift and powerful blow at his foe's crimson-clad heart.

Things started well for Epaminondas with a decisive victory by his horsemen, who easily routed their much inferior counterparts. Cleombrotus' bested riders fell back in confusion and would cause some disorder among their hoplite comrades on the Spartan flank as they escaped around that end of the line. The Boeotian footmen were now coming on at the double, their own cavalry clearing from the path after having hid the unusual infantry set-up. The Spartans also started forward, though not with the sort of fanfare to which they were accustomed, since turmoil in the wake of their retreating horsemen and attendant with the rapid enemy advance had managed to silence the pipers that normally set their pace (Polyaenus 1.10, *Excerpts* 18.1). Meanwhile, a bloodless stand-off was developing on the other end of the field. Epaminondas had ordered his right wing there to hold back from the fight ('refusing' it in military terminology) so as to cut the chance that it might meet defeat before he and his ultra-deep left could win the day. These men, if anything, actually drew back a bit to avoid action. Nor were the allies of Cleombrotus on that side of the field willing to move across and force the matter. Far from enthusiastic, Pausanius claimed (9.13.8) that they actually harbored hostility toward their Spartan overlords and weren't about to endure any additional risk to help them out, and Xenophon noted that some of them "were not even displeased" at Sparta's subsequent defeat (*Hellenica* 6.4.15). The engagement was therefore to be determined solely by events on the Spartan right.

Cleombrotus' hoplites and those of Epaminondas fought on even terms as the battle opened, both sides thrusting spears along the front and pressing into each other with all the strength their files could impart. This strongly suggests that the advantages of formation depth were proportionally less when files got above an optimum range of eight to twelve (or possibly 16) shields. (A phenomenon well documented in 424 at Delium — see "Deeply Massed Othismos" in Ray [2009, 186–187].) In fact, it's likely (as Xenophon observed) that the Spartans actually might have had something of an upper hand as the action opened, fighting hard and having slid rightward during their initial advance in an attempt to wrap around the open end of the Theban front (Plutarch Vol. I *Pelopidas*, 398–399). However, this favorite Spartan maneuver of cyclosis met with failure when the extending spearmen on the far end ran into the Sacred Band. Epaminondas had stationed Pelopidas with this elite unit immediately behind his left flank, and they had wheeled out from that hidden post as the formations closed to then move up and block the Spartan attempt at envelopment.

With no opportunity to roll their enemy's flank, the Spartans were locked in a grim duel of spears that became increasingly dominated by shoving from the after-ranks. In this they were badly overmatched against the famously physical Thebans, who could bring much greater manpower into play. Still, the Spartan hoplites heroically held out for a surprisingly long time. It was only after Cleombrotus fell mortally wounded and his comrades carried him away that his men finally started to wear out and falter. Sensing that the decisive moment had come at last, Epaminondas called out to his fellows (Polyaenus 2.3.2): "Give me one step, and we will have the victory!" And with a final surge of othismos they began to shove their fast-fading foemen rearward. The Spartans yielded ground only very reluctantly at first and kept their array intact, but eventually they had no choice but to give way, breaking from the fight to flee under a fierce pursuit. And no sooner did their reluctant allies see them being chased from the fray than they took to their heels as well.

Epaminondas and his Thebans not only held the battleground at the end of the day, but had dealt tremendous damage to Sparta. A probable 1,000 of its vaunted spearmen lay dead on the field, a full quarter of those that had entered the fight that morning. Worse yet for Spartan society, a high proportion of these casualties might have been full citizens (see "Casualties" below). Thebes had won a complete and shocking victory over the Spartans, one that would turn out to mark the end of Lacedaemonian ascendancy over Greece.

Reflections on Leuctra

Leuctra is one of the most famous engagements in ancient history. Yet its documentation in our surviving sources is surprisingly weak in many key areas. This has imposed the need for any detailed recreation of the battle to employ a great deal of speculation, with the effort along those lines presented here certainly being no exception. It's prudent therefore to explore in greater depth the inputs and reasoning behind critical choices made in formulating this reconstruction.

MANPOWER • Our surviving ancient texts are remarkably stingy with regard to the sizes of the armies that engaged at Leuctra. In fact, we have only two numbers (infantry and cavalry) for the Spartan force from a single author (Plutarch), a lone entry without qualifications for the Boeotians in total (Diodorus) and one more set for the Thebans separately (Frontinus 4.2.6), with perhaps our most reliable source (Xenophon) giving no army strengths at all. It's assumed here that the number for Boeotians present (6,000) refers solely to hoplites. This matches well with indications elsewhere that the Thebans could throw about 4,000 hoplites into the field at most (matching Frontinus here) and draw 2,000–3,000 others from the rest of Boeotia. The lower figure applies in this case due to lack of cooperation from a few of the lesser poleis (Pausanius 9.13.8). Cavalry in the current reconstruction represents strength equal to about 10 percent of that for the spearmen in accordance with common practice. The light footmen are considered to have been some 25 percent of the infantry as a whole, which seems reasonable for a Boeotian muster that was often very rich in light forces. On the other side, the figure for Cleombrotus' cavalry is taken as presented and the ratio of heavy to light foot soldiers is put at 4 to 1 as seems the more usual case among southern Greeks at this time (any Phocian light infantry present likely operated as substitutes for the mercenaries frequently present in Spartan armies). The result of all this is a significant edge for Cleombrotus in heavy-armed troops. Still, it wasn't so great as to discourage Epaminondas from offering battle. (Mutual consent was generally a prerequisite for pitched combat in this era, something that is well attested by the many engagement refusals that took place during the recent Boeotian War.)

Of greater controversy than overall army strength is the size of the contributing contingents. This is especially so for the Spartans. For while most who've looked at the battle would probably be comfortable with 3,000–4,000 hoplites in the muster from Thebes itself, there is a wide range of opinion on Spartan numbers. This stems from great uncertainly about the mora, the largest organizational unit in Sparta's army. This element is frequently cited by ancient authors instead of giving a precise figure for manpower. Granted that it's often stated that the Spartan army consisted of six morai, it seems clear that four of these were present at Leuctra, since we're told elsewhere (Xenophon *Hellenica* 6.4.17) that the Spartans called up "the remaining two morai" in the battle's aftermath. The controversy therefore lies in the exact size of the mora. Our estimates range from about 500 hoplites to just over 1,000. Plutarch, for example, offered the lower of these numbers (Vol. I *Pelopidas*, 395), citing Ephorus. However, he showed a degree of uncertainly in this by acknowledging that other respected authors used different figures (700 for Callisthenes and 900 for Polybios). The impression is that we're dealing in all these varying ancient references with possible generalized use of the term "mora" for what was really a "lochos" (half a mora) as well as parade complements (the *actual* number of men counted in the field). This suggests that true establishment strength was at least a bit above even the highest of these citations in line with a mora of around 1,000 spearmen and close to Lazenby's proposal (1989, 63–64) of a nominal strength of 1,120 (about 25 percent above our top ancient "parade" number). This estimate is based on Thucydides' detailed description of the Spartan army at Mantinea I in 418 (5.68.3) and that of Xenophon for a sub-unit at Leuctra (*Hellenica* 6.4.12). The issue of Spartan manpower will doubtless remain forever in dispute, but other indications at Leuctra lend indirect support to the idea that the Spartans deployed their morai at around 1,000 men strong consistent with there possibly having been a muster of 6,000 hoplites in six morai at Nemea River (394).

The first item favoring a Spartan total of about 4,000 hoplites is Pausanius' note (9.13.9) that "the Lacedaemonians themselves and the Thebans were not badly matched adversaries." While this can be taken as a statement about relative quality of the troops, it might well have referred to quantity as well. Pausanius otherwise made no comment on manpower. The idea of last-minute reinforcements arriving directly from Sparta (Diodorus 15.54.6) also backs the idea of half the army being Spartans. Citizens were much easier to gather on short notice than farther flung and reluctant allies. As a result, they could very well have made up an overwhelming majority of this second "large army." Diodorus clearly made an error in assigning this force to Archidamus (the son of Agesilaos, who actually later commanded troops gathered on the home front), yet otherwise may have been accurate in reporting the sending of considerable manpower by the Spartan assembly. Finally, the best indication that the Spartans might have been around 4,000 in number comes from their casualty figures. These range up to exactly 4,000 (Diodorus 15.56.4), and even the lower estimates are consistent with a total force of that size (see "Casualties" below).

OBLIQUE ORDER • Epaminondas designed a formation to attack the enemy at its strongest point with superior manpower drawn from a select portion of his complement while keeping the rest of it out of combat. Diodorus said that he did this by "arranging his phalanx in oblique formation" (15.55.2) and the term "oblique order" for such an approach is often employed today. While exact details of the Theban's technique are subject to debate, it's widely accepted that he withheld the right side of his formation (perhaps even withdrawing this a few paces as indicated by Diodorus) after filling its ranks with men of lesser quality at a more modest depth than that of the other wing (possibly even below that of normal practice). At the same time, the left side of his formation (whether relatively broad or confined to just a very small stretch at the flank end) deployed with unusually deep files containing the army's highest quality troops. He thus hoped to use greater othismos and any other advantages accruing from his overly deep, left-side array to best the opposition's more thinly aligned right wing. And this is precisely how it all seems to have worked out at Leuctra. Less clear is the role of the Sacred Band. Plutarch's account indicates a station for this unit behind the left wing, from which it moved out to make a surprise attack against the Spartans' standard ploy of extending their right to envelop opponents on that side of the field. This is a change from that elite unit's past practice of forming the Thebans' leading rank(s), yet seems reasonable all the same. Accepting such a post for the Sacred Band, Stylianou (1998, 402–403) has made an interesting proposal for how the rest of the Thebans set up at Leuctra. He offers that the left wing wasn't 50 shields deep, but just 25 as at Delium (and, maybe, Tegyra). However, the Sacred Band made it appear deeper by standing in the back at the same 25 shields in a dozen files. This intriguing idea provides yet a third (and perhaps the best) variant for the Theban deployment.

CASUALTIES • Losses among the victorious Thebans were apparently minimal. Xenophon gave no account, but Pausanius cited 47 (presumably all hoplites) while Diodorus allowed for a rather more believable 300. The former would represent just over 1 percent of a 4,000-man Theban contingent and falls within the bounds of the sort of small losses often associated with the winning side in a phalanx battle. However, the kind of extended action described, featuring stiff Spartan resistance and back-and-forth fights (one waged over the fallen Cleombrotus is described in detail) would seem more in accordance with the higher figure and a 7.5 percent loss.

As for Spartan losses, we have the 4,000 listed by Diodorus, which seems impossible for an actual count of the dead and is almost surely a tradition on the total number of hoplites defeated (per the foregoing "Manpower" discussion). Fortunately, we have two other casualty reports for the Spartans from Xenophon (*Hellenica* 6.4.15) and Pausanius (9.13.12). These are more or less in agreement, with the former claiming "almost a thousand had been killed" and the latter "more than a thousand." Based on a likely 4,000-man deployment, these hover around 25 percent of the total strength exposed in the engagement, quite in keeping with typical damage done to a force broken after a long fight and suffering the level of chase cited at Leuctra. Xenophon elaborated on the Spartans' losses by saying that 700 of those killed (over 70 percent) were spartiates. This is quite astonishing in light of that uppermost class of citizen surely making up a much smaller percentage of the army overall. At the very least, this means that the spartiates present were heavily concentrated in the first few ranks and/or within the rightmost morai, those postings likely having suffered the heaviest casualties. It's also highly likely that Xenophon used the term "spartiate" to distinguish all those that were not from the perioecian class (he seems to have used just this formula in describing Spartan forces the next year [*Hellenica* 6.5.21]). This combination of higher classes might indeed have approached half of the hoplite pool and, added to the foregoing conjecture on positioning, would much better explain such a high representation among the dead.

Lastly, given that contingents other than those from Thebes and Sparta had not really come to action, these would have incurred very few casualties of any sort. Losses were probably limited to just a few men that fell to missiles either along the periphery of the cavalry action or in connection with any light infantry skirmishing that was going on. (This latter is not reported in any of our sources, but was nearly always present around the edges of a phalanx battle.) We thus hear from Pausanius (9.13.12) that among some of the Spartan allies "not a man of them had fallen" and for others there was "but slight loss to report."

Those on the Spartan side who had escaped the battlefield fell back on their camp. They stood to arms there in defiance, the site offering a strong defensive position on a hillside with a ditch in front. Epaminondas was of no mind to launch a disadvantaged attack on such a strong point and gave leave instead for the beaten men to go out and gather their dead. Finally, the Thebans were dissuaded by their allies from making any further attempt on the Spartans at Leuctra and allowed them to depart under a truce. Meanwhile, back in Sparta, news of the defeat had spawned a whirl of desperate activity. The two morai remaining at home were mustered and the reserves were called out as well as any other men who had for some reason escaped serving with Cleombrotus' column. Agesilaos was still hobbled, so Archidamus took command of these citizen levies. He was then able to add allied troops from Tegea, Corinth, Sicyon, Phlius, Achaea and others to form a sizeable new army. It was his intent to confront the Thebans and rescue what remained of his defeated countrymen. However, upon marching into the Megarid, Archidamus meet the Leuctra survivors coming from Boeotia and, leading them home, he dismissed his allies in route.

War Comes to Sparta

The Spartans found their former authority greatly diminished in the aftermath of Leuctra. Jason, the dictator of Pherae, had grown strong in recent years and made it clear now that his region was fully independent of Sparta, going so far as to attack the Spartan colony at Heraclea. Even in the Peloponnese there was rebellion. The recently scattered Mantineans felt free to lay claim to the autonomy promised by renewal of the Peace of Antalcidas' terms and rebuild their city. And when Sparta conceded this but asked that they do so with at least its nominal consent, they haughtily rejected even this relatively minor, face-saving gesture. Such resistance inspired others to do the same and there was soon trouble at Tegea as well. A movement to unite all the Arcadians arose there that led to a fresh round of warfare.

Tegea II and Elymia (371/70 B.C.)

Calibius and Proxenus of Tegea were leaders of the Arcadian union movement and, when their proposals were rejected by the city council, they gathered their followers under arms outside the walls to settle the matter by combat. The unionists took the precaution of sending to nearby Mantinea for help; yet believing themselves to be in the majority, they were willing to enter battle when the opposition took the field under Stasippus. But though those opposing union were indeed fewer, they were victorious. Proxenus fell in the engagement alongside a few others and Calibius fled with the rest. This action would have involved 3,200 or so hoplites at most if the entire citizen roster (including reservists) took part. We might thus propose that these were split something like 1,700 to 1,500 against the winners (Diodorus [15.59.2] indicated that after very minor combat casualties and later executions some 1,400 of anti-unionists would eventually flee into exile) with a few horsemen on either side.

Despite their success in the engagement, Stasippus and his party were to lose in the end. This came about after those defeated gathered near the gates facing Mantinea and let troops arriving from that sympathetic polis into the city. Still having large numbers and now united with these reinforcements, Calibius' forces were able to seize control of Tegea. They then joined with other Arcadians to plan a confederation for their region. Meanwhile, some 800 of Stasippus' followers had reached Sparta to alert it of this threatening development. In spite of the winter season, Sparta's leadership reacted immediately, putting the now healthy Agesilaos in command of an army for a punitive expedition against Tegea. This was to include both Spartan troops and some of the still loyal Arcadians. The king marched to Eutaea on the Arcadian border to await some mercenary peltasts and Phliasian horsemen that were stationed in Corinth near the Peloponnesian frontier. Meanwhile, things were heating up farther north at the polis of Arcadian Orchomenos.

The Orchomenians were among those opposed to an Arcadian League and this stance drew an attack from the League's chief supporters at Mantinea. However, an assault on the walls of Orchomenos failed and the Mantineans under Lycomedes had drawn back to the city of Elymia. It was here where Agesilaos' reinforcements marching down from Corinth came into contact with them. The mercenary commander, Polytropus, set up a screen in front of his spearmen and cavalry and descended on the Mantineans to initiate a sharp action. Fending off swarms of javelins, the Arcadian hoplites (perhaps 1,000 strong) advanced at speed against their foes (likely around 800 peltasts) and managed to get them within spear-length. How they did this is puzzling, as the much fleeter javelinmen should have been able to withdraw and keep a safe distance — perhaps they had crossed over some sort of barrier in their eagerness to get at the enemy that then hampered their retreat. At any rate, the results were decisive. Polytropus' peltasts were no match for the heavy-equipped spearmen at close quarters and the mercenary commander was killed to send his men running for their lives. There would have been a great slaughter at this point had not the Phliasian horsemen ridden past their hoplite line and come up just in time. They were able to threaten the Mantineans' rear and cause them to break off pursuit. (Note that the foregoing follows Xenophon's description of this action [*Hellenica* 6.5.13–14]; Diodorus alternatively outlined a major hoplite battle [15.62.1–2], which seems much less consistent with surrounding events.)

Agesilaos now advanced to Mantinea and united there with the Phliasians and javelinmen from Orchomenos. He sat pat as the Mantineans joined with the rest of the Arcadian League proponents, eschewing confronting these elements in detail toward letting them gather that he might eliminate all in a single, grand action. However, he had camped in poor position within a narrow valley behind the city and was obliged to retreat when the enemy began to muster above on one of the enclosing slopes. Forming his army up in a column, the king turned his men into battle formation facing the enemy. He then executed an anastrophe movement and pulled the distal wing of his formation away from the opposing front. With his entire force now at double depth, he spun toward the valley mouth and exited at quick pace. Agesilaos reformed his men into a phalanx once they gained the plain, setting them up at a depth of nine or ten shields. The Arcadians at this point refrained from engaging him, waiting in hopes of gaining help from Thebes, that city having already accepted some funds from Sparta's old foes at Elis toward financing a foray into the Peloponnese. But this was long in coming and Agesilaos withdrew in the meantime to disband his troops for the season.

Oeum, Tegeatis Pass and Amyclae (370/69 B.C.)

The Arcadians had to content themselves with spoiling the land of Sparta's local allies for a while. But as winter wore on, the Thebans under Epaminondas and Pelopidas finally reached Mantinea to collect a large armament. Plutarch (Vol. I *Pelopidas*, 399; Vol. II *Agesilaos*, 62) put this force at 40,000 fighters and another 30,000 in support. Diodorus (15.62.5) clamed over 50,000 (probably combatants only) and elsewhere repeated Plutarch's 70,000 total (15.81.2). Yet the lowest figure here for fighting men would seem high by a factor of roughly two times. The Thebans most likely sent 10,000 per past complements. This would be 7,000 hoplites (the presence of all seven regimental commanders is implied) plus 2,300 light footmen (25 percent of the infantry total) and 600 in cavalry. (They would bring this same armament on their next incursion into the Peloponnese the following summer.) Add in 1,500 spearmen, 500 skirmishers and maybe 200 cavalry from Locris and Phocis and you get some 12,000 soldiers in all with about 8,500 of them hoplites. As for the Peloponnesian allies, estimates of their strength based on past deployments and common region practice might be as follows: (1) 6,000 hoplites from Arcadia (possibly including a standing body from the its new confederacy 5,000 strong and paid by the state — the *eparitoi*) with 1,500 light footmen; (2) 3,000–4,000 hoplites and 750–1,000 foot skirmishers from Argos; and (3) 2,000–3,000 hoplites and 500–750 light infantry from Elis. Cavalry variously supplied by these less horse-strong states might have come to 300–600 riders at a quarter to half relative to the supply from Boeotia. This suggests a total fighting force closer to 28,000 including 20,500 spearmen. This was a huge army to be sure, but no greater than the largest that the Spartans had marshaled during the recent Boeotian War. And the smaller deployment makes much more sense of Xenophon's comment that the invaders were at this time "by no means eager to proceed into Lacedaemon" (*Hellenica* 6.5.24).

Despite such initial reservations, the Thebans began to gain courage from intelligence being gathered on their enemy's current condition. It was growing ever clearer that the Spartans had much fewer of their own men than usual and had still to gather their allies. Moreover, the invaders were approached by people willing to rebel against Spartan rule, most importantly including some of the perioeci. Deciding now to risk a march on Sparta, the Thebans, Locrians and Phocians headed directly south down the valley floor toward Caryae on the Laconian border. At the same time, their local allies set out as well, with the Arcadians, Argives and Eleans (these last with all the Peloponnesian cavalry in tow) moving along separate tracks.

The Arcadian column came up against a Spartan garrison that guarded the pass at Oeum (Xenophon *Hellenica* 6.5.26). Ischolaus commanded this outpost with half the exiled Tegeans (400 hoplites), a body of freed helot spearmen (maybe 500–600 strong) and at least a few younger Spartans. In addition, he could call upon local men, perhaps adding another 100–200 spearmen and some foot skirmishers (probably less than 50). As the Arcadians neared, Ischolaus made the mistake of not descending to meet them in a narrow part of the pass where his modest force might have prevailed. Instead, perhaps assessing the situation as being more desperate than it actually was, he dismissed his youthful Spartan charges to fight another day (Diodorus [15.64.5], possibly getting them past an advance enemy force by means of a ploy ascribed to him in Polyaenus [2.22.2]). He then set up the rest of his command in phalanx at the edge of town with the intent of insuring that the locals would fight at his side in order to defend their own homes. The Arcadians closed on him there in a confined space that might have permitted them to conventionally deploy at no more than equal strength. Taking advantage of this fair match in numbers, the Spartan's hoplites were able to beat back their attackers for a brief victory in the opening phase of the battle. However, though the opposing spearmen were limited in arraying before Oeum by terrain and (perhaps) man-made features, this was not the case with their light infantrymen. Those, being numerous, were able to overwhelm the handful of light-armed opponents set against them and take possession of surrounding high ground and rooftops. They then used this advantage to pour a deluge of missiles down on the town's defenders. Swarmed by men and darts from either flank as well as the rear, Ischolaus and his troops were slaughtered to the last man. The Arcadians pushed on and descended into Laconia.

Meanwhile, the Argives climbed Mount Parnon through the pass above Tegeatis, where they met a garrison in that entry as well (Diodorus 15.54.2). Alexander of Sparta held this outpost with a complement that might have counted around 1,000 hoplites if it was on a par with Oeum. These apparently also included a group of exiles, this time from Boeotia. We have no details on how the action played out here, but the Argives broke through, killing the Spartan officer and some 200 of his men including all of the Boeotians. Possibly Alexander and the latter had stood on the right wing of an array that was penetrated by much deeper files to send the rest of their formation into flight, with a hard pursuit then running the body count up to a hefty 20 percent. The Argives now moved down the mountain to join the Arcadians and Eleans (who'd traveled with the horsemen via a gentler route) to link up with the Theban column at Caryae. This combined force then marched south on course for the Spartan capital.

The Thebans and their allies arrived on the east side of the Eurotas River across from the Spartans' un-walled city and began to spoil the neighborhood. Spartan hoplites held post at high points and narrow places along their side of the river in relatively small numbers. Shorn of allies and the perioeci for the moment, they probably counted 2,500 citizens of all classes between the ages of 20 and 50 plus another 600 or so older men and youths. There were also 400 remaining Tegean exiles, 200 Boeotian refugees and some light-armed support in the form of the mercenaries from Agesilaos' recent expedition that had remained on the payroll. Given such limited strength, it would have been tactical folly of the highest order for the Spartans to chance an open battle, since that would pit them against a foe with better than four times as many spearmen and all of prime age. Instead, Agesilaos kept his troops within strong positions that acted as significant force multipliers in discouraging any attempt to storm them. He was also able to call upon 6,000 helots, who took up arms in return for a promise of freedom. Some 1,000 of these (Diodorus 15.65.6) must have been outfitted as hoplites while the rest formed a corps of light-armed auxiliaries, though Plutarch claimed that many of the latter ultimately deserted (Vol. II *Agesilaos*, 63).

Avoiding a potentially costly assault on the Spartan defenses, the invaders ranged about and plundered the countryside for several days before moving to ford the Eurotas at Amyclae. This led to a clash which the descriptions of Diodorus (15.65.2), Polyaenus (2.1.27) and Frontinus (1.10.3) combine to paint as a major hoplite action. It seems that the choice of this crossing site was prompted by deception on the part of Agesilaos, who openly displayed a very weak guard there and had these men run away when Epaminondas and his van moved into the stream. The Theban procedure seems to have been to send the heavy elements from the Boeotian and Arcadian brigades across first to set up a beachhead that would then cover passage by the rest of the army. The river was running high, fast and cold in this winter season and proved difficult to wade. Waiting on the other side, Agesilaos sprang from cover to catch his foes by surprise as they emerged from the water in some disorder. His phalanx boasted around 4,700 hoplites (including citizen regulars and reserves, Tegean and Boeotian exiles and helots) along with a strong screen of light footmen off its flanks. The attack closed against maybe 13,000 spearmen under Epaminondas, bringing the 4,000 Thebans that spearheaded the crossing into action first. Fortunately for these veterans, they were well-trained and must have quickly shuffled according to their standard drill into an array filed eight-deep. Advancing that they might cover for their comrades still emerging from the river, they then moved out to engage the fast closing enemy.

Sparta's formation seems to have been the more coherent one as the battle opened, which is understandable given the opposition's initial disarray and short preparation time, and it badly bloodied the Thebans early on in what Diodorus called a "heavy slaughter." Doubtless this claim is somewhat hyperbolic (it isn't repeated in Polyaenus or Frontinus); nonetheless, the invading spearmen took significant damage before their Arcadian and remaining Boeotian companions in the rear could organize and move up to join the fight. These fresh troops were then able to turn the action in Epaminondas' favor, extending his line off either flank to slowly begin encircling both ends of the Spartan front. Agesilaos must have called upon elite troops in his forward ranks and heady old-age reservists at the back to lead the way in now reversing his phalanx's heading (for a description of the disengagement procedure involved see the battle of Chaeronea in 338) and execute a withdrawal. Discouraged from pursuit by his foe's superior light-armed forces, Epaminondas held the battlefield for a technical victory; all the same, Polyaenus said that he'd lost 600 men, nearly 5 percent of those that had crossed the Eurotas. The Spartans' casualties are unreported, but were probably no more than half or less of those they inflicted.

Sparta's Peloponnesian allies were now beginning to arrive and soon had gathered to the number of 4,000 hoplites, and a column was on the way from Athens under Iphicrates as well. In contrast, the army of Epaminondas was shrinking as his local partners broke off for the rest of the winter. With supplies running short and opposing forces having grown to around 8,500 spearmen to rival his own manpower, the Theban elected to leave Laconia. Yet he didn't go back to Boeotia straight away. He instead helped the Messenians found the city of Megalopolis (around which they would federate) and left it with a garrison. When Epaminondas finally did head for home in early spring 369, he thus left behind budding unions in both Messenia and Arcadia as powerful hedges against the prospects for a Spartan recovery.

Corinth and Sicyon Plain (369 B.C.)

Epaminondas' return to Thebes proved brief. Within months he was again marching an army to aid the Arcadians, Argives and Eleans in resuming their war on Sparta. The Spartans and Athenians had in the interim put forces in place across the Isthmus of Corinth, strengthening their positions with earthen and stake field works in hopes of blocking entry into the Peloponnese. Chabrias of Athens had command of some 10,000 men for this task (Diodorus 15.68.1), drawing them from his own polis as well as Megara, Pellene and Corinth. These probably represented 8,000 hoplites backed by 2,000 peltasts and horsemen. The Spartans had joined him with an equal force that was similar in its mix of arms, bringing all the men that had been gathered in Laconia that spring prior to the Theban withdrawal save for the old age/youth citizen reservists. With only 7,000 spearmen and 600 in cavalry plus a likely 2,000 or so foot skirmishes, Epaminondas was therefore facing more than twice his number; however, he saw opportunity in his foes being spread thinly over a fairly broad line of separate outposts. He scouted these and determined that one manned by a mixed contingent from Sparta and Pellene was weakest. Timing his approach to arrive just at dawn when the enemy would be changing watches and least alert, he launched a concentrated assault. The defenders were taken unaware and abandoned their post to make a stand on a nearby hill. They then departed under a truce as the Thebans passed through to join their allies.

Epaminondas now carried out a series of raids against poleis allied to Sparta. In addition to Phlius, these included Pellene and Sicyon, with the campaign being so successful as to bring the latter across into the Theban camp. He also invaded the territory of Epidaurus to the southeast. It was during the return from this foray when a small action took place as his column passed just to the southwest of Corinth. A party of peltasts (perhaps around 800 mercenaries) under Chabrias charged from a gate and attacked the Sacred Band, which had separated from the rest of the army to march very close to the city wall in a foolhardy display of distain for their foes. As the Thebans set up in phalanx to meet the emerging threat, their opponents got atop nearby burial monuments and hurled javelins to deadly effect from these elevated positions, killing "a very considerable number" (Xenophon *Hellenica* 7.1.19) of the hoplites. Lacking light-armed support of their own, the Thebans were unable to retaliate and fled when Chabrias and his men descended to swarm them on open ground. The peltasts pursued for a fair distance before returning to set up a trophy and carry away the enemy dead. The victors gave back the corpses later under a truce that the Thebans requested in formal acknowledgment of their defeat.

Despite this set back, Epaminondas' operations inflicted significant damage; however,

Dionysius of Syracuse had thrown in on the Spartans' side and now sent them reinforcements. These sailed on more than 20 triremes (Xenophon *Hellenica* 7.1.20) that included transport conversions, landing some 2,000 foot soldiers (Diodorus 15.70.1) while a horse-carrier provided 50 riders and their mounts. These troops were mostly Iberian and Celtic shock fighters carrying swords and equipped predominantly with large shields. The Spaniards (and some of the Celts as well) would also have had throwing spears to provide longer-distance strike potential, and inclusion of cavalry indicates a balanced mix that might also have had some light footmen (maybe 25 percent of the infantry). These last would have been Iberian *caetrati* very similar to Grecian peltasts. Dionysius' horsemen, despite their paltry number, proved a great nuisance to the Thebans with general harassment. They also probably contributed greatly along the flank of an engagement at Sicyon. The Sicilian's men claimed a triumph there, besting what was probably a similarly sized force of local hoplites (per the city's contingent at Nemea River in 394). Perhaps turning a flank to break up an otherwise superior front of overlapping aspides, they killed 70 of the Greek spearmen. At around 5 percent, this would have been very typical losses for a beaten phalanx of 1,500 hoplites.

Epaminondas returned to Thebes at summer's end having managed to bloody his foes, yet not able to report a telling blow. Back in Sparta, the hired men from Sicily went home as well, but other foreign help arrived with a delegation from the Persian king Artaxerxes. Philiscus from Abydos led this effort with intent to broker peace between the warring Greek factions. When this unsurprisingly failed to materialize, he provided funds and helped the Spartans gather a force of 2,000 select mercenaries before returning to Asia.

Phlius Crossing, the Tearless Battle (Malea) and Pherae Road (368 B.C.)

The Thebans replaced Epaminondas as army commander after his political rivals successfully advertised the results of his last effort as disappointing. And being then distracted by events in Thessaly, they spared the Peloponnese an invasion in 368. Still, the war there continued as the Arcadians and Argives marched again into Phliasian territory. This time, however, the defenders didn't wait for their foes to reach town; moving out to meet the invaders' vanguard as it crossed a river, the city cavalry attacked in the company of Athenian horsemen and support from a picked unit of hoplites (Xenophon *Hellenica* 7.2.10). The troops caught across the river took a beating and were forced to retire onto high ground for fear of mounted envelopment. They spent the rest of the day there as the horsemen continued to harass even as they kept their comrades from crossing to their aid. This was undoubtedly a small action, involving no more than 300–600 spearmen in the elite lochos from Phlius, while the leading Arcadian and Argive elements are unlikely to have been more than twice that else they probably would have been able to push the Phliasians aside horsemen or not. Pulling back at nightfall, the locals and Athenians retired behind the city walls and had no problem in fending off any subsequent attempts on those stout ramparts.

Meanwhile, the Spartans, taking advantage of their relief from the predations of Epaminondas, were now able to assume a more aggressive stance. The result would be an engagement that forever became part of their lore. This happened when Archidamus (who'd succeeded his elderly sire in command of the polis' army) set out to reclaim Caryae at summer's end. His forces included not only Sparta's citizen hoplites (around 2,500) and maybe 600–700 light-armed men, but also a fresh contingent from Dionysius. The latter might have numbered 1,500 heavy infantry and 500 light plus 50 in cavalry if the tyrant's second sending had matched the first. Taking Caryae, Archidamus shifted next into the Arcadian-Messenian frontier region. He ravaged the countryside there for some time, but upon arrival of a relief force from Arcadia and Argos retired onto a strong position in the hills above an otherwise unknown location called Malea. After a time, the commander of the mercenaries, Cissidas, announced that his men's term of employment was up and they would be departing. He and his troops then headed for Laconia to take ship: however, they found their path blocked at a narrow pass by a force of Messenians. Cissidas was apparently unsure of the opposition's strength and followed a prudent course of sending back for help. But just as Archidamus was coming to his assistance, the Arcadians and Argives suddenly appeared. Their manpower is speculative, but might have included the standing army of Arcadia (5,000 hoplites) and some 2,000 spearmen from Argos (like those later joining the eparitoi in Elis). Typical light support would have been 1,500 in foot skirmishers and 300–400 horsemen.

This convergence of forces led to a battle at a road junction where a broadening of the valley allowed for wide deployment. Archidamus had 4,000 in heavy footmen, with Spartan hoplites occupying his right wing, Iberians likely standing in the middle and Celts on the far left with the light forces arrayed off the flanks. Across the way, the Arcadians would have formed the right wing and center of their formation and set the spearmen from Argos to hold the left end with their light troops outboard either side. The Spartans undoubtedly stood four shields deep against opponents in files of eight, while the foreign heavy footmen adjusted per their own customs to create fronts of near equal length. What followed (Xenophon *Hellenica* 7.1.30–32) seems to have been a classic example of Spartan reputation and demeanor so cowing a foe that they gave way almost without a fight. As the enthusiastic Spartans drew near in their intimidating slow march to pipes, most of the Argives panicked (perhaps still aligning and unready to fight), with those at the rear leading the way in a rush from the field. This left no more than a few brave souls standing their ground to be speared down by the advancing, crimson-clad steamroller. The rest of the enemy array was immediately caught up in the collapse on its left wing and soon joined the mob streaming rearward. Giving chase, Archidamus' allied cavalry and light footmen cut down many of the fleeing men, as did the Celts whose lighter gear allowed good speed.

In light of an ardent pursuit by the Spartans' allies, casualties in this engagement must have run very high among the losers. Xenophon reported "vast numbers" of their slain and we might estimate this at a crippling 20–30 percent. (We can discount here as hyperbole the claim by Diodorus [15.72.3] that 10,000 Arcadians lost their lives. This is probably a reference to the "Ten Thousand," which was the ruling assembly of the Arcadian League. Indeed, this title itself was probably exaggerated, being at best a nominal accounting of total hoplite residency in the region.) Such a cost was in strong contrast to that on the other side, where not a single Spartan had fallen. As a result, there was no need to grieve in Sparta and this victory came to be known most popularly as the "Tearless Battle."

Back in Thebes, the focus in 368 was on Thessaly and Macedonia to the north. The Macedonian king, Alexander II, had been assassinated by his brother-in-law, Ptolemy, who then claimed the throne. Pelopidas, having in the past conducted missions to Macedonia, set out to convince this new king that he should continue his predecessor's alliance with Thebes. But the Thessalian tyrant Alexander of Pherae captured and imprisoned Pelopidas and a companion in route. Incensed at this, the Thebans dispatched (per Diodorus 15.71.3) 8,000 hoplites (probably including at least 1,000 mercenaries provided by Thessalian foes of Alexander, who initially aided the expedition) and 600 horsemen to get their man back. Alexander sent for help from Athens and got 1,000 mercenaries under Autocles, marshalling these with his own forces (possibly 10,000 hired hoplites and 6,000 horsemen if Xenophon's claim is to be trusted [*Hellenica* 6.1.8], though this is probably overstated) in preparation for a pitched battle. However, after marching to the gates of Pherae, the Boeotian commanders saw their Thessalian support evaporate and elected to retreat.

A large body of Alexander's cavalry came up to assault the rear of the Theban column as it moved down the road from Pherae, flinging clouds of javelins to wound and kill some of the hoplites. The heavy-armed spearmen were not only too slow to catch and engage the attacking riders, but their same lack of speed also made it impossible to escape. In the distress of the moment, the Thebans turned to Epaminondas (who was serving in their ranks as a private soldier after his recent removal from office), electing him general again on the spot. He quickly set about trying to extricate the army from its predicament. He succeeded by organizing his own cavalry and light infantry into a trailing screen that could counterattack and then safely retire as needed behind a rearward facing phalanx of hoplites. Fighting off charge after charge and withdrawing by stages, the Boeotians could thus cut their losses while handing out some damage in return. In the end, the Thessalians gave up and Epaminondas was able to lead his Boeotians home without further difficulty. And though this expedition was a failure, Epaminondas would continue to threaten Alexander and the tyrant eventually released Pelopidas and his companion unharmed.

The Corinthian Gate at Phlius (366 B.C.)

In 367 Epaminondas and the Thebans returned to the Peloponnese. They persuaded the Argives to seize the passage past Cenchreae on the Isthmus of Corinth and swept past the Spartan blockade with no difficulty. This was to prove a much less extensive campaign than those in the past, with the main accomplishment being Epaminondas' pressuring of the Achaeans, who had previously stayed neutral, to join Thebes' cause and set up a democratic government. However, this was to go sour after the Thebans returned to Boeotia and the newly established Achaean democracy was overthrown as the region joined in alliance with the Spartans. The Arcadians now found themselves caught between Sparta below and Achaea above as the campaign season came to a close.

There was no invasion the next spring, but the Theban commander of the garrison at Sicyon led a march on Phlius with his own troops as well as a force of mercenaries under Euphron from Sicyon plus men from Pellene and some Sicyonian citizens. The size of this armament isn't detailed, but there may have been 1,000 hoplites from Thebes, 500–1,000 (up to a two-thirds muster) from Sicyon and another 400–600 (one lochos) from Pellene with the mercenaries adding in around 2,000 peltasts. Reaching Phlius, the invaders split into two teams, the Thebans moving out onto the lowland on one side of the city to spoil crops and the rest taking position on a hill near the gate to Corinth (see Pritchett [1969, 96–111] for a discussion of the topography). Observing these dispositions and that the men on the hill were starting to descend toward the plain, the Phliasians sent out their cavalry and picked hoplites (300–400) against them. Xenophon's account (*Hellenica* 7.2.11–14) goes on to describe a lengthy duel at long distance between the light-armed men, with one side and then the other moving up and back in an attempt to enjoy ground or cover favorable to their own capabilities. The peltasts eventually became separated from their hoplites and Phlius' cavalry jumped ahead of its companions on foot to strike the now unsupported spearmen. At first, the hoplites held their ground and the riders fell back a bit; however, once some of the Phliasians' own spearmen came up into the fight, the Pelleneans and Sicyonians were routed, with many of the former and a few of the latter killed at the scene or in flight. All this took place before the Thebans could come across to help their allies or the mercenaries could get back into the action. With dark falling, the Phliasians were left to hold the field and set up a trophy before retiring into the city.

Major shifts in the political situation developed as 366 wore on and the Arcadians decided to form a limited alliance with Athens that called for the latter to aid them if attacked, but not requiring action against Sparta. Corinth responded by ending its own partnership with the Athenians and opening peace talks with Thebes. All of this led to ever wider negotiations and a general armistice was eventually agreed upon that put an end for a while to the conflict in the Peloponnese (what Diodorus termed the Sparto-Boeotian War [15.76.3]).

Datames' Revolt

Persian affairs at this time were also in a state of turmoil as a number of Artaxerxes' satraps sought to establish their own kingdoms in armed revolts. Their weapon of choice in these endeavors more often than not was the Greek mercenary. However, the imperial armies their hired fighters now faced had a more effective design that reflected Grecian models.

Persian Phalanxes

Accounts of the army of Darius III (Arrian 2.8.8; Plutarch Vol. II, *Alexander*, 153; Justin 11.6.2) claim that the host of late-mid 4th century Persia had 600,000 foot soldiers. Probably an exaggeration by an order of magnitude, it's more likely that the imperial roster contained six divisions (baivaraba or myriads) of front-line troops at an authorized complement of 10,000 men each for a total of 60,000. (There was perhaps an equal number of supporting satrapal levies theoretically available, since Xenophon's fictional account of Cyrus the Great indicates that a 120,000-man total might have been rumored in the early-mid 4th century when he wrote that work.) These "regular" units drew recruits to fill out a host as needed from select military colonists settled at key defensive sites. But in reality, the reported baivarabam strengths were no more than "paper" numbers, since most of these divisions were not standing entities and the manpower they actually took into the field varied downward greatly (regularly running from 80 percent of allotments down to 60 percent or even as low as 30 percent). The same held true for cavalry normally organized in nominal 1,000-man regiments (hazaraba). Mounted potential might have come to no more than one hazarabam of horsemen per four hazaraba of infantry, 30 regiments including satrapal bodies for 30,000 riders at establishment strength in line with a claim for Darius in 334 by Callisthenes via Polybios (12.18.1). However, as most of these horsemen were locally derived, availability must have varied greatly as frequent episodes of internal unrest cut off recruiting areas. Having put aside the bow, Persian horsemen now depended on javelins and had added a few pieces of light armor. Overall, however, the form and function of Persia's cavalry in the 4th century was much as it had been since the days of Cyrus the Great in the 6th. It was among the empire's foot soldiers where things had changed.

The Persians had not given up on their past "combined arms" approach to warfare and continued to field infantry units with an organic mix of shock and missile troops. All the same, combat gear had undergone some major evolution since the early 5th century. The system in those days featured a few men with short spears and large wicker shields (spara) fronting for shieldless bow/spearmen and pure archers in the following ranks. This method had come to grief whenever hoplites were able to breach the leading shield wall and get at those behind, which finally led to better protecting men in the after-ranks through provision of a small shield (*taka*). Based on images of ethnic Persian light infantry in later years, diversification of weaponry then followed, with peltast/light spearmen replacing at least a portion of the bow-armed troops within combat arrays. These might have rendered obsolete the former custom of relying exclusively on drafts of light-armed militiamen from the satrapies for attached duties like forward skirmishing, close support of cavalry, screening the rear/flanks and pursuit. Nevertheless, local levies of slingers, light bowmen, peltasts and the like were still around and must have remained the dominant battlefield auxiliaries as well as prime tools for detached assignments like scouting and foraging.

Evolutionary trends among the rearward ranks eventually spread to front-liners as well. Adding aspis-style shields to their spears, these came to resemble hoplites (some even adopting linen cuirasses) and thus provided Persian formations with a stouter, more shock-capable leading edge. (Excellent representations of this type of "Persian hoplite" appear on the famous Alexander Sarcophagus, showing them in action against that renowned Macedonian hero in the 330s). Such transfiguration of the old shield wall into a sort of "mini-phalanx" likely reached its peak with filing of these improved lead fighters at a greater depth. Just how deep is speculative, but we might have a clue in the residual terminology retained by later Greek tacticians for countermarching, the various maneuvers used to reverse the facing of phalanx formations (Asclepiodotus 10.13–15). Both the "Laconian" countermarch (*exeligmos Lakonikos* per the Spartan evolution at Cornea II in 394) and the "Macedonian" countermarch (*exeligmos Makedonikos*) achieved this reversal of front by transforming arrays into mirror images along each rank (the most rightward man becoming the most leftward) and reversing the file order front to back as well (save for the rearmost man in the Laconian maneuver and the foremost in the Macedonian). For these, the entire formation needed to consist of like-armed heavy infantrymen (as was the case in both Doric and Macedonian phalanxes). However, the "Persian" countermarch (*exeligmos Persikos*) seems to have applied to arrays of mixed troop types, since, though similarly exchanging wings, it was also designed to keep its front-rankers to the fore and rear-rankers behind. It did this by having these two groups maneuver in separate halves (those at the rear reversing their file order and the rest then following suit to again take post in the lead). This not only maintained optimum positioning with respect to function for the differing troop types (heavy-armed in front and missilemen in the rear), but also suggests that these categories might well have been equal in manpower. Possibly derived from actual Persian practice, the terminology suggests those stacking into a standard imperial formation ten men deep could have consisted of five hoplite-armed troopers at the head of each file followed by some mix of peltast/spearmen and taka-equipped archer/spearmen rearward. The reformed warriors making up this arrangement (both light and heavy) were "kardakes"—*kardaka* in Persian. (Strabo's claim that "kardaka" came from *karda* or "warrior spirit" appears sound, though Head [1992, 42–43] has suggested otherwise.)

It seems that the foregoing changes might have come to maturity some time after 372 under Datames, satrap of Cappadocia (Sekunda 1992, 27). This general had come forward to take command of the Greek and Persian troops that had gathered a few years earlier to retake Egypt. Iphicrates of Athens had gone home by this point, but his uniquely retooled Greek phalanx seems to have remained. Thus, we can see Datames' upgrading of Persian contingents into kardakes as a logical attempt to supply his Iphicratean legion with a more capable battlefield partner.

Datames was particularly well suited for such a task. Carian by birth and upbringing, he was undoubtedly very familiar with hoplite warfare, that being the dominant combat style of his mixed barbarian/Greek homeland. At the same time, he had served as an "Immortal" in the Great King's bodyguard and was thus equally acquainted with Persian methods of shock fighting. Datames, as it turned out, would never lead the army he designed into battle. Political pressure caused him to abandon his imperial post and return to Cappadocia by no later than early 369. There, he would use Greek mercenaries, likely some of the very men that Iphicrates had re-equipped, to fight against his own kardakes.

Cappadocian Narrows (c. 367 B.C.) and the Cilician Gate (c. 361 B.C.)

Datames was in revolt within a year of leaving the Egyptian campaign and Artaxerxes sent an army against him. Manpower is extremely difficult to judge in this conflict, but we know that Datames had left Egypt "with his own men" (Nepos 14.5.6) and that the core of his infantry consisted of 20,000 mercenaries (Diodorus 15.91.2). The latter was precisely the number assigned by Diodorus to Iphicrates' legion (15.41.1). It's quite possible therefore that some or all of these members of his former command had joined him then or since in Cappadocia. If so, these could have broken down into 10,000 hoplites, 5,000 pikemen and 5,000 foot skirmishers if Iphicrates had adjusted an original 50/50 split to a more shock-capable mix featuring only 25 percent light-armed men. Datames also had a powerful mounted contingent. This could have been 5,000 strong on the basis of a 4 to 1 ratio with his foot soldiers.

As for Datames' foes, Nepos' account provides numbers that are huge beyond any practical possibility. More likely, we're talking here about four imperial baivaraba of infantry at around 80 percent of nominal strength. This would be 32,000 footmen at most. These imperial infantrymen would have been kardakes with half outfitted as hoplite-style spearmen in the front ranks and the rest being missilemen for the rear. Nepos claimed there was a wide array of provincials present as well. Most of these would have been skirmishers (though Nepos mistakenly put them separate from "an enormous number of light-armed troops"). His figures for these in total run about half the count for the kardakes (51,000 versus 100,000). This would put them at some 16,000 if that ratio is applied to the smaller force proposed here. Mounted support perhaps came to 8,000 riders (ten hazaraba) at quarter the manpower of the core kardakes footmen. The resulting host, though much reduced from Nepos, would still have outnumbered Datames by better than 2 to 1 in line infantry, 3 to 1 in auxiliary infantry and 60 percent in the rebel's reputed strong suit of cavalry.

Datames moved to take up a stout defensive position upon learning that the Persian army was approaching. He moved too late, however, to occupy his first choice, the slender valley-entry into Cappadocia known as the Cilician Gate. Instead, he took up a stance behind this in other tight passages. He waged a series of linked actions there that served to keep his foes at bay. Much as Sparta's Leonidas had done to Xerxes in the pass at Thermopylae in 480, Datames used his superior Greek heavy infantry to bar these later day Persians by always fighting "in some narrow defile" (Nepos). It was a serial battle in which he negated mobility factors and superior numbers on restricted ground to win every component engagement. Nepos claimed that Datames lost around 1,000 men (4 percent of his army), yet took out much more among his enemies (we can reasonably project their losses in the range of 10–15 percent).

In time, the Persians had to negotiate a truce and withdraw in order to address an uprising of greater concern that had broken out elsewhere. Indeed, before long the entire eastern coastal belt of the empire was in turmoil with one satrap after another going into revolt. Datames was thus able to maintain his independence over the next several years as Artaxerxes' focus lay in a variety of other areas across his troubled realm. However, when imperial forces began gaining the upper hand in the late 460s, Datames was again faced with a royal army closing on Cappadocia, Artaxerxes' nephew Artabazus having command. And this time the rebel satrap found himself forced to fight a battle on the plain in front of the Cilician Gate when his father-in-law Mithrobarzanes, who commanded his cavalry, deserted at night with most of his troopers. Leading out the mercenary infantry and whoever remained loyal among his horsemen, Datames abandoned his defensive stance inside the Gate and gave chase. He found the traitors just as they were about to join Artabazus' vanguard (maybe no more than a single baivarabam of kardakes with light infantry and mounted support).

Attacking perhaps just as dawn was breaking, Datames caught the wayward cavalry in a crossfire between his own forces and those of the Persians, who thought in all the confusion that Mithrobarzanes had turned coat again. Most of the betraying horsemen ended up being killed by one side or the other while dealing out a fair amount of harm themselves (Diodorus claimed a dubious 10,000 casualties on the day across the board [15.91.5]). Yet there seems to have actually been little interaction between the contending footmen on either side, allowing Datames to disengage and draw back inside his strong position within the Cilician Gate. There, he sat tight to once more block entry into his kingdom. We have no details on what the Persians tried to do that was different in the ensuing campaign, but whatever it was, they proved no more successful in cracking Datames' defenses than before and eventually retreated. Before long, however, the Great King would have all of his Asian holdings back under control. The last of the rebels to hold out, Datames himself would fall to an assassin in 359 without every having tasted defeat in the field.

Lost Leaders: Elis, Arcadia and Thessaly

The long Sparto-Boeotian conflict might have been resolved, but Thebes still had issues to settle by means of arms on its northern frontier. And bloodshed continued in the Peloponnese as well, with a dispute between former anti–Spartan allies Elis and Arcadia now leading them to war on each other and drag other poleis into the fight. Worst of all, Theban ambitions in the south were not yet satisfied and Epaminondas would lead one last crusade against the Spartans and their friends.

Lasion, Elis-Cyllene and Cromnus (365 B.C.)

A new round of trouble hit the Peloponnese as the Eleans seized Lasion. This town had in the past been within their authority, but formed part of Arcadia's holdings in more recent years. The enraged Arcadians responded by sending out an army to descend from a hill onto the Eleans camped nearby this bone of contention. The Elean party was composed of 700 hoplites from two elite contingents (the "Three Hundred" and the "Four Hundred"). Xenophon claimed (*Hellenica* 7.4.13) that these troops were outnumbered "many times" by the force moving down on them, suggesting the presence of Arcadia's entire standing army of 5,000 spearmen (the eparitoi). The badly outmanned Eleans had little chance and (if they even formed up) broke from the fight almost immediately. Their only escape route, however, lay over rough ground and the opposition's light infantry (probably over a thousand strong) easily overwhelmed any screen they could have had (there were surely less than 200 Elean skirmishers). The result was a slaughter among the fleeing men. Diodorus put Elis' dead at 200 (15.77.3), a devastating loss of nearly 30 percent of its very best spearmen.

The Arcadians went on to spoil the countryside before leaving and returned for another round of pillaging when the Eleans elected to join causes with Arcadia's foes at Sparta in the aftermath of the disaster at Lasion. However, after the raiders came back for yet a third pass at ravaging Elean territory, a force from the capital marched on their encampment between there and Cyllene on the northwest coast. The scope of this engagement is unclear, but Elis committed its horsemen and had a spartiate advisor, suggesting that it might have involved much of the polis' surviving army, maybe 2,000–3,000 spearmen with light infantry support. Regardless, the Arcadians, perhaps once more fielding 5,000 hoplites, carried the action (probably pushing through a phalanx filed at only about half their depth) and killed the Spartan along with what might have been another 100–150 of the Eleans.

Having absorbed a couple of beatings, Elis now asked their new ally for more overt assistance. Archidamus answered by bringing his army into southern Arcadia and capturing the town of Cromnus, garrisoning it with three of his lochoi (1,500 hoplites). If designed to divert Arcadian attention from Elis, this worked splendidly. But if meant to discourage the Arcadians from further aggression of any kind, it was an absolute failure, because they now took the force prepared for an Elean campaign and promptly invested Cromnus, surrounding it with a double wall to contain their men in safety. Archidamus took once more to the field and laid waste southern Arcadia hoping to draw the besiegers away. Failing to raise a response, he then moved directly against Cromnus. His force probably consisted of the remainder of the regular Spartan army less one mora left at home. This would have been some 3,500 spearmen (seven lochoi) with support from a few horsemen and maybe 1,000 mercenary peltasts. His cavalry and javelinmen caught a contingent of the Arcadian regulars (smaller than the Spartan hoplite force per Xenophon [*Hellenica* 7.4.24], perhaps at a half-strength of 2,500) outside the stockade. The light-armed troops attacked and forced these spearmen to draw together in a tight body. Archidamus, meanwhile, was unaware of the situation and approaching with his hoplites in column two-abreast. Coming suddenly on the scene, he had no chance to reorder before the Arcadians charged out at him. The Spartans hurried to meet this attack and converted their column into line of battle by a simple 90 degree turn toward the enemy. This left them far too thin (only two shields deep) and they quickly buckled when the densely formed eparitoi struck.

Archidamus took a spear-thrust through the thigh and 30 of his men died in the following melee as the Spartans fell back down the road by which they had come. Eventually, this path opened up onto a field and the embattled Spartan hoplites were finally able to assemble into a proper phalanx as their Arcadian foes took position across the way still in their deep formation. A stand-off now ensued, with the eparitoi confident but outnumbered and the Spartans with a stronger array yet in poor spirits. The end result was a truce, allowing Archidamus and his men to carry away their dead while the Arcadians set up a trophy. Ultimately, the Spartans would manage to break through the stockade at Cromnus in a night attack and rescue most of their men (around 100 were captured before they could escape).

Cynoscephalae I and Olympus (364 B.C.)

Thebes was to take a hard blow the following summer with the loss of Pelopidas. This came about in Thessaly as he led an army north to aid the enemies of his old nemesis Alexander of Pherae. Diodorus' account (15.80.1–6) indicates that the Theban took 7,000 men with him. This probably included 5,000 hoplites, 1,500 foot skirmishers and 500 horsemen. He then added Thessalian allies, perhaps roughly equal to his Thebans in infantry of all types (the spearmen being Greek mercenaries and the light footmen allied tribesmen) and rather stronger in cavalry with maybe 2,000 riders. Pelopidas confronted Alexander where he had taken a strong position behind some steep hills east of Pherae outside of Thessalian Cynoscephalae. Diodorus claimed that the tyrant had an army of 20,000. And Plutarch's assessment is only a bit smaller (Vol. I *Pelopidas*, 405), citing an infantry contingent twice that of his Thessalian enemies. This indicates 10,000 hired hoplites and 3,000 skirmishers. Given an overall cavalry potential for Thessaly of 6,000 riders (Xenophon *Hellenica* 6.1.8), a similar ratio for mounted troops yields 4,000 horsemen and a total 17,000 combatants.

Action opened with a contest between light infantry for possession of the intervening high ground while the cavalry dueled on the plain. Pelopidas' riders prevailed below, but it was Alexander's peltasts that took the heights. When the Theban's Thessalian allies then sent their hoplites up to dislodge the enemy, they took significant losses and fell back without doing any real damage. Seeing this, Pelopidas sent a recall to his horsemen and moved out with his Thebans. He personally joined and reorganized the Thessalians, putting them into long files on the left while sending his own hoplites to form up at similar depth on the right wing. He then led this rearranged array up the hilly terrain to the attack. Alexander and his men repulsed two or three advances; yet each time, Pelopidas' formation drew back, redressed and came on again. Finally, fearful of the now returning enemy cavalry and its growing threat to their rearward approaches, the tyrant and his men took advantage of the opposing phalanx's latest round of reformation to withdraw down the backside of their position. That they did this in some semblance of order says much for the discipline of Alexander's professional spearmen; still, they were in at least modest disarray as they got down onto the flat and tried to recover behind their skirmishers.

Seeking to exploit the temporary confusion among his foes and spotting Alexander directly opposite on the enemy right striving to organize his men, Pelopidas led a charge down the rise. Unfortunately, this advance became a ragged affair in its rush, leaving the eager Theban out in front and an easy target for javelinmen below; thus, though he got among these and killed several hand-to-hand, others had shot him down by the time most of the following Thessalians could get there to help. Pelopidas' hoplites were somehow able to reorder and reengage despite his death and, after their cavalry came up to help, they succeeded in routing Alexander's army. Adding in a thorough pursuit, the victors ran enemy casualties up to 3,000 dead per Plutarch. Costly as this action was to Thebes in the loss of one of the era's truly great commanders, it served its strategic purpose well. Alexander was forced to not only return all the lands he had seized, but had to agree to a Theban alliance as well (perhaps only after a second engagement alluded to by Diodorus but not attested elsewhere — see Stylianou's discussion of this possibility [1998, 499–500]).

Meanwhile, back in the Peloponnese, the Arcadians prepared to host the games at Olympus, having captured that sacred site from Elis. The Eleans were not about to let this pass. They enlisted aid from the Achaeans and launched an attack on Olympus. This took the Arcadians by surprise and they didn't come out to meet it, forming up instead into a phalanx along the Cladaus River within the sacred precinct. Either their heavy array (probably 5,000 hoplites) must have taken up the available space or (as seems more likely) they needed to guard more than one approach, because they seem to have detached 2,000 spearmen from their long-time ally Argos as well as 400 horsemen from Athens (under obligation of the bilateral treaty of 366). The Eleans (on the right) and Achaeans (on the left), likely having 2,000–3,000 hoplites each, arrayed their own formation on the other bank. Advancing (the stream does not appear to have provided an obstacle), the hoplites from Elis and their allies closed into the Arcadians.

Perhaps unnerved by the unexpected enemy mobilization and far from eager for action, the lesser troops on the Arcadian left wing gave way at first contact. This collapse soon sent their entire array into a panicked run for the rear. Keeping well-ordered to give slow chase, the Elean phalanx advanced to now meet the spearmen from Argos coming up in an attempt to rescue their beaten allies. The outmanned Argives could probably file only half as deep as the Eleans and Achaeans that now moved into them, with the result that they were rapidly pushed from the field to break and join the Arcadians in flight. Any Athenian horsemen that might have come on the scene at this point must have been swept along with the frantic mob streaming away from the fight. However, once the pursuit had carried as far as the city center, the invaders' skirmishers began to fire down from the rooftops to good effect. A number of the Eleans were killed, including Stratolas, who led the elite Three Hundred. Under this lethal rain of missiles, the victors broke off their chase and withdrew to their camp outside town. Those defeated spent the night putting up a stockade. In the morning, the Eleans, judging the barrier formidable, prudently retired to their capital.

Spoiling of the sacred site at Olympia by members of the occupation force would ultimately bring an end to the Elean-Arcadian conflict. Condemnation of this behavior by the Arcadian assembly led by Mantinea cowed the Tegeans and other confederacy hawks, leading to productive talks and the signing of a peace accord between Elis and Arcadia in 363. As it turned out, however, hardly a year would elapse before the Peloponnese was to be roiled by an even greater war that would once more greatly shift the power-base in Greece.

Mantinea II (362 B.C.) and the Egyptian Canals (360 B.C.)

The dispute in the Arcadian assembly over Olympus had revealed a deep division within its league, with Mantinea and Tegea heading contending factions. These neighboring poleis were rivals of old and it's not too surprising that they would eventually come to loggerheads again over regional leadership. The new element this time was Thebes. No longer were Arcadian disputes simply that; rather, there now existed the potential for Thebes in its role as hegemon to play a deciding hand in this kind of local issue. Many of the Arcadians resented such interference and had come to see the Thebans less as allies and more as ambitious conquerors. Mantinea was the leading state in this group. On the other side, the Tegeans were eager to use Theban power in promoting their bid to exert local ascendancy. By the summer of 362 this volatile situation led to open hostilities between Mantinea and Tegea, with the former gathering in help from Sparta and Athens and the latter calling upon Thebes. Both camps mobilized for war and Epaminondas again marched south.

Epaminondas entered the Peloponnese and paused at Nemea to block an Athenian contingent from joining the Mantineans. But upon learning that these troops were coming by sea, he went on to Tegea. He found there that the opposition was gathering at Mantinea and awaiting Spartan reinforcements. He attempted to prevent this by marching his northerners against Sparta directly. However, the Spartans under their aged king Agesilaos prepared stout defenses as they had seven years earlier. Assessing the enemy's strong position and fearful of having his foes mass here and catch him without his own allies, Epaminondas returned to Tegea. He organized his forces there and sent parties up to raid the Mantinean countryside. This resulted in a cavalry action that saw the Athenians best his own highly regarded Theban and Thessalian riders.

Epaminondas now decided to settle things in a grand battle. Diodorus put his numbers at 30,000 infantry and 3,000 cavalry (15.84.4). The core of his army was the Boeotians at 7,000 hoplites and 600 riders. The allies he'd brought with him from the north might have been on the order of 4,000–5,000 spearmen. These were maybe 3,000 mercenaries from Thessaly and the rest from Locris and Euboa. The Thessalians would also have provided 1,000 horsemen at a third the strength of their hoplite contribution (added to the Theban cavalry to get the 1,600 horsemen mentioned by Polyaenus [2.3.14]). As for support from the Peloponnese, this probably included 4,000 hoplites (a majority of the Arcadians), another 2,000 from Argos and a combined 2,000–3,000 from Messenia, Sicyon and elsewhere. The Peloponnesians might have thrown in 400 or so riders as well. These all totaled 20,000 spearmen and around 2,000 horsemen. Given the strong presence of light-armed men from the tribal peoples bordering Thessaly that was emphasized by Diodorus (15.85.4–5), Epaminondas might have had 8,000 or more foot skirmishers to approach that historian's overall count of his infantry strength.

For the anti–Theban coalition, we have Diodorus' claim of 20,000 infantry and 2,000 cavalry. The hoplite corps included 6,000 Athenians (Diodorus) and a likely 2,000 from Arcadia plus some 5,000 from Elis, Achaea and elsewhere. Sparta's contribution poses the largest uncertainty. Xenophon reported (*Hellenica* 7.5.10) that only three lochoi had initially gone to Mantinea. However, these were to be reinforced and, after the initial confrontation with Epaminondas had been resolved, it's probable that most of the rest of the Spartan army had now joined its advance party. If we allow for a single mora remaining on home guard, there would therefore have been five morai at Mantinea for a total of 5,000 spearmen. This brings the coalition count to around 18,000 hoplites, not too far below that for the opposition. And with their cavalry at 2,000, the allies had a good match in that arm as well. It was thus only in light infantry where they fell short — Diodorus putting their numbers at only about a third those in Epaminondas' camp and of lesser capability to boot.

Instead of moving straight on his foes, Epaminondas first led his army northwest along the mountain front bordering the valley that held Tegea and Mantinea (see Pritchett [1969, 37–72] for a discussion of the topography). He then put his troops into battle formation, though initially indicating that he might just be setting up camp. The allies had been watching these movements and relaxed briefly when they thought the enemy might be preparing to stand down for the day. But when it became obvious that their foes were actually preparing for action, they too readied their phalanx.

The coalition forces took position across the narrowest part of the valley. The Mantineans occupied the far right post of honor in their own land, followed leftward by their Arcadian supporters and then the Spartans to complete that wing. On the left wing stood the Athenians, leaving the Eleans, Achaeans and others to fill across the middle. Filed at a depth of eight shields, these spearmen would have spanned a front of 2,250m, leaving some 75–125m rising onto higher ground off each flank to be covered by cavalry and light infantry. Some of the Eleans led Peloponnesian mounted forces on the right side and the Athenians had their own riders beside them on the left. In addition, the rest of the mounted contingent from Elis formed a reserve in the rear set to reinforce either flank should that be needed.

Across the field, Epaminondas arranged his phalanx to match. He set up his Thebans on the left extreme in a deep array per their custom of recent years, seemingly 25 shields deep this time. The Sacred Band apparently had their usual station along the first two ranks here, the narrowness of the battle ground and inward position of the cyclosis-prone Spartan contingent removing any need to stand apart as they'd done at Leuctra. As for the rest of his army, the Theban filed it rightward at a depth of eight, completing a formation near equal in width to that of his foes. The remaining Boeotians held post alongside the Thebans, followed in order by the Tegeans and other Arcadians, the lesser allies and, finally, the Argives at the far end of the line. Epaminondas seems to have hoped to again hold back his right wing, but arrayed it at an effective depth. He was no doubt mindful that the Athenian spearmen on the enemy left were not likely to be as passive as their counterparts had been at Leuctra. If they took the initiative and advanced, his weaker allies would have no choice but to fight. Like his opponents, he placed his light forces outboard for flank security.

The arrays closed on signal, opening one of the largest hoplite battles in Greek history. As their spearmen dueled and shoved across the long battle front, the mounted forces and their attached light footmen fought it out off either flank. The importance of light infantry in screening ahead of horsemen in this era is revealed in what happened on the coalition left, where the Athenian cavalry and its skirmisher screen faced Theban riders and supporting missilemen from the hilly regions of Thessaly. Outnumbering the peltasts standing with Athens' horsemen by 200 percent and being more effectively intermingled with their mounted comrades rather than standing apart like those opposed, the javelinmen and slingers fighting for Thebes heavily wounded and pressed their foes, driving them back. The Athenian riders didn't lose good order, however, and were still able to turn with success against a body of enemy troops they found circling through the bordering upland in an attempt to menace the coalition rear. The Theban cavalry, meantime, followed up its skirmishers by wheeling against the enemy phalanx. The hoplites from Athens there had (just as Epaminondas feared) come forward to engage the Argives and others on that part of the field. They were nonetheless tiring in the course of what had been a hard-fought scrum; therefore, this sudden assault on their now exposed flank nearly broke them. It was the Elean mounted reserve that intervened at this crucial juncture to avert disaster. Charging from the rear, it took the Boeotian riders and light footmen by surprise and put an end to their attack.

Elsewhere, Epaminondas' light-armed forces were gaining the upper hand on his left even as his overly deep wing there began to make progress amid a terrible struggle of thrusting spears and shield-shoving. Smashing forward "prow on, like a trireme" in the words of Xenophon (*Hellenica* 7.5.23), the Thebans penetrated at last, driving the coalition right wing from the field as their cavalry turned that flank as well. Yet at the same time, the Athenians, having been rescued by the Elean horsemen, were now carrying the day against the Argives and other Theban allies across the way; and though the extent of their victory isn't clear, they took possession of the contested ground there. Prevented by the enemy's aggressiveness from keeping his weaker wing out of action as he'd done at Leuctra, Epaminondas had at the last been unable to complete his conquest of the opposing right fast enough to prevent an exchange of triumphs on opposite ends of the engagement. And at the very outset of his own pursuit, he received a fatal wound. The Thebans faltered as their general was carried off to die and they became aware of the enemy still in place to their right. No doubt mindful of the costly second attacks at Nemea River, Coronea II and the Long Walls, the Boeotians cut short their chase to bring the action to a close.

Both armies set up trophies immediately after the fight to mark their competing successes on separate portions of the field. They then withdrew, each to later recover their dead under truce. The engagement and its disputed results ended up settling nothing, but Thebes' era as the dominant power in Greece had passed for good with the death of Epaminondas. An armistice emerged in the battle's aftermath that ended fighting on a major scale for a while. The last significant Greek combat of the decade therefore took place in Africa.

Agesilaos may have retired from commanding Spartan armies, but that hadn't meant that he would stay home in peace. In fact, he'd been earning coin for his polis by hiring out as a mercenary leader overseas. First plying this trade in Ionia during the Satraps' Revolt, he went to work for the Egyptian pharaoh Tachos sometime before spring 361 as commander of a 10,000-man Greek mercenary corps. This likely consisted of some 6,000–8,000 hoplites and 2,000–4,000 skirmishers. However, when a coup removed Tachos from power, the Spartan deserted with all his men to the new regime. He then had to face Persian forces invading Egypt on Tachos' behalf. In the campaign that followed, Agesilaos made good use of the well-worn tactic of setting up his spearmen between impassable barriers to best Persians where their greater numbers and light-armed superiority gave no advantage.

This took place per Diodorus (15.93.4–5) and Plutarch (Vol. II *Agesilaos*, 69) after Agesilaos and his men found themselves caught by the Persians in a fortified town. Noting that the enemy's encircling wall and ditch weren't yet complete, the Spartan put his men into a broad column and charged out under cover of night to force his way through the gap in the Persian lines and escape. His foes marshaled their forces the next day and set off in pursuit. However, Agesilaos maneuvered about until he had them following up a narrow route between two canals. He then turned around, formed up his phalanx and advanced to the attack. Caught between the water-filled barriers on either side, the kardakes (perhaps two baivaraba) couldn't use their greater manpower to envelop the Greeks' flanks and had to endure a head-on fight against superior heavy infantry. As Grecian hoplites had done so many times in the past, Agesilaos and his troops broke through the Asian front-fighters and then routed their light-equipped after-ranks in short order to send the entire opposition force into flight with severe losses (likely in the 10–15 percent range) at very little cost to themselves. The geriatric Spartan king thus managed to complete a successful tour in Egypt, but would pass away from natural causes on the way home.

Tactical Discussion: 385–360 B.C.

Theban tactics at Leuctra (371) are far and away the most oft cited example of military revolution in this period. The winning approach to that battle had four prominent elements: (1) exceptionally deep files; (2) concentration of elite manpower on the left wing; (3) refusing of the right wing; and (4) probable semi-detachment of a select unit (the Sacred Band) to counter an enemy attempt at envelopment. In fact, use of exceptional file depths by Theban armies was nothing new, since the tactic dated back at least to 424 at Delium (Thucydides 4.93.4). This practice is noted again in our sources at Nemea River in 394, where the Thebans violated pre-battle planning by stacking well in excess of the agreed upon 16 shields (Xenophon *Hellenica* 4.2.18). It's thus quite possible that similar alignment was a factor in Theban victories at Thespiae and Tanagra III (both 378); what we know for sure is that this method was used with great success in 375 at Tegyra. As for concentration of effort on the left wing rather than the more traditional right, our sources for Thespiae, Tanagra III and, especially, Tegyra can be taken to suggest that this could have been the case in those engagements, but they are not explicit. However, at least one such deployment is attested prior to Leuctra, and Theban troops were on the scene to observe it. (It's likely, in fact, that the Thebans commanding at Leuctra [Epaminondas and Pelopidas] were present as hoplites.) This was in 382 at Olynthus I, where Sparta's Teleutias concentrated his best troops on the left.

Deliberate refusal of the right wing appears to have been something new, perhaps addressing a weaknesses exposed at Olynthus I. The Thebans there probably held the right end of the line and nearly fell to the enemy before victory was achieved on the other wing. Tegyra had proven that you could win a battle without committing your off-wing to combat (or, indeed, even *having* an off-wing), suggesting that one good way to avoid losing a fight on that side of the field was simply to never engage. As for detachment of the Sacred Band elites (if they did indeed maneuver to extend their army's attack wing and head off a Spartan cyclosis maneuver), this certainly resembled what Cleandridas did c. 433. That Spartan was commanding at Thuria in Italy against Lucanian tribesmen and hid a picked unit behind his phalanx (likely in back of the left wing). Wheeling it out at the last minute, he frustrated an enemy envelopment to carry out one of his own (Polyaenus 2.10.4; Frontinus 2.3.12). Overall, Leuctra was a clever mixing of a little that was new and a lot that was old, making it best considered a case of evolutionary experimentation rather than a revolutionary advance.

This era saw greater and more aggressive use of cavalry by the Greeks. While there was not a single case of Grecian mounted troops being decisive elements in actions from 400 through 383, there were eight examples (22 percent of all engagements) between 382 and 362. Whether Greeks deployed overland or by ship (as to Pyrgi in 384), much greater attention was paid to taking an adequate force of horsemen along. And the use of cavalry in battle was becoming more sophisticated as well, with horsemen maneuvering behind cover (Olynthus I) and from reserve (Mantinea II in 362) and providing thinly arrayed frontal screens (Tegyra and Leuctra).

Pelopidas and Epaminondas of Thebes are the best known military stars of this time by a wide margin, leading their polis to its brief interval of hegemony over most of Greece. It's impossible to tell whether one or the other of these men was the prime source responsible for any particular item among their army's successful tactical adoptions, adaptations and innovations. Maybe these were all largely products of mutual collaboration. What we *can* say is that most of what they did was drawn from past traditions (as per the discussion above on Leuctra), yet was brilliant all the same. Nevertheless, this famed pair probably had less impact on future tactical practices than Iphicrates of Athens. While the Thebans' methods largely fell out of favor after their deaths, Iphicrates' necessity-driven invention of the "Iphicratean pikeman" in the late 370s for the short-lived Egyptian campaign would inspire a major step in the evolution of Greek heavy infantry, sending it down a new path that other great generals would both follow and help blaze for the next two hundred years.

* * *

Greece was now a land deeply divided and without a dominant power among its competing city-states. Sparta was badly hurt, having lost all hope of regaining its former influence and struggling just to hold onto a corner of the Peloponnese. Thebes was still strong, but any prospect for establishing a farther flung hegemony had died along with Pelopidas and Epaminondas. It was, in fact, Athens which had prospered most, rebuilding its maritime league to become best situated of the major poleis. Still, even the Athenians were weak by past standards. Strained finances along with a decade and a half of continual bickering and fighting had gone far to wear them down. Fortunately for Greece, the Persians were in just as bad a shape, with all of their own internal disorders killing any enthusiasm for reaching into Europe as they had done in the previous century. However, a threat to Greek freedom more serious than any before was about to arise from a most unexpected source.

III. Finding a Master

Rise of Macedonia; Sacred, Persian and Sicilian Wars; Conquest of Greece (359–336 B.C.)

"Freedom ... do you not see that Philip's very titles are irreconcilable with that? For every king, every despot is the sworn foe of freedom and of law. Beware ... lest, seeking to be rid of war, you find a master."

Demosthenes (*Second Philippic*, 25)

Macedonia sat at the northern fringe of the Greek world, forever fighting an array of barbarian invaders for its very survival. This near constant state of peril served to push its people into accepting a hereditary line of warlord kings. Marshaling all of the land's wealth and arms, they were responsible for both the borders and internal peace. This proved a very hit and miss proposition, with Macedonian fortunes shifting along with the quality of each monarch. So things stood in early 359, when the current ruler, Perdiccas III, took on the Dardanians of Illyria along his western frontier. In a grand action that might have featured 10,000 fighting on either side, the barbarians killed Perdiccas and also took out 4,000 others, including both actual casualties and manpower lost from areas now under Illyrian control. The Macedonians were in the direst of straits, but luck was with them. An untested new king would quickly turn things around and lead them on to unprecedented heights.

Macedonia Reborn

It was Philip II, younger brother of Perdiccas, who came forward during the crisis of 359; acting at first as regent for an underage nephew, he soon claimed the throne for himself. Only 24 years old, Philip was literally facing danger from every quarter. Not only had his western provinces fallen, but Paeonian tribes to the north were threatening as well. And of even greater concern to his personal safety, other aspirants to the kingship had sponsors to the east in Thrace and to the south at Athens, the most powerful Greek state of the day. With barely time to secure his position (slaying or driving away a trio of half-brothers and gaining recognition from the aristocracy), Philip gathered what remained of the national army to his seat at Pella. He then set out to meet the most immediate menace: the pretender Argaios, who had once challenged his father and now sought to seize power with help from mercenary hoplites in Athenian pay.

Methone (359 B.C.)

Macedonia's army was based upon tribal groups spread across a number of geographic districts. Each territorial division yielded an allotment of men, who then served under their own nobles. Suffering from a crippling combination of casualties and the loss of upland levies, Philip could probably gather only some 6,000 foot soldiers and 400 horsemen; yet, small as this force might appear, quality rather than quantity was actually his most pressing concern.

The lowlanders that made up Philip's infantry were unsuited to shock combat. Many carried pelte and javelins for fighting in open order from a distance, while those that had spear and shield lacked both experience and any significant tradition as close-order fighters, at best having been recently organized into some semblance of rank and file by Philip's brother (Alexander II) prior to assassination (Bosworth 2010, 98–99). Philip knew that these men would have no chance leading a pitched battle against the sort of phalanx that Argaios could deploy with a cadre of 3,000 hired hoplites. They probably couldn't even buy enough time to allow his cavalry to be decisive on the flanks. Though Argaios wasn't rich in light arms, he might have fielded at least 1,000 skirmishers and riders — more than enough to delay a decision and allow his heavy footmen to carry the day in the center of the field. Mindful of all this, Philip wisely eschewed conventional engagement in favor of a surprise attack.

Argaios had sailed aboard an Athenian fleet, which landed at Methone, a Greek city at the head of the Thermaic Gulf and allied to Athens. He had then marched his hired men some 28km inland through ridge country to Aegae (Vergina), the old capital of Macedonia. But an attempt to recruit local support there proved fruitless and Argaios headed back toward Methone to consult the senior Athenian on hand, the general Mantias, who had stayed aboard ship. Alerted to these moves, Philip hastened his forces across the 40km between Pella and Aegae and slipped undetected into the hills. He rapidly skirted Argaios' path and (as suggested by Justin [7.6.6] and Diodorus [16.3.6]) got into position for an ambush within the pass to the coast.

Argaios' column moved through the uplands strung out along a narrow track that let his men align just a few abreast. This put the cavalry and some light infantry in the lead, followed by the hoplites and with the remaining foot skirmishers bringing up the rear. This procession made it about halfway to Methone (Hammond 1995, 25) before falling into Philip's trap. The king's troops charged from hiding, hurling their missiles as they poured down to surround Argaios and his men. Taken unprepared, the pretender's van and rear guards disintegrated amid a riot of panic and confusion. The mercenary spearmen, however, proved to be of sterner stuff. Caught out of formation, they somehow drew together and battled their way onto a nearby hill, taking heavy casualties in the process (perhaps 30 percent, including 5–10 percent killed or fatally wounded). Once on high ground, these veteran fighters circled to fend off further attacks.

The tactical situation was a stand-off. Philip didn't have the shock fighting capability to drive these spearmen from their high ground, while they in turn lacked mobility for either a counter strike or escape. The strategic state of affairs, on the other hand, was clearly in the young monarch's favor. All he had to do was sit pat while his foes weakened. But Philip was keenly aware that time spent on such a siege might boost his risks elsewhere; he therefore elected to negotiate. The mercenaries quickly agreed to put Argaios and his fellow exiles into Philip's hands in return for an uncontested withdrawal. The Macedonian leader then applied similar diplomacy to his other problems, signing a treaty with the Athenians and buying off the threats from Thrace and Paeonia. Though these fixes were no more than temporary, they let him settle in at Pella to upgrade his army that winter.

Reforms of 359/58 B.C.

Philip's transformation of Macedonia's military was an exercise in mixing and matching the best martial practices from Greece with unique indigenous virtues. As it turned out, this enterprise also benefited greatly from fortuitous timing that allowed incorporation of important new developments from Asia Minor.

Philip had gained respect for heavy infantry during a hostage stay in Thebes as a teen (probably 368–365). He saw how that polis' hoplites could descend from one side of their phalanx and turn a flank to secure the entire battlefield. Ability to carry a fight from a single wing meant that the rest of their array need only stand on the defensive as shown at Leuctra (371) by Epaminondas, the most outstanding Greek tactician of the day and friend to Philip's Theban host, Pammenes (Plutarch Vol. I *Pelopidas*, 401). Philip was now determined to create an infantry juggernaut that could take a similar approach. Moreover, though Epaminondas had employed light riders effectively enough as a screen for his spearmen, Philip, who had grown up a horseman and was well aware of the latest mounted techniques from neighboring Thessaly (Sekunda and Warry 1998, 9), sought to go the Theban one better. Rather than confine his own heavier cavalrymen to a supporting role, he would have them take direct part in enveloping attacks. Not only could they thus add combat strength, but their speed might well allow him to turn a targeted flank faster than he could with foot troops alone.

The first barrier that Philip faced in reforming his army was Macedonia's shortage of good heavy infantry. This fundamental weakness had denied him the option to engage his hoplite opponents at Methone in open battle despite having superior cavalry and a significant edge in raw manpower. Yet, there seemed little that he could do about it in the short term. It would take a long time to raise, equip and train enough locals to upgrade his heavy foot troops, while there wasn't the money in his treasury to just go out and hire foreign spearmen in sufficient number. But as luck would have it, events in Asia at this moment provided the very resources he needed.

As we've seen, Iphicrates of Athens had prepared a mercenary force for a Persian campaign into Egypt by outfitting enough Greek skirmishers with long spears (called *sarissai*, *sarissa* singular, in Macedonia) and small shields to provide a somewhat shock-capable contingent for the left, defensive wing of his phalanx. These pikemen and their hoplite companions had then most likely joined in the satrapal uprisings of the 360s — especially that of Datames, their former Persian commander. But this work came to an end with surrenders to the Great King in 360 and assassination of Datames the next year. Many from Iphicrates' legion must thus have been on their way home by late 359. There's no sign that these men ever influenced the armies of Greece proper during the 4th century (Stylianou 1998, 342–346); still, similarities between their methods and aspects of Philip's reforms can hardly be a coincidence. At minimum, he copied much of their approach; however, there's a distinct possibility of an even closer tie. The timing of their unemployment plus proximity would have made it ideal for the young king to recruit a few Iphicrateans at a price within his means. And he was assuredly already familiar with what they could do. Iphicrates had served in Thrace after Egypt and there took in Philip along with his mother and older brother (Nepos 11.3.2), protecting them after the death of Alexander II in early 368. The Athenian was formally welcomed into the Macedonian royal family as a reward for this timely assistance. Already a keen student of the military arts, Philip would surely have discussed the Egyptian campaign and its new breed of pike-armed soldiers with his adopted brother at considerable length. He must then have fairly leapt when the opportunity later arose to gain some of these fighters as models for restructuring his own army.

Leading Philip's fresh national levies was a regiment of hoplites to provide more manpower for the offensive wing of his battle line. Philip might have had a small bodyguard of spearmen as early as 364 (Parke 1933, 156–157); if so, these would have provided a core for the new heavy-armed force. Possibly using the title for his guards, he called the select local hoplites *pezhetairoi* or "foot-companions" (Heckel 2002, 24). This denoted an elevated status much as for his guard cavalry (the *hetairoi* or "companions"). Under Philip's son Alexander III, these spearmen were called *hypaspistai*—hypaspists or "shield-carriers." As a practical matter, it's useful to apply this terminology from the beginning. This is due to Macedonia's Iphicratean-style pikemen being better known today by the title of "pezhetairoi." It seems that the rest of the phalanx adopted the old honorific after it was dropped by the hoplites (Heckel and Jones 2006, 31; Bosworth 2010, 98–99). Like their mercenary counterparts, the hypaspists wore a helmet, cuirass and greaves while carrying a dory thrusting spear and aspis.

The green Macedonians must have received instruction from their professional compatriots. They also no doubt found inspiration on the field from those same savvy warriors, who deployed alongside and were perhaps seeded within their ranks as well. This was a vital component of Philip's success in rapidly creating an effective new army. Indeed, a shortage of just such assistance might have contributed to what seems to have been poor results of any attempt at an upgrade by his brother as well as failure of a possible try at something similar even earlier. Arrhabaeus, warlord of Upper Macedonian Lyncestis and Philip's maternal great-grandfather, had fielded a formation of heavy spearmen in 423. Thucydides specifically identified these troops as "Lyncestian hoplites" (4.124.3) and Arrhabaeus lacked both ready access to Greek mercenary spearmen and probable funds to maintain a sizeable company of hirelings for any extended period; therefore, this heavy corps most likely comprised native skirmishers outfitted anew with thrusting spears and large shields (possibly derived from Illyrian gear already near to hand). Probably in operation for a period of at least two years, these tyro hoplites seem to have lacked the sort of adequate role models and intense training that Philip was now providing and fell quick prey to a Spartan-led phalanx.

It's important to confirm the nature of the hypaspists, since this is essential to understanding just how the early Macedonian phalanx really worked. There has been quite a bit of controversy on this issue, with hypaspists having been described variously as either lightly armored peltasts, chosen pikemen or possibly some manner of hybrid warrior. However, though nothing is certain, there are several lines of evidence strongly supporting the idea that they were traditional hoplites.

The first clues about the true nature of the hypaspists come from literary sources. While it's not particularly instructive that all Macedonian phalanx fighters were at times generalized as "hoplitai" (simply "heavy infantrymen" in this case), it's of greater value that the title "hypaspistai" likely refers to their bearing hoplite shields. We are probably dealing here with specific terminology from Alexander's day being repeated by authors of the Hellenistic period, who themselves otherwise used the word "aspis" more broadly. A very strong suggestion that this is so comes in a passage from Arrian (1.1.9), which describes hypaspists plying their aspides in an overlapping fashion possible only for large devices that spanned a full body-width, like the traditional hoplite shield. Likewise, we read of hypaspists extending their shields over a wounded companion; an act that also called for an instrument with size sufficient to cover the entire torso. Men giving this sort of aid carried the label *hyperaspizantes* (Heckel and Jones 2006, 18) in yet another explicit allusion to the aspis. Lastly, Heckel and Jones point out (2006, 41) that hypaspists "are often referred to, loosely, as *doryphoroi* ('spear-bearers')." Relating perhaps to a role as bodyguards, this would appear to be an express nod to their use of a dory of some sort, a weapon better suited to close personal protection than either a pikeman's sarissa or the javelin of a peltast.

Further evidence for hypaspists as hoplites comes from ancient graphics. The "Alexander Sarcophagus," possibly a depiction of the battle of Issus in 333 (Sekunda and Chew 1992, 29–

30) or Gaugamela in 331 (Heckel 2006), shows infantrymen in action alongside the Macedonian king as per the hypaspists' post next to the royal cavalry. These combatants without exception wear elements of hoplite panoply. Each man has an aspis (shown from both front and back) and "Phrygian" helm (with forward curving crown), while those not shown artistically nude sport a cuirass and some have greaves as well. In keeping with use of the aspis, they wield their one-handed weapons (unfortunately lost) in an overhead manner perfectly suited for a hoplite spear, a broken example of which can be seen near the foot of one of these apparent hypaspist figures (Sekunda 1984, 30). Likewise, the monument at Delphi celebrating Aemilius Paullus' victory at Pydna (168) shows Macedonians carrying large concave shields, perhaps a body of hypaspist elites among the contingent of "picked" men that fought to the bitter end in that engagement. One shield shown from the front covers its holder's entire upper body; and, though lacking a reinforced rim, the backside of another has the distinctive and more vital central porpax and shield-edge antilabe suspension of an aspis. Sadly, the Greeks' weapons have succumbed to erosion; yet all are single-handed and one figure is striking overhead with left leg forward consistent with the use of a dory. Anson (2010, 81–82) cites four more depictions of Macedonian hoplites and/or their equipment: warriors with Macedonian helms holding hoplite spears and shields shown in a painting from the "Agios Athanasios" tomb at Thessaloniki; a hoplite aspis displayed on the façade of the early Hellenistic "Tomb of Judgment" in Lefkadhia; hoplite shields appearing on the Macedonian "Shield Monument" at Beroea; and an aspis (with the device "AE") stamped upon on a Macedonian coin dated 325–300 B.C. All of these pictorial displays indicate that native hoplites were standard within the Macedonian military, and hypaspists are by far the most likely troop type with which they can be identified.

Backing up the literary and graphic data are archeological finds. Among these is a sauroter from a late 4th century dory (Heckel and Jones 2006, 18, 20). This slender and simple bronze attachment for a hoplite spear differs significantly from the larger, heavier and more complexly shaped iron butt-spikes of sarissai. Nor does it match the tail-spikes/counter-weights of contemporary cavalry lances. Tellingly, this relic carries the inscription "MAK," marking it as being of Macedonian state manufacture and, thus, standard issue for hypaspists (given that other state-supplied troops — pikemen and horsemen — didn't use this particular tool). Other relevant finds of hoplite gear come from the royal tombs at Vergina (Head 1982, 106–107). These include a dory head and highly decorated aspis, both associated with greaves thought to have accommodated the limp of Philip II (see Worthington [2008, 234–241] for counters to contrary claims). The king must have worn these items when he stood among his similarly equipped guard of royal hypaspists.

The final argument on the hypaspists concerns their function in the line of battle. Comprising the maneuverable, offensive wing, they had to be more mobile than the rest of the heavy formation and we see historical praise for their agility. At the same time, Arrian identified them as the phalanx's prime "shock troops" (per–Selincourt's translation [3.11.9]), marking them as Alexander's most capable hand-to-hand fighters. This called for a repertoire of capabilities best matching those of select hoplites. In fact, by having the hypaspists and mercenary spearmen press an othismos-assisted shock attack on one end of the field while his pikemen used their lengthy weapons to avoid shield-on-shield contact along the rest of the front, Philip created the same sort of "oblique order" that had worked so well for Epaminondas. Only he did so in a much simpler and more effective fashion. Unlike the Theban's method of refusal, which awkwardly restricted advance to a single wing and depended upon cooperative enemy passivity across most of the field, Philip's men could all close in lock-step without concern for how the opposition might react. The totality of information we have from every source therefore lends much credence to Hans Delbruck's long ago conclusion that the corps of hypaspists "was armed entirely in the manner of the old hoplites" (1990, 179).

Elsewhere among his line troops, Philip used similar mercenary-based equipment adoption and training to create a force of local Macedonian pikemen or "phalangites" (phalanx men). Established in even greater numbers than their hoplite comrades, these less costly soldiers and their hired prototypes would actually provide the bulk of his array, making up its defensive center and left. Like the hypaspists, these troops wore a Phrygian helmet. Commonly painted blue, this distinctive bit of oriental-style headwear reflects the Asian roots of Philip's reforms.

Along with the hypaspist as hoplite, the other concept vital to understanding how Philip's infantry functioned in his original version of the Macedonian phalanx is the role of the phalangite pikeman as a defensive specialist. Summarized in the earlier discussion of Iphicrates' reforms and assumed above, we can expand here on the reasoning behind this critical determination. In fact, the arguments favoring pikemen primarily being defenders mostly revolve around offensive limitations of the sarissa.

Hoplites facing a phalangite array would have stopped at the outer limit reachable by the front rank of opposing pike points, it being physically impossible to advance any farther. At that stage, compared to what they would have had to absorb from dory-armed foes, they took much fewer strikes from the pikemen. This reflected that phalangites could attack with only their foremost rank, while traditional spearmen were able to employ at least their first two rows in hitting at an enemy front. Nor was reduction in strike frequency the only shortcoming of the sarissa in projecting force compared to the dory, as both strength and location of the blows that could be made were hampered by a required underhand grip.

Measurements reported by Gabriel and Metz (1991, 85) and elaborated upon by Schwartz (2009, 80) show that spear strikes delivered underhand are much less forceful than those directed overhand: 18 Nm (Newton-meters) versus 96 Nm. (Note that these numbers are for spears, not sarissai having greater mass. But a heavier pike would have been jabbed at lower velocity. Since mass acts as a single multiplier in calculating force while velocity multiplies as a square, these figures remain informative and, if anything, might actually overstate the relative strength of a sarissa blow.) Thus, with fewer and weaker strikes, a phalangite array must have imparted considerably less force of weaponry than a dory-armed phalanx. And its inability to apply the sort of othismos push available to an aspis-equipped formation then served to further compound this shortcoming. Finally, men dueling along the front of a pike phalanx could not land blows where they would count the most. This was due in part to an inability to engage targets other than those directly ahead because "the angle of the leveled sarissa cannot be changed by more than about five or ten degrees, if that" (Heckel et al 2010, 105). Worse yet, thrusting on low denied strikes at the more vulnerable areas exposed above or just behind the top of the aspis of even an immediately opposite hoplite foe. As Gabriel and Boose note: "Unless the soldier was fortunate to land a blow directly to the face, under the chin, or in the space between the neck and chest armor, the spear was not likely to be a terribly lethal weapon in phalanx combat, at least as long as one's opponent stood his ground" (1994, 21).

Add the foregoing to flexibility restrictions common to a sarissa array (even compared to the traditional phalanx, which wasn't very agile itself) and you get quite a low attack capability against a formation of hoplites. Yet, it was a very different story when it came to *defense*. Unless a spearman could cut past the intervening layers of pike points (a task ever harder to do as sarissai grew in length over the years) then he could project no offensive force himself. Thus, simple analysis of the faults and strengths of Philip's pikemen inevitably leads one to conclude that their intended role in fixed battle was to prevent (or at least delay) close contact with facing foes toward giving other components of their army time to win the day.

In contrast to what was required to upgrade his native infantry, Philip had no reason to make great changes among his crack corps of heavy cavalry — the hetairoi. These were outstanding riders, who had slightly sturdier mounts than the Grecian norm (Head 1982, 172–173). Their gear included a helmet (painted white like those of Epaminondas' horsemen), cuirass and long lance (*xyston*)—all designed for shock combat. A sole focus on fighting in this way was critical to Phillip's plans for his cavalry and unique among the Greeks, though the techniques must have sprung in the beginning from methods widely employed for spearing game from saddleback.

Methodology with the xyston probably evolved over time. Maybe less than 3m long, protoypical versions of the weapon were likely employed for the most part in an over-hand fashion just like hunting weapons of similar proportions. This allowed for more forceful strikes and gave a broad radius of reach by preventing the torso of one's own mount from getting in the way. An overhand style also folded the forearm back in recoil, thus protecting the bicep and presenting the smallest possible target to a facing enemy. (This contrasted with an underhand grip, which did not cover the bicep in contraction and, when fully extended, exposed the arm from shoulder to wrist.) Finally, a down-sloping lance held over-hand further shielded the arm and kept the butt-spike from accidentally damaging the horse's rear flank. Still, despite all these considerations, under-handed thrusting must have found use from the beginning as well, especially against low-lying targets. And, as efforts over time to extend its reach resulted in a xyston of greater length with a heftier counter-weight (thus allowing the grip to move back), underhand use likely became predominant.

Beyond promoting younger nobles to replace losses, any retooling of hetairoi tactics by Philip would have been on a modest scale. It perhaps amounted to little more than practice in mass maneuvers as a way of improving formation integrity. These drills also probably put greater emphasis on wedge arrays copied from Thrace and Thessaly. Rather than the horsemen, it was undoubtedly their light-armed infantry support that actually saw the greater reform at this time.

Their shorter ranged missiles and vulnerable mounts had always put horsemen at a disadvantage against foot skirmishers. Most armies countered this by setting screening forces in front their cavalry, and the Macedonians followed the most common practice of assigning javelinmen on foot for this task. These were nearly as mobile as mounted troops and could either cover at the rear during retreat or get out in front of a charge. The latter called for thinning out opposing skirmishers and forcing them to use up their supply of missiles. Evidence for how this was done comes from Arrian's account for Granicus River in 334 (1.16.1), where the light infantry was mixed intimately with its riders in the same superior manner that Xenophon praised for the Theban cavalry's supporting skirmishers at Mantinea II (362). In the past, each aristocratic horseman must have provided his own retainers for this duty. Philip would have recognized such a system as being amateurish and a breeding ground for inconsistency. It's probable therefore that he now moved to organize a dedicated cavalry screen, investing it with up to half of his light footmen. Trained as a team, these troops could provide a cohesive replacement for what had been a haphazard mob of individuals.

By early 358, Philip had amassed around 10,000 infantry and 600 hetairoi (Diodorus 16.4.3). His native foot troops most likely counted 1,000 hypaspists and 3,000 phalangites (one regiment or taxis of the former and two taxeis of the latter per strengths of later years) plus 2,000 skirmishers, about all that the lowlands remaining under royal control could provide. This suggests that there were at least 4,000 mercenaries, just enough to replace Perdiccas' losses and probably matching the homegrown heavy corps at 1,000 hoplites and 3,000 pikemen. Philip had by this point also taken steps to install a better system of logistics. Engels notes (1978, 12) that he forbade the use of wagons, reduced the number of servants (one for each horseman and per file of ten foot soldiers), had his infantrymen carry their own gear and wouldn't allow women to accompany the army into the field. The result of all these changes was a leaner force capable of vastly greater operational mobility. Therefore, as winter drew to a close, Philip prepared to debut his new "Macedonian" phalanx, not knowing just how well it would work nor even dreaming of the lofty heights to which it would take him.

Paeonia (358 B.C.)

Philip led his army out in the spring, passing through the mountains on his northern frontier and entering Paeonia. His selection of an opponent for this campaign is instructive. The Paeonians were probably contemplating no more than border raids against Macedonia, and even such modest plans would have been in flux at the moment due to the recent death of their king. This clearly wasn't the most imminent threat on the horizon. It thus seems likely that Philip had a greater focus on further improving his military capabilities than on securing a border.

Fashioning an effective phalanx called for more than just supply of the right equipment and time to drill. Minimum training for a phalanx fighter was, after all, reasonably modest. Sure, he had to learn a few formation maneuvers, but these often amounted to little beyond lining up and marching straight ahead. At that point, the requirement was to stand firm in the ranks and either prod (with a sarissa) or shove and jab (with aspis and spear). The whole process was not overly complex, perhaps not greatly above what a modern marching band might have to master in a few months of part-time practice. But Philip was well aware that even very basic actions become difficult under the extreme stresses of mortal combat. It took a good deal of confidence and discipline for an army to perform in such dire circumstances. Knowing that only solid victories in the field would breed and reinforce these traits, Philip was setting out to initiate a tradition of success by opening against his weakest foe.

The Paeonians had a military much like those in nearby Thrace, relying on a mix of javelin-armed light cavalry and peltasts (Alexander the Great's storied Agrianian peltasts were closely related). Unfortunately, we have no record of Paeonia's total manpower. Still, it's possible to project numbers from a report that, when finally gathered at strength in Egypt, around 600–650 of Alexander's cavalrymen were Paeonian (Head 1982, 14). If this was no more than half the full levy (consistent with another 600 Paeonian riders arriving later in Syria and roughly in synch with the percentage of Thessaly's mounted contribution to the same expedition), then there might have been at least 1,200 horsemen nation-wide. A heavy mobilization would have had most of these riders on hand to confront Philip's invasion. As for foot soldiers, we know that they could compose as little as 60 percent of a lowland Thracian army (Webber 2001, 35), but 80 percent is more likely for a single highland tribal group like that of the Paeonians. This implies that they might have fielded on the order of 5,000 infantrymen.

Philip marched into Paeonia spoiling for a fight. However, his marked superiority in manpower begs the question of why the Paeonians would ever accommodate him. Surely they could have avoided a confrontation, retreating before the Macedonians and ultimately forcing them to give up and go home. Maybe this kind of passive strategy was too costly or perhaps it wasn't culturally acceptable to a warrior people. It's even possible that the new Paeonian ruler felt that he had to be aggressive in order to prove his mettle in battle and fitness to lead. Yet the answer might be simpler still: the Paeonians most likely believed that they could win.

The reality was that Philip's army didn't have a favorable reputation at the time, while its greater numbers applied only to infantry. The Paeonians actually had many more horsemen, who represented their very best troops. If the tribesmen could elude defeat for just a little while in the center of the field, it wasn't unreasonable to think that their outstanding cavalry would drive its less numerous mounted opponents from the wings and then go on to envelop and rout the Macedonian phalanx. With something like this in mind, the Paeonians must have awaited Philip on ground that gave their horsemen plenty of room to maneuver. It's also probable that the chosen site had tree-covered uplands not too far in the rear. These would provide vital avenues of escape and shelter should things turn out badly.

Seeing his foes gathered in the distance, Philip signaled to turn his troops out of their marching column and into phalanx formation. Use of the term *dekka* or "ten" for the phalangite file in later years (when it commonly held 16 men) suggests that this was the depth of Philip's original array where sarissa-armed at center and left. But on the right, where the king stood with his hypaspists and hired hoplites, the phalanx would have been either eight or twelve men deep. His heavy infantry thus fronted across maybe 650m at about 1m per hoplite and perhaps two-thirds that per phalangite once fully closed for combat. (Note that the narrowest width assumed here for the phalangite is only slightly broader than that of his pelte, but this device would have, in fact, been held at an angle to permit use of the sarissa alongside. Polybios [18.28.2] cited approximately 1m spacing for pikemen in the 2nd century, during the phalanx's final, more attack-oriented phase. His interval fits the "intermediate" spacing of Asclepiodotus [4.1], whose 1st century work incorporated that of his teacher Poseidonius and, hence, of the older Polybios and a plethora of even more ancient military manuals. Thus, pikemen of earlier times might well have converged to less than 1m spacing. Indeed, the separation for Asclepiodotus' "closest order" was only around 0.5m, allowing phalangites to square up nearly shield-rim to shield-rim with the sarissa held tight against the body much as done by unshielded Swiss pikemen of the 15th and 16th centuries A.D. [Oldfather, 269]. Comparisons of calculated formation widths to manpower estimates and citations from the literature for all pike deployments during the 4th century suggest that a 2/3m spacing matches well with the apparent frontages of that era.) As for Philip's cavalry and light footmen, they must have split off either wing. The Paeonians divided their own supporting troops in a like manner as the bulk of their infantry (maybe 4,000 men) spread across the intervening stretch to confront the phalanx.

There is no surviving account of the ensuing battle; nonetheless, the size and nature of the forces involved plus Arrian's descriptions (1.1.11–13, 1.4.1–4) of actions with similar armament mixes suggest a likely course. The opening phase was surely dominated by fighting along the flanks, where Philip's peltasts got out ahead of their cavalry to engage the opposing skirmishers and horsemen. Now better organized and drilled, the Macedonian light footmen fought to good effect, largely exhausting Paeonian missile supplies. The hetairoi moved up at this juncture, charging among the enemy to drive them back and beyond a wing of their infantry formation. Up until then, the barbarians in the middle of the battleground had been holding their own, hurling javelins into a phalanx that couldn't advance with its flanks still at risk. This began to change when the hetairoi and their escorts were able to envelop one side of the line. Those few among the tribesmen who had spear and shield must have made a desperate attempt to fend off this assault, but their efforts came to naught as the Macedonian horse soon broke through on the other flank as well. With both ends of their alignment at last safe from attack, Philip and his shock troops were finally free to move ahead. They swiftly closed on their foes, who in all likelihood gave way long before the more numerous and heavily armed Macedonians could come into lethal contact.

Scattering into the backing hills, most of those defeated should have made good their escape. This reflects the fact that Philip's skirmishers alone were able to give extended chase, yet undoubtedly refused to do so for fear that they would be badly outnumbered once into the woods. Paeonian fatalities therefore probably amounted to only around 5–10 percent. Nearly all of these came from the 3,000 or so riders and peltasts that had dueled so fiercely along the flanks. Macedonian losses were no doubt even lighter, perhaps less than 200 dead. Again, most of those who lost their lives were light-armed men that had gone down off the wings. However, a few phalangites must have fallen to javelins as well, their small shields offering inadequate protection during what had been a fairly lengthy barrage. Whatever the relative casualties might have been, one thing is clear: the Paeonians were convinced of Philip's superiority. They therefore accepted terms that for the moment left their nation subordinate.

Philip's victory in this battle was the product of a well balanced mix of arms that progressed in an orderly sequence, culminating in his phalanx's advance to seize the field. And it's notable that that last infantry action was absolutely crucial. This was because the Paeonians' loose array of peltasts, unlike a close-ordered formation, could turn and confront a lateral mounted attack such as the hetairoi had launched, but at the same time were quite helpless against a frontal push from heavy footmen.

Lyncus Plain (358 B.C.)

With his northern frontier safe for the time being, Philip turned westward that summer to regain the territory lost by his brother. The Illyrian tribesmen there presented a daunting challenge, able to match his manpower with 10,000 foot soldiers and 500 riders of their own (Diodorus 16.4.4). Moreover, their infantry had a strong component of shock fighters, possibly making up 7,000 of the total. These warriors used a heavy-headed *sibyna* spear and bossed shield. Philip had to have known that they would put his as yet untried hypaspists and native phalangites to a stern test of hand-to-hand combat. Finally, there was the matter of their leader. The Macedonian wasn't facing a newly enfranchised king like himself this time, but rather a grizzled veteran of many a war. Bardylis, the Dardanian monarch, might have been 90 years old (Wilkes 1992, 120), yet was still sturdy enough to take the field on horseback.

Bardylis at first tried to head off the conflict by offering a treaty that would preserve the status quo. Philip, however, would have nothing to do with any deal that left his western provinces in enemy hands. Perhaps expecting this response and confident from past successes against Macedonia, the Illyrian moved to offer battle on open ground. Hammond suggests (1994, 26) that this was just west of the Kirli Dirven pass on the plain of Lyncus. Philip arrived and deployed his phalanx much as he had in its first action, with the phalangites at left and center, hired hoplites and hypaspists from the right in that order and cavalry and light infantry split off both wings. As for Bardylis' arrangements, Diodorus' claim of a square formation (16.4.6) is confused even in context of his own battle description and, since such tactics are unattested elsewhere save in retreat for either barbarians or Greeks in this era, the version of Frontinus (2.3.2) is to be preferred. This indicates that the Illyrian leader set up in a linear fashion, his heavy infantry matching the phalanx's width with even deeper files and having the best men fronting in the middle with horsemen and skirmishers outboard.

If the victory in Paeonia had been the product of various arms finely mixed in sequence, then the probable scenario at Lyncus Plain seems to call for an even more impressive work of synchronous combination. The formations had closed together, Illyrian at a quick pace and Philip's slowly so as to keep good order. When they finally met, a vicious melee was set in motion from one end of the field to the other. All the elements of the phalanx at this point moved in chorus to execute their deadly tasks. Left through center, the pikemen held firm, their long weapons keeping enemy spear points out of range even as they wounded at least a few among those leading the barbarian effort. At the same time, Philip and his spearmen made progress on the right, striking furiously into their foes as othismos from the rear ranks pushed them relentlessly ahead. In contrast, the front-fighters opposing them got much less help from behind and were powerless to resist the intense, file-length pressure coming at them. In the end, these men had no choice but to yield ground. As the Dardanian left began edging back, it was the hetairoi and their skirmishers that now excelled, easing the way for their hoplites and hypaspists by clearing all enemy horsemen and light foot from that flank. Exposed and put upon beyond endurance, the Illyrian left now gave way completely and sent the rest of the barbarian formation into frantic flight under fierce pursuit.

Frontinus' account of the battle focuses on the turning by Philip's heavy infantry on his right, tying it to the subsequent break-up of the Illyrian array. This suggests that it was the hypaspists and foreign hoplites that carried the day. But then there's the report of Diodorus (16.4.6–7), where the hetairoi seem somewhat the more decisive element, skirting an enemy flank to trigger the rout. Yet, even here, Philip and his elite spearmen receive strong praise for their contributions as well. In truth, any discrepancy between these stories is perhaps not so very great. Much like the disparate tales told by the fabled blind men trying to describe an elephant, no version is strictly wrong, but all are required to paint an accurate picture of the entire animal. Without doubt, this victory on the Lyncus Plain derived once more from a combination of arms working in concert, with each contributing its share to Philip's ultimate success.

Diodorus' tally of 7,000 slain among the barbarians in this action (16.4.7) is clearly an exaggeration. It might be better seen as a reckoning of the heavy infantry defeated than as an actual toll of the dead. (There is an odd account in Polyaenus [4.2.5] that tells of Philip slaughtering Illyrians in violation of a post-battle truce. This possibly reflects an attempt to rationalize the fantastic figure of Diodorus.) All the same, Dardanian casualties must have been very high ("several thousand" per Justin [7.6.7]), with a likely 20–30 percent killed. Philips' cost would have been quite a bit lower, perhaps some 3–5 percent going down in the fight or dying shortly thereafter. Bardylis appreciated the scope of his defeat and lost no time suing for peace.

Philip next turned toward Thessaly. In the years following the death of its tyrant Jason of Pherae in 370, that region had split into hostile camps. By 358, this division pitted a federation of inland cities, the Thessalian League led by Larissa, against Jason's successors at Pherae, who controlled the lucrative coastal plain. Frustrated and the poorer/weaker faction, the League sought a partnership with Macedonia. Free to act in the fall after his victories against Paeonia and the Dardanians, Philip took on this obligation and made a show of force by marching into Thessaly. Staying barely long enough to marry a local noblewoman in affirmation of the new alliance, Philip returned home without a battle, but having put Pherae on notice.

Along with his Thessalian demonstration, Philip also signed a treaty with the Molossians, those Greek tribesmen whose kingdom lay just west of Thessaly in Epirus. (He marked the deal with another marriage, this time to the Molossian princess Olympias. She would soon bear him a son — the future Alexander the Great.) Thus, the Macedonian king had acquitted himself well in his first months in power. Not only had he restored his nation's borders and honor, but he had spread its influence into Greece as well. Moreover, he had also regained a huge pool of manpower vested in the western provinces. Suborning those districts' nobles into his cavalry, Philip drafted the commoners into the phalanx. This influx of fresh troops let him significantly boost his strength (Polyaenus 4.2.17), likely doubling his home-grown fighting force within a year to match expansion of territory and subject population on that same order of magnitude (Hammond 1994, 20).

Ortygia (357 B.C.)

The region around Philip's realm in the far north wasn't the only section of the Greek world to see hostilities at this time, with even more far-flung Hellenic outposts coming into conflict as well. On Sicily, Dionysius II had followed his father as tyrant of Syracuse, but had proven less capable than his famed sire and, after nearly a decade in power, faced revolution. Leading this uprising was his son-in-law (and his father's brother-in-law), Dion. This ambitious fellow had sought to enlighten the tyranny with help from Plato (whom he had relocated to Syracuse), but had seriously overstepped his bounds and been forced to flee to Greece. There, he conspired to return with Heracleides, another exile and former commander of Dionysius' mercenaries. Staging on Zacynthus with some 3,000 troops (Parke 1933, 116, citing Anaximenes), Dion sailed out in 357 with half his men in tow, leaving Heracleides to follow with the rest.

Dion landed in western Sicily to find that Dionysius and his general Philistus were in Italy with their fleet. Exploiting this bit of luck, he took off right away for Syracuse. Dion had some 1,500 fighters at most to begin this march. These likely included 500 hired skirmishers and 1,000 hoplites, the last including nearly 800 veteran professionals (Parke [1933, 116–117], derived from Plutarch [Vol. II *Dion*, 550]) plus a handful of Syracusan outcasts and some mainland volunteers. A swarm of local men (Plutarch said about 5,000 [Vol. II Dion, 553]) joined in route, maybe running the spearmen up to something like 2,000 (a figure that Diodorus' source perhaps escalated times ten in citing a force of 20,000 [16.9.6]).

Dion's opponents were mostly mercenaries, Dionysius I having long ago limited arms among the citizenry (Diodorus 14.10.4). Our sources provide fantastic numbers for this host, but it's likely that it didn't much exceed 10,000 fighters (Parke 1933, 114), with the claim by Plutarch (Vol. II *Dion*, 545) of 10,000 guardsmen being a nominal figure at precisely a tenth of Diodorus' infantry estimate (16.9.2). Based on prominent mention of peltasts by Plato (Parke 1933, 115), light footmen probably were a heavier than usual component, possibly forming a quarter or so of the tyrant's armament. While some of the mercenaries must have been Greek, many came from Spain (Iberians) and Italy. The latter were chiefly Campanian Oscans, though a few Etruscans and Gauls might have been present as well. Mercenary shock troops would have fallen into two categories. Iberians made up the smaller of these; wearing leather helmets and carrying large, center-grip shields, they used throwing spears and sabers (the *falcata*, with a downward curved blade much like the Grecian machaira). The larger class of heavy footmen was for the most part Campanian with some Greeks, all sporting hoplite or roughly comparable Oscan equipment. In support of these line troops were maybe 1,000 light horsemen (again, exactly a tenth of Diodorus' inflation), the aforementioned peltasts, some slingers and, possibly, a few archers.

As Dion approached Syracuse, he managed to detach a portion of its defenses. A contingent of perhaps 1,500–2,000 men from nearby Leontini and Aetna held the plateau of Epipolae along the northwest side of the city. Dionysius had settled many of his Campanian mercenaries at these sites to provide a useful local recruiting pool; however, this also gave these men a concern other than Syracuse. By threatening their homes, Dion now pressured them into withdrawing, which left him free to take Epipolae. Having lost its high ground, the remaining garrison fled onto Ortygia, a fortified peninsula set apart beyond a narrow neck between the city's main harbor to the south and a smaller one on the north. Dion quickly spanned the connecting isthmus with a low wall to seal off this citadel.

Dionysius landed on Ortygia a week later along with the balance of his army. Despite the desertions from Epipolae, he still had at least 6,000 heavy infantry, 2,000 foot skirmishers and a strong cavalry force with which to break the siege. However, though this included nearly three times the spearmen that Dion had first led into the city, the rebel leader had since grown stronger. Crowds of Syracusans had joined his cause and he was able to supply many of these with gear brought from Greece, including 2,000 shields (Plutarch Vol. II *Dion*, 551) for fitting out hoplites plus a store of spears and javelins. Added to the mercenaries and allies, these volunteers brought his foot troops up to something like 4,000 hoplites and 1,000 light missilemen. (The total of

5,000 infantry is, once more, a tenth of Diodorus' maximum. It also parallels his note that Dion had carried exactly that many panoplies to Sicily [16.9.5–10.3].) Throwing in some riders plus his siege wall and a literal mob of men with make-shift arms, Dion had the strength to make it very difficult for the tyrant to break out.

Seeking to improve his odds, Dionysius made a show of negotiating to put the rebels off guard. Then, suddenly, he opened the gates of Ortygia and sent his army out to attack the Syracusans along their cross-wall. It seems that this construction wasn't all that substantial, having been thrown up in a couple of days at most; in fact, it very probably was like those deployed on Sicily in the past as temporary field works (Ray 2009, 230–232, 235). These were waist-high piles of stones that served as a hardened front, hindering any attempt to shove into those behind it while leaving them clear to ply their spears above. Such conditions tended to stall a battle's leading edge and therefore favored the defense. However, a key to this tactic's success was to deploy in strength along the rampart, thus forcing attackers to constantly fend off an opponent rather than leaving them free to go after the wall itself. In this, the surprised and poorly mustered Syracusans failed miserably. The result was that the dictator's men pulled down portions of the flimsy barrier and pushed through.

Seeing the enemy pour past the cross-wall, a party of Dion's hirelings moved up to slow their advance. Men fleeing from the wall disrupted the ranks of these well-seasoned fighters, throwing their counterattack into disorder; still, they bought Dion time to mobilize the bulk of his troops from their nearby camp. Meanwhile, Dionysius' soldiers were reacting to the initial resistance by hustling into some semblance of formation as well. Amid all the confusion, Dion was eventually able to move his hastily formed array into engagement along a narrow front (the isthmus being just over 1km long, but only about 300m wide). Crowded into this space, the rebel spearmen probably filed at ten to twelve shields against opponents standing up to 20 deep.

What now ensued must have been a fairly disorderly fight; the Syracusans had been caught unaware and many lacked experience, while their generally more seasoned opponents had rushed to form up with very little preparation. Dion played a prominent role at the head of his mercenary troops, perhaps half of these being on hand with the rest stationed back in the city. Having superior hoplite gear and being better schooled in close-ordered combat than either their amateur companions or barbarians on the other side, the rebel professionals were able to lance and shove their way ahead for a space; however, the enemy's considerable depth absorbed this pressure without breaking and the front soon stalled as Dion's troops tired and intensity of their weapon-strikes and othismos faded. It was at this point that an already battered Dion took a wound to his right hand from an enemy spear.

The veterans ranked about Dion managed to get him clear and to the rear. Hurt but still thinking clearly, the rebel leader saw that the contest was now stalemated, with neither force able to drive its foe from the field and both rapidly nearing exhaustion. Sensing an opportunity, Dion mounted and rode to fetch his remaining mercenaries (perhaps 400 spearmen plus some skirmishers) as well as any men fled from the wall that he could rally. He then returned to the battleground, where he found the armies still locked together like spent prizefighters clinching toward the final bell.

Dion swiftly massed his heavy-armed reinforcements into a compact body and launched them at the enemy, likely targeting the wing where the less shock-proficient Spaniards held post. Tightly arrayed in phalanx, Dion's improvised tactical reserve moved past tired companions, who stumbled out of the way as these fresh troops charged into the frayed enemy line. Hitting with telling force, they smashed through to roll up that flank and send the tyrant's men into flight along the entire front. What followed was a slaughter, with the Syracusans cutting down their beaten foes from behind as they scrambled to get back across the fallen counter-wall and safely within Ortygia's defenses. This defeat cost Dionysius dearly, with 800 of his men giving up their lives per Diodorus (16.12.5); in contrast, Plutarch (Vol. II *Dion*, 556) claimed that the rebels lost just 74 hoplites. Though Dion's victory in front of Ortygia failed to deliver Syracuse into his hands immediately, Dionysius would eventually withdraw to Italy. However, factional disputes then led to Dion's assassination and subsequent rebel disunity eventually allowed the dictator to return in 346 and resume control of the city.

Chios (357 B.C.)

The insurrection at Syracuse saw its match that same year when a revolt of Athens' allies erupted on the other side of the Greek world. The islands of Rhodes, Cos and Chios in the eastern Aegean raged at what they felt were oppressive aspects of the maritime league known today as the Second Athenian Confederation. The Athenians had founded this union 22 years earlier as a means to insure that Greeks in the East kept their autonomy from Sparta; however, it had since turned into a vehicle for empire, complete with tribute and political interference in the form of imposed governors and garrisons. Encouraged by the Carian ruler Mausolus (who had his own designs on the region) as well as the independent city of Byzantium, these poleis overthrew their democracies and broke from Athens. This led to a two year fight with the Athenians in what is now called the "Social War" (from *socii*, the Latin term for allies).

Athens sent out its generals Chares and Chabrias with 60 ships (Diodorus, 16.21.1) to mount an attack on Chios, strongest of the rebel states. Our sources don't record their armament's manpower, but comparison to a fleet that put down a similar uprising on Lesbos in 412 could give us some clues. Transports made up about 30 percent of the vessels in that comparable effort, suggesting that the fleet of 357 might have had 18 such troop carriers if designed along the same lines, with the other ships being fast triremes. This would have let the Athenians land nearly 4,000 hoplites on Chios at 150 per transport and 30 per trireme (ten heavy marines remaining aboard each of the latter). These probably came ashore on the northeast just above the island's capital (also called Chios). Beaching the troop carriers to form a temporary camp, Chares took charge of land operations. In addition to his spearmen, he would have had just over 1,000 rowers from the transports for use as light infantrymen.

As Chabrias led the now cargo-free triremes off to threaten Chios' harbor, Chares marched his army down toward the city walls. Based on past fleet capacity, the islanders could probably muster around 4,000 prime-age hoplites in total, with perhaps another 1,000 being available in old age/youth reserves. However, it's likely that no more than a third or so of these were attached to Chios city, the rest residing around (and concerned with defending) the large island's numerous other settlements. As such, Chares presumably expected to come against something less than 2,000 spearmen from the targeted town and its very nearest neighbors. What he got was much more. Not only had Cos and Rhodes sent ships and troops to aid Chios, but other reinforcements had come from both Byzantium and Caria, likely including many veteran mercenaries. These allied troops plus the Chians were enough to later man 100 triremes at a probable 40 hoplites each and still leave an adequate defense ashore, thus indicating that 4,000 spearmen may be about right for the reinforced garrison sans reserves. Therefore, when the Chians rushed out to form up before their city, Chares and his men found that they didn't have the expected better than 2 to 1 advantage; rather, they were facing a foe with equal or even slightly greater heavy-equipped manpower, at least some it well-experienced. Moreover, the defenders would have had a decidedly hefty edge in light footmen against the Athenians' modest corps of armed rowers.

What little we know of the following battle via Diodorus (16.7.3) supports the idea that the combatants were fairly evenly matched, as neither proved able to dominate for a decisive victory. All the same, it was the exhausted invaders from Athens who ended up giving way at day's end, pulling their phalanx from the engagement to retreat toward the beach. No doubt equally drained, the Chians and their allies let them go, content in having repulsed any attempt on the city's walls. With neither side broken and pursued, casualties must have been light all around (maybe 2–3 percent). Nonetheless, it was a serious strategic set back for the Athenians. Nor did the bad news stop there, as their fleet had also hit greater than anticipated opposition in its run on the harbor. The result was a defeat that cost Chabrias his life, that famed general having committed suicide to avoid capture after his trireme had been rammed and rendered unable to flee with the rest (Diodorus 16.7.4; Nepos 12.4.2). Fearful of being trapped on the island, Chares embarked his surviving force and withdrew.

Eastern Expansion and a Proxy War with Athens

As Philip continued to drill his military throughout the winter of 358/57, he was able to further hone its tactical skills even as the restored highland levies began to swell his ranks. His sarissa-bearing troops soon came to number around 9,000, perhaps still including a couple of thousand foreign hires. These phalangites formed six regiments (taxeis) of equal size. The hoplites, meanwhile, grew in strength until they filled three 1,000-man units (possibly two of hypaspists and one of mercenaries). At the same time, light-armed foot troops rose to a probable 3,000 strong, with some making up the dedicated cavalry screen and the rest providing advance skirmishing and flank support. As for the hetairoi, they reached a count of 1,200, probably forming six squadrons of 200 lances apiece.

Given Philip's shortage of cash when he gained the throne, he must have issued only small sums to his local levies in payment for relatively brief terms of service. However, early on during the army's expansion, he took the momentous step of turning it into a true professional force. He probably had little option on this. The intensity and length of his training regimen required nothing short of a paid, fulltime commitment from the native troops, who would also have wanted compensation on a par with what their hired companions were getting. From this time forward, all Macedonian military units became standing entities.

Philip went on the offensive again that spring, besieging Amphipolis and taking it by late summer. During the course of this operation, he made a secret pact with the Athenians, who were eager to regain that city along their route for vital grain imports from the Black Sea. The deal required yielding Amphipolis to Athens in return for Pydna (a town on the Thermaic Gulf that had come under Athenian influence in the mid 360s). However, once he had Amphipolis in hand, Philip ignored this arrangement and went on to capture Pydna as well. Outraged, the Athenians declared against him despite already being freshly involved in the Social War.

Pherae I (357/56 B.C.)

As the Thessalian League had appealed for help that winter, Philip now made a second incursion into Thessaly. He was to meet armed opposition this time. The site of the battle that followed is not known; however, keen to force a confrontation, the Macedonian might have marched directly on the enemy's center at Pherae. It's a good bet then that the engagement took place somewhere on the plains near that city. Philip would have had about two-thirds of his army along (leaving the rest to guard the many hazards still in play at home). We have no data on allied Thessalian League troops, but they must have consisted of some native light horsemen and *hamippoi* (javelineers accustomed to working with cavalry) in similar strengths (1,000 or so each) as well as mercenary forces to the tune of perhaps 500 additional light infantrymen in support of a couple of thousand hoplites.

Pherae's phalanx must have been quite a bit smaller than Philip's, possibly boasting no more than 4,000 hoplite hirelings. The latter represented less than half of what the tyrant Jason had reportedly been able to employ with the resources of a united Thessaly (Xenophon *Hellenica* 6.1.8). These spearmen were nonetheless seasoned pros that posed a real threat to the still green Macedonian phalanx. And elsewhere, the Pheraeans might not have been too far behind the Macedonians in their number of light-armed men. These would perhaps have included a little over 1,500 horsemen (around 50 percent of the region's full potential per a later estimate by Isocrates [8.118]), a like number of hamippoi and maybe 1,000 professional peltasts (one for each four hoplites).

The northerners likely filed much as they had before, using depths of ten for their phalangites and eight to twelve for the hypaspists/hoplites. As for any League spearmen that might have been present, Philip probably extended his offensive wing by placing them left of his own mercenaries and for the first time having the hypaspists take the far right, all as per later known deployments for these troop types. Assessing the opposing array, the Pheraeans would have approximated its breadth by standing their own line infantry six deep across the entire front. The mounted and light contingents for both armies took post off the flanks, with the allied Thessalians next to Philip's pikemen. This latter is particularly notable in that it let the hetairoi and their screen deploy in full alongside the hypaspists, putting them in position to apply their entire strength against a single end of the opposing array.

Going into action near simultaneously, both formations would have advanced with caution. However, once within a few dozen meters, the Pheraeans must have taken the lead, charging on signal to crash into the slower moving Macedonians, whose phalangites in particular had to keep a very deliberate pace to maintain their exceptionally close order and multi-layered array of spear points. Yet, within seconds of shock contact, the fight from Philip's center through left would have stalemated. The opposed light horsemen and skirmishers off that flank were more or less evenly matched, while the Macedonian pikemen were well able to absorb the opening blow and then fix their hoplite foes in place. It's probable that the phalangites had great benefit at this juncture from a certain amount of confusion among Pherae's mercenaries. Experienced though these were, they had never come up against an obstacle quite like that posed by the dense hedge of sarissai now barring their way.

With action stalled elsewhere, Philip and the elite fighters on his right wing now must have set about their lethal work. This delivered a swift victory that would have had both infantry and mounted components. The king's heavy footmen surely led the way, using their greater depth to push through the opposing ranks. And even as this was happening, his companion cavalry must have chased away its opposite numbers and curled in to further disrupt the enemy line. Overwhelmed, the Pheraean left would then have fallen back to set a wholesale withdrawal into motion. Given heavy pressure from surging hoplites and darting hetairoi alike, there had to have been some serious bloodletting around the flank where the initial collapse took place. However, both the center and right side of the beaten army faced less mobile phalangites and, with a good bit of help from their light forces, they should have taken lighter damage. Overall, Pherae's losses might have come to around 1,000 hoplites, horsemen and skirmishers killed (roughly 12 percent of its army). The butcher's bill for Philip was no doubt much lower at perhaps 200 men or fewer each from his heavy and light contingents.

Though far from an even match, this first encounter between the new Macedonian and old Doric phalanxes was a clear-cut victory for the former. And it certainly impressed the Thessalian League cities. They were now more eager than ever to maintain their relationship with Philip and his formidable military machine.

Crenides, Grabaea and Odrysia I (356 B.C.)

Recovered from his southern foray, Philip turned in early spring toward Crenides. This Greek colony, a recent foundation sitting inland some 65km east of Amphipolis, was seeking his help to fend off a Thracian coalition that included both local tribesmen and western Odrysians. Led by Cersobleptes, the latter were part of a now divided people that had long held sway over much of Thrace. The main appeal of this undertaking was the opportunity to gain control of Crenides' underdeveloped gold and silver mines, which held the promise of financing Philip's growing ambitions.

Philip must have moved out with most of the armament recently employed against Pherae plus a few men from Crenides. The Thracians seem to have taken position in force nearby. Their leader, Cersobleptes, was one of a trio of Odrysian kings and thus likely had only a third the numbers later ascribed to his tribe as a whole. His infantry therefore would have amounted to no more than 8,000–9,000 peltasts and other skirmishers (6,000–7,000 of his own plus some allies from the immediate area). Not only were these fewer footmen than Philip could deploy, but their light arms denied them the shock potential needed to challenge a phalanx head-on. Cersobleptes did, however, hold an edge in the size of his mounted contingent, which probably had 3,000–4,000 riders (including a thousand or so locals). He therefore must have taken his stand on open terrain. This gave his horsemen free rein off the wings, where they might achieve dominance while their infantry compatriots kept the enemy at bay with missile fire in the middle of the field. Having encountered similar tactics in Paeonia, Philip was able to duplicate his victory there with relative ease. Mounted cover and ready routes for escape would have allowed for a running retreat that limited Thracian losses somewhat; regardless, the engagement was still decisive and taught an obvious lesson: light-armed forces like those of Thrace had little chance in pitched battle against Macedonia's potent new blend of heavy infantry and shock cavalry.

Philip next besieged Potidaea, a key site on the tri-pronged peninsula of Chalcidice. Surviving sources present a confused chronology at this point, but the most consistent interpretation is that Philip became aware in early summer of a pending Athenian bargain with several of his regional foes. These were the Illyrian Grabaei (under Grabus), some resurgent Paeonian tribes (led by Lyppeius) and eastern Odrysians (under Centriporis). Once agreed, these three parties would act as Athens' proxies in its war with Macedonia. It would take the speediest of actions to preempt this developing menace and, rather than abandoning the ongoing investment, Philip took the bold step of splitting his forces. Thus, the king's most trusted general, Parmenio, immediately headed west with the bulk of the national host. He was to first strike the Illyrians and then move against Paeonia. Meanwhile, Philip himself would finish off Potidaea before dealing with the new Thracian threat in the east.

Parmenio was well qualified for this job, having gained a wealth of experience commanding the left side of the phalanx in all its previous actions. We can only guess at manpower for his campaign, but a force similar to that sent to Illyria two years earlier seems reasonable. This would have been around 6,000 phalangites (nearly all Macedonian citizens by this time), 2,000 hoplites (maybe still a mix of hired men and hypaspists, though mostly the latter), 2,000 light foot troops and 800 hetairoi. The horsemen were a bit over half the companions in service given likely growth over the last year. Standing on the other side was a tribal gathering that could have nearly matched the earlier army of Bardylis at something like 6,000–7,000 spearmen, 2,000–3,000 foot skirmishers and 300–400 horsemen.

Diodorus' brief account of the Macedonian campaigns of mid-356 (16.22.3) indicates that the Illyrians, having lost to Philip two years ago, gave way without much effort. Yet it was actually the Dardanians who had suffered that defeat and not the Grabaei, whose lands lay untouched well north of Dardania. Moreover, Plutarch claimed (Vol. II, *Alexander*, 141) that Parmenio bested the Grabaei in a "great battle" that Philip heard about on the same day that he learned of his son Alexander's birth. Thus, we can be fairly certain that a major action did indeed take place, likely resulting in a near point for point repeat of Philip's triumph at Lyncus Plain. As for the king, he had by this time taken Potidaea, which he promptly turned over to its rivals in the Chalcidian League (Diodorus 16.8.3, 5–6; Demosthenes 6.20). This shrewd move was requisite if Philip was to put a second army of adequate strength into the field, Potidaea being the price for an alliance with the Chalcidians' muscular military, which likely amounted to 10,000 hoplites and 1,000 horsemen (Demosthenes 19.230, 266) plus 2,000–3,000 foot skirmishers. Now in possession of a deep pool of allied manpower and with Parmenio securing his rear, Philip set out for Thrace.

The Macedonian ruler's first stop was at Crenides. Here, he further locked down the surrounding area and then marched against Centriporis and his Odrysian tribesmen. The army that accompanied him likely boasted a little over 6,000 Macedonians (2,000 hypaspists, 3,000 phalangites, 500–1,000 light infantrymen and 600 companion riders). And it probably had an even larger contingent from the Chalcidian League in the form of an allied muster approaching two-thirds, including some 6,000 hoplites, 600 light cavalry and 1,000–2,000 foot skirmishers.

Much like for Parmenio's campaign in Illyria, the summary of Diodorus again describes a foe beaten in the past and unwilling to take the field. Yet once more this is surely wrong, as it was western Odrysians under Cersobleptes rather than these easterners under Centriporis that had incurred that earlier pounding. And while we don't have an explicit reference to a pitched battle this time, it seems quite improbable that one of the dominant tribes among a race long known for ferocity and martial prowess would simply cede its homeland without putting up a fight.

Needing to incorporate so many foreign troops, Philip must have adjusted his usual battle order. It's very likely that this called for deployment of the Chalcidian cavalry off his left wing and assignment of the League hoplites to the formation center. Neither of these posed much of a challenge to his tactical scheme; indeed, he had used light horsemen in this same way in Thessaly and the allied hoplites were merely subbing for phalangites, themselves replacements for just such traditional spearmen. On the other side, the Odrysians surely had a strength and array similar to those of their kinsmen in the previous action at Crenides. And as then, their javelin-armed riders would have sought to carry the day from posts outside a loosely ranked line of light infantry. If so, Philip's system once more proved up to the challenge, with the hetairoi on the right probably running off their lighter-armed opponents in a brief duel and the Chalcidian horse on the left then keeping pace as the phalanx moved up. A final decision must have come quickly as minimal effort from the Macedonian and Greek heavy footmen chased their overmatched foes into the hills. Casualties were doubtless modest all around. However, the clearly repeatable nature of this triumph utterly demoralized its victims and cleared the way for Philip to seize the entire Thracian coastal belt.

The last Athenian proxy, Lyppeius of Paeonia, probably fell to Parmenio late that summer. It's here where Diodorus' tale of cowed barbarians simply giving way strikes its most believable chord. The Paeonians had indeed suffered in pitched battle against Philip's phalanx and can't really be blamed for not wanting to risk another such thrashing. Moreover, word had certainly reached them by now of the recent Macedonian victories in Illyria and Thrace against armaments that were considerably more powerful than their own. It's therefore easy to imagine that Lyppeius came to terms after no more than token resistance — a response that some sources might then have mistakenly assigned to Grabus and Centriporis as well.

Adding to Philip's successes in this period was an impressive string of investments as one city-state outpost after another fell before him. In fact, the Macedonian army was proving just as adept at siege-craft as on the battlefield. By late 355, Philip was going against Methone, the only Greek center in the region still outside his control. The king would suffer a fearsome wound here (Worthington 2008, 49), struck in the face by a catapult bolt (*toxeuma*). Though this cost Philip an eye and left a frightful scar from cheek to forehead, he soldiered on to take Methone in 354. Yet, even as he was making these gains in the far north, a major conflict was underway in central Greece that would soon draw Macedonia deep into Grecian affairs.

Sacrilege and War

The Third Sacred War (the first two being 6th and 5th century events) arose out of a petty rivalry between Thebes and Phocis. It seems that in the fall of 357 the Thebans were in the throes of righteous anger over their recent expulsion from the island of Euboa (Hornblower 1991, 246). The Phocians became the focus for this rage because, despite being erstwhile allies, they had refused to come to Thebes' aid. The Thebans elected to avenge this perceived insult through the Delphic Amphictyony, a regional league overseeing Greece's most revered shrine at Delphi. This oracle sat naturally within Phocian territory, but the league dictated its affairs and Thebes had firm control of that body. It was thus a simple matter to have the Amphictyony assess a fine on Phocis for cultivating land set aside for grazing shrine sacrifices. Doing this in the spring of 356, the Thebans made sure that the penalty was outrageously costly so as to justify further action when the Phocians refused to pay. Seemingly trivial, this act of spite would have a surprisingly significant impact on Greek history.

Phaedriades and Amphissa I and II (356 B.C.)

Philomelus, the Phocian leader, now seized Delphi. He had prepared for this act by using a sum of 30 talents (half his own and the rest from Sparta) to secure a band of mercenaries for that summer's campaign season. These likely consisted of 2,000 hoplites (each paid one drachma per day for 90 days), whom he supported with some of his own men, perhaps 500 peltasts and a few hundred horsemen. The Ozolian (western) Locrians marched straight away to free the shrine. As members of the Amphictyony closest to hand (their lands lying just south and west of Delphi) they might have felt the need to do this in order to prevent abuse of the sacred precinct. However, enmity toward the Phocians, bitter rivals of long standing, must have been a factor as well. And it's probably this intense hatred that best explains why the Locrians were willing to chance a battle at this time despite having an inferior force of perhaps no more than 1,500 hoplites, 750 peltasts and 150 cavalrymen.

The armies came to blows on a gentle incline leading down to Phaedriades, a circle of rocks on the south side of Mount Parnassos that formed a cliff plunging toward Delphi. Approaching from the east, the Phocians aligned their phalanx down the slope, likely making use of greater numbers to stand at a depth of twelve shields along both wings while only eight in the center. This compelled the Locrians to avoid an overlap by filing less than eight-deep along their entire front. With light-armed contingents offsetting each other at the edges of the fight, Phocis' deeply stacked and better seasoned mercenaries appear to have carried the day on their right by making the most of natural drift to sweep that flank. This caused the Locrian array to break apart in a downhill progression as men came under attack from the side and tossed shields to run. The Locrians took heavy losses, some suffering capture but many more (perhaps 20–30 percent) being either slain in flight or driven over the nearby precipice.

Philomelus had been able to inflict a crushing defeat on Locris at trivial cost to his own forces (a percent or two in fatalities at most). This encouraged him to punish his foes by descending on their home territory. To this purpose, he called up the Phocian national levy, which let him put around 5,000 men into the field (Diodorus 16.25.1). These would have included the peltasts and hired spearmen from Phaedriades as well as some 1,500 native hoplites and Phocis' full complement of 500 light horsemen.

Philomelus struck at Amphissa, the main town of Ozolian Locris, which lay but a short distance to the west of Delphi. He did this by sending out separate raiding parties so as to better spoil the surrounding croplands, each detachment having a core of hoplites backed by cavalry and light footmen. Such a dispersion of strength was common for Greek invaders when encountering little or no opposition; still, it was a course fraught with peril, since these detachments could easily end up far from the main body of their army and make tempting targets for resistance fighters.

This theoretical risk soon turned real as one of the raiding groups did indeed come under attack. The size of this unit is speculative; however, 600–800 men appears reasonable on the basis of reported casualties. This suggests a lochos of 400–500 hoplites (perhaps Phocian militia) working with 150–200 peltasts and maybe 50–100 horsemen. Hiding within the wooded district around Amphissa, the Locrians sprang an ambush with a force likely about equal in size to that of the Phocians, using survivors from Phaedriades plus old age/youth reservists. Caught unprepared, the raiders fled after a sharp action that ended before aid could arrive from the central Phocian column. Though the fight was brief, it still cost the lives of 20 of Philomelus' men (Diodorus 16.25.2) and, perhaps, even more, since this figure might represent only hoplite losses at a rate of 3–5 percent. By the time Philomelus came to the rescue, the victors had withdrawn, carrying away the Phocian dead along with their own.

In the aftermath of this minor triumph, the Locrians chose to add insult to injury by refusing the Phocians a truce to recover their slain, claiming that those who had defiled a holy site like Delphi didn't deserve honorable burial. It was a bold move that came back to haunt the Locrians when they tried to repeat their ambush tactic. This time, the targeted troops (mercenaries?) were ready and inflicted a stinging defeat. Philomelus was now able to claim a number of Locrian bodies, which he then traded for his own dead before wrapping up the campaign and heading home.

Argolas and Neon (355 B.C.)

Following his victory in Locris, Philomelus faced an invasion by Thebes and its allies in the coming year. He was well aware that Phocis' army was hopelessly inadequate to meet this threat without massive mercenary help, but lacked adequate funds to hire the required troops. This compelled him to take a drastic measure. Delphi was actually much more than just a religious site — it was also a repository of immense riches. Nearly every polis in Greece donated to its famed oracle in return for highly prized state prophesies. No doubt feeling already damned for his previous acts such that no greater infamy seemed likely to accrue from further sacrilege, Philomelus used the shrine's treasury to pay for forces needed to protect his homeland.

As summer 355 approached, the Thebans were moving closer to all-out war with Phocis. They had hesitated to take this step to date out of fear for what Athens might do. But Athens, despite being the Phocians most powerful supporter, had its own worries. The still raging Social War was draining the Athenians of means to fully engage in another conflict, whether in Macedonia (where they had to settle for rather feeble proxy campaigns against Philip) or now in central Greece. With courage bolstered by this, Thebes was at last ready to move against Philomelus.

With the Thebans set to enter the fray, attention shifted from the south of Phocis to that state's upper reaches. Here, below the northern slopes of Mount Parnassos and bordering on Opuntian (eastern) Locris, the land lay open to invasion. Yet defense of this region was imperative in that it held the vast majority of the Phocian population, which resided along the valley of the Cephissus River. Philomelus therefore moved his entire armament northward to await the pending enemy advance.

The opening round went well for the Phocians when their cavalry defeated a team of riders from Boeotia and Opuntian Locris. Sometime after this, a major battle took place on the Locrian plain near a hill called Argolas. Philomelus fielded a force of over 10,000 men for this action (Diodorus 16.29.3). These probably counted around 8,000 hoplites that included mercenaries (5,000), Phocian militia (1,500) and perhaps allies from Achaea (1,500, though this reinforcement might have arrived after the battle). Light support would have been on hand to the tune of 2,000 peltasts and 500 horsemen. In opposition was a 6,000-man army from Thessaly (Diodorus 16.29.4). This likely consisted of hirelings in the form of 4,000 spearmen and 1,000 peltasts plus 500 militia riders with a matching force of hamippoi. The Thessalian League and Pherae (in rare harmony) sent these troops along with a small contingent from local allies. As the armies prepared to fight, Philomelus must have put his numerical advantage to use by setting up his heavy formation twelve-deep along its full length, sandwiching the less experienced Phocians in the middle and forcing the enemy to reply with files at half his depth.

The following engagement seems to have resulted in a fairly rapid triumph for Phocis. Undoubtedly a prime display of othismos, concerted shoving by the Phocians' spearmen must have projected much greater muscular energy that powered through the thin opposing line. Panic on the other side would have fueled this penetration as well, rising quickly to fever pitch as soldiers found themselves stumbling awkwardly backward at an ever increasing pace. Within a few minutes at most, terror-struck men began peeling away to bolt from the Thessalian rear. Luckily for those trying to flee, their mounted comrades, who were of outstanding strength and quality, must have intervened to screen the retreat and drastically cut losses from pursuit. Casualties were likely on the order of 1–2 percent killed for the victors and 5–8 percent for those defeated.

Philomelus followed up by advancing into the passes over Mount Kallidromon, thus blocking all direct paths onto the Phocian plain from Thebes' northern staging area. However, Philip's old Theban host, Pammenes, frustrated the ploy by looping around to enter from the east. This compelled Philomelus to withdraw southward toward Mount Parnassos. As the Phocian and Theban armies shifted position, they lost track of each other only to then have their advance elements inadvertently make contact while marching through a densely wooded area near the foothill village of Neon. This chance meeting of vanguards soon led to a full scale battle, which took place across open ground on the far side of a deep ravine holding the Kachales River where it flowed to the northwest in front of Neon.

Diodorus claimed that Pammenes brought 13,000 men to Neon (16.30.4). If true, it's probable that some 10,000 of them were hoplites from Thebes (3,000), elsewhere in Boeotia (4,000) and the hired ranks (Parke [1933, 135] from Pausanius). The rest would have been peltasts/hamippoi along with 700 horsemen. As for Philomelus, he stood across the way with the same force that had fought at Argolas. This gave Pammenes a decided numerical edge, which would have let him deploy the spearmen from his native polis at 25 shields deep. A disciple of Epaminondas, the Theban probably positioned these troops on his left wing while filing the remainder of his hoplites at a depth of only eight. Seeking to avoid being outflanked, Philomelus now had to arrange his entire formation at eight shields deep. It's likely that these preliminaries weren't complete until late afternoon, at which time the phalanxes finally began to advance. Closing deliberately at first, the spearmen on both sides would have rushed over the last few meters to precipitate a desperate melee.

Diodorus' account of the battle at Neon (16.30.3) indicates that it turned on the Boeotians' greater manpower. If this was actually the case, then the climax likely came on the Phocian right wing. The Thebans could have used their superior depth there to steadily push back and eventually pierce the facing array. With what were presumably its best troops beaten, the Phocian phalanx must have collapsed in short order, sending men flooding rearward toward the Kachales defile and the mountain beyond. It seems that Philomelus was among those who escaped to higher ground; however, looking down from the sheer cliff that sat above Neon town, he could see the bodies of 30 percent or more of his men strewn over the rugged terrain below. These lay in heaps near the abandoned line of battle and scattered along the path of retreat all the way onto the lower mountain slopes. Dismayed and disgraced, the Phocian commander sought to atone by leaping over the rock face to his death. Yet, all was not lost, as another general, Onomarchos, now led the bulk of the beaten army to safety.

Neon might well have marked the end of the Third Sacred War if not for three conspiring factors. The first was Onomarchos, who would emerge as a more than adequate replacement for Philomelus. The second factor was the largely mercenary nature of the Phocian military. No matter how often it might suffer defeat or how many casualties it took, the seemingly inexhaustible pool of unemployed fighting men in Greece enabled Phocis to keep throwing new armies into the field as long it had the funds to pay for them. This brings us to the last factor: the riches of Delphi. The Phocians remained firmly in control of that vast reserve of wealth, thus guaranteeing their ability to continue the war. As a result of this confluence of elements, the events of 355 terminated no more than the opening phase of a conflict that was destined to last a full decade and have the gravest consequences for all of Greece.

Philip Marches South

Onomarchos made good use of Delphic funds to restore strength to his fighting force over the fall and winter. He then struck back with a punitive campaign in spring 354 that dealt a good deal of damage to Opuntian Locris and the Boeotians. But the most fateful event at this time proved not to be tactical, but rather diplomatic. This occurred when Pherae and the Thessalian League, who had found common cause at Argolas, renewed their long running civil war in Thessaly. In decline and seeking to stave off defeat, the Pheraeans turned to Athens and Phocis for an alliance. Their agreement would soon create a seismic shift in the balance of power by bringing Macedonia, an ally of the Thessalian League, into the Sacred War.

Pherae II and III, The Crescent Hills and Hermeum (354 B.C.)

Philip marched south with what was likely a full national muster as Diodorus' account sets no limitation, simply saying that he "entered Thessaly with his army" (16.35.1). At this time, his forces probably totaled on the order of 3,000 hypaspists, 9,000 phalangites, 3,000 skirmishers and up to 1,600 hetairoi, all at nominal unit strength. Allied troops would have met him shortly after entering Thessaly. These could have been as many as 2,000 hoplites, 500 peltasts, 1,000 light horsemen and 1,000 hamippoi — the League's full hired levy and around two-thirds of its native cavalry with light infantry support. Philip must then have closed on Pherae that he might invest the enemy's seat of power. It was near here where Phayllos, brother of Onomarchos, confronted him, having marched up from Phocis with 7,000 men (Diodorus 16.35.1). Adding in a full mobilization of local resources, Phayllos might have had roughly 8,000 hoplites (what his polis had fielded a year earlier plus 3,000 more from Pherae) — all mercenaries. His supporting forces likely amounted to around 2,000 peltasts along with at least 1,500 native Pheraean horsemen and an equal number of hamippoi.

Meeting Phayllos, Philip would have turned his column to spread out its heavy infantry in battle formation. This probably had his hypaspists stacking at a depth of eight shields on the right wing, foreign hoplites eight-deep in the center and pikemen far left in their usual ten-man files. The hetairoi and their screening light footmen would have posted alongside the hypaspists, while the horsemen from Thessaly and remaining light infantry did the same beyond the phalangites. This presented Phayllos with an opposing array on the order of 1,200m across. To avoid being outflanked, he would have split his own riders and light footmen off each wing and filed most of his hoplites at a depth of less than eight.

The following clash must have been a grueling affair, yielding Philip a tactical victory most likely gained through either a real or threatened frontal penetration of the Phocian left wing. However, it seems to have been a success that his played out men couldn't exploit with a proper pursuit due to still intact enemy screening forces off either flank. As a result, casualties must have been modest (fatalities at perhaps 5 percent for Philip and no more than 10 percent for his foes) and Phayllos retired with an army sufficiently whole as to be able to again take the field in short order. It was at this moment that Onomarchos arrived with reinforcements. And maneuvering with skill, he lost little time in bringing about a rematch, no doubt once more close to Pherae where the Macedonians would have been preparing their siege. Assuming a strength having some of the same elements as at Crocus Plain the next year, Onomarchos could probably call upon healthy survivors from Phayllos' retreat to field around 14,000 hoplites, 3,000–4,000 foot skirmishers and close to 2,000 horsemen with matching hamippoi.

The dynamics for this action differed from the one just past in much more than better balanced manpower. Leadership and experience were factors as well. The tactical skills of Onomarchos made for a markedly greater challenge than Philip had dealt with in his sibling (a man later to become notable for losing in the field). At the same time, many among the Phocian's mercenaries had increased experience against the Macedonian phalanx. In fact, some had tangled with this formation twice, having served with Phayllos as well as in Pherae's earlier loss to Philip. Unprepared to cope with the new and exotic pike array in those actions, these savvy professionals were surely by now devising better ways to counter sarissai. This would be crucial to their fighting the next battle in a much more effective manner.

Diodorus claimed (16.35.2) that Onomarchos enjoyed numerical superiority, though the foregoing projections suggest that any such edge was extremely modest with respect to overall manpower. However, the Phocian probably *did* have around three times as many traditional hoplites, an advantage which let him take the initiative and deploy his heavy corps at a uniform depth of eight shields while dividing the light forces off either wing. Philip then had to respond with a line approaching equal width. This required him to thin a portion of his phalanx below what would otherwise be optimal. And rather than sacrifice offensive potential by handicapping his hoplites on the right, he probably chose the less risky approach of reducing depth for the rest of his formation, which normally stood ten men deep. The phalangites there had a role that was not really much affected by diminished files. This was because they didn't physically support each other beyond overlapping their weapons, and even this involved only the front three ranks. It's therefore likely that not only Philip's spearmen but his pikemen as well ended up arraying eight-deep or less.

When finally locked into shock combat, these formations turned out to be very closely matched, battling long and hard with neither achieving a penetration or envelopment. Sadly, there is no surviving account of just why this action at last took the decisive turn that we know it did in favor of the Phocians. However, we do have a detailed discussion from an expert observer on the strengths and weaknesses of the Macedonian phalanx which suggests a plausible scenario.

Polybios, a veteran Greek general, noted (18.30.5–11) that a Roman swordsman of his era desiring to engage a phalangite had the near impossible task of getting inside at least ten pike points. This reflected that he faced two opponents (since it took roughly twice as much width to swing a blade as to thrust a pole arm) and these foes had the aid of overlapping sarissai from four rows behind. Romans therefore couldn't best an intact phalanx frontally and had to rely on superior flexibility to hit at side or rear. But the chore for Onomarchos might have been much easier. Macedonian pikes at his earlier date were shorter, putting just three points out in front, while an almost as tightly-ranked hoplite faced but a single foe. Moreover, his spear had greater reach than a Roman sword. All this meant that a spearman probably had to break off or push aside no more than two pike points in order to then step in and strike at a phalangite. The pikeman would then be in real trouble, forced to drop his now useless sarissa and defend with a short sidearm and undersized shield. Doubtless with just such observations in mind, Onomarchos and his hoplites must have drawn out the fight, hanging tough until they could make this sort of deadly penetration at several spots along the enemy line. Philip's leading rank would then have begun deteriorating, with some stretches awkwardly struggling to keep sarissai in play even as others were reduced to using swords at great disadvantage. And all so put upon in the front rank had to have felt a rising panic, which would have quickly spread rearward. The phalangites' unusually thin files for this action now emerged as a liability, creating an unnerving sense of vulnerability and making it easier for shaken men to escape from the front.

With center and left wavering, Philip seems to have realized just how dire his predicament had become and signaled to disengage and withdraw. To attempt such a difficult maneuver in mid-battle says a great deal about the faith he had in his army's professional skill. That he actually pulled it off with what must have been only minor losses says more still, not only on how highly disciplined Macedonian troops had grown in recent years, but also about how utterly exhausted his opponents were as the arduous duel dissuaded any real post-battle chase. Onomarchos was thus able at day's end to claim the field and the distinction of handing Philip his first defeat. Still, his inability to pursue and punish the Macedonian meant that the larger, strategic issue remained unresolved. This set the stage for yet another engagement — one that would prove to be among the most unique ever waged on Greek soil.

In casting about for a way to deal Philip a mightier blow, Onomarchos hit upon a plan that called for drawing him up a box-canyon. The exact location of this feature isn't known, but it probably lay along the western fringe of the Mount Pelion complex above ancient Lake Boibeis to the northeast of Pherae. The hills surrounding the canyon formed a crescent that opened to the west, and it was into this entrance that Onomarchos led his army with the Macedonians close on his tail. Nearing the defile's back wall, the Phocian commander turned his soldiers about and put them into a phalanx that anchored against the slopes on either side. Philip's troops pulled up when they realized that their quarry was forming for battle and quickly followed suit. This left the two armies facing each other in formations much like those used previously at Pherae, save for having all of their mounted men and light foot troops in the rear.

Keen to get at a pinned foe, Philip and his phalanx must have begun closing upon the stationary enemy line. At that instant, a signal sounded to trigger an ingenious trap described in some detail by Polyaenus (2.38.2, *Excerpts* 36.3). It seems that Onomarchos had prepared this site in advance by hiding "*petrobolous mechane*" (rock-throwing engines) on the enclosing heights. These were likely non-torsion cross-bows of an advanced design (Marsden 1969, 59), which at a length of nearly 9m could hurl stone shot more than 250m on the flat and farther still from the sort of elevated positions occupied here. Now, having enticed his opponent within range, the Phocian unleashed a lethal crossfire from these machines. The account of Polyaenus has Onomarchos firing on his opponents while they are still in full chase and only then reversing his course to form up for a fight, but it's much more likely that he turned before springing the ambush so as to bring his foe into line of battle. This let him "cross the T" on either end of a nearly static target, giving his artillery a much deeper and therefore easier mark, correct range being harder to achieve than direction.

Philip's advance staggered to a halt as cascades of stones crashed into his wings from either side. Weighing around 2.3kg (5lbs), these projectiles broke bones and crushed skulls, smashing men to the ground as they tore ragged holes in the king's array. Seizing their chance as the enemy milled in some disorder, Onomarchos and his men mounted a charge. The battle that followed must have come to a decision in mere minutes as the wrecked Macedonian line gave way under shock assault, with the less flexible and more lightly protected phalangites in particular being unable to stand fast after the preliminary battering had cut fatal gaps in their front. It was only the mutual rearward stationing of skirmishers and cavalry that then prevented a wholesale slaughter, since this hindered pursuit at the same time that it helped the losers screen their retreat. Philip got away, but at the cost of perhaps 20–30 percent of his men plus a fortune in shields, sarissai and other gear tossed in haste.

Onomarchos' twin victories put Philip out of action for the rest of the year, so damaging the bravado of his troops that a rebellion broke out. Forced to leave Thessaly, the Macedonian vowed to return and spent that winter replacing physical losses as well as mending his army's broken morale. Our sources are silent on just how he did the latter, but his process might have included improving phalangite defenses with longer (4.6m) sarissai that projected an additional row of pike points and required an exclusive two-hand grip. In fact, our first archeological evidence for such attenuated pikes comes from the battle of Chaeronea 15 years later; still, these kinds of finds are haphazard at best and really only set a latest possible date for the weapon's appearance. That its introduction came earlier in direct response to shortcomings exposed by the setbacks against Onomarchos seems to make a lot of sense. What we know for sure is that Philip would return to the field in 353 with an army refreshed in both strength and spirit.

As for the other contestant at Crescent Hills, Onomarchos came away from his great triumph full of confidence. He had earlier forced the Ozolian Locrians into alliance and thus secured his nation's southern and western boundaries; now, holding the mistaken belief that he had done the same in the north by taking Macedonia out of the war, he turned against Boeotia. It must have looked like he might be able to pacify his last remaining hostile frontier by year's end if he could just gain one more victory along his eastern marches.

Thebes and some of the other Boeotians soon gave Onomarchos just what he wanted by engaging him at a location called Hermeum. The Thebans could have deployed up to 7,000 hoplites for this action as well as 700 horsemen and 2,500 peltasts and hamippoi. (Notably missing was their best general, Pammenes, who was preparing to earn funds for his polis by supporting the satrap Artabazus' revolt against the Persian king. Pammenes had 5,000 soldiers in hand, but these were hirelings that would have had no effect upon native manpower available [Parke 1933, 124].) As for Onomarchos, he must have fielded all of the troops that had come away in good health from the campaign against Philip. These might have totaled as many as 8,000 mercenary, Phocian and allied Achaean spearmen along with 2,000 in light foot soldiers and a few hundred horsemen. There also would have been a contingent from Pherae, likely a two-thirds muster consisting of hired men at 2,000 hoplites and 500 skirmishers plus 1,000 each in homegrown cavalry and hamippoi.

Onomarchos managed to carry the day at Hermeum. With his more abundant foot skirmishers keeping the potent Boeotian horse at bay, he probably was able to use deeper files on his right wing to break the opposing phalanx. Yet any strategic gain seems to have been short lived at best. This likely owed to a low casualty count among those defeated, their withdrawal having been amply protected by a cavalry force of good ability and superior strength. The reality was that Phocis was no closer to resolving the war in its favor despite three straight battlefield successes.

Crocus Plain and Pagasae (353 B.C.)

Philip marched back to Thessaly that spring with an armament not only replenished in terms of its native manpower, but actually much expanded by the addition of foreign soldiers. The latter were a benefit from the mining operations around Crenides, which had grown over the last couple of years to yield a great deal of wealth. Philip had put that resource to use in hiring large numbers of mercenaries (Diodorus 16.8.7), swelling his hoplite forces and upgrading his light foot troops with professional missilemen. Nor was this all he did to ensure success, going on to persuade the Thessalian League to give him sole command over its army as well. Gathering the latter as he moved south, Philip now closed on Pherae to put it under siege. In dire straits, the Pheraeans called upon Athens and Phocis for help.

Onomarchos responded by drawing on Delphic monies to gather another large, mercenary-rich armament of his own. Once having assembled this powerful host, the Phocian leader quickly departed; however, rather than heading straight for Pherae, he first made for the lower shores of the gulf that stretched below that city's port of Pagasae. Here, he met the Athenian general Chares, who led a fleet of triremes loaded with hired men tasked with liberating Pagasae (Philip had captured it in the autumn of 354). With Athens' naval force in the distance off his right shoulder, Onomarchos then turned up along the beach that he might rendezvous with his Thessalian allies. But Philip had no intention of waiting for these foes to join forces. Setting out swiftly, possibly at night (Hammond 1994, 47), he rushed to catch Onomarchos in transit. It must have come as quite a shock to the Phocian when he found that a large force lay in wait just ahead, formed up for action across a broad coastal expanse known as the Crocus Plain. Electing to fight over flight, Onomarchos swung the head of his column landward, rushing to transform it into a battle-ready phalanx.

Diodorus gave Onomarchos a total of 500 riders and 20,000 foot soldiers (16.35.4). The latter probably consisted of 16,000 hoplites (some Phocian, but mostly mercenaries) and 4,000 skirmishers. (Note that Chares made no contribution. The reason for this isn't recorded, but it's possible that he simply had no chance to land before the fight got underway.) Onomarchos spread out his formation from the shore, stacking hoplites eight-deep and stationing all the missilemen off the inland flank. Fronting for what few horsemen he had, the latter would need to buy sufficient time against the enemy's own light forces for his heavy footmen to carry the fight.

On the other side, Philip is said to have had more than 20,000 infantry plus 3,000 cavalry. Given that the infantry number is but a partial accounting, it likely represents just the heavy troops at 3,000 hypaspists, 9,000 phalangites and up to 8,000 hired men (2,000 from the Thessalian League). Philip would have arrayed his pikemen at a depth of ten with their flank resting on the sea, the paid hoplites in eight-man files in the center and his hypaspists at that same depth on the far right. Like his opponent, he then must have set up all of his riders landward (full levies of maybe 1,600 hetairoi beside the hypaspists and 1,500 Thessalians outboard). Leading for these were around 3,000 of the king's own skirmishers plus 3,500 hired peltasts and League hamippoi.

Closing on signal, the armies entered into a combat that Diodorus described as "severe" (16.35.5), suggesting a bitter melee of some duration. Given strong similarities in arms, experience and numbers from west through center, it's not surprising that that part of the front immediately stalemated. Men frantically speared and pushed here, but could make little headway. Meanwhile, the phalangites on the seaward end of the line were facing a stern test. Laced with green replacements for last year's casualties, they were going against men who had twice before gotten the better of their kind. And it was imperative that they now stand fast, since only a repeat of their past vulnerability would give Onomarchos any real hope for victory. Maybe their sarissai fared better in a briefer fight or perhaps they did indeed have new weapons with longer reach. Whatever

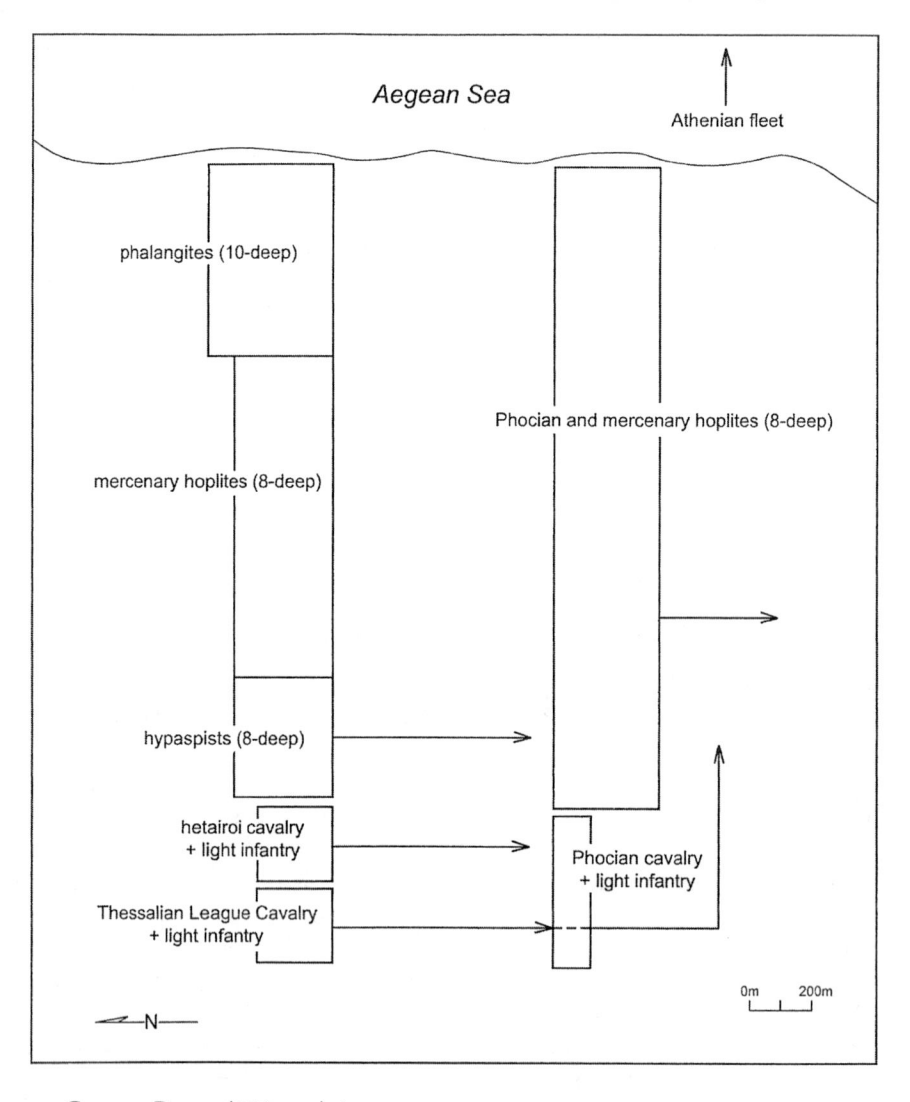

BATTLE OF CROCUS PLAIN (352 B.C.) (BOXES REPRESENTING FORCES ARE EXAGGERATED TO SHOW RELATIVE SIZES.)

the reason, Philip's pikemen held long enough against the very best Onomarchos could throw at them and effectively sealed his fate.

With phalanxes stalled in place, the light-armed battle inland proved decisive. That this contest hadn't instantly been resolved probably reflects the kind of dynamic seen at Mantinea II (362), highlighting just how much cavalry needed infantry support in this age. Philip had a six-fold advantage in mounted troops, but they couldn't go into action until their skirmishers had cleared the way. And since the two sides were better matched in light footmen, it took a while for this duel to play out. As it happened, the fight in front of the hetairoi seems never to have been conclusive enough to let them take the lead. Rather, Diodorus' account informs us that it was the Thessalians on the far western fringe who prevailed once their light infantry finally drove off its opposition. The situation turned quickly after these expert horsemen brought their superior numbers to bear, chasing away the few Phocian riders on hand and then wheeling against the enemy's proximal flank and rear.

The hoplites on the Phocian left had been struggling mightily against the hypaspists that were shoving and thrusting into them; all of a sudden, barrages of javelins flung by the Thessalian horsemen began hitting them from behind. This embattled sector rapidly began to fail as men spun about to protect themselves and bled strength out of their push at the front, allowing the elite northern spearmen to break through. At this point, collapse began rippling along Onomarchos' line from left to right and had soon carried all the way to the beach. As the victorious Macedonian right wing curled inward, defeated troops tossed their shields and tried to flee, with most of those rearmost and closest to the sea getting clear. The rest were less fortunate, spears and pikes claiming many at the front as they turned to crowd into what had become a terrified mob behind. And even as this unfolded, Philip's horsemen worked their way down to the water's edge, severing the last avenue of escape.

With nowhere to run, some of the beaten soldiers tried to give up, while others shed their gear and plunged into the sea in an attempt to reach a few Athenian ships that had rowed close to shore. A horrific massacre now took place that saw thousands either cut down where they stood or drowned, Onomarchos himself being among those meeting a watery death. The final price for the Phocians and their hirelings reached 6,000 dead (30 percent) with another 3,000 surrendering. Philip lashed out afterwards with great brutality, crucifying the Phocian leader's lifeless body and drowning his captives in the prescribed punishment for sacrilege.

Rather than moving south against Phocis in the battle's wake, Philip instead resumed his siege of Pherae. With that city's garrison and Chares' fleet still intact, it must have seemed sound to deal with these right away lest they come to menace his route home. And Chares would shortly validate that concern by striking for a small but galling victory. Our sources are quite sketchy on this action (see the excellent summary of Pritchett [1974, 80–81]), but the most logical and consistent interpretation suggests that the Athenian took advantage of Philip's withdrawal after Crocus Plain to pursue his original mission against Pagasae. Landing nearby, he was able to rapidly unship his men and advance on the port. Based on going rates and the fact that Chares later received a sum of 60 talents to cover the cost of his troops, he probably had as many as 4,000 hired hoplites with him. Light support for these would have come from some ship's archers and a large number of javelin-armed rowers.

Standing in opposition was Adaios, who normally led Philip's mercenaries. He had apparently remained behind at Pagasae to guard against just this kind of problem. Adaios' strength is highly uncertain, yet must have been but a portion of his usual command, consisting of somewhat fewer men than Chares had brought. The Macedonian should have kept within his walls until help arrived, but patience wasn't his long suit. Known as "The Cock" for his aggressive style, Adaios emerged to challenge Chares in open battle. Perhaps aided by a third or better edge in heavy-armed manpower, the Athenian's phalanx delivered a crushing defeat to Adaios, taking his life in the process. Still, things could have gone worse for Philip, since Chares lacked proper light-armed resources to mount an effective pursuit. As a result, the king's men probably took less than devastating losses (5–10 percent) before retiring inside Pagasae.

Athens' leaders had reacted rapidly after learning of Onomarchos' defeat, sending 5,000 citizen hoplites and 400 horsemen to block the pass at Thermopylae and preempt a march on Phocis. This proved prudent when Philip gained a quick surrender from Pherae in return for allowing its dictator, Lychophron, to leave with 2,000 of his mercenaries. There was no way now for Chares to sustain a threat to the Macedonian rear and his retreat freed Philip to head south. However, he chose to go home instead, satisfied with having added Thessaly to his domain. The way was then clear for Phayllos to pick up his brother's mantle at Phocis and promptly put together another army. Taking in combat survivors and the escapees from Pherae, he also tapped the wealth of Delphi to contract fresh troops. The Sacred War was thus destined to drag on in spite of what had looked like a decisive battle at Crocus Plain.

Phrygia and Lydia

In the same period that Philip II was overcoming the initial challenges to his career and country, another new monarch was facing like trials overseas. Artaxerxes III (Ochus) had come to the throne of Persia upon his father's death in 358. Mindful of his nation's woes during the recent satrapal revolts, he moved to head off more of the same by instructing that the last of the mercenary garrisons used to challenge royal authority be disbanded. Timing of this order isn't certain, but it likely came no later than 356. However, rather than precluding a new uprising, the decree actually reenergized open conflict when two of the affected governors refused to obey. Thus, Artaxerxes unexpectedly found himself having to send troops out to once more deal with mutinies strong in paid Greek fighters.

Phyrgia I, Sardis II and Tmolos Camp (355 B.C.)

How large was the counterinsurgency effort? At the start of Artaxerxes' reign, hoplite-fronted units of kardakes like those created in the late 370s by Datames likely cored Persia's regular army. Drafted out of special military colonies, divisions (baivaraba) of these warriors formed a combined-arms force along the main line of battle while cavalry and screening footmen supported forward and off the wings. Based on past campaigns and others from later in the 4th century, an all-out effort would have been on the order of eight baivaraba with additional bodyguards should a monarch be present. But for a lesser expedition such as that of 355, a force of only about half that size seems more probable. This suggests no more than four divisions of footmen and a like number of cavalry regiments with supporting skirmishers. Wishing to deal at once with both revolts, and no doubt expecting only weak resistance, the royals split into two columns, one headed for Phyrgia and the other marching on toward Mysia. Each of these task forces at 80 percent establishment strength would have had 16,000 line infantry and 1,600 cavalry plus some light footmen. This is consistent with a report (Olmstead 1948, 425) that Artaxerxes ordered a force of 20,000 men (nominal for two baivaraba) be deployed into Phyrgia.

Artabazus led the revolt in Phyrgia as governor of that satrapy. He gathered cavalry from sympathetic local Persian settlers, enrolled native Phrygian javelinmen and sought to obtain a force of heavy infantry. He did the latter by reaching out to Chares, the general prosecuting Athens' ongoing Social War against its rebellious Asian allies. Chares duly delivered an army that seems to have had both Greek and (per Isocrates 8.42) Asian troops, the latter presumably including Ionian and Carian spearmen recently put on the market by the Great King's ban. Seeing some potential advantages, Athens turned a blind eye to this move, doing so in part because it lacked funds to pay the mercenaries anyway. Artabazus, who on his own had "only a few soldiers" (Diodorus 16.22.1), could now surprise his foes with quite a large hoplite phalanx under an experienced and able field commander.

What was the size of the rebel armament? Parke (1933, 122) has proposed that Chares headed a force in which some 10,000 mercenaries taken in from former satrapal garrisons formed only a portion. This would fall into line with the suggestion of Demosthenes (4.19) that Athens' hired armies at this time could have some 10,000–20,000 men "on paper." Likewise, Diodorus described the 5,000 soldiers that Artabazus later acquired via Thebes as "an auxiliary force" (16.33.4), implying that the satrap's army (inherited from Chares) was larger still. We might then propose a possible parade strength of some 15,000 men. This would likely have been around 12,000 hoplites and 3,000 (20 percent) in light infantry. Local troops would then have added to Chares' muster in the form of the aforementioned Phrygian peltasts and horsemen.

Chares was able to defeat the troops sent against Artabazus, a feat that he compared to Athens' victory at Marathon in a boastful letter home (Parke 1933, 123). Unfortunately, we lack details on this action, and Diodorus' spare report seriously overstates the scale of the fight in citing a Persian deployment of more than 70,000 men. Nevertheless, even the much smaller armies proposed here suggest quite a sizeable engagement. In fact, battle lines likely stretched more than 1.5km for the heavy corps alone (filed ten-deep for the kardakes and at around eight for Chares' hoplites). The rebels seem to have kept Persian cavalry from sweeping their flanks, either through use of terrain or by exploiting an advantage in light footmen. This let their hoplites break through the kardakes' leading rows of spearmen. The lightly armed Persian after-ranks would then have rapidly lost an uneven fight and beat a swift retreat. Given their strong edge in mounted forces for cover, the imperials no doubt got away without undue slaughter. Their dead might thus have been some 10–12 percent of the infantry deployed. Fatalities among the insurgents would have been significantly less, yet may still have reached 5 percent. Toward the upper end for victors in a phalanx battle, this reflects casualties inflicted by the kardakes' missilemen in addition to those normally absorbed as a result of shock combat. As it turned out, this action would earn Athens considerable blowback. The Great King threatened to retaliate with a large naval force and compelled the Athenians to bring Chares home and concede the Social War.

Meanwhile, things initially took quite a different turn for the other insurgency in progress. Here, the satrap Aroandus (Orontes) had awaited the king's response to his uprising on open ground near Sardis in Lydia. He had a force of 12,000–13,000 Greek heavy infantry that he backed with horsemen (and probably javelinmen as well) from his home province of Mysia. It seems that Aroandus suffered a defeat in his first encounter with the king's men. Again, we have no details, leaving it open as to why the rebel effort fell short. However, given Aroandus' strength in spearmen, this most likely was a case of poor flank security allowing Persian mounted forces to envelop a wing. All the same, the satrap seems to have escaped with a good portion of his army intact (losses perhaps approaching 20 percent versus 3–5 percent for the opposition).

Aroandus took up a strong position with his surviving troops inside a fortified camp on nearby Mount Tmolos (Polyaenus 7.14.2, *Excerpts* 19.2.5). Investing this site, the Persians couldn't prevent their foe from making a nighttime sortie with his cavalry against their supply line along the road to Sardis. The renegade satrap then coordinated a sally out of the camp with a surprise strike from his horsemen against the enemy rear. Taken front and back, the besiegers fell apart as the Greeks killed many and captured others at little cost to themselves (maybe 1–3 percent fatalities). Aroandus later tested the discipline of his remaining contingent of about 10,000 hoplites, having them hold fast against a large-scale cavalry attack near Cyme (Polyaenus 7.14.3). He next ravaged Lydia and marched on Ephesos, where the fearsome reputation of his mercenaries gave him a bloodless triumph. This came when he disguised some of his Asians as Grecian spearmen and their foes fled after seeing these faux fighters maneuver to commands in Greek (Olmstead 1948, 428)

Phrygia II and III (354 B.C.)

Artabazus cast about for a Greek partner to replace Athens and found the Thebans willing. Thebes sent Pammenes to Phrygia along with a 5,000-man mercenary force, probably consisting of 4,000 hoplites and the rest light infantry. Their pact no doubt called for the rebel leader to pick up the tab for both the general (directly enriching Thebes) and his men. The agreement gave Artabazus not only an excellent phalanx tactician to lead his army, but also pumped that force up to something like 15,000 hoplites, 3,000–4,000 skirmishers and a small yet effective contingent of cavalry. It's likely that the imperial reaction was to double down on a single front. This called for gathering the four baivaraba split between two efforts during 355 into a united force, ignoring Aroandus for the moment so as to concentrate entirely on Phrygia. As a result, Persia now marched on Artabazus with something like 32,000 kardakes and 3,200 horsemen plus proportional light infantry support.

These armies clashed twice in what Diodorus called "great battles" (16.34.2), the rebels winning out each time. That there were two engagements indicates that, regardless of how clearcut a tactical success the first might have been for Pammenes, its strategic impact was modest enough to require a rematch. Once again, we might suspect that the Greek hoplites enjoyed enough flank protection to allow their penetration of the kardakes' fore-ranks, yet screening by its much larger mounted contingent then let the Persian host retreat at less than ruinous cost. If so, perhaps only about 10 percent of the imperial footmen died against 1–3 percent among their foes. Accounts in Frontinus (2.3.3) and Polyaenus (5.16.2, *Excerpts* 19.3) of what must have been Pammenes' second action in Phrygia appear to support this idea. Though a bit confused on some points, these seem to portray the Greek commander's countering of horsemen as being critical to then gaining a decisive victory with that Theban tactical specialty of long standing, an unbalanced hoplite array.

The most straightforward reading of our sources suggests that Pammenes faced off against the kardakes (these standing in what Polyaenus called a "phalanx") along a front some 2.5km wide. This reflected around 26,000 Persians (a roughly 20 percent reduction due to deaths and wounds from the previous action) filing ten-deep and some 14,000 Greek spearmen (reduced about 5 percent) in an arrangement favoring their right wing (that half of the formation standing eight-deep versus only four on the left). Cavalry took post off either end, with the imperials targeting a heavier mounted effort against Pammenes' left. Closed into combat, the wily Theban withdrew the light forces shielding his left, playing upon his foe's hopes that they could turn the battle on that wing. Keeping enough skirmishers to check enemy cavalry on his right, he then sent his own horsemen from there to attack the rear of the pursuing Persian riders and foot skirmishers across the way. This caught these foes in a vice when their supposed quarry spun about to hit from the front as well. With the opposition's mobile units now broken on the left and stalled elsewhere, Pammenes and his deep right wingers broke through the kardakes and put them to rout. Having been at least partially enveloped and with more than half their screening cavalry in disarray, the Persians must have suffered serious casualties (possibly 20–30 percent killed and many more wounded).

Despite its triumphs on the field of battle, the Phrygian revolt ultimately came to naught when Artabazus put a relative in Pammenes' place. This caused his army to eventually fall apart and sent him into exile at the court of Philip II. As for Aroandus, his uprising seems to have persisted for some time, as we hear of Athens concluding a commercial treaty with him in 349 (Olmstead 1948, 435). However, Artaxerxes appears to have regained control over the rebel satrap's territory by the mid-340s.

Phocis, Boeotia and the Peloponnese

The Sacred War continued to rage as Phayllos replaced the fallen Onomarchos and drew funds from Delphi to hire yet another army. He spread gifts around and called upon his allies in this. Per Diodorus (16.37.1–4), Sparta sent 1,000 foot soldiers, Athens 5,000 infantry and 400 horsemen, the exiled tyrants of Pherae threw in with 2,000 more mercenaries and some of the lesser states gave support as well. Adding these assets to what might have been another 1,500 footmen and 500 riders from his own militia, the Phocian warlord thus fielded perhaps 7,500 hoplites, 2,000 skirmishers and 900 in cavalry for a march into Boeotian territory.

Orchomenos, Cephissus River, Coronea III and Naryx II (352 B.C.)

Phayllos met the Boeotians along the shore of Lake Copais near the city of Orchomenos. We've no figures for the Boeotian force in the campaign of 352; however, based on past deployments, it might have been at worst only slightly smaller than that present for Phocis at some 7,000 hoplites, 700 horsemen and 2,500 in light infantry. In the ensuing battle, the Boeotians proved superior, besting Phayllos and causing him to lose "a great number of men" (Diodorus 16.37.5). What this means is debatable, but a heavy beating might well have cost the Phocian around 10–15 percent of his army at the price of a mere 1–3 percent for his foes. Still, Phayllos and most of his troops managed to get away in good enough shape to fall back westward and fight again alongside the Cephissus River just north and east of Chaeronea. But the Phocian wasn't able to do any better than before, going down to defeat with the loss of more than 900 killed and captured after probably inflicting no greater damage on his enemy than in their first engagement, though he did escape once again with most of his army intact. In both these encounters we can suspect that the Boeotian hoplites had been able to carry the engagement by rolling up a wing with a heavier allotment of troops along that part of the line per their standard practice since at least the days of Epaminondas. However, effective cover from the Phocians' skirmishers and cavalry let them retreat in reasonably good order that they might live to fight another day.

Though twice bested in the field at full strength, Phayllos was unwilling to give up on his campaign and seems to have settled on hitting back at the enemy by sending out small raiding parties. A common enough practice for invading Greek armies when holding a numerical advantage (as seen in Ozolian Locris in 356), this was a questionable approach where the Phocians had no such edge. Close to Coronea, the Boeotians (perhaps a full regiment of 1,000 hoplites, 100 riders and 350 light footmen) caught maybe 400 or so spearmen (an under-manned lochos) operating detached from the main body of their army with some 100 skirmishers and a like force of cavalry. The Boeotians overwhelmed these troops, quite possibly pulling off a double envelopment, and killed 50 while taking another 130 prisoner.

Finally, despairing of success in Boeotia, Phayllos turned northward into Locris. His luck now improved, as he was able to capture several cities there by one means or another. However, he had a setback at Naryx, which he'd taken by treachery only to then be expelled with a loss of 200 men. Leaving elements behind to prosecute a siege, Phayllos retired with his main force on Abai just inside the Phocian border. He then took heavy losses in a Boeotian night attack on his encampment and chose to retreat deeper into his homeland. The Boeotians followed with a sweep into Phocis' territory that netted a fair amount of booty. They next swung back to break the investment of Naryx with an army that after three victories in the field and a successful camp assault still probably numbered some 6,000 hoplites, 600 riders and 2,000 light infantrymen. But Phayllos wasn't through and had trailed his foes with a still potent host that might have counted 5,000 spearmen, 1,000–1,500 skirmishers and 600–800 horsemen. Taking advantage of the Boeotians' laxness, he sprang an unexpected attack that chased their hurriedly formed array from the field and probably inflicted fair casualties (5–10 percent) at very little cost (1 or 2 percent). Phayllos went on to re-take and plunder Naryx, but this would prove the swan song of his less than glorious career when he shortly thereafter died after suffering from a wasting disease.

Though Phocis had now lost its third warlord in as many years, it was still game. Phalaeccus, the son of Onomarchos, advanced to the leadership in accordance with the deathbed wishes of his uncle, who also directed that the youth be overseen by Mnaseas, an experienced general. This arrangement was short lived, however, as Mnaseas soon fell victim along with some 200 other Phocians to a Boeotian night attack reminiscent of the one at Abai. Now on his own, the inexperienced Phalaeccus then suffered a reverse in a mounted fight near Chaeronea, losing "a large number of his cavalry" (Diodorus 16.38.7). Still, the war would not end. Phalaeccus managed to retain his position through the rest of that year and the next four as well by engaging in numerous small actions while avoiding a major battle.

Orneai I and II, Telphusa and Messenia I–III (352 B.C.)

Even as the Sacred War devolved into a series of minor border clashes in the later half of 352, another conflict arose in the Peloponnese. Sparta had chosen this time when its old enemy Thebes was busy in central Greece to wage war on the Theban-allied Messenians of Megalopolis. The Megalopolitans couldn't match the Spartans and called for help. This came right away from their fellow Messenians plus Sicyon, while Argos also joined the cause and more distant Thebes sent 4,000 hoplites and 500 cavalry to their aid. But before the Argives could muster and the Thebans arrive, the Spartan king Archidamus III (Agesilaos' son now on the throne) led out his army.

Archidamus had perhaps 4,000 of his own hoplites (four of six morai), nearly 500 cavalry and some modest light infantry when he advanced out of Sparta to meet reinforcements from Phocis (3,000 mercenary hoplites) and the exiles of Pherae (150 horsemen). Striking with dispatch, he invaded Argos and took Orneai. It was outside that city where he then fought a battle with the Argives. Based on casualties, Argos had gathered only about 60 percent of its army on short notice, fielding some 4,000 hoplites with maybe 1,000 or so foot skirmishers and a mere handful of cavalry. Considering this estimate of strength, the Argives' decision to accept battle appears rash. However, it might well have been colored by high passions (in the wake of so sudden a strike on their homeland) as well as poor scouting that missed the mercenaries attached to Sparta's usual manpower. Regardless of the odds, the men of Argos assembled their formation, engaged Archidamus and promptly got beat. Argos seems to have lost 200 of its men in this action (Diodorus 16.39.4). In fact, at 5 percent of its hoplites, this would have been quite typical for a bested phalanx that suffered the sort of weak pursuit normally associated with Spartan victories. Archidamus' losses must have been very light in contrast, perhaps amounting to no more than 1–3 percent.

The men from Thebes now arrived under Cephision, who regrouped the Argives and collected the rest of his allies. Replacing casualties and adding perhaps 2,000–3,000 hoplites from Sicyon and 3,000–4,000 Messenians, he now had twice as many spearmen as Archidamus. Yet Diodorus claimed that his collection of militiamen was "inferior in discipline" (16.39.4); and, indeed, when finally engaged against the more steady Spartans and mercenaries, it came up short. In an action once more near Orneai, the armies must have spent most of the day organizing, with Archidamus setting up by late afternoon in a phalanx four or six shields deep to counter enemy files of eight or twelve. The ensuing fight proved to be both stubborn and lengthy. With exhaustion setting in, Cephision saw that his troops had made very little progress despite their edge in heavy manpower and decided to withdraw. Backing away behind a screen of cavalry and skirmishers, the Theban ceded both field and fight to Sparta. Neither party was likely to have been badly hurt, with losses maybe coming to less than 3 percent on either side. Yet in now disbanding, the allies would give Archidamus a strategic success to go with the tactical one his crack hoplites had so brilliantly earned in combat. Turning about, the Spartans sacked the Messenians' Arcadian ally Helisson and marched home.

When the coalition army broke up, its Peloponnesian troops went back to their own cities while the Thebans relocated to Megalopolis. At this point, it seems that the Spartans began spoiling districts tied to Megalopolis using small contingents of their Phocian hirelings and Thessalian cavalry, but the Boeotians caught one such raiding party near Telphusa in Arcadia. The mercenaries, maybe a lochos of 400–500 men, were likely badly outmanned by a Theban regiment of hoplites and horsemen with nominal complements of 1,000 and 100 respectively. The Boeotians drove their foes off, killing perhaps 20 percent of them in an action with chase that also took more than 60 captive along with their commander. Nor did this turn out to be an isolated incident, as two more of these detached elements fell victim to the Thebans under what must have been similar circumstances, the only likely variation being that they were probably operating on actual Messenian rather than nearby allied soil.

This infuriating string of minor reverses spurred the Spartans to action. They marched out in search of a decisive engagement and found their enemy obliging. We've no details on the resulting combat, but Diodorus distinguished it from the foregoing small encounters by calling it "an important battle" (16.39.6). This suggests that it pitted the full strength immediately to hand on both sides. As such, the Spartans (presumably once more led by Archidamus) could have deployed some 6,000–7,000 hoplites (4,000 of their own and the rest mercenaries) and better than 600 horsemen (including over 100 from Thessaly) along with a force of foot skirmishers. The Thebans and Messenians were able to match this with 6,000–7,000 spearmen, 500 riders and plenty of light infantry. Tellingly though, the disparity in troop quality that had brought Cephision to grief at Orneai had not gone away. Therefore, the Spartans, who had essentially equal manpower this time, carried the day with what must have been relative ease. As before, we might suspect that there were less than devastating casualties on the losing side as a consequence of enduring no more than a short pursuit. Whatever the costs, this battle brought the current round of warfare in the Peloponnese to an end, sending the bested Thebans home and allowing the Spartans to gain an armistice to their liking from Megalopolis.

Chalcidice, Euboa and Central Greece

Other conflicts came to the fore in the early 340s as fighting dropped to low ebb in the Sacred War. The first of these was in the far north, where the Greek cities of the Chalcidian League had a long record of interfering in Macedonia and now once more took to meddling with their neighbor's affairs in violation of the treaty that they had signed with Philip back in 357. It seems that their offense was to harbor the king's two surviving half-brothers, whom he had chased into exile when first coming to the throne. Philip naturally took strong exception and promptly invaded when the Chalcidians failed to give these men over.

Olynthus III and IV (348 B.C.)

Philip moved against the Chalcidice in 349, bringing 4,000 hypaspists, 12,000 phalangites, 3,000 of his own foot skirmishers and 1,200 hetairoi as well as perhaps some 7,500 heavy and light mercenary infantry. His initial victim was the town of Stageira, which he razed so brutally after a siege that several other sites then gave up peacefully and accepted garrisons of Philip's hirelings to avoid the same fate. Philip briefly broke off to deal with trouble in Thessaly, but came back by spring 348. Meanwhile, the Chalcidian center at Olynthus, clearly his ultimate target, sent for help to Athens, where Demosthenes presented its case. The Athenians (Spence [1993, 125] from Philochoros) sent Chares with a contingent of mercenaries that totaled 2,000 javelinmen and 150 in cavalry. Later, they pulled Charidemus from the Chersonese to replace Chares along with another 4,000 peltasts and 150 horsemen (Worthington 2008, 197). Operating in the company of strong local forces, Charidemus hit some of the places that had fallen to Philip, yet couldn't prevent a final descent on Olynthus.

When the Chalcidians finally confronted Philip as he closed on their capital, they probably fielded around 10,000 hoplites, 1,300 horsemen (including the 300 from Athens) and up to 9,000 peltasts (Athenian mercenaries plus locals). The Macedonian monarch would have set up to meet this menace with his hypaspists on the far right at a likely depth of twelve and mercenary spearmen (maybe only 4,000 after providing garrisons) next left standing eight-deep, completing his phalanx with phalangites in files of ten. The companion cavalry must have then split off either end of the line to be joined after some forward skirmishing by all the light infantry. Compelled to match fronts, the Chalcidians no doubt filed their own heavy infantry at under eight shields, dividing riders and foot skirmishers outboard on either side. There is no surviving description of the battle that followed; yet, given their vast strength in light footmen, it's doubtful that it was a failure on the Greeks' flanks that brought about their defeat. The Chalcidians more likely found themselves stymied on the right, where there was nothing to be had regardless of how hard they raged against the overlapping rows of opposing pikes. At the same time, Philip's deeper array had been steadily forcing back League spearmen on the other wing. Breaking through the Chalcidian left, his hypaspists must finally have sent the whole enemy formation into retreat with a threatened turning around that flank. Their edge in foot skirmishers would then have again favored the Greeks, cutting losses by giving cover to allow a withdrawal absent strong pursuit.

Having battered the enemy without delivering a knockout blow, Philip pressed on toward Olynthus only to have the Chalcidians regroup and combat him once more. Scope of this second engagement could have been very similar to that of the first, with that earlier clash likely having claimed but few casualties (possibly no more than 1 percent in fatalities for the winners and at most 5 percent for the losers). However, the rematch would yield more decisive results. Again probably besting the Greek left wing, Philip's men undoubtedly instilled much greater panic in their beaten foes this time. The Chalcidians failed to screen as effectively and/or keep any semblance of order in their retreat as the Macedonians dealt them severe damage, taking tolls both physical (possibly 12–15 percent killed) and mental that drained much of the remaining fight from the Greeks. Following up this victory, Philip invested Olynthus while the Athenians sent yet another allotment of troops that tallied 2,000 citizen hoplites (more or less equal to combined

Chalcidian losses to date) and 300 horsemen. Unfortunately for Olynthus, these reinforcements wouldn't arrive in time, as the city fell to internal treachery within a month and put an end to the Chalcidian League.

Tamynae (348 B.C.)

The other major conflict of the early 340s outside the Sacred War arose on Euboa, The Athenians had pulled that large island on their eastern coast back under their control in 357, but a new independence movement arose under Callias, tyrant of the Euboan city of Chalcis. Athens dispatched Phocion to Euboa with a modest force, intending for him to fill out his ranks with local men and then put an end to Callias' plans. But once on the scene, the Athenian general found the situation much worse than expected and was forced to fight for his very survival.

Euboan manpower might have come to some 3,000–3,500 hoplites based on the force sent in concert by the islanders to Nemea River in 394. Callias seems to have held the upper hand and may have had 2,000–2,500 of these, leaving his foe, Plutarch of Eritrea, with some 1,000–1,500. Both would have had small local cavalry forces as well as bodies of hired spearmen. Callias' brother had brought in mercenaries from Phocis (Aeschines 3.87) and Plutarch's account (Vol. II *Phocion*, 253) attests to the like-named Euboan leading such troops in battle as well. Again, we've no numbers, but can hazard a guess that there were around 1,000–2,000 hirelings on each side. As for Phocion, he probably sailed with only the tribal taxis of Pandionis (Aeschines 2.169) of no more than 1,000 hoplites along with what was likely a squadron of a hundred horsemen (Demosthenes 21.132-4). If so, he would have at best merely evened the odds.

Phocion had obviously expected stronger support; moreover, his allies were muddled, with everything being "in confusion" per Plutarch. This led him to take up a defensive stance near Tamynae where he could organize. Here, he sent to Athens for reinforcements (Demosthenes 21.162) and built a fortified camp on high ground set apart by a water-cut ravine from the level plain near town. His situation was very precarious, with no easy escape route through the highlands behind and the enemy moving into Tamynae to entrench and cut off access to the sea forward. Some of his local allies deserted at this point. Seeing his position deteriorate, Phocion realized that he needed to break out and, wary of the town's defenses, had his men stand to arms while he extended pre-battle sacrifices so as to give the opposing army time to emerge onto open ground. However, his local compatriot Plutarch lost patience. As soon as a portion of the rebel force emerged, he sallied with his mercenaries, apparently hoping to isolate and defeat the opposition's vanguard (likely some riders and their own hired spearmen). As a hasty infantry battle opened, Phocion's horsemen rushed forth to aid Plutarch, but did so in a haphazard fashion that caused their leading elements to be turned back and trigger a rout. And once the cavalry began to flee, Plutarch and his hoplites were soon to follow as Callias' mercenaries pressed on in a body, hoping now to follow up by capturing the Athenian fortification. It was at this crucial juncture that Phocion finally led out the remainder of his troops and went on the attack.

Phocion smashed into the hired men of Callias as they rushed ahead in poor order. Killing some outright, the Athenian forces cut down others as they tried to run. Phocion then pulled back and rapidly redressed his best men, these being the taxis from Athens and the more outstanding of his allies. Leaving a still jumbled Euboan majority behind to collect those of Plutarch's beaten corps now straggling back, he next led his 1,000–1,500 select troops against the enemy remnants of some 2,000–2,500 heavy militia under the Chalcian tyrant. A sharp action then ensued on the outskirts of Tamynae near its hippodrome. Phocion's horsemen rallied there to join their foot skirmishers on his flanks as the Athenians "showed themselves brave men, and conquered the enemy in a pitched battle" per Aeschines (3.88). Given that Aeschines, who fought here as a hoplite, went on to characterize those defeated as being "unworthy foes," it's likely that these inexperienced amateurs, despite probably standing nearly twice as deep, lost heart and simply gave way to hand Phocion the victory. However, Phocion's success on the battlefield did not end the rebellion, and Athens finally had to drop its hold on all the island's cities save Carystus.

Hyampolis, Coronea IV and Western Boeotia (347 B.C.)

The Third Sacred War had for some time been simmering without a significant field engagement, but in 347 things came to a higher boil. The Boeotians at that time crossed into Phocis to plunder the area around Hyampolis (Hya) where they defeated a counterstrike. Apparently of modest proportions, this action cost the losers 70 men, suggesting that they might have had 1,000–1,500 troops to start the fight, these perhaps being 1,000 or so hoplites with a few hundred light footmen and some cavalry. The Boeotians likely were operating with a full regiment of up to 1,000 spearmen, 100 riders and 300–400 foot skirmishers. If so, this was a relatively even match and we don't have a record of how it was resolved; however, success on a wing by a larger and more capable Boeotian mounted contingent seems the probable solution.

The Phocians responded quickly to this setback. Regrouped and probably reinforced, they returned to chase the raiders back into Boeotia, bringing them to battle near Coronea. Perhaps very similar in scope to the action at Hyampolis, the combat went in Phocis' favor this time and Diodorus noted (16.56.2) that their foes "lost many men" (maybe 100 or more at 10–12 percent). This exchange of small victories was followed by another raid by the Boeotians, who reacted to the loss of several towns by marching into Phocis and destroying grain fields. The Phocians again responded by mounting a pursuit that caught the raiding force on its way home. The resulting battle probably was much like the summer's earlier actions in size, involving less than 2,000 hoplites on either side with proportional light-armed support. Phocian arms gained yet another small triumph in this engagement that let them pay back their foe's spoiling of crops by killing maybe 5–10 percent at but a small price to themselves (no more than 1–3 percent lost).

These border clashes had turned up the heat, and in 346 the Sacred War threatened to once more explode into a wider ranging conflict as Phocis appealed to Sparta and Athens while the Boeotians turned to Macedonia. The Spartans obliged by sending their king Archidamus with 1,000 men (seemingly a mora of citizen hoplites on this occasion) and the Athenians provided a fleet of 50 well-manned ships. Philip trumped this aid by then marching south with a large army. Phocis' Phalaeccus had some 8,000 hired spearmen to go along with his allied forces in opposition, but still felt that he was no match for the Macedonians. He therefore negotiated a settlement that let him retire with his mercenaries to the Peloponnese (some of these hirelings would attach themselves to Archidamus a few years later and campaign with him on behalf of Taras in southern Italy, where the Spartan fell in a skirmish at Manduria in 338.) Phocis was now left with neither warlord nor army and surrendered to Philip, bringing an end at last to the Third Sacred War after ten long and bloody years.

Phoenicia and Egypt

Persia's Artaxerxes III had failed in a campaign against Egypt in 351 and was not able to mount another effort to regain that highly prized holding until the mid-340s. At that time, he began gathering troops and caching supplies for a truly massive expedition. However, he suffered an annoying setback in these preparations when the Phoenicians suddenly revolted in 345.

Sidon (345 B.C.)

The satraps Belesys of Syria and Mazaeus of Cilicia were first to respond to the uprising in Phoenicia, moving against the rebel center at Sidon in hopes of quickly resolving the situation. Their army's makeup is extremely speculative, but might have consisted of royal units on hold in their provinces pending the march on Egypt. These likely would have been two infantry divisions plus two regiments of cavalry with supporting light footmen. At 80 percent nominal strength, such an armament would have had some 16,000 kardakes and 1,600 riders backed by a force of peltasts.

The Phoenicians added hired fighters to their citizen soldiers and asked for aid from Egypt. That ally sent 4,000 hoplites under a Rhodian named Mentor (Diodorus 16.42.2). Perhaps fielding a Persian styled division of native heavy footmen (similar to hoplites, but with dual-purpose spears) beside a force of locally subscribed mercenaries to equal those obtained from Egypt, the insurgency could more than match the invading satraps. No account survives, but had all filed at a depth of ten, the armies would have spread their heavy units across 1,600m or so with cavalry and skirmishers off the wings. After engaging, Mentor and his men (probably on the far right) are likely to have rapidly broken their immediate foes, thus carrying the fight before any enemy mounted advantage could affect the outcome. Losses were no doubt quite light for the rebels (1–2 percent) and modest (3–6 percent) for even the losers in that they should have had a strong light-armed screen for their withdrawal. As it turned out, this action didn't achieve a lasting effect due to Mentor and his troops switching sides once the Persian monarch arrived with his whole host. Their defection set off a round of surrender that swiftly ended the rebellion and freed Artaxerxes to head on to Egypt.

Pelusium and Nile West Bank (344 B.C.)

The Persians reached the Nile after a difficult march and invested the fortress of Pelusium. Diodorus gives some overblown numbers for native elements of their army (16.40.6); however, these are more likely to have been eight baivaraba of kardakes plus another of royal guards along with nine regiments of cavalry (one a guards unit) and screening light infantry. Prior to any losses on the march, this provided something like 74,000 kardakes, 7,400 riders and as many as 16,000 foot skirmishers. Adding to these were a number of Greek contingents. Three of them were allied (Diodorus 16.43.2–4): 1,000 Theban spearmen under Lacrates, 3,000 hoplites from Argos under Nicostratus and 6,000 Ionian spearmen from various cities. Also on hand was Mentor, the traitor at Sidon, who brought his band of around 3,000 hoplites. This yielded more than 100,000 combatants in an army larger than any seen since the invasion of Greece in 480.

Huge as the Persian host was, the Egyptian king Nectanebos (Nekht-har-hebi) had gathered a counter force of nearly equal magnitude (Diodorus 16.47.5–6). This included 20,000 Grecian mercenaries (perhaps 80 percent hoplites), nearly 20,000 Libyans (mostly Carthaginian-style heavy footmen) and six divisions of Egyptians with spears and large shields (60,000 men nominal, but perhaps more like 48,000 actual) from the caste known as "The Warriors." These troops held post within a number of strong points that guarded entrances to the Nile and other key sites. At Pelusium, 5,000 Greeks (likely 4,000 spearmen and 1,000 in light infantry) under the spartiate Philophron formed the garrison's backbone. And it was these hired men that drew first blood when Lacrates' Thebans, camped close to the city's walls and, eager to display their skills, recklessly made an unsupported late day attempt on the fortress. Maybe 1,000 hoplites defending that portion of the walls sallied to engage the men from Thebes. Diodorus claimed (16.46.9) that these bitter rivals battled severely, with the fight coming to an inconclusive end only with the fall of night.

Artaxerxes broke his Greeks into three teams the next day. He let them keep their own generals, but paired one of his own men with each so as to prevent any more adventurism like that of Lacrates and his band. The rash Thebans and 4,000 Ionians comprised one group, Mentor and his contingent another and the troops from Argos along with the rest of the Ionians made up the third. It was this last unit that shortly afterwards fought the campaign's pivotal engagement. This came after Nicostratus carried his men on 80 triremes through a canal to land and set up camp in a secluded district on the western side of the Nile. Unknown to him, the local mercenary chief, Cleinius the Coan, had this area under watch. Moving quickly, Cleinius attacked with at least 7,000 soldiers, possibly 5,000–6,000 hoplites with light infantry support. Undoubtedly posting large numbers of armed rowers on his flanks, Nicostratus formed up his 5,000 spearmen into phalanx formation and closed for a combat that saw his men earn a brilliant and crushing victory. Diodorus' figure of over 70 percent lost among those defeated (16.48.5) seems too high; still, it at least indicates that the losses were exceptional. The best explanation for such a lopsided result is a double envelopment. Aided by an overwhelming edge in light-armed troops off the wings (the triremes could supply many thousands of skirmishers), Mentor's Argives probably folded in from either side to slaughter Cleinius and a startling number (maybe 30–60 percent) of his men.

Though Nectanebos' losses were to date far from crippling, he appears to have fallen into a profound funk. Ignoring his Greek military advisors, he retired to Memphis. His ensuing inactivity then led to one city after another falling to the Great King. Finally, Nectanebos accepted that his situation was hopeless and fled into Ethiopia as Artaxerxes reclaimed all of Egypt.

Timoleon's Campaigns on Sicily

Dionysius II was still holding onto power in Syracuse in his second tour as the city's despot; however, pressure had been building to once more overthrow his rule. Working with the tyrant Hicetas of Leontini, a group of Syracusans went to their mother city of Corinth for help. The Corinthians agreed to limited aid and sent out 700 soldiers (men who had served Phocis in the Third Sacred War [Parke 1933, 170; Trundle 2004, 70]) under Timoleon. In his mid-60s at the time, this still hardy and energetic soldier had quite a reputation for hating tyrants, having been involved in the killing of a brother accused of plotting dictatorship.

Syracuse/Leontini (344 B.C.)

Hicetas had not stood idle during the discussions in Corinth, moving to invest Syracuse with an army perhaps approaching 10,000 strong. This was "a large force" per Diodorus (16.68.1), who was to later characterize 5,000 troops gathered at Adranum as being only the tyrant's "best soldiers" (16.68.9). On the upside, we might suspect 6,000–8,000 hoplites with 1,500–2,000 foot skirmishers and a few hundred horsemen. When this effort stalled after running low on supplies, Hicetas broke off and headed back to Leontini. Dionysius mounted a hot pursuit with a force that was probably not much smaller or he wouldn't have exposed it. As such, he may have had 6,000–6,500 spearmen and 1,000–1,500 light infantry plus some cavalry. But disaster was to befall the Syracusan despot as he overtook and struck at the rear of the retreating column. Without warning, his prey put about, formed a phalanx and counter-attacked to deadly effect. The Leontines promptly routed what must have been a shocked and unready opposing array, pursuing to bring down 3,000 among its broken remnants (Diodorus 16.68.3). Having lost perhaps 40 percent of his army, Dionysius could no longer offer an active threat and holed up on Ortygia while Hicetas overran the rest of Syracuse.

It now became clear that the Leontine tyrant meant to claim Syracuse on his own behalf and had for some time been secretly conspiring with Carthage toward that end (Plutarch Vol. I *Timoleon*, 330). With Dionysius shut in on Ortygia, he sent word to Timoleon (who had reached Rhegion three days after the fall of Syracuse) that he should turn back as there was no longer any need for his help. At the same time, a Carthaginian fleet arrived to bar the Corinthian's way. But Timoleon was able to slip past the blockade and make landfall on Sicily at Taruomenium. Meanwhile, Hicetas was operating against Adranum (Hadranum), which had rejected his rule. Sensing an opportunity for a surprise attack, Timoleon gathered up his Corinthian spearmen, added 300 hoplites from Taruomenium along with some foot skirmishers plus a few horsemen and set out for the siege site. Arriving undetected, he found Hicetas with 5,000 men encamped before the city. The Corinthian and his small force hit while their foes were at dinner; capturing the camp, they killed more than 300 men and took about 600 more as prisoners (Plutarch Vol. I *Timoleon*, 334)..

Before the dust had settled on this success, Timoleon marched with all possible speed to Syracuse. He was thus able to seize half of that city before those bested at Adranum could reach home and give warning. This left Syracuse cut in three pieces, with Timoleon holding the southern boroughs, Hicetas in control of Achradina on the northeast plus Epipolae to the northwest and Dionysius still in place on Ortygia. Further complicating matters, a Punic fleet then sailed into the Great Harbor. Yet the situation was to turn in a flash, as Corinth sent more assistance (2,000 hoplites and 200 horsemen), local allies began flocking to Timoleon's cause and the Carthaginians, only reluctantly committed and suspicious of Hicetas, went home. Dionysius then went into exile for the final time and Hicetas, left with little support, fell back upon Leontini. Timoleon was now master of all Syracuse, where he set up a fairly inclusive, moderate oligarchy (Hornblower and Spawforth 1996, 1464, 1528; R.J.A Talbert in Tritle 1997, 155) and began restoring the city's depleted population.

Crimisus River (341 B.C.)

Timoleon continued to war with Hicetas and other tyrants in Sicily's Grecian east and became strapped for funds with which to pay his mercenaries. Launching a raid on Carthaginian holdings in the western corner of the triangular island, he restored Entella from Punic control and made away with a good deal of loot. Timoleon was thus able to put his hired troops on long term contract, but reaped considerable trouble for this affront when the Carthaginians retaliated. Their punitive campaign most probably came in the summer of 341, though alternative dates as late as 339 have been proposed.

The generals Hasdrubal and Hamilcar landed at Lilybaeum in westernmost Sicily with what Nepos called "a huge force" (22.2.4). Diodorus (16.77.4) and Plutarch (Vol. I *Timoleon*, 345) gave them 70,000 men (with Timaeus their likely common source) and Polyaenus 50,000 (5.12.3). However, overblown Greek claims for barbarian hosts are the norm and seem certain here. Plutarch's comment (and the implication of Diodorus) that the Punic foot soldiers came on a fleet of 200 oared ships with horses and other gear traveling aboard sail-driven transports sounds a much more realistic note and allows for a reasonable calculation of manpower. The

Punic galleys cited in our sources were undoubtedly triremes. Though larger vessels had been introduced by the early 4th century, these were generally reserved for specialized tasks and were maintained in only very small numbers until Hellenistic times. Thus the trireme, which was more versatile as well as cheaper to build and run, remained the standard warship (Rodgers 1937, 203, 212). The trireme's carrying capacity was, in fact, only some 150 soldiers at most. This called for boosting its regular top load of 40 by replacing 110 rowers in two of its tiers of oars with passengers, thus relying on only a single tier for propulsion. As such, 200 of these vessels could have carried no more than 30,000 troops. Sabin (2007, 163) has proposed the same upside for this armament using a different set of criteria, while Warmington (1960, 46) likewise came up with an identical strength for the Punic host that sailed to Sicily in 480 by means of a similar 200-trireme fleet. Interestingly, these figures also nearly match Diodorus' toll of the expedition's losses (16.80.5). He pegged these at 27,500, possibly repeating a tradition on total manpower rather than just those who died and fell prisoner.

Common mixes of troop types indicate that the Carthaginians might have had a rough 60/40 ratio of heavy to light infantry with at least 3,000 riders (equal to 10 percent of their footmen). Hoplite-style shock fighters cored the infantry. These probably were divisions with nominal strengths of 3,000 and counted full citizens (an elite division known among the Greeks as The Sacred Band), Liby-Phoenician perioeci (two divisions) and Libyan mercenaries (three divisions). Mounted troops included both conventional cavalry as well as three-man driver/archer teams. These latter rode on four-horse chariots, possibly 200 of them per Diodorus' claim for captured rigs. The lighter infantry consisted of hired Iberians, Celts, Italian Gauls and Numidians as well as teams attached to the chariot corps.

Timoleon met this menace by first calling upon his Syracusans, but got a pitiful turnout of only 3,000 hoplites. Fortunately for him, Sicilian allies stepped up to fill the gap with another 5,000 spearmen. And in a shocking sign of how dire things were looking, Timoleon's foe Hicetas chipped in to bring the Corinthian's hired hoplites up to 4,000 strong. Adding 1,000 horsemen and maybe 3,000–4,000 foot skirmishers, Timoleon set out to preempt the enemy by meeting them in their own territory. He had a setback in route when a thousand of his mercenaries deserted, yet was still able to approach the Punic army without being seen. Cresting a hill in a pre-storm mist that helped hide his presence, Timoleon saw the enemy host to the west on the other side of a ford along the Crimisus River. The Carthaginians now handed Timoleon a great tactical gift. Dividing their forces by divisions, they began to wade through the water right below his position, setting events in play that would lead to a grand engagement put down in some detail by both Diodorus (16.80.1–5) and Plutarch (Vol. I *Timoleon*, 345–348).

First across the river were the chariots with their squads of foot skirmishers. Next came the best heavy infantry, consisting of the Sacred Band and the Liby-Phoenicians. At this point, there were something like 10,000 troops on the eastern bank of the Crimisus. (Note that Diodorus put the Sacred Band at 2,500 to fit this calculation in round numbers; however, Plutarch listed 3,000 citizens [presumably the Sacred Band] among his casualties for a better match with what seems to have been the normal establishment for a Punic division. The difference is fairly small, but remains worth marking, as the lesser figure might account for a sub-unit of bodyguards initially posted with the expedition's leadership.) Seeing a chance to take on just half of the enemy's heavy footmen and but a third of their total manpower, Timoleon struck with dispatch, sending his cavalry on ahead as he followed with the infantry.

A fierce mounted action opened on the east side of the Crimisus. Timoleon's horsemen darted in and out against the charioteers, who cycled back and forth in front of their foot soldiers as these formed up for battle. The Greek riders couldn't break past the opposing machines and wheeled away on command to turn instead against the flanks of the Carthaginian infantry. As the chariots drew off in pursuit, Timoleon and his phalanx of 11,000 hoplites closed into shock contact with the Punic heavy array, which stood fully formed along the river with the Sacred Band in its accustomed slot on the right (Diodorus 20.10.6). The Greeks were likely filed at eight shields with Timoleon and 1,000 of the most capable of his mercenaries rightmost, the other 3,000 hired spearmen next left and then 1,000 of the best allied Sicilian hoplites completing that wing. The Syracusans held the center with the remaining allies on the left wing. Their foes stood somewhat thinner. Plutarch's account says that the Sacred Band had a front of 400 men, indicating a depth of seven to eight at most (if 3,000 strong), but maybe only six (if only numbering 2,500).

Whatever the formation mechanics might have been, Timoleon and his men held a strong hand going against troops caught by surprise and psychologically unprepared for combat. Adding to this and their small advantage in numbers was the weather. It seems that the storm that had been pending finally broke from the east over the battlefield, providing a wild display of lightening and driving sheets of rain and hail into the faces of the Carthaginians. Nearly blinded, being bested in front and perhaps suffering from cavalry on the flanks, the Punic phalanx "shattered at first onset" in the words of Diodorus. The resulting slaughter was intense as the Greeks drove their broken enemies into the river. The rest of the Punic host was meantime struggling to cross and join the fight. This was to prove an impossible task.

Moving to the river's edge, Timoleon's men played havoc with their foes as they tried to scramble up and engage. Plutarch's often anachronistic retelling makes much of their heavier armor and drenched clothing in explaining the Carthaginians' problems. Yet both their burden of gear (for the Libyans and, perhaps, a last detachment of the Sacred Band) and soaked garments would have been no worse than for the Greeks. In fact, it's much more likely that the real culprit was a bane familiar to attacking armies from time immemorial — mud. Clay-rich soil turned to paste and destroyed footing as a dense downpour saturated the riverbank. With their enemy suffering on even the slightest slope, Timoleon's hoplites had a field day as they thrust spears into anyone overcoming gravity and bad traction to top the bank. Occasionally they dealt a wound or even death, but always sent their foes sliding back into companions still struggling in the wet and slime below. Whether cut down in action or drowned in the rising flood, the Africans died in great numbers (10,000 per Plutarch and 12,500 in Diodorus' estimate). Timoleon's forces laid claim to a total victory in the end as the Punic survivors drew back across the Crimisus and retreated all the way to Lilybaeum. Shortly thereafter, Carthage brought its battered army home, having neither punished the Greeks nor taken so much as a hectare of their land.

Hierae (c. 339 B.C.) and Damyrias and Abolus Rivers (338 B.C.)

Timoleon's campaign against tyranny on Sicily had great success, but endured some tough moments in its early stages. During this period, he was sending out mercenary troops in small bands that they might support various operations in Syracuse's interest. An account by Plutarch (Vol. I *Timoleon*, 149) relates how such efforts sometimes met with failure and gives some details on what might have been the most costly of these at Hierae in the territory of Messana in the island's northeastern corner. A 400-man lochos of hired hoplites under Euthymus of Leucadia met its doom here in an ambush, said by Plutarch to have been sprung by another group of Greek mercenaries, these being in Carthaginian pay. Caught out of order, the Leucadian and his men were apparently surrounded and wiped out entirely by a force that might have outnumbered them by two or three to one.

Timoleon moved in 338 against allies of Hicetas at Calauria to the northeast of Syracuse. No sooner had he done this than the Leontine tyrant descended to raid into Syracusan territory with an army that might have had 4,000 spearmen and 1,000 skirmishers plus horsemen. Seemingly contemptuous of his aged opponent, Hicetas returned from this foray by a route that passed near Timoleon's position. This was a fatal mistake. Timoleon watched the raiders go by and then followed with a contingent of cavalry and light footmen in the lead. Aware of these on his tail, Hicetas crossed the Damyrias River and set up in a phalanx likely eight-deep along the steep far bank to receive the Corinthian's men. Timoleon and his hoplites (perhaps around 3,000 strong) caught up with their vanguard and deployed to ford and engage in files of probably no more than six.

With the terrain in his favor, Hicetas must have been quite confident. But that doesn't appear to have been the case with his soldiers, who seemingly lacked the kind of intense fervor for battle that was manifest among their foes across the river. Eager to get at the opposition, Timoleon's thinly arrayed troops charged with such élan that they overcame the waterway's sharp rise and its hesitant defenders in a single rush. Probably broken more by fear than steel, Hicetas men threw down their arms and fled. The initial clash and subsequent pursuit took the lives of 1,000 (20 percent) among the losers (Plutarch Vol. I *Timoleon*, 350) and broke their will for good. Timoleon was thus soon after able to capture Hicetas with his entire family. Duly executing all of these, the people of Syracuse put paid at last to their longest running Greek enemy.

Timoleon followed up his destruction of Hicetas with a victory near the Abolas River. This came against Mamercus, despot of Catana, in an action that perhaps featured 6,000–10,000 combatants on either side. The Syracusans most likely took advantage of superior cavalry and light infantry to execute an envelopment and hard chase that slaughtered some 3,000 (30–50 percent) of the tyrant's men (Plutarch Vol. I *Timoleon*, 351). Most of these casualties were Greek mercenaries provided by Carthage and this disaster soured its taste for further Sicilian adventures. The Carthaginians therefore made peace with Syracuse, promising not to stray beyond their old limits in the west.

The Fourth Sacred War: Greece Falls

The late 340s saw Philip's forces engage a wide variety of foes all across the northern span of his realm. We're told by Justin (8.6.3) that he reorganized his homeland at this time, shifting entire communities into frontier areas that he might better guard his borders. He would accompany these internal moves with a series of campaigns against the regions past those boundaries. These expeditions had the aim of not only further securing his kingdom, but were also meant to gain sway over large new populations. Philip would move some elements of the subjected people inside Macedonia so as to refill recently emptied sectors with fresh reservoirs of manpower. Others would remain in place, but with an obligation to provide allied reserves and auxiliaries. Either way, Philip was set on growing his military strength with an eye to pushing his conquests farther into Greece and beyond.

Ardiaea (345 B.C.), Odrysia II and III (341 B.C.) and Strymon Valley (340 B.C.)

Philip's opening border campaign in this period was against the last Illyrians still eluding his control. These were the Ardiaei, a tribal group living within the Adriatic coastal region near the Rhizon Gulf in what today is northern Albania. The king marched a "large army" (Diodorus 16.69.7) into Ardiaea (perhaps resembling that employed against the Chalcidice in 348) and bested the tribesmen and their leader Pleuratus in a set battle. We know little about this engagement, but it was probably much like the actions at Lyncus Plain (358) and Grabaea (356). This time, however, the Macedonians would have had superior manpower with at least twice their opponents' strength in heavy infantry. Philip therefore likely used his deeper array to break the Illyrian left wing and initiate a rout. The primary shock fight was surely brief and decisive in favor of Philip's side, yet took at least a small toll in that we hear of the king receiving a broken right collarbone that led Isocrates to chide him for taking needless risks in combat (Worthington 2008, 108–109). And what looks to have been an extended pursuit claimed a price as well. It seems that some 150 of the hetairoi took wounds in this chase (Hammond [1994, 117] from Didymus). Damage of better than 10 percent suggests that these chosen riders suffered 30 or so fatalities. In the end, the Ardiaei bowed to Philip and a good many must have added to other tribal men and boys transplanted into Macedon as a future source of hardy spearmen (Polyaenus 4.2.12).

The next round of fighting began three years later when Philip invaded the farther interior of Thrace. The Odrysians there under Cersobleptes and Teres had attacked neighboring Greeks, which gave Philip all the leave needed to take action. He did this with a host much larger than that fielded only a decade earlier. Absorbed peoples and relocated captives had joined good times under Philip's rule to give him a population fit for doubling his native pool of soldiers, and he had the means to add a lot of mercenaries as well. Most of this newfound strength now came down on Odrysia as Philip led out an infantry force 30,000 strong (probably some 5,000 hypaspists, 15,000 phalangites, 5,000 hired/allied hoplites and 5,000 foot skirmishers) as well as both companion and light (Thessalian and/or mercenary) horsemen. All we really have on the combats that followed is Diodorus' note that the Macedonian king "overcame the Thracians in several battles" (16.71.2). What seems likely is that most of these actions were small, but events peaked in 341 with two major engagements. The first involved Cersobleptes, who had lost to Philip at Crenides (356) and surely realized that he had even less chance this time around. Indeed, only extreme desperation could have led him to abandon holding actions and finally risk open battle. With no greater manpower than he had at Crenides, the Thracian's defeat was inevitable and must have come with a long pursuit and severe losses. Teres and his tribesmen would shortly fare no better under almost identical circumstances, leaving Philip clear to reduce a last few remaining hilltop fortifications and claim the entire Odrysian realm by 340.

Secure throughout the north, Philip now decided to bring to a head his long-running duel with Athens for leadership among the Greeks. He therefore went after Athens' allies in the Hellespont, investing Byzantium, Perinthus and Selymbia as a gross provocation. So great was his manpower at this stage that Parmenio and Antipater as well as his son Alexander could operate separate columns at the same time that the sieges were ongoing. We've no details on these forays, but they must have been of modest size. It seems most probable that each campaign involved columns of 5,000 heavy footmen (2,000 hypaspists and mercenary hoplites plus 3,000 phalangites) backed by cavalry and light infantry. While Parmenio and Antipater led splits from Philip's main force, the prince had troops left at home for just such an eventuality. It was this latter, reserve element that seems to have fought the only significant combat, defeating the Paeonian Maedi in the Strymon Valley above Amphipolis. Alexander was still in his teens, but seems to have done well in this first battlefield test, no doubt with aid from senior officers assigned by the king to provide oversight. Lacking particulars, we might assume that this victory bore strong likeness to that of Philip over the Paeonians in 358. The only real difference would have been one of scale, with the father having faced a multi-tribe effort maybe half again to twice as large.

Dobruja Plain and Hister Valley (339 B.C.)

Philip's investments in the northeast dragged on into 339 without success, and when Athens and some of the Persian satraps sent aid to those besieged he made terms and withdrew. Before doing this, however, he took another bold step against the Athenians by seizing their annual grain shipment as it sailed south from what is today the Ukraine. Destroying all the Athenian ships while letting the rest go, Philip caused a food shortage that drove hostility toward Macedonia to high pitch in Athens. He then turned northward on the way home to attack Atheas, the Scythian king whose lands lay immediately above Odrysia. That geriatric monarch (said to be 90) not only posed a threat to the recent Odrysian conquests, but had also reneged on sending supplies in support of the Macedonian siege efforts. Marching into Scythia, Philip fought an action on the Dobruja Plain along the west side of the Black Sea.

The Scythians were mounted archers, who normally avoided shock fighting. Their favored approach was to either perform repeated charges and retreats against foes with a fixed flank or make a running assault that circled around and fired flights of arrows into troops exposed on open ground. We can deduce what happened from a probable misreport by Frontinus (confusing infantry for cavalry [2.8.14] as per Hammond [1994, 136]) and likely similar tactics used by Alexander against the Scythians a decade later (derived from Arrian [4.4.6–7]). Philip had his phalanx (perhaps partially anchored) form a bulwark at the rear while his cavalry and light footmen advanced in mixed order. This kept the Scythians from surrounding his mobile vanguard for fear of being pinched between that and the spears and pikes behind. At the same time, his riders and skirmishers, their rear now well protected, dashed out to turn back every enemy charge at the front. With their tactics frustrated, being out-ranged by the Macedonian peltasts, slingers and archers and with no screening infantry of their own, the Scythians took a sound beating to yield both the field and their dominion to Philip after Atheas fell during the course of the fight.

Philip gathered booty from his Scythian triumph and headed home. He moved up the Hister (Danube) Valley with the intent of entering Macedonia from the north by passing through the territory of the Triballi. These were notoriously fierce and unruly people so influenced by neighboring Scythians and Illyrians that they were almost distinct from their fellow Thracians (Webber 2001, 10). The Triballi demanded a share of Philip's loot in return for a peaceful transit of their land and attacked when he refused. Possibly repeating schemes employed in Scythia, the king charged out on horseback with his cavalry and light footmen to engage riders leading the enemy attack. The Triballi fell back before this onslaught to cover behind their infantry, especially those men wielding a long spear ('sarissa' in Macedonian parlance). One of these lengthy weapons took Philip in the thigh, passing through so deeply as to kill his mount (Justin 9.3.2). Seeing their king go down, many thought him dead, leading to disorder among the Macedonians. The Triballi took advantage to make off with most of Philip's hard-won goods before he was able to rally his men for an orderly retreat. He did this by having the rear ranks of his phalanx stand fast with weapons deployed while the rest of the army drew back behind them, the rearguard then joining their comrades to clear the field with minimal loss (Polyaenus 4.2.13). (This may be similar to the tactics employed in 368 by Epaminondas along the road from Pherae.) Philip thus escaped with his army intact and returned home, but having a permanent limp to mark his third (and last) battlefield defeat — the only one he would ever suffer against a barbarian foe.

Chaeronea (338 B.C.)

While Philip was in the final stages of his operation in Thrace, problems were once again arising with regard to fields near Delphi. In a repeat of the sort of dispute that had sparked the

Third Sacred War, the Ozolian Locrians of Amphissa stood accused of using land set aside for the shrine. The Macedonians and their allies in the Amphictyony voted in the winter of 340/39 to declare against the Locrians, thus igniting the Fourth Sacred War. This gave Philip authority to act against Locris and its chief supporter Athens. The Athenians for their part had already set aside an existing peace with Macedonia in outrage over the attacks on their allies and the grain fleet. Philip, whose leg had healed somewhat, marched into Phocis late in the fall of 339 to threaten not only Amphissa, but Thebes and Athens as well. At this juncture, he offered a choice of submitting to his hegemony or facing attack. The decision was to fight. Since Philip's troops were recovering from their last campaign and he was still not fully fit, the king withdrew to ready a major effort. In the meantime, he sent small detachments to wage a guerilla war along the Cephissus Valley in Phocis and Boeotia.

Philip set out in force late the next summer. The national army was now roughly triple what it had been upon the reunification that followed his victory at Lyncus Plain in 358. The phalanx stood 24,000 strong with the backing of perhaps 2,400 hetairoi (one per ten heavy footmen in a dozen 200-horse squadrons) plus 3,000–4,000 light infantrymen. This count of line troops matches that for 334 given by Diodorus (17.17.3–5) and likely represents 6,000 hypaspists and 18,000 phalangites in the same 1 to 3 ratio detailed by the historian for Alexander's expeditionary force. (Note that a popular view, see Hammond [1994, 150] for example, has been to cap the hypaspists at 3,000 in 334 and send all of them against Persia, filling the rest of the heavy corps with 21,000 phalangites. This appears less likely in that it ignores clear tactical needs for the army left in Macedonia and is out of step with documented expansion in every other part of the Macedonian military.) As for the host Philip had in tow for this particular campaign, it must have included the entire national phalanx plus some 6,000 hired hoplites. But his shock cavalry doesn't appear to have been at full strength, maybe amounting to a third or so of the hetairoi. Thessalian light horsemen (presumably the "laggard confederates" mentioned by Diodorus [16.85.5]) made up the difference, bringing the king's mounted contingent up to 2,000 in all. Several thousand foot skirmishers must have been present as well to push his infantry above 30,000.

A modest coalition of Greeks prepared to meet the invasion, gathering near the western Boeotian city of Chaeronea on Philip's projected route along the Cephissus River. The allies had around 28,000 hoplites, maybe 2,000 horsemen and up to 7,000 in light infantry for 35,000 foot troops in all. Their spearmen came from Athens and Boeotia (10,000 apiece) with another 2,000 each from Corinth, Megara and (per Hammond 1994, 148) the mercenary ranks. There were also troops from a number of other poleis representing Euboa, Achaea, Leucas, Corcyra and Acarnania. These lesser levies totaled an additional 2,000 spearmen. Athenians and Boeotians made up the cavalry for the most part and were of good quality. Diodorus said that Philip outnumbered this allied muster (16.85.6), which appears marginally true of the heavy infantry. Yet, Justin's claim (9.3.9) of greater manpower among the allies looks slightly more accurate overall. In truth, the opposing forces were so close in size that confusion as to their relative strength is not surprising.

As Philip's army drew near on the morning of September 1st, the Greeks set up across his path in combat formation within the valley of the Cephissus. The allied line faced northwest and stretched from an anchor along the marshy bank of the river on the northeast to the other side of the plain, where that flank was equally fixed against a slope leading up to the acropolis of Chaeronea. The phalanx covered a front of some 2.3km with its hoplites standing in twelve-man files. The Athenians took the left wing, having the lesser allies alongside with the hired men to complete the array through center. On the other wing were the Boeotians with the hoplites from Thebes rightmost and their 300 elites of the Sacred Band at the very end. Since

132 III. Finding a Master

both flanks of this phalanx abutted terrain barriers, part of the light-armed men spread into the hills to the southwest. The rest moved across the Cephissus, where their cavalry sat to block any attempt at a wide envelopment around that side of the valley.

Seeing this arrangement, Philip set up in phalanx as well, taking post with his hypaspists on the right, placing the mercenary spearmen next left and with his pikemen on the far wing under the leadership of the young Alexander. The Macedonian line would have matched the enemy front by filing its hypaspists twelve-deep, the other hoplites at ten to twelve and the phalangites at their usual depth of ten. (Note that files of eight for both hoplites and hypaspists could have achieved the same frontage had the latter been only 3,000 strong.) With the ends of their heavy formation anchored on the same topography as the Greeks, Philip's cavalry and its screen of footmen crossed the river to engage their opposite numbers while the remaining skirmishers moved against the Greek light infantry scattered over the uplands.

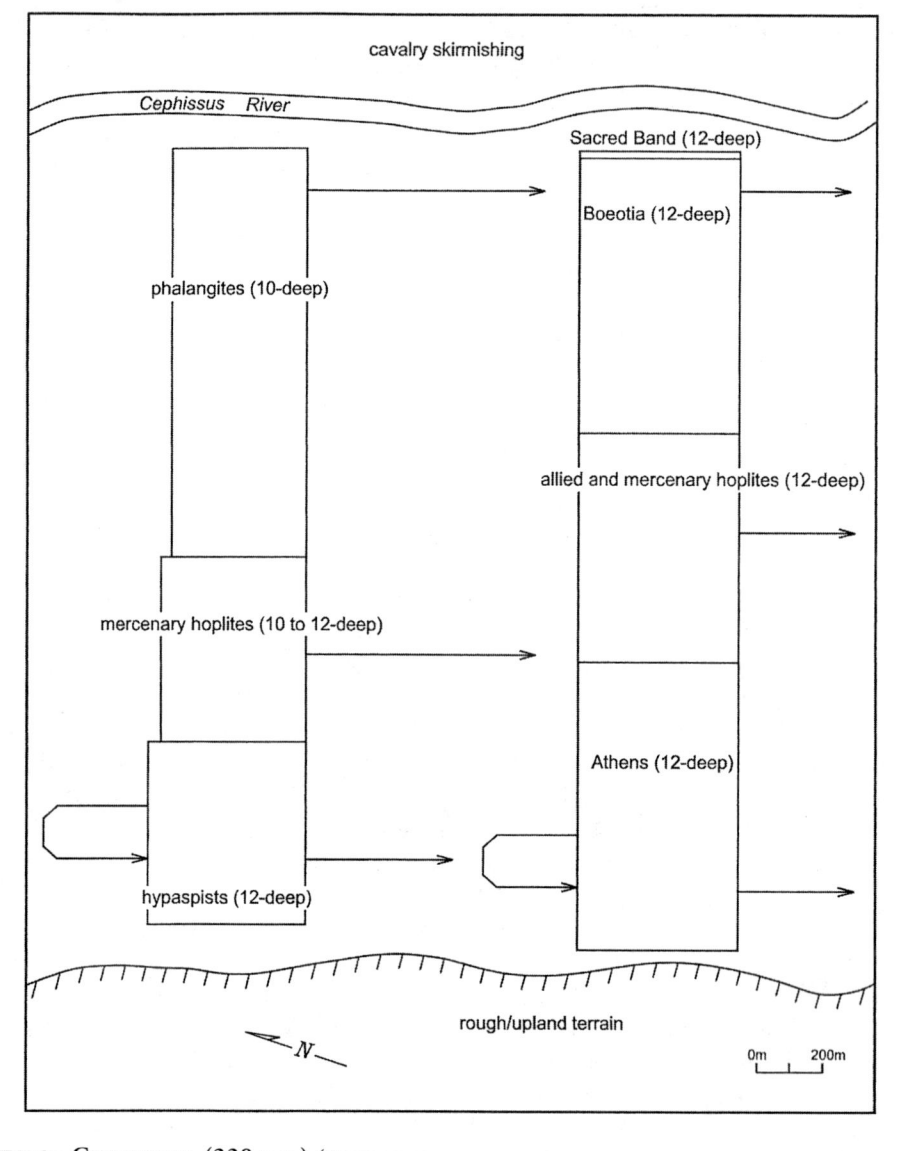

BATTLE OF CHAERONEA (338 B.C.) (BOXES REPRESENTING FORCES ARE EXAGGERATED TO SHOW RELATIVE SIZES.)

Philip's troops advanced in good order to initiate a hard-fought shock action that raged across the valley floor for quite a while. The Boeotians and their mercenary comrades found themselves stymied on the northeast side of the field by the long pikes of the Macedonian phalangite array as they tried to push in tight and ply their shorter weapons. Yet some of the hoplites did manage to penetrate and deliver fatal strikes. This is attested by the remains of pikemen that have been found interred nearby and there can be no doubt that, once inside the pike front, a hoplite's shield and spear were superior for close combat, letting him lance down lightly protected foes whose elongated pole-arms were now useless. All the same, such successes by the Greek fighters were way too few and far between to overcome the Macedonian formation. Meanwhile to the southwest, Philip's seasoned hypaspists were fairing no better in their attempt to push through or turn the Athenians opposing them. Stabbing with spears or shoving with their shields all along the front, the facing formations were equal in depth and desire; straining, sweating, bleeding and dying, neither side would give way. Nor were these the only stalemates on the day, as neither the skirmishing light infantry in the hills nor the cavalries and their fronting footmen across the river were any more decisive.

It was at this crucial moment that Philip gave a signal by horn for his hypaspists to draw back. Starting from the rearmost, each rank spun about in turn and calmly moved away, the leading row (now at the rear) edging backwards to swing at last and join an orderly retreat that was heading toward rising ground. The king's mercenary hoplites on the left of this withdrawal must have played an important role at this point, holding station as the hypaspists marched off, with the rightmost few files pivoting slightly to keep well-shielded while presenting spears cantered toward their now abandoned flank. Stunned, the Athenians facing this maneuver hesitated for a moment in surprise. Then, thinking the fight won, they gave shouts of triumph and, ignoring the mercenaries opposed to their right, moved out in a pursuit led by their general Stratocles. Perhaps a few of the more experienced, like those who had fought at Mantinea in 362, felt that something was wrong, but they had no hope of holding back the green crowd that dominated their ranks and were carried along as the Athenian array became jumbled in an increasingly enthusiastic chase. That's when Philip and his men reached higher terrain and a second signal blared out. With frightening precision, the finely drilled hypaspists once more swung around from rear rank to front, reversing direction to redress for a beat and then advance upon a third signal.

Caught out of formation in premature pursuit, the hoplites from Athens were broken and scattered by the well-ordered line of shields and spear-points that now smashed into them. A thousand Athenians (10 percent) died right there and 2,000 more would surrender as Philip and his hypaspists cleared that end of the allied line and folded around to envelop the remainder of the enemy left. This triggered a pulse of panic that surged along the Greek formation toward the northeast, tearing it apart contingent by contingent as weary men sensed the fight was lost and shed shields and weapons alike to flee lest their foes cut them off from behind. On the far end of this collapse, the Thebans, already battered in their efforts against Alexander and his pikemen, saw their fellow Boeotians bolt and ran as well — all but the Sacred Band. These picked troops fought to the bitter end, battling desperately as the phalangites closed about and broke into their ranks. Taking hits from every side, they died to the last man, with 254 being buried in a single mound near where they went down. Total casualties from the allied center and left wing were probably not quite as bad as those of the Athenians due to this concentration on the Sacred Band and a shorter chase overall; still, they likely ran well above 5 percent fatalities to mark a severe beating. Thus, the day closed on Philip standing thoroughly triumphant and poised to claim mastery over all of Greece.

Reflections on Chaeronea

Chaeronea is where the Greek city-states lost their independence and thus stands as a counterpoint to the Persian invasion of 480–479 when Grecian arms had preserved that same freedom. It's therefore a pity that we have no involved account such as those Herodotus left behind for the key engagements of that earlier conflict. This forces us to piece together events on the battlefield from an all too short and general description in Diodorus (16.85.2–86.6) and even briefer segments scattered throughout our other sources. Any resulting reconstruction is therefore unavoidably speculative and worthy of closer examination on some important points.

THE FALSE RETREAT • Diodorus' description of the battle gives major place to Alexander's exploits on the Macedonian left wing, placing his victory there ahead of that of Philip on the right. But this may better reflect the young hero's glorious later career than actual timing of events at Chaeronea. Chaeronea's own Plutarch, who commended the prince for breaking into the Sacred Band's ranks (Vol. II *Alexander*, 145), made no mention of where that feat came in sequence nor (tellingly in a tract otherwise lavish in praise) claim it as decisive. And, while Justin gave no credit either way, Strabo (9.2.37) mentioned only Philip with regard to Chaeronea and Frontinus' version (2.1.9) clearly grants the determining role to the king in a prolonged and grueling engagement. Most detailed and convincing of all is the description of Polyaenus (4.2.2,7). This shows Philip wearing his foes down in a long slug fest and then withdrawing in tight order until reaching elevated ground. At that moment, "turning around, he attacked the Athenians vigorously and, fighting brilliantly, he conquered." Here, as well as in Frontinus and Justin, there are signs that Athenian lack of experience helped Philip's ploy to succeed. As it turns out, this "false retreat" maneuver is a well documented hoplite tactic of old, lending much credence to Polyaenus' tale.

Herodotus cited several faux withdrawals at Thermopylae (480). Sparta's Leonidas and his men there "would turn their backs and feign flight all together" and, when the enemy finally caught up in disorder, they would "then suddenly turn around and face them, at which point they would slay countless numbers" (7.211). Similarly, Plato reported a dialogue between his old tutor Socrates and the general Laches (both veteran spearmen) that dealt with this tack (*Laches* 191 B-C). Socrates points out here that the Spartans at Plataea (479) "ran away," but when their foes broke ranks to pursue, "they turned and fought … and so won that particular battle." It thus seems highly likely that Philip used the same trick to disrupt and rout the Greek left wing, rolling around then to break apart the entire opposing phalanx. If so, it was only when flank support collapsed on their left that the Thebans faltered and their Sacred Band then fell prey to penetration from Alexander's pikemen.

CAVALRY ACTION • As a practical matter, anchoring of the phalanxes at Chaeronea against terrain barriers impassable for cavalry pretty much rules out any participation by Philip's horsemen along the edges of the battle. Nor did they launch an assault on the allied rear, as our sources (though they might differ on the critical wing being left or right) all insist that the decision came at the front (as per Justin 9.3.10). With regard to a direct mounted charge, Rahe makes the key point that horses will not initiate physical contact with a solid formation of infantry and says "it seems unlikely that the Macedonian cavalry played a decisive role in the struggle" (1981, 87). Given that any attempt at it would be intrinsically suicidal, we can thus fully discount the idea that riders could have broken an intact allied array through a frontal attack. Moreover, even had gaps appeared in the Greeks' phalanx, there would have been no way for horsemen to exploit them. This is because Philip's own heavy infantry was already engaged along the entire line, blocking all possible access to the front ranks.

Though Diodorus placed cavalry at the scene and archaeological evidence exists suggesting that it could have been involved in the fight (Rahe 1981, 86), there is nothing in our sources to indicate that cavalry in any way determined the outcome. Indeed, all references to combat appear to describe infantry actions. In this vein, Gaebel has looked at the various arguments on the topic of horsemen at Chaeronea (2002, 154–157) and concluded that "it is most likely that Alexander was in command of the infantry on the left wing and that the struggle was primarily one of infantry with cavalry in some subordinate but unknown role." This makes the old tale of Alexander shattering the Sacred Band by means of a gallant charge on horseback into a myth — a fiction that Plutarch should have squelched long ago with his note that the bodies of the Sacred Band lay opposite to the remains of sarissai left by the phalanx that killed them (Rahe 1981, 85). Adding this to what we know of the battlefield's topography, it's therefore probable that the riders and attached foot screens for both sides were confined to a sidebar duel across the Cephissus River. This skirmish was likely inconclusive and kept the Macedonian horsemen from all but the latest stages of the main action, in which they did some clean-up and pursuit after the Greeks gave way.

A NEAR-RUN THING • The foregoing reconstruction suggests that the fight at Chaeronea may well have turned under very tenuous circumstances, due just as much to Athenian error as Macedonian prowess. This finds independent support in evidence of contemporaries seeing it that way as well. Such a view has emerged from the discovery of fragments of a speech by Hyperides of Athens, who died in 322. Hanson (2008, 34–35) describes the orator's recently found statement that there was no inferiority in Greek strategy or prowess at Chaeronea and it was mere "chance" that handed Philip the victory. This is something in which Hanson believes Hyperides "might well have been right," going on to support that judgment with his own analysis from other sources. If so, this stands as an example of chance favoring the better prepared — those best able to adapt and make their own luck.

Philip dealt harshly with Thebes in the wake of his victory at Chaeronea, making the city pay an indemnity, stripping it of its Boeotian League and installing a narrow oligarchic ruling body supported by a Macedonian garrison. In short, the Thebans were reduced to a subservient state that was every bit as low as that to which they had sunk before throwing off the yoke of Sparta more than half a century earlier. Interestingly, it was their old Lacedaemonian enemy (which had been neutral in the Fourth Sacred War) that would now suffer next most. Seeking to reward his Peloponnesian allies and discourage this always threatening presence from rising to give him trouble in the future, the Macedonian king ravaged Spartan territory, driving the polis' influence inward until spanning little more than its traditional homeland.

Beyond Thebes and Sparta, Philip mostly kept direct interference at a minimum in favor of using more diplomatic measures of control. These included backing takeovers by local pro–Macedonian factions in places like Corinth, Megara and Acarnania. Most notably, he did not come down hard on Athens. That city was fully expecting to be besieged, but Philip chose to settle on favorable terms. Though he dismantled the Athenians' naval league, he allowed them to retain their democracy and fleet as well as sovereignty over certain island holdings. The reason for this gentle handling of a bitter foe of such long standing is to be found in the king's plans for the future. These included an invasion of Asia Minor for which Athens would prove a useful ally.

Tactical Discussion: 358–336 B.C.

Though Philip II had clearly been honing his new-style phalanx over a period of two decades prior to Chaeronea, that battle stands as the centerpiece of his efforts. It's therefore often touted as the decisive culmination of a major revolution in tactics — the new Macedonian phalanx over the old Greek/Doric one. Yet, what role did innovation really play at Chaeronea and in other Macedonian combats?

Philip's tactical advances had two major aspects: (1) substitution of pikemen for hoplites within at least a portion of the battle formation (a concept likely adapted from Iphicrates of Athens); and (2) the use of elite, shock-capable cavalry on the wings, especially the right. Since, as we've seen, horsemen played no significant role at Chaeronea, we can assess only the impact of Philip's infantry there. There's no doubt that his phalangites performed quite well on the left wing of his phalanx. The pike array carried out its mission of holding the best enemy spearmen in check as long as needed to ensure success; all the same, this was maybe no more than good quality hoplites might have done in the same place. The battle actually seems to have stalled before Philip and his hypaspists maneuvered on the other wing to bring about a decision. And in this, those old fashioned spearmen were executing a routine that dated back more than a century. In fact, both here and elsewhere, Philip's tactical approach to infantry combat was essentially an improved version of the old Spartan cyclosis maneuver. These methods were thus incremental and evolutionary advances rather than revolutionary changes to traditional phalanx warfare.

It was actually the coordinated use of shock cavalry in Philip's engagements prior to Chaeronea that seems the more profound tactical step. Greek armies had been steadily increasing and diversifying their use of horsemen during the 4th century and Philip was following that trend in kind. Yet he plied cavalry to effect with much greater frequency and it played a decisive role in a full 75 percent of his engagements after Methone. Moreover, bringing his nation's unique shock-oriented lancers into the process was something completely new. It seems that as substitutes for conventional, javelin-armed riders, his hetairoi would have upped attack potential most against opposition cavalry. This was because foot soldiers were more at hazard from mounted missilemen than lancers who had to get within reach to do any damage. However, chasing off screening riders was generally just what was needed to turn a flank, and horsemen armed with lighter javelins were at serious disadvantage once a heavy lancer could close into contact. Again, this was a sequential improvement. Traditional cavalry could turn a flank too (even for Philip, as his allied Thessalians did at Crocus Plan in 353) — it's simply that the hetairoi often did it better.

All the same, Philip's greatest contributions to the Grecian art of war might well have been in the areas of training and supply. He married a large and patriotic national army like that of Thebes with the concept of professional soldiering. And, unlike seasonal hires in the mercenary hosts of states like Phocis or Pherae, his native troops served full-time, allowing for exhaustive drill toward skilled execution of his own system of tactics. Going on to support these men with superior operational logistics, he then created an army not only capable of defeating any size or type of opponent, but one that could also go anywhere in his world to do so.

The foregoing makes it clear that Philip II of Macedonia stood far above his contemporaries. But was there *any* other figure in his era that could qualify as a significant shaper of the Greek way of war? It seems that the best candidate is a man much reviled in his lifetime and little known today — Onomarchos of Phocis. His career as a commanding general was brief (a mere two seasons) and encompassed only four battles, the last of which being a fatal defeat. Nonetheless, the Phocian warlord conquered both Philip and Thebes in the same year (353). And his victories over the Macedonian phalanx were not only very likely responsible for its later modification, but also introduced the Greek world to the concept of field artillery. This last was to have only limited impact during the 4th century (Alexander the Great employing the concept much less spectacularly on a couple of occasions), yet still remains a stroke of genius. (It also raises the question of just where his rock-throwing devices came from. Paul Bardunias [2011, personal communication] has intriguingly suggested that prototypes were among items "liberated" from Delphi. He points out that Iphicrates seized a quantity of catapult bolts along with some statues meant for that shrine aboard one of the Syracusan ships captured in 372 [Cole, 1981]. This is a good indication that Dionysius likely had dedicated gifts of the associated launchers as well.)

* * *

In 337, Philip created a nearly pan–Hellenic confederacy, the League of Corinth. This was to serve as a platform for confirming his control over Greece as its elected *hegemon* (leader). It would also provide drafts of manpower for his planned campaign into Asia. Philip formally proposed this as a grand League project to liberate the Ionian Greeks and punish Persia for past transgressions, though Worthington argues persuasively (2008, 168–169) that the prospect of looting Persian wealth might well have been the king's true primary motivation. With no known dissent, the League membership quickly agreed to mount this effort and duly appointed Philip as its commander. He sent an advance force to Ionia the next year to prepare the way. However, Philip fell to the dagger of an assassin that very summer, leaving both his empire and any prospects for an Asian war of conquest in the hands of his son, Alexander. Very young and facing the immense political turmoil created by so sudden and unexpected an ascension to the throne, that newly crowned king would rise to the occasion in legendary fashion.

IV. Action and Glory

Battles in the Era of Alexander the Great (335–324 B.C.)

"Whenever he heard Philip had taken any town of importance, or won any signal victory, instead of rejoicing at it altogether, he would tell his companions that his father would anticipate everything, and leave him with no opportunities to perform great and illustrious actions. For being more bent upon action and glory than either upon pleasure or riches, he esteemed all that he should receive from his father as a diminution and prevention of his own future achievements; and would have chosen rather to succeed to a kingdom involved in troubles and wars, which would have afforded him frequent exercise of his courage, and a large field of honor, than to one already flourishing and settled where his inheritance would be an inactive life, and the mere enjoyment of wealth and luxury."

Plutarch (Vol. II, *Alexander*, 140)

Alexander III began his reign at the age of 20. Such youth wasn't all that unusual for a successor in an era when disease could claim someone at any time and in a land where assassins or warfare always offered lethal threats. After all, Alexander's father had become king at only four years older following the murder of one brother and then the death of another in battle. What sets Alexander apart is not that he was successful from so early an age, but that his level of achievement was such that he gained far greater acclaim than his sire, a man who, after all, had become the first conqueror of Greece. Many a son had fallen well short of a famous father in the course of Greek history (Dionysius the Great and Dionysius II offered a prime recent example); however, Alexander was to shatter that pattern to such an extent that the title "Great" became his rather than Philip's. One might in all fairness argue as to whether father or son was actually the more skilled general, yet the overall scope of Alexander's accomplishments remains unparalleled.

European Campaigns

The death of Philip II in 336 set off a round of rebellion throughout his empire. The Athenians refused to recognize Alexander's rule, as did the Thebans and Thessalians. Garrisons were expelled from the Cadmea in Thebes and in Ambracia in northwest Greece. Elsewhere, Acarnania, Elis, Arcadia and Argos all broke away. Even beyond Greece proper there were problems. The tribesmen of Illyria to the west of Macedonia and the Thracians to the east had become restive and rumors were flying that Attalus, an officer in the force that Philip had sent to Asia Minor, was subverting his troops in an attempt on the throne. Alexander met these challenges quickly and effectively. He sent a team to assassinate Attalus and, leaving some troops behind to guard against any incursion from Illyria or Thrace, he marched out with the remainder of the Macedonian army to deal with matters in Greece.

The Thessalians were the closest of the Greek dissidents to hand and they tried to block the new monarch's entry into their land at the pass of Tempe. Alexander's victory there was bloodless. He outfoxed his foes by circling a portion of his army through the mountains to come out in their rear and, hopelessly outnumbered and facing threats now from both front and back, the Thessalians gave up. Their League declared for Alexander and went on to provide him with mounted troops. The young ruler continued southward into Boeotia, and as he then marched about on or near their soil, the other Greek states caved in quick succession rather than again face a Macedonian phalanx on the field of battle. (Note that Sparta had always been an exception in having never formally accepted Philip as hegemon. It would now retain that unique distinction by not bowing to Alexander either.) Alexander next called a meeting of the Corinthian League. This assembly confirmed him as his father's successor, both as leader of the League and as commander for the still pending expedition into Persia. Having thus solidified his position among the Grecian poleis, the new king turned north to deal with the upstart barbarian peoples in that direction.

Haemus Pass I, Lyginus River, Hister River (335 B.C.)

Alexander set out to subdue Thrace in spring 335. He first marched east along the coast from Amphipolis and then headed north toward the Hister (Danube) River. The size of his army isn't fully documented, but it might have had a third of the complete Macedonian muster, the rest being split among the men that Philip had sent to Asia under Parmenio and others left at home with Antipater to keep an eye on the Illyrians. If so, those from the national host that went with the king were likely 2,000 hypaspists and 6,000 phalangite pikemen plus 800 hetairoi with perhaps 300 recently formed and lighter-equipped horsemen. The latter were *sarissophoroi* or "lancers" also known as *prodromoi*, probably Thracians that had been absorbed into the Macedonian realm. We know that the cavalry was nearly 1,500 strong (as later seen across the Hister) and included riders from Amphipolis, thus there were probably almost 400 other mounted troops as well as allied and mercenary hoplites (perhaps 3,000–4,000 at eight to ten for each allied horseman). As for foot skirmishers, something like 4,000 appears reasonable. These consisted of men attached to the cavalry, around 1,600 excellent Agrianian peltasts and others that included perhaps 400 archers along with some slingers.

Alexander's route led him across Mount Haemus, where he took on the local Thracian clans. These had set up on the crest of a ridge along the Macedonians' path, very likely in the Shipka Pass, though another, the Trojan, has also been proposed (English 2011, 22–23). Gathered maybe 5,000–7,500 strong (based upon subsequent casualties), the tribesmen were sheltering behind a barrier of carts and planned to use those vehicles as weapons by rolling them down against any attempt by their heavier armed foes to attack in close-order (Arrian 1.1.7). The barbarians hoped in this way to disrupt the phalanx and make it more vulnerable to their javelins. But judging by Alexander's anticipation of this tactic, the Macedonians must have seen or heard about a similar ploy at some time in the past.

The solution to the Thracians' scheme was for Alexander to advance with only his hoplites (Macedonian hypaspists and allied/mercenary Greeks) and the best of his light footmen up what seems to have been a modest grade. Where the approach was narrow, the spearmen were closely ranked with each man's aspis nearly edge-to-edge against those on either side, but filed loose enough to cower when the carts careened near. They could thus shelter beneath their broad shields as the vehicles rolled over on a road of aspides without doing any damage. Elsewhere, where the path was wider, men could simply open ranks and let the carts roll harmlessly through.

Having negated the enemy's opening trick, Alexander formed his men into a Doric-style phalanx before the Thracian battle line, standing among his hypaspists on the left with the Agrianians outboard and placing hoplites from Amphipolis on the other wing with his bowmen off their flank. He then had the archers shift to take post on flatter ground in front of the Greek spearmen, putting them in position to shoot down any sally the Thracians might make on the open, right side of the strike wing as it charged. The king and his hypaspists plus the Agrianian javelineers then closed on the barbarians at speed, the hoplites intent on putting them to the spear as the peltasts added their heaver missiles to the arrows already pelting the opposition's front-fighters. The Thracians didn't wait to die in a shock action for which they were ill-equipped; instead, they plunged in mass down the backing mountainside. Giving hard chase, Alexander's skirmishers killed 1,500 of the tribesmen (20–30 percent) and captured their camp, including all of its women and children.

Alexander crested the Haemus range and descended against the Triballi beyond. Crossing the Lyginus River and advancing, he found that the Triballi leader, Syrmus, had withdrawn north with some allied Thracians to take refuge on an island in the Hister River; however, most of his warriors (maybe 12,000–15,000 of them) had moved down to a spot along the Lyginus. The king therefore reversed course to catch the enemy main body by surprise. As the Triballi spread out through the woods along the north side of the river and prepared to launch a shower of javelins, the Macedonians came on in column with their archers and slingers in the van. Alexander's missilemen could far outrange the barbarian peltasts on the other side and he halted his trailing column to let them spread out and begin inflicting damage from afar while the Triballi were helpless to hit back. This drew the tribesmen out from the trees to form up for a charge so as to get their unarmored antagonists within javelin-reach. A portion of the hetairoi under Philotas (son of Parmenio) now rode out to attack the enemy's right wing while other Macedonian horsemen combined with the Greek light cavalry from Amphipolis to attack the left. Meanwhile, the remaining companions got out in front of the phalanx and moved forward as their shock infantry followed. We've no description of the Macedonian heavy formation, but a reasonable guess is that it featured hypaspists and allied hoplites in that order from the left with pikemen lining the rest of the array and foot skirmishers off either wing.

The Triballi held up for a while in a duel with the Macedonians' leading peltasts and light cavalry, exchanging missiles at a distance. (It's interesting that Arrian's note here on the exchange of javelins in front of the hetairoi off Alexander's right flank offers some of our best evidence for organic attachment of light infantry to those riders at this time.) However, once most of the tribesmen were down to the last javelin for hand-to-hand use, both the lance-armed horsemen on the wings and the phalanx at center were able to close into shock contact. It was no contest from there on as the better-equipped Macedonians and Greeks put the Triballi to rapid rout. And despite the fact that darkness now cut pursuit short, some 3,000 (20–25 percent) of the barbarians died before the last of them got away (Arrian 1.2.7). Alexander took few casualties, losing only eleven hetairoi and 40 foot troops, though the latter are likely only the heavy infantry, thus there might have been more severe losses among his foot skirmishers.

Alexander next swung east to rendezvous with ships dispatched from Byzantium. He loaded these with hoplites and archers and took them upstream for an attempt on Peuce (Pine) Island where Syrmus had holed up. However, the river's swift current along with the island's steep banks and its Thracian defenders kept his small flotilla from coming ashore. Moving on, the young king switched targets and led his army across the Hister into the territory of the Getae.

These were some of the most feared Thracian fighters, whose bravery in combat rested in part on a belief that they were immortal (Arrian 1.3.2 — also, see Webber [2001, 10]). The Getae had gathered to the tune of nearly 4,000 horsemen and 10,000 infantry to take up station along the north side of the river where they could best block a Macedonian fording. To foil this tack, Alexander used his ships, a large number of dugout-type fishing canoes and make-shift rafts (formed of tenting material filled with straw) to transit the river at night, using high-standing grain for cover on the far bank. He thus assembled a modest force across the flood that consisted (per Arrian 1.3.6) of nearly 1,500 cavalry (probably all he had, the horsemen getting across by holding onto their swimming mounts) and 4,000 foot soldiers. These last were most likely just the shock troops (half the available Macedonian heavy infantry). A fair number of foot skirmishers attached to the horsemen must have landed as well, presumably among those using the straw-filled rafts.

Alexander's heavy corps likely had one taxis of hypaspists and two of pikemen. Some of the phalangites put their lengthy pole-arms to novel use in flattening the tall stalks of grain to clear a path for their column, which marched out with the cavalry following at the rear. Having so small a force of line infantry, Alexander set it up in a rectangle once beyond the fields. His formation was perhaps just over 60 shields wide and stood an equal number of ranks deep, having 2m or so between men along each file on the march. Everyone faced forward on the move, but were able to huddle into a compact square if attacked. The heavy infantry could then turn and face out on all sides so as to protect flank and rear from large numbers of light-armed foes. The hypaspists fronted this arrangement in 16-man files, Arrian's account noting that the Getae faced a phalanx with "locked shields" (1.4.3) in what would appear to be a description of abutting aspides. As for the cavalry and foot skirmishers, Alexander led these from horseback as they moved off the right flank (the left being anchored on the river).

It seems that once the Getae became aware of the Macedonians' approach they went into a panic quite contrary to their fearsome reputation, never having suspected that the enemy could get across the Hister so quickly and without detection. Moreover, they were also intimidated by the fearsome appearance of the bronze-shielded, spear-tipped phalanx bearing down on them with murderous intent. As a result, the tribesmen broke in fear as soon as Alexander and his horsemen charged out from alongside their hoplites. The barbarians fled first to their city, which lay a short distance beyond the river. Collecting their families and whatever goods they could carry, they then escaped into the interior. Alexander plundered and burnt the town before pulling back to join the rest of his army, which had now also crossed the flow. The local Thracian tribes, the Triballi and even some Celts from farther north soon sent representatives to Alexander with offers of alliance. He next turned about and marched down into the Agrianian and Paeonian lands that lay just north of Macedonia. From here, he would stage to deal with some of the Illyrian peoples farther west that had recently joined in the revolt against his ascension to the throne.

Pelion (335 B.C.)

Cleitus, son of Philip's old opponent Bardylis, was leading his Dardanians against the new Macedonian king, and another tribal leader, Glaucias of the Taulantians, was moving to join him. At the same time, yet a third group of Illyrians, the Autariates, were also readying an attack. Alexander arranged for Langaros, king of his allied Agrianians, to occupy the Autariates with a raid on their home territory. He then set off to deal with the Dardanians before they could receive reinforcement. Cleitus had occupied Pelion, a fortified city to the west, and it was here where Alexander caught up with him. A Macedonian assault on Pelion was met by the Dardanians sallying out for a fixed battle. Backed by perhaps 2,000 javelineers and slingers, up to 8,000 Illyrian shock fighters engaged Alexander's phalanx with their heavy-headed spears and large, center-grip shields in a close combat. No details are known for this action, but the barbarians ultimately gave way and withdrew into the city. As such, the battle must have been hard-fought with the Macedonians giving a little better than they got (maybe taking 3 percent losses against twice as many for the Dardanians), but not able to mount an effective pursuit as their enemy pulled away.

Having shut up his foes in Pelion, Alexander prepared to surround the place with a siege wall and force its surrender. At this juncture, the Taulantians under Glaucias arrived and threatened to strike at the rear of any attack against the city walls. Making matters worse, the Illyrians moved to cut off Macedonian supplies, going so far as to trap a large provisioning party until Alexander came to its rescue with his hypaspists, Agrianians, archers and 400 hetairoi horsemen. (There was only one squadron of 400 riders. This was the royal company of the companion cavalry, which had twice the usual number of troopers and was a mounted counterpart to the royal agema of hypaspists.) Short on food and facing a large and determined enemy force in the surrounding forested uplands, Alexander decided to retreat. However, this was much easier said than done. The escape route was narrow, being bordered on one side by steep cliffs and on the other by a river. What followed was a brilliant display of the Macedonians' training and discipline that let their king bluff past this tricky situation.

Alexander drew up his native heavy footmen in an oblong formation. This was 60 shields wide and 120 ranks deep, having two times the manpower that he had arrayed along that same frontage on the bank of the Hister a few weeks earlier. He then deployed 200-rider bodies of hetairoi off either flank along with the usual light infantry support. Next, he led his superbly drilled hypaspists (at lest half of them being in the van, the rest maybe forming the rearmost ranks) and pikemen through a dazzling series of parade-ground maneuvers as they worked their way toward the exit from Pelion. These complex evolutions so impressed the Illyrians that most of them simply ran away when the Macedonians finally drew near and made a threatening move on their blocking positions. After the hypaspists and a few select horsemen scared off the last of the barbarians from a hilltop, the army was clear to march away.

In the ensuing retreat, the hypaspists acted as vanguard and the Agrianians and archers (2,000 men total) as rearguard while the Macedonians made a key river crossing, (This was also covered from the far bank by the fire of both archers and bolt-throwing mechanical bows). Alexander thus won his way clear, but wasn't content. Learning that the Illyrians thought him gone for good and had set up a poorly arranged camp in his wake, he re-crossed the river at night with the hypaspists, Agrianians, archers and two taxeis of pikemen (3,000). These caught the tribesmen unprepared and in their beds, slaughtering many on the scene and killing and capturing others as they fled in confusion. The Illyrians were so shaken that they abandoned Pelion and burnt it down as they took to the hills. Alexander was now able to return to Macedon with a relatively quiescent territory at his back.

Once home, Alexander found that he had to contend with a new crisis. This was at Thebes, where a group of anti–Macedonian exiles had taken advantage of a rumor that the young king had died during his northern campaigns to raise a revolt against the Corinthian League. Alexander responded with a lightening march to capture Thebes, placing League troops in the Cadmea as he razed the city around it. It was a brutal object lesson that soon had other poleis eager to pledge loyalty to Macedonia, allowing Alexander to turn toward Persia at last.

The Persian Campaign I

Parmenio had crossed into Asia in 336 with what might have been 2,000 hypaspists and 6,000 phalangites plus 800 hetairoi and 1,200 light infantrymen (probably 1,000 associated with the heavy infantry and the rest attached to the cavalry at 50 per 200-horse squadron). This totaled 10,000 troops in line with Polyaenus (5.44.4). The Macedonians set up at Abydos on the Hellespont and began moving down into Aetolia, raiding Persian assets, collecting more troops from the Ionians and hiring mercenaries. The Persian response was slow. Artaxerxes III (Ochus) had been poisoned in 338 and his successor, Artaxerxes IV (Arses), was assassinated as well in 336; therefore, it was Darius III who now ruled as Great King. A grand-nephew of Artaxerxes II known for bravery and prowess in single combat, this new monarch was at first encouraged by the death of Philip, thinking that the youthful Alexander couldn't follow-up on his father's plans. But as soon as it became clear in the summer of 335 that Philip's heir was highly capable, Darius began to prepare for defending his kingdom. This was an involved process that called for the many units forming the empire's huge roster on paper to be filled with real soldiers. Darius' first task, therefore, was to buy the time needed for his lengthy mobilization program. He did this by gathering mercenaries already present within some of the eastern garrisons of the empire and putting them under Memnon, who was a Greek from Rhodes and his best general. Memnon's assignment was to march against Parmenio on the coast, where he was to limit the Macedonian's operations while the imperial host mustered inland.

Granicus River (334 B.C.) and Sagalassos (334/33 B.C.)

Memnon moved to meet Parmenio and his men with a modest mercenary army. This probably consisted of 4,000 hoplites (per Polyaenus' estimate of his total strength [5.44.4]) and 1,000 foot skirmishers for a 5,000 man total (Diodorus 17.7.3). Arriving at the Greek city of Cyzicus on the southern shores of the Propontis (Sea of Marmara) above the Hellespont, the Rhodian menaced and nearly captured the place in an attempt to draw his foe out of Persian territory. When this failed, he dropped into Aetolia and chased Parmenio and a contingent of his men away from a siege operation at the coastal city of Pitane. Too weak to tackle the enemy's fortified outposts or even risk a large-scale engagement, Memnon then set about waging a clever campaign of maneuver, bedeviling his opponents at every turn. He even managed to catch smaller enemy detachments in isolation on a couple of occasions and send them into bloodied retreat (Diodorus 17.7.10; Polyaenus 5.44.4). The Macedonians thus accomplished much less than anticipated before having to fall back on Abydos at the end of the summer. Leaving adequate garrisons in place, Parmenio and his original expeditionary column withdrew over the winter. They were thus able to rest and refill their ranks back home in preparation for the coming invasion.

When Alexander set out across the Hellespont the following spring, he had a powerful armament at his back for which Diodorus (17.17.3–5) has left a detailed order of battle. His troops included half of the full Macedonian infantry muster (3,000 hypaspists [three taxeis] and 9,000 phalangites [six taxeis]), a like-sized force staying behind with Antipater. There were also 1,800 companion horsemen. These were three-fourths of the hetairoi in seven 200-horse squadrons and one of 400 (the other 600 companions apparently remained with Antipater, who had 1,500 total cavalry). Macedonia's light infantry is not listed, but must have been around 2,000–3,000 strong. The Greek allies added some 7,000 foot soldiers (maybe 5,000 hoplites and 2,000 skirmishers from Boeotia and the Peloponnese). There were also 5,000 mercenaries (perhaps 4,000 spearmen and 1,000 light-armed). Barbarian levies totaled 7,000 men from Illyria and Thrace as well as a team of archers and Agrianian javelineers (elite troops 1,000 strong at half those that had served in the campaigns of 335). This adds up to more than 30,000 infantry in all, which is consistent with our other ancient accounts from Arrian (1.11.3), Justin (11.5.12) and Plutarch (Vol. II, *Alexander*, 149). (Wells [1963, below 164–165] points out that Plutarch also cited similar numbers given by Aristobulus and Ptolemy while claiming Anaximenes as a lone dissenter with 43,000 footmen. Perhaps this last included non-combatants.) Additional cavalry came from Thessaly (1,800) and the rest of Greece (600 Boeotians and Peloponnesians) along with some barbarian riders from Thrace and Paeonia (900, including maybe 300 Thracian/Macedonian lancers) for a total mounted corps of around 5,000.

The Persian national host was still gathering under Darius as Alexander marched into Phyrgia. This left defense of the realm's western provinces in the hands of five satraps on the scene and a few generals. Memnon was the most capable military mind among the latter and he wisely advised greeting the Macedonians with a "scorched earth" policy. This called for refusing pitched battle and falling back while destroying all supplies along the enemy's path. They could thus stall Alexander's advance through shortage of food. (He had set out with only 30 days worth of provisions and would soon need copious local foodstuffs to sustain his men and animals). At the same time, naval forces sent into Greece could raise enough hell that it might compel him to return home. This was a sound plan, but the other commanders wouldn't go along with it. They saw such an approach as undignified and too costly for those whose assets would be torched. It was decided instead to offer battle at a site favorable for a defensive stand. They chose a location along the Granicus River in western Phyrgia where they could set up on high ground behind that stream.

Most claims in our sources for Persian manpower at Granicus River are significantly overblown. In truth, it seems likely that imperial strength was a bit less than Alexander's, thus prompting the defensive strategy of Memnon as well as the actual Persian tactics used in the battle. Our lowest ancient numbers of 10,000 cavalry (Diodorus 17.19.4) and 20,000 infantry (Arrian 1.14.4) are probably closest to reality. The horsemen might have represented ten hazaraba, both satrapal and imperial, which at 60–80 percent of their nominal 1,000-man complement probably totaled only 6,000–8,000 riders. As for the foot soldiers, Memnon had brought his 5,000 mercenaries (including 4,000 spearmen) while small contingents of bodyguards from each of the five satraps present would have raised Greek hoplite strength to around 6,000. (This assumes an average 400 spearmen per guard unit in line with the one documented by Xenophon [*Anabasis* 1.4.3.] for the satrap Abrocomas.) The remaining infantry would have been non–Greeks. These could have included some Carian and/or Lydian hoplites, but most would have been light-armed. Considering the satrapies involved, the light footmen likely included Carian, Mysian, Cabelee, Phrygian (Paphlagonian) and Cappadocian peltasts (the last two nationalities also carrying a small spear for hand-to-hand use instead of a "last javelin"). These skirmishers probably split in some fashion to provide support for the cavalry as well as a flank screen for their heavy array.

Both armies set up for battle on their respective sides of the Granicus. The Persians had their phalanx of hoplites back a fair distance from the water's edge, with the cavalry and light infantry posted in front and off either flank. This let them take advantage of a rising slope that would force the Macedonians into an unfavorable uphill attack should they get across the river. The alternative of locating directly along the bank was less desirable, because that lower position would expose them to Alexander's archers (including men with mechanical bows) and slingers. These could easily outrange any rearward-standing Persian javelineers and their fire would be devastating if allowed to continue for a sufficient length of time. The only solution in that case would be a disadvantaged cross-river assault against a larger enemy infantry force. The current deployment was much better in that the Macedonian missilemen had to ford the Granicus to get a reasonable shot. And once on the far side, the Persian cavalry and its attached peltasts could launch javelins on them from above and then mount a powerful counterattack down the slope.

Alexander wasn't daunted by this arrangement and fixed upon making a bold attack. He therefore set up his bowmen and Agrianians outboard on the right, followed inward by seven of the eight hetairoi squadrons and then a grouping of the final hetairoi unit (200 riders) leading the Paeonians and Thracian/Macedonian lancers. His heavy infantry phalanx came next. The three hypaspist regiments formed its right wing, half the phalangites (three regiments) were in the center and the rest of the pikemen made up the left wing. Beyond the heavy array, his remaining cavalry took post with the Thracian horsemen standing inside, the mounted Greek allies next and the Thessalians on the far flank. There is no mention in our sources of where the allied and mercenary infantry were, but they might have formed another phalanx at the rear. (Arrian noted [1.13.1] that Alexander advanced on the Granicus "having arrayed his phalanx in two rows." Possibly a reference to a 16-man depth [twice eight], this may actually denote the presence of a second, parallel formation.) Such a reserve arrangement would have been a new tool in the Macedonian box of tactics, added to meet specific challenges presented along the Granicus. His enemy's much smaller force of heavy footmen (the Macedonians alone outnumbered them by 50 percent and had a wider frontage) gave him the luxury of having a back-up battle array. This could counter an encircling attack from the unusually large Persian cavalry force on hand or, should his daring thrust across the river prove a bust, cover a retreat.

While we have descriptions of the lateral arrangement for the Macedonian units, this is not so for their depth. The hypaspists had probably filed at eight to twelve shields under Philip and the phalangites at ten. In Alexander's previous formations the depth had been unusual (up to 120) to accommodate special circumstances during his European campaigns. Clues as to the probable depth of file at Granicus River come from an assumption that an effort was made to match the enemy's frontage. Taking a Persian strength of around 8,000 horsemen, the imperial array would have stretched along 2km at eight deep (maximum useful depth for mounted troops per Polybios [12.18.2], himself a cavalry commander, and Asclepiodotus [7.4]) and 2m lateral spacing. Given similar dimensions for the horsemen with Alexander, they would have stood across 1,250m. By filing eight shields deep for the hypaspists (375m) and 16 deep for the pikemen (375m) he could then equal the Persian front even as he matched his heavy array's width with that of the 6,000-man phalanx at the enemy's rear, which probably stood eight-deep. (His 9,000 reserve hoplites might have had a similar frontage using files of twelve.)

The armies faced off across the river, eyeing each other in silence for some time. This allowed the Persians to adjust their order and increase the concentration of cavalry on their left wing, which was opposite where they saw Alexander riding with the hetairoi to mark the likely focus of his opening attack. And this was indeed the case, as the Macedonian king gave signal and led his horsemen across with the specialist light infantry (right) and the agema of royal hypaspists (left) advancing alongside. The leftmost of the Macedonian cavalry (the squadron of companions with the Paeonians and lancers) crossed first to meet a storm of javelins as their opponents charged down into them. While this lead element drew the enemy in, Alexander drifted rightward and took the rest of his wing over the stream before swinging left to hit the already engaged Persians from that side. Once at closer quarters, the lances of the hetairoi were much more effective than the Persians' shorter and less robust javelins in hand-to-hand combat; moreover, the Asians took a lot of damage from the foot skirmishers that were mixed within the Macedonian array (Arrian 1.16.1).

As Alexander and company were gaining the upper hand on one flank, a similar story was playing out at the other end of the battlefield. The king's allied cavalry had crossed and engaged there as well, working its way up the far bank despite also meeting "showers of darts thrown from the steep opposite side, which was covered with armed multitudes of the enemy's horse and foot" (Plutarch Vol. II, *Alexander*, 150). The Thessalian horsemen particularly distinguished themselves here, so much so that they would trail only Alexander himself in post-battle acclaim.

And as the mounted action swirled upslope off either flank, the Macedonian phalanx took its cue from the royal agema and also waded over. Once on the Persian side of the Granicus, the hypaspists and pikemen quickly restored their battle array and began to advance. By that time, many of the imperial commanders had fallen along with a good number of their fellow riders and, badly battered and seeing the phalanx now coming on, it was more than the remaining Persian horsemen could bear. The last of the imperial cavalry broke from the fight and their oriental infantry joined them in a mass rush eastward. So sudden was this collapse that it left the Greek mercenary hoplites behind. With flanks exposed and facing overwhelming numbers, most of these gave way as well to be mercilessly slaughtered in place by the enclosing wall of spears and pikes or cut down from behind by a swarm of pursuing horsemen and skirmishers.

The satraps that had ignored Memnon's advice and engaged Alexander with an inferior force paid a high price for their folly. Only 2,000 out of 6,000 or so Greek spearmen survived to surrender. (A loss of 67 percent is unusual, but not unreasonable for an encircled force pressed to the end.) And while Diodorus' claim (17.21.6) of 12,000 imperial dead looks high in light of there being only a brief pursuit (Alexander cut it short to concentrate on the mercenary hoplites), losses above 3,000 (15 percent) in addition to those among the Greek hirelings wouldn't be out of line. For Alexander, the reported casualties are suspiciously low. Still, damage was probably minimal for the lightly engaged heavy infantry and no more than modest for the cavalry and foot skirmishers (likely below 5 percent killed). Alexander took Sardis in the battle's aftermath and claimed all of Lydia. Memnon and other survivors from the Persian side escaped to the coast and sought refuge at Miletus.

Alexander marched south from Sardis to liberate Ephesos and then dropped down to capture Miletus, forcing Memnon and his fellows to flee once again. With Lydia and Ionia under control, the Macedonian moved next against Caria. He took Halicarnassus after a siege that featured a number of unsuccessful sallies and skirmishes by the defenders. Leaving his officer Ptolemy behind to hold Caria with 3,000 mercenaries and 200 horsemen, Alexander then went back north. Through fall and winter 334/33, he secured the coastal region of Asia Minor and advanced up the Eurymedon River toward Phyrgia. On the way, he found it necessary to fight a battle before Sagalassos, which lay in rough country west of the Eurymedon headwaters.

Sagalassos was a large city of the Pisidians, whose warriors were peltasts. These mobile fighters used small shields covered with rawhide and wore no armor save for bronze helmets (fashioned with horns and ears like a bull). The Pisidians and a few allied troops from Termessos to the south (also javelineers) had taken a strong position atop lofty terrain in front of town. Alexander arrayed his phalanx, standing with the hypaspists on the right and having his pezhetairoi pikemen filling out the center and left wing. He placed the archers and Agrianians in front of his right wing and Thracian peltasts in front of the left, but kept his cavalry out of the fight due to the unfavorable ground held by the enemy. As the Macedonian formation advanced upslope, the Pisidians struck at both wings, driving off the archers that were at the fore on Alexander's right and killing 20 of them (10 percent) as well as their commander. However, the Agrianians came up to replace the bowmen and were able to withstand this assault, as were the Thracians on the other end of the battle line. Once the phalanx closed into shock combat, its heavier equipped troops began to take a serious toll on the lightly armed barbarians while suffering little harm in return. The Pisidians eventually gave way after losing men all along the front, running from what was clearly a hopeless fight. But though they easily escaped the Macedonians, who were slow in their weighty gear, Alexander followed close behind and took their city by storm.

Once into Phyrgia, Alexander negotiated the surrender of a well-placed force of 1,000 Carian and 100 Greek mercenaries and laid claim to the province, garrisoning it with 1,500 soldiers. He wintered there at Gordian (of the famous "knot"), where he received reinforcements from home. These consisted of 3,000 pikemen along with cavalry from Macedonia (nearly 350), Thrace (200) and Elis (150).

Issus (333 B.C.) and Memphis (333/32 B.C.)

Having no success on land, Memnon set out in 333 to counter Alexander from the sea. This began with an attack on the Greeks of Lesbos, but the Rhodian had hardly gotten the campaign underway when he contracted a disease and died. Still, his forces were able to seize Mytilene, and Pharnabazus then came out to take over the Persian effort in the Aegean. He continued his predecessor's strategy by capturing the island of Tendos. Spending the summer in Phyrgia, Alexander finally began marching out of Gordian toward Cilicia in the fall, accepting surrenders from the Paphlagonians in route. Arriving at the Cilician Gate gorge, he made a nighttime sortie with his hypaspists, Agrianians and archers to frighten off the blockading troops there and gain easy passage. Once in Cilicia, Alexander sent an advance force on to seize the Syrian Gate (the narrow entry into Assyria) while he made a foray into the mountains to deal with some hostile local peoples. He quickly completed this task and headed for the coast to move along until reaching Myriandros, which lay just to the northwest of the already secured Syrian Gate. Alexander camped here to wait out a bout of bad weather (it was now early November and winter was setting in) before entering Assyria.

Darius had by now assembled the imperial host and was waiting to engage Alexander on the open Assyrian plain where his large numbers of cavalry could have the advantage. However, growing impatient, the Great King gave up his favorable position and marched instead to go though a pass known as the Amanic Gate, which lay inland to the north and a bit east of the Syrian Gate. He therefore ended up coming down to the sea north of Myriandros in Alexander's rear. Neither army seems to have been aware of the other until they suddenly found themselves only a short distance apart on the coastal plain. Marching to engage, the forces of Darius and Alexander converged on a point below the seaside town of Issus.

Alexander advanced up the coastal flat in column. As the area began to open up approaching Issus, he shifted his heavy infantry units one by one into a phalanx that stretched from the bounding hills on his right to the sea on the left. Starting with the elite agema, his hypaspists formed across the right wing at 3,000 strong. The phalangite regiments then spread along the middle and left down to anchor against the water's edge. There were now nearly 12,000 pikemen counting those that had arrived in the spring, these latter apparently forming up within the original six taxeis to raise them to around 2,000 men each. Initially, the narrow shoreline strip had demanded that the heavy footmen file four times their minimum (at 32 for the pikemen and 16 for the hoplites), but they were able to spread out as it broadened, going to half that depth. The mercenary and allied hoplites (reduced due to garrisoning for the former and returns to Greece for the latter) remained in the rear with the light footmen and all the cavalry; however, as the plain kept on expanding, rather than extend his phalanx, Alexander chose to post his best horsemen (the hetairoi and Thessalians) off his right wing. There wasn't room there for both contingents to spread out, so the Macedonians rode in front with the Thessalians tucked behind. Elsewhere, some of the other mounted units now took position alongshore on the left side of the heavy array.

The Great King, meanwhile, had come down from the north and stopped to set up camp above the Pinaros River, which flowed westward into the sea. Temporarily posting his cavalry across this small stream, he carefully arranged his foot troops just below his tents in a line above the riverbank, throwing up some field works as well (probably shallow trenches backed by the mounded dirt, though these must have been very minor and/or limited as we hear nothing about them in the ensuing battle). He deployed his phalanx with roughly 15,000 Greek hoplite mercenaries in the center. (This considers that the 30,000 cited in several ancient sources was a nominal figure sans significant reductions for casualties and dispersions to garrison and bodyguard duty. Alexander [Arrian 2.7.6] refers to only 20,000 mercenaries here, which might mean 15,000 hoplites if light footmen made up a typical 25 percent of the mix.) To either side of these, Darius evenly divided the hoplite-armed men from six baivaraba of kardakes, likely his empire's full muster. Arrian claimed that there were 60,000 men in these, but this was an establishment strength and probably twice what was actually present, while using only the heavy element ("hoplites" per Arrian [2.8.6]) cut the number down to more like 15,000. As for the approximately 15,000 rear-rank kardakes bowmen and peltasts from these same units, they massed to the left of their hoplite-armed comrades. Darius covered his flank on the seaward/right side by repositioning nearly all of his horsemen there once the heavy-armed phalanx was set. His cavalry might have numbered 15,000 (citations of 30,000 being subject to reductions similar to those applied to both the mercenary and kardakes elements of the imperial host).

The Persian spearmen had to form long files due to the narrowness of the battleground. They thus probably spanned 1,700m in all, the Greeks covering 950m at twice normal depth of 16 shields and 750m for the kardakes hoplites with similarly doubled files for them of 20. And given that the coastal plain here was only about 2.6km wide (per Callisthenes via Polybios [12.17.4]), deployment of cavalry and light infantry at either end of the line must have been even more crowded. The horsemen on the right therefore probably formed up 60-deep (contingents stacked one behind the other) while the kardakes archers/peltasts leftward likely stood 30-deep. The satrapal infantry levies (perhaps 30,000 in all) mostly gathered behind their phalanx, but some light-armed contingents completed the left wing onto rough terrain, spreading out from there into the hills beyond and well up the Pinaros valley. As for Darius, he is reputed to have taken post on his chariot in the center of the phalanx. Darius was probably surrounded at the rear by two 1,000-man units of heavy-armed kardakes-style bodyguards (these elites are attested at Gaugemela two years later and must have always have been present whenever the Great King took the field).

Alexander was able to observe the Persian formation as he drew near and the plain continued to widen. He took advantage of these developments to shift some of his men, adjusting his formation and tactics to counter the enemy's arrangements as he filled the added space. He stretched out his phalanx, thinning the files to minimums of eight-deep for the phalangites (Polybios 12.19.6) and four for the hypaspists. This spread the heavy infantry across some 1,750m in order for it to match frontages with that of the opposing hoplites and heavy-armed kardakes. At the same time, he had the Thessalian cavalry transfer to the seaward flank to address the dense concentration of Persian horsemen on that side of the field, doing so without the enemy's knowledge behind cover of the phalanx. He would continue to adjust his supporting units as he closed, with archers and Thracian peltasts finally ending up on the left between the pikemen and cavalry there and the Paeonian horsemen and lancers adding on to his right wing. He also had archers, the Agrianians and some of his Greek mercenaries come up to support his cavalry force on the right (where he himself held post), these having chased some of the enemy's light footmen back into the hills (he had then posted 300 cavalrymen behind on that side to make sure these beaten skirmishers didn't return). The rest of the allied and mercenary hoplites and foot skirmishers remained in the rear, there being no more room at the front.

Alexander led his formation toward the Persians standing firm on the other side of the Pinaros, advancing at first at a walk to maintain orderly ranks; then, as the distance closed and the massed kardakes archers on his right began to rain down arrows, he came on at the double

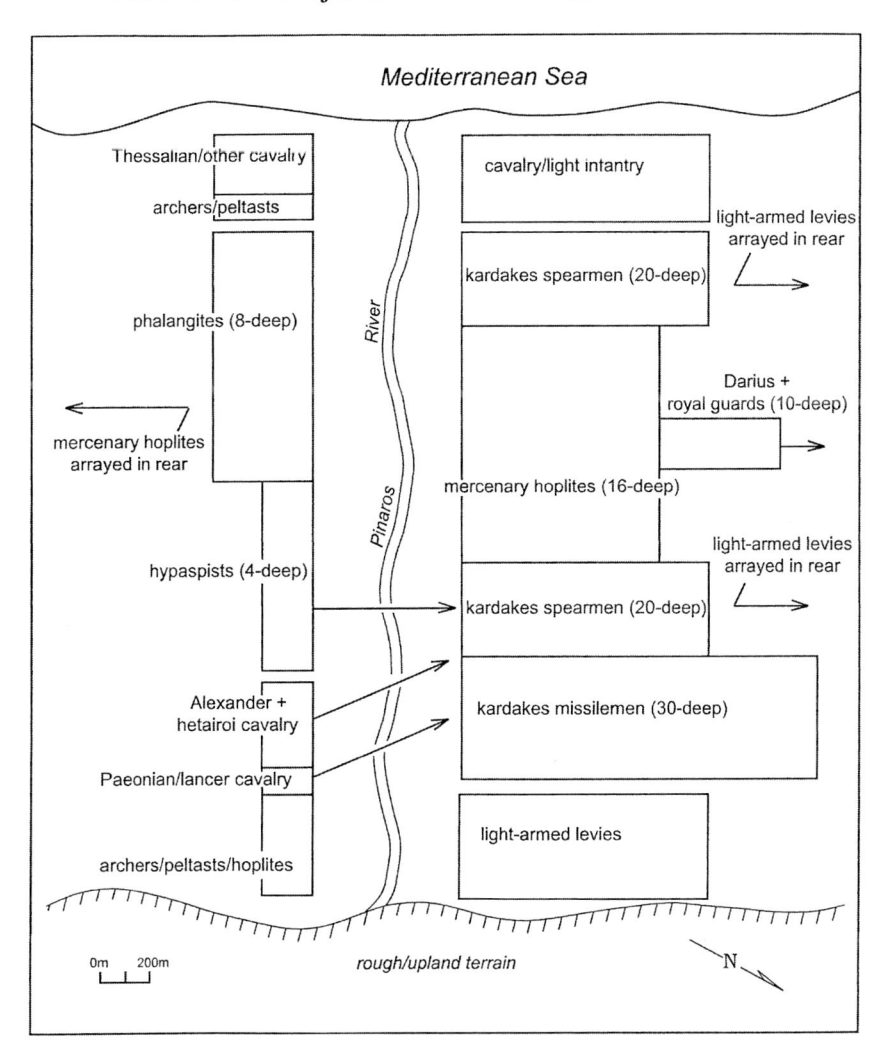

Battles in the Era of Alexander the Great (335–324 B.C.) 149

BATTLE OF ISSUS (333 B.C.) (BOXES REPRESENTING FORCES ARE EXAGGERATED TO SHOW RELATIVE SIZES.)

across the stream. However, while this helped to reduce exposure to missile fire for the horsemen and light footmen around his person, it was difficult for his heavy infantry to avoid some disarray at such a pace in traversing the streambed. A gap thus opened in the Macedonian line, most likely between the hypaspists and the first regiment of pikemen on their left. Here, the Persian mercenary hoplites opposite were able to flank the pike hedge and take down a regimental commander and 120 (8 percent) of his now disadvantaged phalangites in a close-in fight. It's a tribute to the adjacent Macedonians' heart and discipline that they maintained formation and didn't break at this development. And elsewhere along the heavy-armed front, Alexander's men were holding their ground as well, staving off the enemy despite having a very thin array. The pikemen were able to use their long weapons to good effect against the kardakes hoplites on the left and the mercenaries across the center. Meantime, the hypaspists' spears took a toll among the remaining hirelings and the heavy-armed kardakes facing their part of the line on the right, all the while resisting any shield-pushing pressure coming that way. Next to the shoreline, a fierce cavalry action was raging. The Persians had charged there, crossing the Pinaros to go on the attack in hopes that they could win the battle by turning the Macedonians along that flank.

Again, Alexander's outmanned forces hung tough, giving him a chance to carry the day on his right.

The Macedonian king and his shock cavalry had weathered the initial missile fire from the light-armed kardakes on their side of the ground through a mix of determination and speed; now, they put those foes to the lance and drove them away in a brief melee. As the bowmen and peltasts fled under pursuit from the Paeonians and lancers, Alexander and his hetairoi turned against the freshly exposed side and rear of the Persian hoplites on that end of the field. The kardakes were unable to withstand this sudden lateral assault along with renewed pressure from the hypaspists; as a result, their formation began to disintegrate. Whether the Alexander Sarcophagus depicts this moment at Issus or a similar one from Gaugemela, its images perfectly illustrate the scene that now unfolded, with the kardakes struggling against Macedonian hetairoi and hypaspists as a few Persian cavalrymen come up in an attempt to cover their withdrawal. Some of the Persians still held aspis and spear, while others were down to broken shafts with sauroters or swords as they were washed to the rear in a swirl of hand-to-hand combat that saw Alexander himself take a cut to the thigh. In short order, the Persian spearmen were shattered and they streamed rearward to join the light-armed members of their regiments already on the run.

The hetairoi moved next to take Darius' Greek hoplites from behind as the hypaspists, having cleared the last of the kardakes on that side, folded around to envelop the denuded left end of the mercenary line. This is the moment shown in such romantic fashion on the Alexander Mosaic, with the famed Macedonian riding with xyston in hand toward an alarmed Persian king. Whatever the reality might have been (the two monarchs more likely being well separated), Darius saw that his left wing was defeated and his hired spearmen were being cut off, making it high time to take advantage of his unblocked rearward position and beat a speedy personal retreat. It was a wise move that might well have saved his life.

Behind the fleeing Great King, his battle line rapidly collapsed from left to right, with the mercenaries giving way, then the kardakes hoplites on the seaward side and, finally, the imperial cavalry that had up until now been making some progress along the beach. The resulting rush to the rear was a nightmare, with masses clawing to get away along the narrow coastal plain under hot pursuit. The Thessalian horsemen were especially effective in that sector, chasing and cutting down so many enemy riders that their foes (quite unusually) lost a higher percentage in mounted men (both Arrian [2.11.8] and Curtius [3.11.27] indicate a third) than foot soldiers (15 percent). Across the field overall, infantry casualties must have been greatest among the kardakes and hireling Greeks. For the latter, we hear of only abut 10,000 getting away (Arrian cited 8,000 deserting over the mountains to Phoenicia with their exiled Macedonian commander, Amyntas, and another 2,000 later joining Darius). This suggests the loss of a third, consistent with Arrian's claim that infantry and cavalry casualties were about equal and assuming that by "infantry" he meant only heavy footmen. As it was, the Persian death toll would undoubtedly have been even higher if night hadn't begun to fall at the battle's end. As for Macedonian losses, they were surely modest; still, the extremely low fatalities claimed by Curtius are dubious. These also conflict with the damage Arrian reported among the phalangites that had been penetrated. We might more reasonably suspect that some 3 percent of the heavy infantry lost their lives along with perhaps 5 percent of the mounted troops and a similar cut of their intermingled foot skirmishers.

Further trouble would hit the Persians following Issus in the form of marauding by some of their defeated mercenaries. The men who had escaped the battle with Amyntas ended up taking ship in Phoenicia, 4,000 of them then joining that Macedonian refugee in sailing to Cyprus (Curtius 4.1.27) and the rest accepting service under Agis, king of Sparta, for a campaign on Crete (Diodorus 17.48.1–2). (Note that Diodorus gives all of the mercenaries that Arrian said had followed Amyntas to Agis, but adds 4,000 more that stayed with the Macedonian. Curtius' account can be taken to mean that these latter were merely a split of the original 8,000, suggesting that Agis actually took only half of the hirelings that reached Phoenicia. Alternatively, it's possible that some of the mercenary counts in our sources include light infantry [perhaps at 25 percent of the total as suggested above for Alexander's own assessment at Issus] while others do not.) While the fighting on Crete would be on behalf of Persia, Amyntas and his hoplites went rogue and were willing to prey in any manner that yielded profit. They thus recruited more troops on Cyprus (likely a force of 1,000 or so missilemen for skirmisher support) and sailed off to attack Egypt, hoping to take advantage of confusion in the wake of the death of that satrapy's governor (Sabaces) at Issus.

Pretending to be an advance party for Darius, the Greeks gained the harbor at Pelusium and captured that city. They then marched on Memphis where the local garrison came out to offer battle. Given their willingness to engage openly, we can suppose that the defenders were at least even if not actually superior in numbers. And, indeed, a baivaraba at the 30–60 percent parade strength common for long-standing garrisons might well have put enough men into the field at a depth of ten to equal fronts with Amyntas' spearmen filed at eight. The Memphian troops were most likely heavily equipped Egyptians. These used a large, elongate, wooden shield held by a combination of center-grip and shoulder strap, wearing linen body armor and wicker helmet and carrying a long spear (Nelson 1975, 20–21). Though otherwise a fair match in a shock fight, the Memphians couldn't hope to long hold their ground under the sort of pressure that the Greek hoplites could impart via othismos; therefore, once dueling with spears gave way to a shoving match with shields, they must have given way. The mercenaries chased their foes back inside the city, probably having inflicted fair damage (5–10 percent) at considerably smaller cost (2–3 percent). Yet all then went bad for the Greeks when they lost discipline while ravaging the surrounding area and the defenders sallied once more to catch them scattered and unready for another bout. The result was a massacre without quarter that wiped out Amyntas and his raiders to the last man.

Back in Asia, Alexander had now laid claim to Cilicia and marched into Phoenicia, where he put the imposing island fortress of Tyre under siege. This developed into an epic operation that wouldn't see the city fall until the summer of 332. But the effort proved highly worthwhile, since it brought the region under Macedonian sway and took away home bases for the conscripted Phoenician fleet of Darius. This destroyed the Persian naval effort in the Aegean within a matter of months. Having grown more fearful as the siege at Tyre progressed, the Great King sought a negotiated solution. However, an offer of half his empire was rejected by Alexander, who had his sights on the entire realm. Alexander moved toward Egypt that fall, attacking and capturing strong-walled Gaza. There, much like his father had been struck by a catapult bolt outside of Methone, Alexander was hit by a mechanically thrown missile, which resulted in a serious shoulder wound. Recovering sufficiently, the hardy young man pushed on, founding Alexandria at the mouth of the Nile and spending the winter consolidating control over Egypt.

Gaugamela (331 B.C.)

Antipater sent 500 Thracian horsemen and 400 mercenaries to Egypt during the winter of 332/31 and Alexander arranged a major recruiting campaign back in Greece toward further boosting his mercenary manpower for a final confrontation with Darius. Once reinforced that spring, the Macedonian left a garrison behind and marched back into Asia. Darius had elected to await his arrival on favorable terrain near the small town of Gaugamela, which lay close to the Boumelos River, a tributary of the Tigris. The Persian monarch had learned from his disastrous first encounter with Alexander and was sticking to a wide plain this time, where his large cavalry force wouldn't face the kind of restrictions that had so seriously limited it at Issus. Going even further, he had taken the step of artificially altering the ground, having teams of workmen clear and level it into a surface ideal for his horsemen.

Our data on the Persian army at Gaugamela is especially poor, with ancient sources giving fantastic figures. Infantry claims range from 200,000 (Curtius 4.12.13) through 400,000 (Justin 11.12.5) and 800,000 (Diodorus 17.53.3) to 1,000,000 (Arrian 3.8.5). None of these figures appear even remotely realistic. We know that Darius had recovered at least 2,000 mercenary hoplites from Issus and there might have been heavy-armed kardakes as well. Even assuming that the latter had suffered as heavily as their Greek comrades at Issus (perhaps a third lost), there could have been 10,000 still on hand. We can also add 2,000 heavily equipped bodyguards for the Great King. These last manned two select units at full strength, having undoubtedly replaced any casualties sustained earlier. Losses at Issus for the other infantry (light-armed kardakes and satrapal levies) probably ran about 5 percent, including a third of 5,000 or so men that would have served alongside the fiercely pursued cavalry. Still, over 40,000 light footmen could have been present, with casualties and dropouts having been compensated for by troops from Darius' eastern provinces. We might then project that the imperial army at Gaugamela had at least 50,000 foot troops and more likely some 60,000–65,000. This was down about 20 percent from Issus, with only around a quarter of the total being heavy-armed versus 40 percent or so at that earlier engagement.

As for cavalry, Arrian said 40,000, Curtius 45,000, Justin 100,000 and Diodorus 200,000. The first two numbers are thankfully non-astronomical and we might take the lower as a basis for projection. Arrian's figure here is a third above what he claimed for Issus. Halving this for the same reasons as proposed there, we get 20,000, which is quite possible. Fresh manpower, including replacement of casualties, seems to have come from satrapal sources not previously tapped. Beyond boosting their numbers, Darius had tried to improve his horsemen's weaponry as well, supplying many with sturdier spears that could better match the Macedonian xyston. He also had taken steps to add a new horse-borne element in the form of scythed chariots such as those that had so damaged the Greeks at Dascyleium in 395. Arrian's order of battle indicates 200 chariots at Gaugamela, which is consistent with reports of 150–200 of these potentially lethal vehicles seeing action at Cunaxa in 401. And Darius actually had even more exotic weapons in his mounted arsenal: 15 Indian elephants. However, while Arrian included these animals in his Persian deployment, he seems to have derived this from a written plan captured afterwards (3.11.3). In fact, he later reported that the pachyderms (and some camels) were captured in camp, thus they missed the battle.

Alexander stopped well short of the Persian position and set up camp so his army could recover from the rigors of its march. Then, after four days, he left his baggage train and men unfit for battle behind and struck out at night, intending to open battle at dawn. Darius learned of this and arrayed his forces on the plain, ready to fight; however, Alexander suddenly halted his advance on the slopes of some hills within sight of the Persian lines and set up a field camp in order to scout the situation. There was some consideration given at this time to attacking Darius under cover of darkness, but Alexander rejected the idea and rested his forces in place. The Persians, fearing an assault after sundown and not having a fortified encampment, spent the night in discomfort fully arrayed for action. The Macedonians were therefore fresher when dawn broke on the day of decision.

The imperial host stretched across the plain with its horsemen posted at the fore and the infantry set up behind. There were likely around 8,000 horsemen on each wing of the main alignment, combining to front along approximately 4km at a depth of eight and 2m spacing. Behind the riders in the center of this formation was a second line composed of foot soldiers that had 2,000 elite spearmen of the royal guard standing ten-deep in its middle with the Great King at their rear. Divided into 1,000-man splits on either side of the guards were Greek mercenary hoplites eight shields deep and there was a contingent of archers in place on the left flank to complete the infantry array. In addition to these footmen immediately rearward of the main line of cavalry, there were screening forces in advance of it as well. On the left, some 2,000 riders held post outside of 100 chariots, the combination covering the last 1.5km of the battle front on that side with the vehicles in single file at 10m spacing. Another 50 chariots sat across 500m before Darius and his infantry units in the Persian center. And over on the right wing, the final kilometer was preceded by 50 chariots with 2,000 cavalrymen outboard. As for the rest of the footmen on hand, they massed some distance to the rear. The kardakes (both heavy and light-armed), if present, must have centered these in a phalanx ten men deep stretching across maybe 1km. The various satrapal levies would then have projected off either side. These latter were mostly light missilemen, but some armored Babylonian spearmen with large shields were on hand as well.

Arrian gives us a detailed description of how Alexander set up his forces in response to this imposing Persian array (3.11.8–12.5). He put his companion horsemen on the right, placing before them a screen of Thracian peltasts along with half the Agrianians and their normally attached archers. The agema of royal hypaspists stood beside the hetairoi; next in line came the other hypaspists and then the pike regiments filled out the rest of the phalanx leftward (with 2,000 men each as at Issus). Some of the allied Greek horsemen held station alongside the last unit of phalangites on the far side with the Thessalian cavalry lined up beyond to complete the battle line. Probably filed at four (hypaspists) and eight (phalangites) much as at Issus, the heavy infantry began the day in open order that kept wide spacing between files.

Even thus spread out, Alexander could see that once his phalanx closed ranks for combat and his cavalry adjusted inward accordingly, he would face an overlap on either flank from the long opposing array of Persian horsemen. He therefore made special deployments off both ends of his main formation. On the right, he posted the other half of the Agrianians and associated bowmen, refusing them at an angle from the companion horsemen's flank. He then placed cavalry (a mercenary squadron leading the Paeonians and lancers) in front of these foot skirmishers and added a contingent of hoplites to their right side (the "Old Mercenaries," presumably a picked unit of maybe 1,000 from the hirelings that had come over in 334). This mixed-arms team was to either extend the main line or fend off any enemy attempt at envelopment as circumstance might dictate. Alexander similarly refused a force from the other flank that was mostly mounted. Consisting of the remaining riders of the 7,000 or so Arrian claimed were on hand, these had another squadron of mercenary horsemen standing in front of allied Greeks and Thracians, with the latter accompanied by their javelineer footmen. (Note that contingents of foot archers and mercenary hoplites might have been present to support the horsemen on the left wing as per Fuller [1960, 171] and Green [1991, 291]. This is logical and attractive, but is derived from Curtius [4.13.29] and Diodorus [17.57.3], who both seem to actually be describing cavalry squadrons in agreement with the battle order of Arrian that is preferred here.)

Alexander's mercenary spearmen, like their mounted counterparts, had greatly increased in numbers thanks to plunder-financed recruiting over the last couple of years. Attached to the allied hoplites, they probably boosted the Greek heavy-armed corps up to around 12,000 in addition to the Old Mercenaries already deployed. These troops formed up behind the Macedonian heavy array, creating a second phalanx at eight shields deep that might have spanned 1.5km not counting screens of light footmen off either flank. (This formation supports the idea

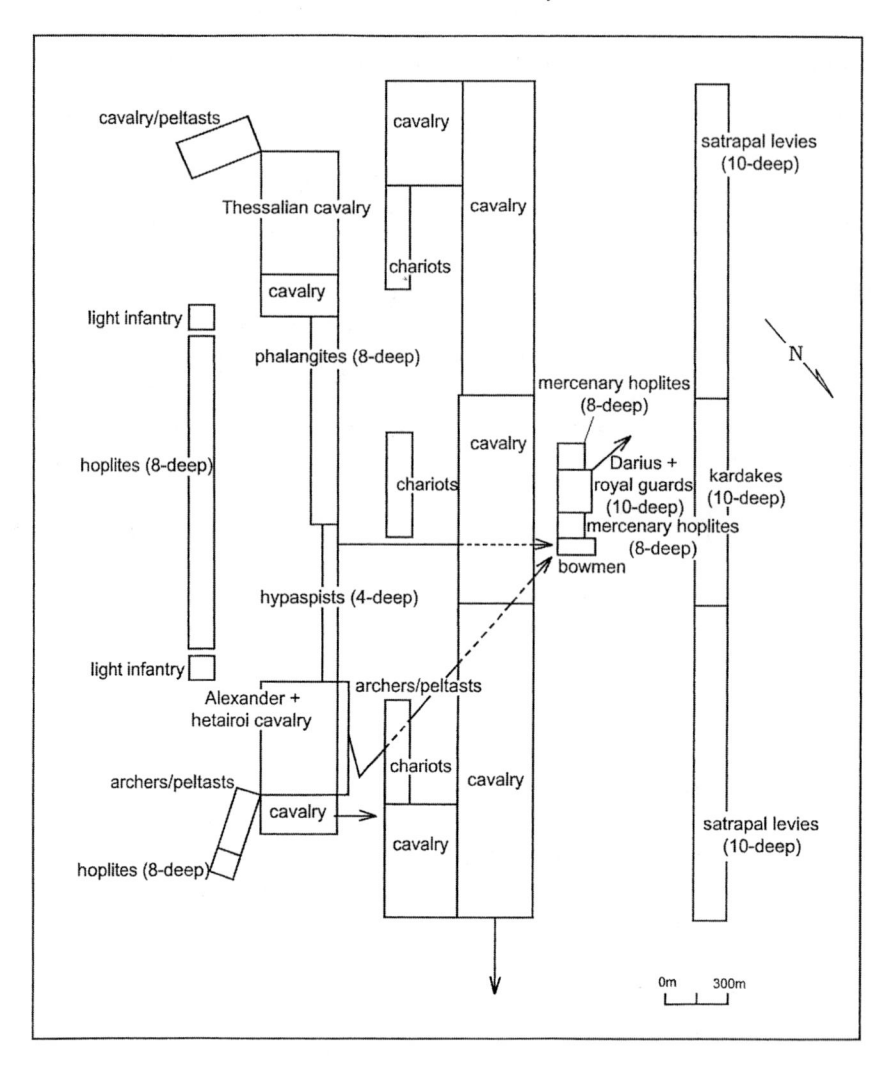

BATTLE OF GAUGAMELA (331 B.C.) (BOXES REPRESENTING FORCES ARE EXAGGERATED TO SHOW RELATIVE SIZES.)

that something similar was done at Granicus River, where there was also great fear of envelopment by a cavalry-rich opponent unconstrained by lateral terrain barriers.) By turning about, such an arrangement could counter any mounted threat from the rear. It was also able to advance to meet enemy forces should they penetrate the forward battle line or, in the worst case, stand as a bulwark in support of a retreat. Rearward of these reserves sat the army's baggage train with a guard of Thracian peltasts. Considering both these various backing forces and the main phalanx, Arrian gave Alexander 40,000 infantry at Gaugamela, a third less than Darius, but 70 percent heavy-armed in contrast to the Persian's 25 percent.

As the armies closed on each other, Alexander and his hetairoi drifted rightward, moving toward less level ground beyond the enemy left. Their intent seems to have been to repeat the flanking maneuver that had worked so well at Granicus River. However, the Scythian and Bactrian cavalry (sitting next to the 100-chariot deployment and farthest left among the Persian front-screen on that side) moved to head this off. Alexander countered by having his right-flank mercenary horsemen charge to engage these foes before they could block his end run. The mercenary riders were outnumbered by better than 2 to 1 and took a terrible beating, but as they fell back, the Paeonians and lancers behind came up in replacement. A fierce fight developed forward on Alexander's right, with the Macedonian riders first gaining the upper hand. The Bactrians then rebounded and the Scythians eventually returned as well to use their superior armor against the more lightly equipped European horsemen (Arrian 3.13.4).

At this point, all three of the scythed chariot contingents raced out to attack. Alexander's peltasts on the right took a heavy toll on the charioteers and their horses before these engines could reach the front; and there, along the phalanx, the hypaspists and phalangites were still in open order and shifted files to form lanes down which the vehicles could be channeled. Many of the chariots were thus disabled while others passed harmlessly through the lines, though some did find the mark with their whirling blades. Diodorus (17.58.4–5) said that "they severed the arms of many, shields and all, and in no small number of cases they cut through necks and sent heads tumbling to the ground with the eyes still open and the expression of the countenance unchanged, and in other cases they sliced through ribs with mortal gashes and inflicted a quick death." Yet the phalanx kept cohesion and, after the chariots had passed and been captured at the rear, it closed ranks and advanced into the enemy front. (Note that the practicality of phalangites creating the sort of avenues described in our sources has been fairly questioned [Heckel et al 2010]. This suggests that the chariots were able to pass through only forward-posted light infantry and, in fact, met defeat [at least against Alexander's right and center] without ever penetrating his phalanx.)

The Paeonians and lancers had by now pushed the Thracian and Bactrian mounted screen back and to its left, driving ahead to cut into the main line of enemy horsemen. This pulled the Persians toward them, which combined with movement that direction in response to Alexander's opening rightward shift to create a gap in the imperial cavalry front where it bordered Darius and his infantry array. The aggressive Macedonian king saw this opening and charged with the hetairoi. Angling back across the open field, he hit at the thinning spot just as his phalanx's bristling weapons were closing into shock contact. The Persian horsemen gave way and Alexander and his riders drove through with their xysta along the left flank of Darius' infantry. Scattering the last of the enemy cavalry and foot archers there, the horse companions wheeled to take the mercenary and guard spearmen from side and rear even as the hypaspists thrust and shoved into them and the pikemen down the line extended their sarissai to lock the other Persians in place. (If not Issus, then *this* is the moment captured on the Alexander Sarcophagus, with hypaspist and Persian hoplites dueling while hetairoi led by their warrior monarch lance down footmen and stray riders alike.)

In a repeat of his defeat in Cilicia, Darius could see enemy cavalry spilling out around the back of his line and the hypaspists beginning to roll up his spearmen's left flank. A rout was clearly imminent and he once more chose to flee. And no sooner did the king take off than his entire left wing through center collapsed to follow suit, the stampede carrying the large infantry formation at the rear along with it. Alexander and his accompanying riders delayed for a few critical minutes to clear their side of the field of the last resistance and then set out in pursuit.

Over on the Macedonian left, things were still dicey. Parmenio commanded that wing and was having a devil of a time fighting off swarms of Persians that had gone on the attack behind the chariot charge. Some of the enemy riders had skirted his position (or, much less likely, cut through it) and raced for the baggage train only to have the reserve phalanx turn about and put them under attack. But so occupied, the allied and mercenary spearmen were not then able to react to Alexander's leaving the field. His departure thus denuded the right side of Parmenio's part of the line. There, cavalry that had stood left of the Persian center were still unaware of Darius' flight and pressed the Macedonian so that he now faced the prospect of simultaneous assaults from the front and both flanks. In fear of encirclement, Parmenio sent a courier to

Alexander begging for help. The king responded, halting the chase to rescue his endangered left wing. On the way back, he met enemy horsemen fleeing rearward and some of the day's most ferocious cavalry action ensued as the Macedonian and his troopers made their way past foes desperate to go the opposite direction. In a mounted variation on Agesilaos' costly second assault at Coronea II (394), Alexander bloodied the enemy before they broke through and escaped, but took heavy casualties in return as some 60 of his companion riders lost their lives and many others fell wounded. As it turned out, by the time that Alexander reached Parmenio, the action had turned. The Thessalian cavalry had done a masterful job and managed to drive off the Persian horsemen, who were retreating even as the hetairoi arrived on the scene. Reversing course once more, Alexander went back to pursuing Darius; however, it was too late, and though chased until dark, the Great King made good his getaway. Meanwhile, Parmenio had finally advanced with his battered wing to flush the enemy from his sector and capture the Persian camp.

Our sources give a variety of numbers for the Persians lost at Gaugamela: Curtius 40,000 (4.16.26), the Oxyrhynchus Historian 53,000 (1798), Diodorus 90,000 (17.61.3) and Arrian 300,000 (3.15.6). Even the lowest appear grossly overstated. And reduced to percentages, a wide range still persists: 9 percent for Diodorus, 16 percent for Curtius and 30 percent for Arrian. Given that only 1,500 of the 2,000 mercenary hoplites later gave up (Diodorus 17.76.1), a loss of 25 percent among the Persian heavy infantry looks realistic. Yet, the more mobile light infantry and cavalry (over 90 percent of the Persian army) surely took much less damage. This suggests something in the 10–15 percent range as a more likely overall loss. As for the Macedonian dead, we get 100 from Arrian, 300 from Curtius, 500 from Diodorus and 1,200 from the Oxyrhynchus Historian. At 2.5 percent, the last figure would be well within the normal range for a fairly hard-fought victory in this era.

The Peloponnese

While Alexander was besting Darius, problems were mounting for his rule back home. Memnon, who was governor in Thrace, had decided to break away from Macedonia and carve out his own kingdom. Antipater marched against him with his entire army, but had to settle for a negotiated resolution, keeping Memnon in his position in return for a renewed pledge of loyalty. This lenient settlement was prompted on Antipater's part by his urgent need to address an uprising in southern Greece.

Vs Corrhagus and Megalopolis (331 B.C.)

Antipater had garrisoned the Peloponnese under the general Corrhagus, who was perhaps headquartered at the center for Alexander's Greek league in Corinth. The Spartan king Agis III led a force of mercenaries against him during the summer of 331. Agis' troops probably numbered 8,000, Diodorus having recorded (17.48.1) that he used that many on Crete two years earlier. The Spartan's army might have included 6,000 hoplites and 2,000 foot skirmishers, with the latter mostly peltasts (though a few Cretan archers might have followed Agis home as well). Corrhagus would also have had a largely mercenary force, maybe with 4,000 of it heavy-armed in line with detachments often used in the past for minor Macedonian expeditions. Corrhagus' spearmen likely enjoyed support from 1,000–1,500 in light infantry. Agis thus might have had an edge in manpower, but not one so overwhelming as to entirely discourage his enemy from accepting battle. Still, he must have used his greater numbers to carry the action either with deeper files pushing through at a critical point or longer ranks wrapping around a flank. The latter, being a typically "Spartan" approach, is maybe a bit more likely. At any rate, Agis gained a crushing victory that "destroyed" his foes (Aeschines *Against Ctesiphon* 165) and killed Corrhagus. We might put the Macedonian's losses at 20–30 percent and those of Agis at 3–5 percent.

The Spartans now became champions of Greek independence and attracted troops from other discontented poleis. Diodorus (17.62.7) put this uprising's total strength at 20,000 infantry and 2,000 horsemen. The foot soldiers probably broke down into 4,000 light infantry and 16,000 hoplites. Among the spearmen there were likely almost 6,000 hirelings and 4,000–5,000 Spartans (their entire muster) with the rest (5–6,000) being allies from Elis, Achaea and Arcadia (the latter perhaps the more numerous). Cavalry primarily came from Sparta and Elis, though some renegades from Phocis and Thessaly might have been present as well. (Demosthenes boasted of having brought some Thessalians into revolt [Aeschines *Against Ctesiphon* 167].) Agis led this coalition army and took it into Messenia. Megalopolis had remained openly loyal to Alexander there and the Spartan king put that city under siege.

Antipater was delayed by the situation in Thrace, but by summer's end had returned to regroup and lead out his entire homeland force to deal with the Greek revolt. He collected some still loyal allies on the way south until he had 40,000 men in all (Diodorus 17.63.1). About a quarter of his troops were Macedonians: 3,000 hypaspists, 9,000 phalangites, 3,000 foot skirmishers and 1,000 horsemen. (This cavalry count represents 600 light lancers and only 400 hetairoi, Antipater having just sent off a third of his native horsemen to reinforce Alexander [Diodorus 17.65.1].) His other soldiers might have numbered 15,000 hoplites, 5,000 light infantrymen and 4,000 riders. The allied cavalry was Thracian, Thessalian and Boeotian, while the infantry came from Boeotia, the Peloponnese (especially the northeast) and mercenary ranks (maybe up to a third). Therefore, it was a powerful armament that arrived with Antipater to disrupt Agis' siege of Megalopolis; one that, in fact, reversed the manpower advantage that the Spartan had held over Corrhagus.

Caught in open country by an enemy much superior in both numbers and quality of horsemen, Agis had no real option for escape and formed up instead for a pitched battle. He faced an opposing heavy infantry formation that likely stretched across more than 2.6km of the plain before Megalopolis, forcing him to file thinly if he was to avoid a dangerous enemy overlap. He thus must have lined up only five or six shields deep. His phalanx probably had the picked men from Elis (the Three Hundred and the Four Hundred) on the far left with their other countrymen and the Achaeans and the Arcadians next in that order across the center. Agis and his Spartans took the post of honor on the right wing. Antipater likely set up his phalangites at either ten or 16-deep. The former had been common under Philip, but the latter, thicker array might now have become standard practice under Alexander; moreover, even in files of 16, Antipater could still compel the enemy to stretch out at non-optimum depth. These pikemen would have held the far left to anchor the battle line on that end. As for his spearmen, the Macedonian probably deployed them in eight-man files. He and his hypaspists no doubt took their customary station on the right, with the mercenaries next in line and allied militia spearmen filling in down to where the phalangites stood. (Note that Antipater could have filed his pikemen at eight-deep just as Alexander sometimes did in Asia during this period. However, there, the king's sarissa-armed troops, which weren't as well suited as hoplites for envelopment maneuvering, assumed these thinner arrays to stretch out his line against larger opponents, which wasn't the case here. Therefore, it's more likely that Antipater used his phalangites in their traditional defense-oriented role and stacked them as deeply as was practical.)

With cavalry and light infantry screening off their flanks, the phalanxes closed into shock combat to initiate what was to prove a long, grinding fight. Agis and his Spartan spearmen had not been able to outflank the phalangites on their end of the line nor could they gain sufficient penetration into the bristling hedge of serried pike-points to do telling damage. As for the Macedonian pikemen, they patiently stuck to their knitting, fixing their foes in place and jabbing away with their ungainly weapons to do whatever harm they could against men whose armor and large, overlapping shields offered precious few targets of opportunity. It was slow, strenuous work and not destined (indeed, not even designed) to be decisive. Nonetheless, it exacted a price from the enemy as, here and there over time, the sarissai found rare openings and laid a few Spartan front-fighters low. And at some point, Agis, who stood somewhere in the forward ranks, became one of those victims, going down with a wound serious enough to keep him from regaining his feet.

The Spartans kept on fighting with equal measures of fury and frustration as their king was carried to the rear. The battle thus remained hopelessly stalemated along one wing while the light-armed fray was apparently no more decisive off either flank, making it action on the other wing that would be critical. Here, on the Macedonian right, it was hoplite against hoplite with part-time militiamen for the Greeks (albeit some of them elite) spear-fighting against full-time soldiers, whether they be Macedonian or mercenary. This was a contest of endurance and willpower in which Antipater's well-seasoned and more deeply filed professionals finally prevailed. Unable to resist any longer, the allies on Agis' left wing lost heart at last and broke away in flight, forcing the still game Spartans to also give way too lest they be surrounded.

Antipater's large cadres of horsemen and foot skirmishers may have underperformed during the main action, but they now executed a thorough and deadly chase. As a result, the rebel death toll rose to nearly 25 percent (5,300 per Diodorus [17.63.3]). It was at this stage where Agis actually met his end when a group of pursuing peltasts caught up with the men trying to carry him to safety. The king ordered that his comrades flee to fight another day; then, rising to his knees, he made a solitary last stand. Diodorus claimed that Agis managed to kill a number of his lighter-armed attackers before a thrown javelin took him down for good. The stubborn battle had been costly for Antipater. He lost 3,500 men (almost 9 percent), which was very high for a victorious force in this period. However, Megalopolis was even more devastating for his opponents as, having taken horrific casualties and with a king dead, the Spartans were broken and their uprising finished.

The Persian Campaign II

Alexander advanced from Gaugamela to enter Susa, site of a huge imperial treasury. Seizing those riches, he rested and received reinforcements from home that were badly needed to replace losses to date. Per Curtius (5.1.40–41), these included 6,000 Macedonian infantry, 3,500 Thracian peltasts and 4,000 Greeks (probably mostly hoplites). There was also cavalry, amounting to 500 Macedonians, 600 Thracians and 380 Greeks. It was at this time that the hetairoi reorganized, setting up two companies within each squadron (four within the double-sized royal unit). Thus refreshed, Alexander set out to capture the rest of the Persian realm. This called for passing through a number of choke points that were defended either by independent local tribal forces or still effective segments of Darius' army. The first challenge came from some of the Ouxioi tribesmen east of Susa. The mountain dwelling Ouxioi tried to extort a fee for passage through their land, but Alexander outmaneuvered them and gained their surrender. He did this with a night action using some 11,000 men (the hypaspists, perhaps four regiments of pikemen [once more at 1,500/taxis] and 2,000 others [most likely Agrianians, archers and horsemen]).

Gaining a position in the mountainous terrain above the enemy, he persuaded them to end their resistance.

Alexander next raced to secure the Persian capital of Persepolis and its riches. He sent the bulk of his army toward the city via the wagon route, which required a long trek through flat country. Alexander himself set out along a rugged, yet more direct path that led through the mountain pass known as the Persian Gate. In this way, he hoped to speed his arrival and prevent any treasure from being spirited beyond his grasp. Along with him were the Macedonian infantry, the Agrianians with attached archers, the hetairoi and the prodromoi lancers. He found a large body of imperial troops holding the Gate. Curtius put these at 25,000 infantry (5.3.17) while Diodorus added another 300 cavalry (17.68.1) and Arrian claimed 40,000 infantry and 700 horsemen (3.18.2). Once more employing a night departure with picked troops, Alexander used a local guide to gain a position above the enemy forces in the pass. At the same time, he detached some of his men to seal off the passage's backside. The Macedonians then struck from front, back and above to clear the pass for an easy descent.

Reunited with his army at Persepolis, Alexander added more treasure to his coffers and was ready to resume his pursuit of Darius. This sent him back north toward Ecbatana in Media, which lay just below the Hyrkanian (Caspian) Sea. It was rumored that the Persian king was gathering an army there. However, unable to find sufficient strength, Darius fled before his foe could arrive. Giving chase once more, Alexander followed with the Macedonian infantry, the Agrianians and archers, his companion cavalry, the prodromoi and a contingent of mercenary horsemen. But the Persian ruler was not destined for capture. Even as Alexander drew near, Darius fell to assassination, victim of a conspiracy of his followers led by Bessos, satrap of Bactria (modern Afghanistan). Most of Alexander's men now considered the war over; still, the monarch's ambitions remained unsatisfied. Though he duly noted the end of the original campaign and excused his Greek allied troops from further obligation, he enrolled many of them for further service on a voluntary basis. He then exerted both his popularity and authority as king to persuade the Macedonians to stay aboard as well.

Aria (330 B.C.)

Alexander began consolidating his Persian conquest by moving east into Hyrkania and then Mardia in 330. The Mardians put up some resistance. Alexander found them attempting to hold a pass with 8,000 men, but yet again executed a successful maneuver, marching to get above the defenders and drive them from their position with heavy loss. Bessos, meanwhile, had proclaimed himself Great King and was trying to assemble an army back in his home province of Bactria. Alexander had to deal briefly with an uprising in Aria to the south, using a flying column of cavalry and light infantry to scatter rebels under his traitorous governor, Satibarzanes (Curtius gives the fullest account of this action [6.6.20–26]). He then moved against Bessos that winter, marching across Bactria and into the Indian Caucasus (today's Hindu Kush range). He founded a city (another Alexandria) in that gateway to India and crossed the mountains into modern Pakistan before turning back upon learning that Bessos had now fled northward. It would take until the spring of 329 to finally run the faux monarch down west of the Caspian Sea in Sogdiana. It was there where Persians seeking Alexander's favor betrayed and turned Bessos over to Ptolemy. He would eventually be tortured and put to death for his part in the murder of Darius.

As these events were playing out in the farther eastern regions of Persia, things had turned ugly once more back in Aria. Satibarzanes had returned to foster another revolt bringing 2,000 horsemen (who had joined in his earlier flight from Alexander) and having added a few more back in his old satrapy (he'd escaped with only "the most he could muster on short notice" [Curtius 6.6.22]). He also must have regained some of the light-armed foot soldiers that had remained behind. Curtius claimed that these originally numbered at least 13,000 (6.6.24), but this seems exaggerated and we might suspect that the renegade leader probably had just a couple of thousand footmen. At any rate, Alexander thought another modest column should be adequate to address the renewed threat and dispatched the Macedonian Erigyius, commander of 600 allied Greek horsemen, along with Stasenor, another of his inner circle. The latter likely led a contingent of Thracian peltasts. Also on the expedition was Arsaces, the replacement for Satibarzanes as satrap of Aria, and Phrataphernes, Alexander's Parthian governor. The latter would have brought sufficient Asian levies to provide a garrison and more than match the insurgent cavalry and infantry.

There were several small engagements and skirmishes before a major battle was finally fought. This settled into an inconclusive, cavalry-dominated action in which the rebels "were holding their own" (Diodorus 17.83.5). Seeking to break the impasse, Satibarzanes, a rather courageous character it seems, rode out to make an astounding offer if we are to believe Diodorus and Curtius. This was to settle the issue by single combat in a throwback to heroic times past. Erigyius accepted the challenge, though being an older man with white hair. The two champions removed their helmets and went at it on horseback, one wielding a javelin and the other with his Macedonian xyston. Dodging the rebel leader's cast, Erigyius took him through the throat with his lance then dismounted to pull the weapon free and finish his kill. He thus ended the rebellion with minimal losses on either side as Satibarzanes' men surrendered. Arrian had a different take on this affair, describing a "fierce battle" in which the aforementioned duelists just happened to meet, with the rebel chief's death then causing his troops to flee "pell-mell" (3.28.3). If this were the case, casualties on the losing side would have been much higher, probably in the 25–35 percent range.

This was a period in which Alexander became increasingly concerned about plots against his life. In October of 330, he discovered that his cavalry commander Philotas had been aware of an assassination scheme yet hadn't taken action against it. The king not only had Philotas executed, but went on to order the murder of his father Parmenio as well. The latter had been Philip's best general and, as second in command to Alexander, a key figure in the conquest of Persia.

Jaxartes, Alexandria Escalate and Polytimetos River (329 B.C.)

Alexander rested his forces a while in Sogdiana and then set out that summer to push his travels to the very edge of the Persian realm. This took him northeast to the Jaxartes River, considered in that era to mark the western boundary of Asia. One of his foraging parties was attacked there by sling and bow-armed tribesmen that were said to number 20,000 (Curtius 7.6.2) or 30,000 (Arrian 3.30.10). The barbarians withdrew to take up a defensive stance on high ground surrounded by steep cliffs and Alexander went after them with a select column. His contingent was highly mobile, probably consisting of his hypaspists, the Agrianians and attached archers and the companion cavalry, possibly with the lighter Macedonian lancers as well. Given the relatively small size of this command (less than 6,000 men), we might question whether the barbarians were really as numerous as claimed, though their position on high ground was to prove more critical than any manpower advantage they might have held.

Both of our sources agree that Alexander was repulsed attempting an uphill assault on the enemy, who showered his troops with missiles until they had to retreat. Alexander himself took a shaft in the lower leg that fractured his fibula, and it was probably the sight of their commander being carried from the field with arrowhead still imbedded that finally prompted the Macedonians to retire. What happened next is unclear. Curtius said that the tribesmen met with Alexander and surrendered. Arrian, on the other hand, claimed that the king returned to capture the barbarian stronghold in some unknown manner and slay all but 8,000 of its defenders. To be frank, Curtius' version seems much the more likely, with that of Arrian probably a contrivance meant to keep Alexander's undefeated combat record intact. If so, the 8,000 citation for surviving tribesmen is better seen as a full count of how many were actually present, nearly all of them living to tell the tale.

Alexander spent the next few weeks building and fortifying a city, Alexandria Eschate (the "furthermost"), which he intended to mark the northeastern frontier of his empire. There were also talks at this time with the people thereabout, who were ethnic Scythians. However, rightly disturbed by the ongoing Macedonian construction project as a sign of long term occupation, these rose up in a revolt that rapidly spread until it included most of Sogdiana. Alexander attacked and took down the nearby rebel strongholds. He also dispatched a relief expedition to the Sogdian capital, where a garrison he'd left was reported to have come under attack. This effort contained 60 hetairoi (an under-strength company) and an allotment of mercenaries including 800 horsemen (former Greek allies now serving for hire) and nearly 1,500 infantry (perhaps 300 of them light-armed and the rest hoplites). Meanwhile, a large group of mounted Scythians appeared on the Jaxartes' eastern bank. Having heard that their kinsmen were in action, these men had come to join (and profit from) the fray and took to firing both insults and arrows across the stream.

Determined to put the Scythians in their place, Alexander brought up his bolt-throwing catapults and laid down a barrage to drive the enemy horsemen back from the riverside. He then crossed with his archers and slingers, who set up a perimeter, their missiles keeping the barbarians at a distance while the phalanx came over followed by cavalry. Alexander next sent one squadron of mercenary horsemen and four of lance-armed riders (prodromoi, maybe 500 men in all) against the Scythians. But the tribal fighters proceeded to encircle these mostly shock-oriented troopers, riding around them while loosing arrows. Moving to rescue his vanguard, Alexander mixed archers and peltasts with his remaining cavalry and charged. The mounted javelinmen (perhaps over 4,000 strong) split out to attack off either flank in company with four squadrons of the hetairoi. Meanwhile, the king himself led out the royal unit of companions, taking them straight up the middle at the enemy.

Caught between the prodromoi landward and Alexander's advance, the Scythians nearest the river broke right and left, barging into their compatriots in either direction to then be driven before the galloping wings of javelineers and hetairoi. As their entire complement now joined in a state of panic, the barbarians fled under hot pursuit. This turned into a long and grueling run in the summer heat that saw thirsty men and horses drinking whatever they could find in their haste. And when Alexander fell ill from bad water, the action was finally called off. The Scythians had left 1,000 dead alongside the river and lost many more during the extended chase, with their fallen perhaps totaling 10–20 percent of a 15,000–20,000 strong gathering. This sound beating brought the Scythian chief to terms, Alexander acquiescing if for no other reason than it would be too difficult for him to effectively sustain further hostilities.

The mounted circling tactics that had so bedeviled Alexander's advance units on the Jaxartes soon brought the Macedonian even greater grief along another river, the Polytimetos. This waterway flowed on the north side of the Sogdian capital of Marakanda, which rebel forces had attacked under Spitamenes, a Bactrian or Sogdian who had led the betrayers of Bessos. The insurgents went after the Macedonian garrison in the citadel, but a sortie had driven them back. They then withdrew east along the Polytimetos upon learning of the approach of the troops that Alexander had sent to relieve the city. This column pursued Spitamenes all the way to the Sogdian border and caught him on level ground at the edge of desert country.

Spitamenes had allied with the nomadic Scythian tribesmen in this region to add 600 mounted archers and bring his horsemen up to around 2,000. Taking advantage of greater numbers and open terrain, he waited while his foes set up in phalanx. Their array was probably composed of 1,200 Greek spearmen filed eight-deep across a 150m front. The cavalry and light footmen would have split off either flank, perhaps with the small band of hetairoi beside their heavy infantry on the right. But before the hoplite formation could advance, Spitamenes charged and, rather than closing directly against the phalanx, his bowmen began to circle it on the broad plain. The Scythians rode round and round as they pelted the closely ordered spearmen and their light-armed comrades with clouds of shafts and the other Asian riders added in more arrows and javelins for good measure. This was the same sort of thing that Philip had come up against years before on the Dobruja Plain and that his son had faced just days earlier. Unfortunately for the men now confronting Spitamenes, there was no one of Philip's or Alexander's caliber among their leaders to devise an adequate countermeasure this time. Thus, the phalanx and its auxiliaries found themselves in a hopeless trap, with swift moving enemies easily skipping back from each slow sally by Greek horsemen on march-weary mounts and then closing back to lethal effect on the befuddled heavy infantry formation regardless of whether it chose to advance or retreat.

Unable to stand such pummeling, the Greeks formed a square and retreated toward the river in a desperate effort to gain relief. Once at the water's edge, the cavalry plunged in and made its way to the far side while the infantry tried to follow, wading in as a disorderly mob. The barbarians closed about from all directions to chase those who had already gotten across and pin the rest mid-passage. Firing missiles from up and down stream as well as from both banks, the attackers drove the men still in the flow onto a small island and shot them down, going on to kill even those few who lived long enough to surrender. In the end, only 40 horsemen (less than 5 percent) and 300 foot soldiers (20 percent, probably almost exclusively light-armed) managed to escape the slaughter. (This is per Arrian [4.6.1]. Curtius [7.7.39] claimed that infantry losses were greater [2,000, this maybe being more men than were actually present], but cut cavalry deaths to only 300.) Arrian noted that there was a variant on this tale, which he attributed to Aristobulus. Here, the Scythians launched a surprise attack from wooded cover after the battle was already joined (and following an argument among the Greek officers in which none was willing to assume overall command). Curtius likewise proposed an ambush (7.7.31–38), though with different details.

Learning what had happened on the Polytimetos, Alexander went there with a strong armament to get revenge. However, he was unable to catch Spitamenes and had to settle for ravaging the countryside along the river to punish locals said to have joined in the action. He then retired into Bactria to set up winter quarters and receive some reinforcements. Among the new troops was a group of Greek mercenaries having 4,000 infantry and 1,000 cavalry. Another 4,000 foot soldiers and 500 riders came from the Lycian coast and a force of equal size arrived from Syria. Finally, Antipater sent 8,000 Greeks that included 600 cavalry.

Xenippa (328 B.C.), Gabai (328/327 B.C.) and Pareitakene (327 B.C.)

Over the course of the winter and into the next year, Alexander pacified Sogdiana and Bactria. This included campaigning against the still defiant Spitamenes and his band of Bactrian exile horsemen. Operating as bandits, these outcasts had allied with the Massagetae (a tribe from beyond the Jaxartes similar in their habits to the Scythians). These provided 800 bow-armed riders. Combining the tribesmen with 2,500 of his own cavalry, Spitamenes managed in the summer of 328 to wipe out 300 Macedonian and mercenary riders under Attinas. This came either in a sneak attack near a wooded area (Curtius 8.1.3–5) or by overwhelming most of them in a fortified position (Arrian 4.16.4–5). He killed a few hetairoi and mercenary horsemen in an ambush shortly thereafter. Amyntas, who was serving as Alexander's satrap of Bactria, came up against the rebels that fall (the Massagetae having gone home at the end of the summer campaigning season) and fought them in a major engagement.

Amyntas had two regiments of pikemen (3,000), two squadrons of hetairoi (400) and all the mounted javelinmen (*hippakontistai*, perhaps 3,000–4,000 strong). He also fielded some loyal Bactrians (probably several thousand light footmen). Sallying with this force, he was caught by surprise and compelled to accept combat on open ground near the Sogdian city of Xenippa. A sharp cavalry action followed in which the Macedonian phalanx played only a small role as a rearward bulwark. The Bactrians managed to hold their own for some time (Curtius 8.2.16–17), but gave way at the last, losing 700 killed in the fight and flight (nearly 30 percent with another 300 captured). Macedonian damage came to 80 dead and 350 wounded (around 10 percent casualties; but, if all horsemen, only 2 percent killed from the cavalry force). This indicates a fierce engagement in which most of the fatalities came, as usual, among the losers during pursuit.

Another action between Alexander's forces and the Bactrians followed near Gabai, a location otherwise unknown. Once more reinforced by the Massagetae, who brought 3,000 riders, Spitamenes attacked a detachment under Coenus that was holding Sogdiana for the winter. The Macedonian had essentially the same force that Amyntas had fielded and he led this against the enemy's advance. Spitamenes had 4,000–4,500 horsemen including 1,000–1,500 survivors from Xenippa. The barbarians lost 700 men (above 15 percent) in a fight that must have followed along much the same lines as the one against Amyntas. Probably retiring more quickly this time, Spitamenes and his allies did less than half as much harm to the Macedonians as they had in that earlier action, killing just twelve foot soldiers and 25 horsemen (Arrian 4.17.6). (It's notable both here and in the preceding clash at Xenippa that the Macedonian heavy infantry consisted solely of phalangite taxeis. If those units carried their usual pikes, then these combats record the first instances of Macedonian phalanxes that had no hoplites in their ranks. Alternatively, Anson [2010] has made the interesting proposal that under Alexander at least one taxis initially and up to half of all phalangites eventually may have adopted hoplite gear, the latter expansion coming as part of improvements made after the battle of Gaugemela in 331 [Arrian 3.18.5; 4.25.1,5]. He suggests that these men might have carried the title of *asthetairoi* from their aspides bearing the symbol of a six-sided star or *aster*, hence "ast-hetairoi" or "star-companions.")

Spitamenes would take refugee after Gabai with his Massagetae friends. This proved fatal when the tribesmen elected to give him up in return for a peace accord. With his capture and execution, Alexander was finally clear to begin considering new conquests and began preparations over the winter and into the spring of 327 to tackle the most distant Persian territory of them all — India.

One major reform that Alexander might have instituted at this time was outfitting his hypaspists with sarissai. He had plenty of hoplites, having taken on massive numbers of mercenary and allied spearmen in the last year, thus his current priority was to boost available strength in pikemen. This arm was limited to men he'd brought over in 334 and from home in a couple of reinforcements since, and these had suffered a fair amount of attrition. Planning now to leave a portion of his remaining phalangites behind to help secure Persia while campaigning in India, Alexander may have decided that the best way to create replacements was to cross-train his other Macedonian heavy footmen, the hypaspists, in use of the pike. This would allow him to employ them as hoplites in the sort of mobile "flying" columns used in the past, yet also field an additional 3,000 pikemen if needed in the main line of battle. In fact, the light-armed nature of Indian warriors must have had him contemplating an increased role for such troops in the near future. Sarissai would clearly fare well against the poorly protected javelineers and swordsmen of India, whose short weapons made penetrating into a pike array very difficult. And having captured some elephants, it must also have been obvious that those mainstays of Indian warfare could better be handled by sarissai in conjunction with missile fire rather than by using traditional hoplite spears.

Our best clue that Alexander altered the hypaspists' weaponry going into India might be what he did with their defensive gear. These were his picked shock troops, men who had great pride in their special standing, and that status was marked above all by equipment that differed from what their less lionized Macedonian comrades used (even had the asthetairoi been outfitted as aspis-bearing spearmen). Alexander maintained this tradition by issuing new panoplies that continued to set them apart as picked men. The smaller shields they now carried were shod in silver rather than being of common, painted bronze like those of everyone else. This let them adopt the lofty title of agyraspides (*agyraspidai* or "Silver Shields" [Justin 12.7.5]). Furthermore, their cuirasses were to be decorated with precious metals (Curtius 8.5.4); after all, Alexander certainly had enough gold and silver on hand from his plundered Persian treasure troves. Of course, he couldn't slight his equally select horsemen in doing this, so he gave them elegant fittings too. The hetairoi got gilded bits for their horses and breast plates with ornamentation up to the Silver Shields' standard.

This period also saw Alexander make a significant move beyond the military realm when he finally took a wife. She was the Bactrian princess Roxanne. Many of his advisors had been urging him to marry since before he left Macedonia, fearing that their combat-happy king might die without siring an heir. The only legitimate successor at the moment was his older half-brother Arrhidaeus (Philip's son by Philine of Larissa), who had been born mentally deficient. In truth, however, given that Roxanne was only twelve years old, Alexander seems to have now accepted a bride less to find a quick solution to the problem of succession than to cement an important relationship with the Bactrians, who would be at his back once he set off for India. After all, such diplomatic marriages had been one of his father's specialties.

In the spring of 327, Alexander carried out a final round of campaigning in southeastern Persia prior to setting out for India. This included the capture of an elevated stronghold at the Sogdian Rock. He took this site by having a small band scale the height at night to get above its defenders and bluff them into surrender. Alexander then moved into Pareitakene, which lay immediately southeast of Sogdiana and northeast of Bactria. Here, he chased opposition forces off yet another fortified "rock" and co-opted their leader into an alliance, receiving provisions in return. Still, other local chiefs remained opposed to a Macedonian takeover and Alexander, eager to get on toward his Indian objective, left the general Craterus to deal with them. Craterus had command of 600 hetairoi (no doubt with some light infantry support) and four taxeis of pikemen (6,000 men). He engaged the resistance forces in a pitched battle of which we have no description beyond its being "fierce" (Arrian 4.22.2). Judging by reported casualties, the barbarian force might have numbered 600–800 in cavalry and ten times that many footmen, yielding a fair match in numbers for the Macedonians. Craterus must have been able to engage the enemy infantry so that his phalangites could pin them in place while his superior cavalry eventually carried the day on one or both flanks. Barbarian losses were 120 riders and 1,500 footmen (20–30 percent). We've no casualty report for Craterus, but can assume only minor losses (1–3 percent), mostly among the hetairoi. The Macedonians captured some of the defeated men, including one of their leaders, and returned to deliver these to Alexander in Bactria.

The Indian Campaign

Alexander finally set out for India in the summer of 327 with a force of 120,000 men per Curtius (8.5.4). In assessing this number, we can assume that he might have had some 15,000 Macedonian heavy footmen. These were the 3,000 cross-trained hypaspists in three regiments and 12,000 pikemen now in eight taxeis. There were probably some 3,000 foot skirmishers as well for a total of around 18,000 native Macedonian infantry. Greek allies and mercenaries might have added about 8,000 hoplites. (This is based on 13,000 at Gaugemela plus nearly 20,000 subsequent arrivals less combat casualties and detachments including garrisons and settlements. These reductions came to some 17,000 [Holt 2005. 97. 107] in the Sogdian/Bactrian campaigns alone; and had the spearmen equaled their share of the army [55 percent], they would have kicked in around 9,000 to that sum. Other dispersals since Gaugemela had taken at least 8,000 hoplites and about as many were left behind with Amyntas.) Allied and mercenary foot skirmishers probably supplied another 6,000 men. These counted Greek and Thracian peltasts (including 1,000 Agrianians) and archers (Cretans and those normally with the Agrianians, maybe 2,000 combined). All of this suggests that there were perhaps 32,000 foot soldiers in Alexander's host.

As for horsemen, between replacements from home, folding in the prodromoi and adding elite Asian recruits, Alexander might have brought his hetairoi contingent up to around 2,000 strong. His Greek and Thracian riders had numbered nearly 5,000 at Gaugemela and around 4,000 more had arrived later. Therefore, even if we subtract 3,000 for reductions and another 2,000 as being among 3,500 cavalry remaining with Amyntas, we might suspect around 4,000 Greek mercenary and Thracian horsemen were still on hand, perhaps split 40/60 in favor of the latter. Bactrian and Sogdian levies probably added another 2,000 troopers and there were 1,000 or so Scythian (Dahae) mounted archers. This suggests around 9,000 cavalry in all. Fighting men would thus have totaled no more than 40,000; therefore, if accurate at all, Curtius' tally must have included two non-combatants for each fighting man.

Aspasia, Massaka, Bazira and Ora (327/326 B.C.)

Alexander marched into the Hindu Kush and emerged on the south side of the mountain range that fall to demand fealty from those living west of the Indus River. This was the region of India formerly claimed for Persia by Darius I and a number of its tribal peoples quickly came to terms. There was also a pledge of support from the ruler of the important Indian city of Taxila, which lay beyond the Indus along the invasion's intended path. At this point, Alexander divided his army, sending his commanders Hephaestion and Perdiccas on with three taxeis of pikemen, half the hetairoi and all the mercenary horsemen (2,000) to clear the way and build a bridge over the Indus. Meanwhile, he moved with the rest of the army to secure his rear by putting down those locals still resistant. This campaign yielded early success with the capture of a series of cities by force, surrender and abandonment, though Alexander suffered a minor wound in one action when an arrow penetrated his armor to enter his shoulder.

With winter nearing, reports came in from a foraging expedition that hostile Aspasian tribesmen had gathered in great numbers. Alexander tackled this by splitting his force. Leonnatos, one of his bodyguards, led a contingent with two regiments of pikemen. Ptolemy headed another with two pike taxeis, one regiment of hypaspists (probably armed in hoplite fashion), the Agrianians, all the archers and half the cavalry. The king himself commanded a third division. This had the final taxis of phalangites, the other two regiments of hypaspists (the royal agema as spearmen and the other perhaps with pikes), all of the Greek hoplites, most of the light infantry and the rest of the cavalry. Finding the Aspasii sitting on high ground, Alexander dispatched his subordinates' contingents to make indirect approaches to either side. He then led his own element straight at the enemy across an open field.

The size of the opposing force is uncertain. Arrian's account seems dubious about Ptolemy's claim of more than 40,000 Aspasii prisoners taken in the battle's aftermath; still, it's clear that the barbarians must have outnumbered at least Alexander's division, since they held its size in contempt (Arrian 4.25.1). This suggests something on the order of 20,000–30,000 men (a third more to twice Alexander's strength) with 25,000 a fair average guess. Perhaps around half of these troops (12,000) might have been light archers that also carried javelins (thrust into the ground while using the bow) with a single-handed sword as a weapon of last resort. Another third or so (8,000) of the footmen were javelineers that held long, narrow shields, wore sparse body armor at best (confined to officers) and were also equipped with a sword. The rest of the infantry (3,000) was probably composed of swordsmen with wide-bladed, two-handed weapons. The horsemen (2,000) were mounted archers that also carried javelins (discharged first) and swords as a sidearm. (Head [1982, 135–139] has an excellent discussion of these various warrior types.)

If he had advanced with his hoplites eight shields deep and pikemen anchoring his left in files of 16, Alexander's heavy array would have been a little more than a kilometer in width. His Asian horsemen (1,500) likely stood outboard of the pike units. This put the Greek and Macedonian cavalry (1,000 and 500 respectively) on the right with the light footmen split among their mounted comrades on each flank. The bulk of the Indians eagerly rushed down to engage, javelineers and swordsmen leading the way for their archers as the cavalry spread off either wing. What followed was a short and decisive clash in which Alexander's troops proved superior in all phases and prevailed "without much trouble" (Arrian 4.25.1). Indian horsemen don't seem to have been very formidable at any time and it must have been fairly easy for the savvy Central Asian riders to hold them at bay on one side of the line while the European cavalry drove them with ease from the other. Then, even as the hoplites and pikemen closed through a relatively ineffective spray of missiles to threaten an extremely unequal shock fight, the tribesmen fled toward the rear.

Ptolemy had meantime approached the Indian position from one side, doing his best to pick his way across the rougher terrain there and find a reasonably accessible path. Facing a deeply filed but very lightly equipped enemy, his men were able to fight their way upslope under cover of their own missilemen. Mostly unarmored, the Indians had no chance in such an action, the slender shields plied by their leading ranks proving wholly inadequate against the spears and sarissai being thrust and jabbed up into them by much better protected foes. In the end, they had to give way. At the same time, Leonnatos and his phalangites, though probably standing more on the defensive rather than attacking up over what must have been worse ground than on Ptolemy's front, were successful as well. This all served to funnel the Aspasii down onto lower ground, where the cavalry herded them together to be captured in large numbers.

Alexander continued campaigning that winter. He now moved out front with a modest detachment against the Assakanians, whose territory lay just above that of the Aspasii. His detachment included the hetairoi (1,000), two taxeis of pikemen (3,000) the mounted javelinmen (2,000 Greeks, Bactrians and Sogdians) and the Agrianians and archers. The Assakanians were said to have 2,000 horsemen, 30,000 infantrymen and 30 elephants (Arrian 4.25.5); yet, they refused open battle upon the Macedonians' approach and withdrew to their cities. Once the rest of the army had caught up with him, Alexander went against the largest of the enemy towns, Massaka, which had hired 7,000 mercenaries from farther east in India to aid its defense. Alexander was confident in the ability of his men to rout anything that the enemy could throw at him and wanted to fight far from town so that he could mount a long pursuit. He therefore turned about shortly after forming up in front of Massaka and fell back toward a hill that sat at a distance from the city walls. And just as expected, the Assakanians took the bait. They ventured out to attack, giving chase as fast as they could and in great disorder.

Alexander waited until the enemy had almost gotten within bow range and then wheeled his phalanx about. If fully deployed, his heavy formation might have featured the phalangites on the left over a front of better than 600m at eight-deep and the hypaspists on the right in files of four across another 750m, all backed by a second phalanx of hoplites in case the highly mobile Indians tried to encircle. This reserve formation could have been either eight shields deep or only six, the latter allowing for a similar width as for the fronting array. Closing with the heavy footmen, Alexander sent out his mounted javelineers supported by the Agrianians and archers to skirmish in front. It seems that the Indians didn't stand to meet the phalanx, but turned tail before that deadly heavy array could even get near. Thus, despite Alexander's best efforts to deal them a severe blow, they escaped leaving just 200 dead behind — a mere 3 percent if only the mercenaries (in the lead) were brought to combat by pursuing skirmishers. The large numbers of Indian bowmen present must have been a key factor in screening this retreat by firing arrows to discourage a tight chase. Indeed, even Alexander, who was standing with the royal hypaspists, had a shaft graze his ankle.

Denied a crushing victory in the field, Alexander put Massaka under siege and, after a hard fight that cost him 25 of his men, gained a negotiated surrender of the Indian mercenaries. These emerged under an agreement to serve the Macedonians; however, when they attempted to escape instead, Alexander slaughtered them using his entire army. He then took the weakened city by storm. After this, Alexander reduced other strong points in the region, during which at least two other small battles were fought. One of these took place at the city of Bazira. Coenus was in command of the investment there, but had been ordered to join Alexander. Establishing a guard force in a fortified position to maintain the siege, he marched away. The Bazirans saw this as their best chance to break out and sallied against the troops Coenus had left behind. Our sources don't give a scope for this engagement, but it likely involved a garrison of 2,000–3,000 hoplites and some light infantry. The Indians might have had around 5,000 men, these being mostly bowmen and javelineers with a lesser number of swordsmen and cavalry. What followed was a sharp fight that gave the Greeks a victory and cost the losers nearly 500 killed (10 percent or so) with 70 more captured. This was no doubt another case of lightly equipped Indians collapsing once faced with shock combat against heavy, European-style infantry, with a majority of their casualties then coming at the hands of peltast pursuers. A similar tactical scenario likely played out at about the same time when the inhabitants of Ora sortied against a couple of taxeis of pikemen supported by some cavalry and light infantry. The Macedonians bested the attackers, "routing them easily" (Arrian 4.27.6) to keep the siege intact. The general size and results of this action probably closely resembled those at Bazira.

Alexander was eventually able to secure the entire region between the Indus and the mountains, taking Ora by storm and seizing the remaining cities after their defenders ran away, those at Bazira doing so in the middle of the night. The final pocket of resistance was on the Aornos Rock, a huge and lofty fortified site. The Bazirans and others holed up here for a last stand. However, Alexander and his men had already overcome such obstacles in Persia and did the same here, undertaking impressive engineering works to bring their bolt-throwing artillery to bear and force the site into surrender. From Aornos, the Macedonians marched to the Indus, arriving there intact after finding that the remaining hostiles in their path had fled.

Hydaspes River (326 B.C.)

Alexander crossed the bridge built over the Indus by his advance force. He then regrouped in the land of Taxila, which was the largest city between the Indus and Hydaspes rivers. Having already allied himself, the ruler there provided funds and food, joining other locals in adding 5,000 soldiers (including at least 700 horsemen) to the Macedonian host. Alexander incorporated these men into his army and did some minor reorganization. One alteration was to consolidate the pikemen into seven taxeis, cannibalizing the eighth to bring these up to full strength. Another change involved the hetairoi, who were now grouped into five units, each around 400 strong. News arrived at this time that the most powerful monarch beyond the Hydaspes River, Porus, was massing his forces in opposition. Alexander set out in the spring of 326 to take him on and camped on the Hydaspes directly across from the Indian's position. Porus was set up there on the defensive, using the river's monsoon swollen flood to advantage as he waited for promised allied support to arrive.

We have various claims for the size of Porus' army from Diodorus (17.87.2), Curtius (8.13.6) and Arrian (5.15.4). The most realistic estimate would seem to be a conservative combination of figures from these sources, leaning toward intermediate values and those most in agreement. This suggests 30,000 infantry, 3,000 cavalry, 300 chariots and 130 elephants. The infantry was probably 15,000 light bowmen, 10,000 shield-bearing javelineers and 5,000 two-handed swordsmen. The cavalry consisted of low-quality mounted archer/javelineers, while the chariots were large, four-horse devices that carried two bowmen and two drivers. The latter pair provided a key redundancy and allowed the driver that was not currently in use to fight with javelins. Each vehicle had an escort of two javelineers with shields on foot. (See Head [1982, 178–179] for a discussion of what is known about these unusual vehicles.) The elephants had a driver (mahout) and passenger, both men being armed with javelins and the passenger plying a sword as well.

Alexander was determined to fight this already impressive host before even more enemy soldiers could arrive. Concerned, however, about making a frontal attack on so strong a position, he sought an easier approach and carried out a series of troop movements up and down the river. This was meant to confuse the opposition as to just where the Macedonians might come across and included several feints toward discouraging close scrutiny of every move. A rumor was also floated for Porus' consumption that any offensive was going to wait until the river was below its current spring flood stage. Alexander then split his forces into three segments for a real attack. One division under Craterus was to remain in camp straight in front of Porus so as to keep his attention while Alexander led a strike contingent across the Indus at some distance upstream. The third group was to stand well back in reserve, ready to intervene should the enemy come over the river themselves. The reserve division consisted of three regiments of phalangites (4,500), the Greek hoplites (maybe 7,000 or so at this point) and the mercenary cavalry (about 1,600). Craterus had two taxeis of pikemen (3,000), the Indian allies (around 4,000–4.300 mostly light infantry and 700–1,000 horsemen), one squadron of hetairoi (400) and the Sogdian and Bactrian horsemen (2,000). For his attack force, Alexander had the hypaspists (3,000, apparently all with pikes), two taxeis of phalangites (3,000), peltasts (2,000, half of them Agrianians), all the foot bowmen (2,000), the remaining companion cavalry (1,600), the Thracian horsemen (maybe 2,400) and the Dahae horse-archers (1,000).

Taking advantage of a monsoon storm to help cover his departure, Alexander set out at night to ford the Indus. He came over the flood (maybe unplanned) at a spot where a large island partially hid his passage; nevertheless, enemy scouts spotted this movement and sent word to Porus. The Indian leader reacted cautiously to the news of a possible crossing and didn't immediately commit his entire army. Instead, he dispatched his son to address what he thought might be yet another feint, sending him out with 40 percent of his chariot force (120) and most of the cavalry (2,000). By the time that this detachment arrived, Alexander had already gathered his phalanx on the east side of the river and was beginning to advance. Hypaspists held the right wing of the Macedonian array and phalangites the left, with the javelineers split along either flank. While this infantry formation came on at marching pace, Alexander led the cavalry ahead in a column by squadrons, having horse-archers in the van and bow-armed footmen trailing closely. Upon seeing Alexander and his riders breaking for them at speed, the outnumbered Indians turned and fled. However, their chariots proved fatally slow on the muddy ground and were easily caught from behind, leading to a massacre in which almost all aboard were killed (nearly 400 dead including Porus' son).

Porus learned of this initial engagement and the death of his son; yet, facing Craterus' large force across the river, he remained unsure of what to do. Finally, he elected to leave about a third of his infantry (10,000) and elephants (40–50) behind to check Craterus and led the rest of his army against the Macedonian king. Moving out with the Indus on his left, he arrayed with the elephants (80–90) in a line at the fore. Spaced every 15m (Polyaenus 4.3.22), this yielded a frontage of just over 1,200m that had squads of javelineers and swordsmen backed by archers filling in densely (perhaps 20-deep) on each side of the pachyderms. His horsemen stood across 200–250m on the ends of the line with the chariots leading.

As the Indians closed toward Alexander, he paraded his cavalry out front. This bought time for the phalanx to arrive and catch its breath. He then carefully evaluated the enemy formation and spread out all his horsemen save for two squadrons of hetairoi on the right side of his foot array. These riders covered a span of just over 1km at eight-deep and were supported by the Agrianians and foot-archers. The phalanx next stretched along another 500m in files of eight and then the last couple of hetairoi squadrons under Coenus took post at eight-deep on the far left in company with the remaining peltasts. Alexander was thus able to match up with the Indian line's extent. It was his intention to initially refuse his left, consisting of the phalanx and the hetairoi on the far end, holding it back until he could use his superiority in cavalry on the right to break the enemy beside the Hydaspes.

The Indian horsemen charged out as their infantry came into bow range. Alexander then launched his contingent of Scythian horse-archers at the enemy's left-side riders, putting them into some confusion. He himself followed this up with a flanking attack using the right-wing hetairoi. Meanwhile, Coenus and his horsemen were threatening the other end of the Indian array so as to keep the hostile cavalry there from withdrawing to counter Alexander. But as the Macedonian king drove the enemy riders before him, Porus and his main line came forward. The phalanx troops, aware that the foe's horsemen were in flight near the river to secure that flank, moved up to meet Porus' advance and pin their portion of the opposing front in place. Diodorus noted that "they used their sarissai to good effect against the men stationed beside the elephants and kept the battle even" (17.88.2). As for the pachyderms themselves, "the phalanx also proceeded to exert relentless pressure against the frightened animals" (Curtius 8.14.25) and flanking javelineers took deadly aim at their mahouts. Along other parts of the front, the hetairoi prodded the great beasts back with their lances as attached skirmishers gave support and the foot-archers chipped in from the rear. Some of the Macedonian light infantrymen even hacked away at the elephants' feet with axes and curved blades taken along for this very purpose. The massive creatures charged individually as best they could and, here and there, did some significant damage. Diodorus described this carnage (17.88.1), with men trodden underfoot "armor and all," others lifted by trunks to be fatally dashed down and even more "pierced through by tusks" to die instantly. Still, these monsters ended up being largely stymied by both the tight phalanx and fluid up and back flow of agile horsemen and foot skirmishers elsewhere. While this was going on, the Indian cavalry attempted to rejoin the fight, but again proved no match for Alexander's much more numerous and better-equipped horsemen on one side and Coenus and his riders on the other.

Porus' lightly armed men were taking serious casualties and most of the elephants, which had lost their riders and accumulated many wounds, began to rampage about in the tight battle space, trampling and killing indiscriminately to deal harm to friend as well as foe. As it turned out, given their closer proximity to the beasts, it was the Indians who actually took the greater damage from them. With the Macedonian cavalry completely triumphant on either end of the battle front and wrapping around to envelop, the phalanx now closed ranks that had become somewhat jumbled in the fight and its men moved forward in unison, finally breaking the enemy array for good. The Indians, under assault from ahead and around both flanks, raced rearward through the only remaining opening. But death awaited them in that quarter too, since Craterus had by now brought his holding force across the river to bar the way (what happened to the Indians left behind to block such a move is unknown, most likely they remained in camp or simply ran away). These fresh troops dealt out heavy losses to the fleeing men to make Alexander's victory even more decisive.

Arrian's claim (5.18.2) of almost 20,000 Indian foot soldiers killed along with some 3,000 horsemen is clearly a tally of the total host defeated (two-thirds of Porus' army) rather than actual casualties. All the same, the death toll must have been steep. Diodorus' figure (17.89.1–2) of 12,000 killed (roughly 50 percent) seems possible. He also noted another 9,000 captured (35–40 percent of Porus' combat troops). As for the Indian monarch, he was seriously wounded, having been shot off his elephant while fighting cavalry and light footmen in the center of the battle line. He would, however, recover and keep charge of his kingdom under Alexander. With regard to Macedonian losses at Hydaspes River, Arrian put them at 80 (1 percent) of the 8,000 infantry with the king's main force (the phalanx and peltasts), 20 hetairoi (just over 1 percent) and 200 other horsemen (nearly 6 percent). But Diodorus' report is much more realistic for such a hard-fought action. This puts the dead at 700 infantry (almost 9 percent) and 280 cavalry (about 6 percent).

His victory at the Hydaspes was to mark the height of Alexander's career. He set out that summer to work his way eastward across the Indian subcontinent, capturing cities and lands along the way while occasionally turning about to put down a rebellious site at his rear. However, his army soon had had enough. Assaulted by the steamy climate more than overmatched enemy soldiers, the men didn't want to go any farther away from already distant homes. Despite every attempt to change their minds, including a three-day sulk in his tent, Alexander had to relent and turn back. He got reinforcements at this time of allied and mercenary troops from Greece, including 7,000 infantry and 5,000 cavalry, who arrived with 25,000 panoplies in tow per Curtius (9.3.21). (Diodorus [17.95.4] claimed a rather less believable 30,000 footmen and 6,000 riders, perhaps putting bodies into all the suits of armor.)

Leaving Porus to govern the conquered Indian territories, Alexander moved down the Hydaspes-Indus river system to the Indian Ocean, with part of his men aboard a fleet of small ships and others on foot. He lashed out along the way to take strong points and eliminate hostile native elements refusing to come out and fight a fixed battle. Alexander continued his habit of exposing himself to danger in some of these actions, personally leading his troops in assaults on two walled cities during the winter of 326/25 and being first up the scaling ladders. The second time, it nearly cost him his life. This happened when he was briefly isolated on the far side of the wall against a swarm of attackers, who put an arrow through his cuirass and into his lung. Fortunately, more Macedonians climbed over to his rescue and, though the wound was very serious, he recovered to resume the march.

Sending off a portion of the army with more cumbersome elements (including captured elephants) to take an alternate route, Alexander reached the sea with the rest in late summer of 325. He then divided his men again and started for the Persian Gulf, with some aboard ships brought down-river while he and the remainder moved along the beach. Eventually, the need to seek food and water led the party on shore to divert inland. Separated from the fleet, it would endure a horrific trek through desert country, losing many men before reuniting with the ship-borne division as well as the group that had split off along the Indus for the journey's final leg.

Persia 324–323 B.C.

Back in Persia, Alexander set about restoring order where problems had arisen in his absence. This called for either executing or chasing off officials (like his treasurer Harpalus) who had become corrupt. Most of the mercenaries that had acted as guards for these renegade officials fled the realm as well. The king then began preparing for his next grand campaign. This was to focus on the Arabian Peninsula as a prelude to conquering North Africa beyond Egypt. His plans for this project included the use of Asian soldiers to replace his dwindled and aging European troops. He had arranged before departing for India that some 30,000 picked men from the Persian provinces be recruited, equipped and trained in Macedonian warfare (Curtius 8.5.1; Diodorus 17.108.1–2). Likewise, he now collected 1,000 Persian and Median riders to form another division of hetairoi (Arrian 7.6.3) and brought in 20,000 local bowmen and slingers to combine with the other Asian troops into a new imperial host nearly devoid of European content (Diodorus 17.109.2; Arrian 7.11.3–4).

These moves naturally raised an outcry from the Macedonian soldiers and commanders that still formed the backbone of his army. Addressing their concerns, Alexander sought to create more of a blended force in which he would use manpower from both Asia and Europe. To this end, he sent Craterus home with a large number of veterans who were to be dismissed. His instructions were to take charge of Greece and have Antipater bring back replacements from Macedonia for the retirees. Alexander's revised plan was to reorganize the phalanx to contain both phalangites and missilemen. This called for a file of 16 that featured three Macedonian pikemen up front and twelve Asian archers and javelineers behind followed by a final rank of Macedonian file-closers (Arrian 7.23.3). In fact, this appears to be a variant upon the previous kardakes concept. The main differences were that the new array would have fewer heavy footmen at the fore (three versus five) and more light infantry (twelve versus five) while being closer geared to defensive tactics in substituting phalangites for hoplites.

Alexander made one brief campaign in this period, attacking and destroying a troublesome mountain tribe in the winter of 324/23 before retiring to Babylon. It was here where he intended setting up a forward base for the campaign into Arabia. But all his plans for military improvements and new conquests came to an end that summer when the still young king (only 33) took ill and died.

Tactical Discussion: 337–324 B.C.

Alexander the III of Macedonia is the most accomplished and highly regarded military figure not only of the 4th century but of all ancient history. However, was his success in battle a product of great tactical innovation or more the product of skilled application of inheritances from his father?

With regard to heavy infantry techniques, there's no reason to think that Alexander varied significantly from Philip's practices in any of his larger phalanx battles, since all featured the same sort of arrangements documented at Chaeronea for the older man. However, Alexander was more creative than his sire in the use of light infantry. And his invention of a second, reserve phalanx behind the first was definitely something entirely new. Still, it's probably the unusual deployments of heavy footmen in a number of lesser actions that best illustrate his creative talents. We have no record of Philip fighting this kind of engagement after the pre-phalanx ambush at Methone, thus there's no way of saying for sure how he would have reacted to such challenges. Nonetheless, Alexander masterfully adapted his arrays to each unique situation in very novel and successful ways. Therefore, when it came to infantry combat, he relied heavily on previous routines, but definitely advanced the art in that area, adding enough new wrinkles to qualify as a major innovator.

All the same, Alexander is probably most lionized today for his cavalry attacks. This too moved along an already established trajectory; indeed, 75 percent of Philip's successful phalanx actions saw cavalry play a significant role in their decision and the figure for Alexander's victories is actually slightly lower at 67 percent. However, Philip won only twice with horsemen as his sole element of decision while his son did so eight times (44 percent of all his victories). To a large extent, this reflects the different theatres in which the two men waged their battles, since Alexander's Asian campaigns played out in venues much more suited for horsemen than the European environs of his father's portfolio. Yet, whether forced upon him by his opponents or not, Alexander employed cavalry with a boldness never before seen in Greek warfare. He personally led his horsemen out in front of the phalanx in all of his largest actions save Issus, where the terrain wouldn't permit it. If his father had raised mounted forces to something approaching an equal partnership with his heavy infantry, then Alexander had by career's end promoted them to senior partners.

Alexander was thus highly creative in his tactics, improving on older techniques and adding some unique twists of his own. Nonetheless, there were other areas where he came up short. For one, his logistical planning could leave much to be desired. Carrying only a 30-day supply of food into Asia probably would have cost him the campaign had the satraps followed Memnon's plan for a scorched earth response. This is all the more questionable when we consider that Agesilaos, when faced with a similar task some 60 years earlier, had taken along a full six month's worth of provisions. Unlike Alexander, the crafty Spartan couldn't be starved out of the field. This same failing looms over the costly march from India. If that disaster had come from someone with any less illustrious a battle record, then it would more frequently be cited as one of the worst military blunders of all time. Nor was Alexander always prudent in his attacks. He ignored sound advice before Granicus River not to charge over the stream and won despite doing the wrong thing. And a similarly risky advance dealt him the only defeat of his career at Jaxartes (329). Alexander was also fortunate in his opponents. Beside the satraps throwing away Memnon's strategies in 334, that worthy foe died unexpectedly the next year and Darius later chose not to fight on the open plains of Assyria the only time he had both the cavalry *and* heavy infantry to make a successful challenge. Therefore, it's fair to say that Alexander was nearly as lucky as he was great. But, then, maybe that's no different than can be said for many another of military history's giants.

* * *

At the time of his death, Alexander the Great's empire stretched across portions of three continents. His realm was, however, a fragile entity. It was once said of Napoleon Bonaparte that the only part of Spain that he really controlled was that which fell within the shadow of a French bayonet. Thus, the minute any region lacked active occupation it reverted to the enemy. Much the same was true for a lot of the conquests that Alexander left behind. Even in his lifetime, he never really had a hold on India. He had given its administration over to Porus less in recognition of the man's loyalty and skill as a governor than in acknowledgement of the reality that it was too distant to rule. Some areas, like Cappadocia, were still effectively independent while others were more like private fiefs being run with little beyond a nominal nod to the central government. In truth, it seems unlikely that Alexander could have kept so large and complex a construct intact even had he lived. As it was, his passing without a clear heir bequeathed that impossible task to a cadre of very capable, but still much lesser men with strong ambitions of their own. The result would be nearly a quarter century of conflict as one after another of Alexander's former subordinates strove in vain to lay claim to the vast legacy he left behind.

V. Many Great Combats

Battles of the Successors (323–301 B.C.)

> "When [Alexander] was quitting life in Babylon and at his last breath was asked by his friends to whom he was leaving the kingdom, he said, 'To the best man; for I foresee that a great combat of my friends will be my funeral games.' And this actually happened; for after the death of Alexander the foremost of his friends quarreled about the primacy and joined in many great combats."
>
> Diodorus (18.1.4–5)

The scene in Babylon in early June 323 offered a foretaste of disputes to come. The native Macedonian infantry proclaimed the late king's half-brother Arrhidaeus to be the new monarch, while the army's elite cavalrymen backed Roxanne's unborn child (having miscarried at the age of 14 in 326, she was again pregnant). The contending groups managed to reach a compromise in which Arrhidaeus would co-rule as Philip III along with the expected offspring should it prove male. In fact, it was Perdiccas, Alexander's former chief-of-staff, who was really calling the shots. He divvied out the realm's 20 satrapies to the most prominent imperial subordinates. These men, known as the Successors (Diodochi), would become major players in a violent contest for control of Alexander's patrimony. Most of them were present to receive their bequests, including Ptolemy (Egypt), Lysimachus (Thrace), Antigonus (Phrygia), Peithon (Media) and Eumenes (granted Cappadocia, which was not yet under Macedonian control). Also on hand was Seleucus, Perdiccas' second-in-command and a future satrap. Two other major figures were out of town — Craterus and Antipater. The former was in Cilicia with the arsenal and a large army; he would be named a roving commander of the empire. Antipater was still in Macedonia gathering reinforcements for the planned Arabian campaign and would stay there to administer the Greek mainland.

The Lamian War and Cyrene

When word spread of Alexander's demise, many resentful of Macedonian dominance took the opportunity to rise up in revolt. Most prominently, this took place back in Greece, where the Athenians and Aetolians declared against the empire and issued a call for others to join them. But trouble also arose in Asia as the Greeks who had moved into the far northeastern districts (the "Upper Satrapies" as they were known) sought their independence as well.

Upper Satrapies, Plataea II, Thermopylae-Lamia and Odrysia IV (323 B.C.)

The rebellious settlers in the Upper Satrapies raised an army of 20,000 foot soldiers and 3,000 cavalry per Diodorus (18.7.2). Parke (1935, 203) considered these figures an exaggeration unless there were a good many Asians included, something he thought improbable. However, given the extensive nature of foreign settlings in this region, such a levy just might have been possible. If so, the infantry likely consisted of 15,000–16,000 hoplites and 4,000–5,000 skirmishers. The Greeks chose a certain Philon as their general. Perdiccas dispatched Pithon, one of Alexander's bodyguards, to address this threat. He started out with only two regiments of phalangites (3,000) and 800 (two squadrons) of hetairoi (Diodorus 18.7.2–3), but got more troops from the local satraps. These amounted to 8,000 infantry (perhaps 6,000 hoplites and 2,000 light-armed) and 800 javelineer horsemen.

Pithon proved a savvy operator and was able to bribe a rebel officer, Letodorus, prior to battle. The nature of Letodorus' command isn't specified beyond containing 3,000 men; however, this strength exactly matches Diodorus' claim for the rebel cavalry, which also fits well with what happened on the field. There, Pithon advanced his phalanx with the pikemen on the left and hoplites on the right. He must have spread both divisions thin (files of eight and four respectively) to counter a long opposing line that likely stood eight shields deep. (Alternatively, should we honor Parke's suspicions and cut the rebel force in half on all counts, Pithon could have matched the enemy with all of his heavy infantry in eight-man files.) This would have seen both phalanxes fronting over a 1km span. Once engaged, the battle was "doubtful" (Diodorus 18.7.6) as the rebel array must have offered a strong challenge, especially on its left where Pithon lacked the stouter defense provided by his pikemen on the other wing. Just then, Letodorus pulled his troops from at least one flank (maybe both if he indeed led horsemen) and took them off. (His ability to disengage and cleanly leave a fight still in progress lends credence to the idea that he led mobile, mounted units.) With their enemy now free to envelop (the hetairoi and others perhaps already doing so), the rebels fled in confusion and panic. They would surrender afterwards only to be treacherously shot down by javelins in accord with Perdiccas' instructions.

Meanwhile in Greece, the Athenians enlisted 8,000 (Diodorus 18.9.1) of the veteran mercenaries that Alexander had expelled upon his return from India. (Pausanius improbably gave them 50,000 [8.52.5].) These had gathered in the Peloponnese and were recruited by Leosthenes. He had also gone to Aetolia to arrange an alliance and picked up another 7,000 soldiers there, taking the opportunity to also solicit the Phocians, Locrians and others to his polis' cause. For their part, the citizens of Athens called up all those fit for duty under the age of 40 (perhaps 7,000 hoplites and 700 horsemen from a pool of roughly 10,000 middle-upper class residents). These represented ten tribes (taxeis), three of them standing to defend the city while the others made ready for distant campaigning. From the latter, 5,000 hoplites and 500 cavalry set out along with 2,000 additional mercenaries to aid Leosthenes' blockade of the pass at Thermopylae. Additional insurgents had already joined him there, including troops from both the mainland and the islands as well as from Illyria and Thrace.

The Boeotians backed Macedonia and gathered near Plataea to intercept the troops coming from Athens. Their army had no more than 7,000 spearmen and 700 in cavalry, though there could have been a couple of thousand mercenary hoplites from Macedonian garrisons on hand as well. Still, this would have provided a good match for the approaching Athenians if Leosthenes had not now upset the odds by marching down with part of the army he had at Thermopylae. Diodorus describes his command as "his own men" (18.11.5). This might mean no more than that they were distinct from the Athenians; however, these might well have been the soldiers he had personally recruited: 8,000 mostly (if not all) hoplites. Likely adding some light infantry and allied horsemen (maybe 1,000 each), he hooked up with the column from Athens. Leosthenes was then able to employ his edge in manpower to defeat the Boeotians with files pushing through foes stacked only half as deep. We've no details on the action's casualties, but might suspect that the Boeotians gave way fairly quickly and took but modest losses (5–10 percent) in a cavalry-covered escape. The victors would have paid only a very minor price on the day (maybe under 3 percent killed).

Having sent to Asia for help, Antipater felt that he could delay no longer and marched out in the fall of 323, leaving the general Sippas behind to find more men. His army had 13,000 Macedonian heavies, probably 9,000 pikemen and 4,000 hypaspist hoplites. There were also 600 hetairoi, and some light footmen (perhaps 3,000 or so) must have been present as well. Moving down the coast to Thessaly beside a large fleet, Antipater met Leosthenes on the plain north of Thermopylae and south of the city of Lamia. The Thessalians had by now gone over to the rebel side to leave the Macedonian short of troops, yet he still accepted battle. Leosthenes would have had better than 30,000 infantry (he had 22,000 the next year after losing 7,000 Aetolians and some others). His mounted arm included at least 3,500 horsemen (again, attested in 324), including 2,000 Thessalians. The mercenaries, Aetolians and Athenians could have given him around 17,000 hoplites and 5,000 light footmen, while other allies might have contributed at least 4,000–5,000 more in heavy infantry along with 3,000–4,000 foot skirmishers.

Antipater must have set up no more than four-deep to avoid an extreme overlap. And even then, the enemy's large force of cavalry and light footmen offered a serious mismatch off his flanks. Braving such opposition appears insane and, whatever inspired him to do so, Antipater's men paid a heavy price for his mistake. Leosthenes drove them from the field, killing perhaps 3,000 (30 percent) of their infantrymen. (This reflects that the heavy-armed force of 40,000 fielded by the Macedonians the next year included 30,000 new arrivals and only 10,000 from Antipater.) Losses on this order indicate that there was at least a partial envelopment followed by a thorough chase. Those who survived took refuge with Antipater inside Lamia (from which the name "Lamian War" for this conflict comes) and promptly came under siege.

A conflict arose at this time in Thrace as well. Seuthes, the Odrysian king, had taken the field to oppose that province's governor, Lysimachus. The latter had a garrison force of only 4,000 foot soldiers (maybe 3,000 pikemen and 1,000 hoplites) and 2,000 horsemen plus some foot skirmishers. He was facing what Diodorus claimed (18.14.2-3) to be 20,000 barbarian peltasts and 8,000 cavalry. That Lysimachus came out to fight against these odds strongly suggests that he chose ground where his heavy infantry had terrain protection on its flanks. The ensuing clash was "a stubborn one" with the Macedonians repelling repeated assaults and "killing many times" more than they lost (maybe 10–12 percent versus 1–3 percent). Nightfall must have brought the action to a close with neither side a clear victor. There's no record of further combat, but Seuthes would ultimately become an unwilling ally of Lysimachus.

Lamia, Rhamnus, Cappadocia and Crannon (322 B.C.)

Leonnatos crossed over from his satrapy that spring to aid Antipater. After recruiting in Macedonia, he marched to Lamia with an army of more than 20,000 infantry and 1,500 cavalry (Diodorus 18.14.5). Composition of this force is speculative; however, it seems reasonable that it had something like 9,000 phalangites and 6,000 spearmen plus 5,000 light infantry. The latter must have been a mix of peltasts, archers and slingers, many of them Phrygian. As for his horsemen, he maybe had 800 lancers (two squadrons) with the rest javelin-armed. Leonnatos' approach caused the rebels to break off their siege and move up to meet him. Leosthenes had lost his life beneath Lamia's walls and Antiphilus now led the Greek effort. Part of his force having dispersed that winter, he retained some 22,000 footmen (perhaps 16,000–18,000 of them hoplites) and 3,500 riders (Diodorus 18.15.2). Still, this allowed for a modest edge in manpower as long as he could engage before the newcomers linked up with Antipater.

Both armies set up in phalanx at some ways apart on the plain above Lamia and the cavalries advanced to open a fierce mounted battle. Leonnatos was a devotee of Alexander's style and led his horsemen into this fight to send it swirling across the flat. A portion of the ground was marshy, and it was here where Leonnatos found himself cut off as the highly skilled and more numerous Thessalian horsemen gained the upper hand and shot him from the saddle. As its soundly defeated cavalry retreated with the general's body, the Macedonian phalanx withdrew as well lest it be enveloped and destroyed. Taking up a defensive stance on high ground, it was then joined by Antipater the next day. Though well supplied with infantry, Antipater was wary of engaging a foe so much stronger in horsemen; he chose, therefore, to retire, doing so across rough terrain so as to discourage attacks from the enemy's riders. Antiphilus had gained a stunning strategic triumph at very little cost (no doubt less than 200 horsemen to maybe twice that for the opposition).

About the same time that Leonnatos was meeting defeat to the north, another Macedonian was faring no better along the coast of Attica. Micion (probably Antipater's admiral) had come ashore there to deal some payback to the Athenians for besieging his comrades in Lamia. Plutarch characterized his landing party as "a large force" (Vol. II *Phocion*, 261). Given a fleet of 110 triremes (Diodorus 18.12.3), he could have had nearly 4,500 heavy-armed Macedonians and mercenaries (40 or so per ship). Oarsmen with javelins (maybe 1,000) provided light support. The Athenian general Phocion (nearly 80 years old at this time) led out his city's three available taxeis of prime-aged men (just above 2,000 hoplites and 200 horsemen) along with the spearmen over 40 years of age (3,000). He also had 300 or so cavalry and light footmen drawn from the baggage carriers (maybe 1,000–2,000). Catching the enemy near the town of Rhamnus, Phocion formed up his phalanx and engaged in a pitched battle.

Micion might have fielded up to 3,000 pikemen (two regiments) on his left and center with about 1,500 hired hoplites forming his right wing. The armed-rowers would have split to screen along either side. Phocion likely set up his slightly larger force at eight shields deep across a 625m front, putting younger men at the fore and the oldest at the rear. This would have led Micion (had he kept his phalangites eight-deep) to stretch out his mercenaries using files of four in order to avoid an overlap. (Note that this assumes a 2 to 1 preponderance of pikemen over hoplites. If the ratio had been the reverse, Micion could have achieved the same frontage and kept his spearmen at a more competitive six-deep.) In the combat that ensued, we might suspect that it was on the thinner and pike-less Macedonian right where Phocion's men won the day. Perhaps aided by a sweep off that flank by their cavalry and more numerous light infantry, Athens' spearmen pushed back and enveloped the Macedonian commander and his hirelings where they stood on that wing. The Athenians "entirely routed the enemy, killing Micion and many more on the spot" (Plutarch), giving chase to probably claim a death toll of 20–30 percent among those beaten before they got back to their ships. Still, despite the success here and at Lamia, things began to turn against the insurgency as it now suffered a pair of defeats at sea.

Back in Asia, Perdiccas (with Arrhidaeus the king in tow) was engaging the Persian satrap Ariarathes for control of Cappadocia that he might deliver that province into the hands of Eumenes as promised. This pitted him against a force of Asians and mercenaries. Based on their subsequent casualties (at around 15–30 percent), his foes likely numbered 13,500–27,500. (Though Diodorus said there were more, putting them at 45,000: 30,000 infantry and 15,000 cavalry.) A reasonable projection toward the upside would give Ariarathes something like 10,000 Greek hoplites. The equivalent of a baivarabam, he had hired these over a period of years, taking advantage of having "amassed a great sum of money" (Diodorus 18.16.1). Likewise, he'd been able to afford a strong local force that included perhaps 15,000 foot soldiers. These were mostly helmeted spearmen with small shields who also carried javelins. Finally, his mounted arm probably consisted of 2,000–3,000 light horsemen based on the Cappadocian riders sent to Gaugamela back in 331 having been only a partial levy.

Perdiccas' army had some 18,000 phalangites and 3,000 hypaspists along with perhaps 5,000–6,000 light footmen and 3,000 horsemen (including 2,000 hetairoi). Given that so many Macedonian troops were in Europe at this time, it's likely that at least a narrow majority of his men were Asian. This included all of the light-armed (mounted and afoot) and half the hetairoi and pikemen. The latter, outfitted in Macedonian fashion, were prototypical *pantodapoi phalangitai* (native phalanx fighters who would become common in Successor armies). These were a portion of the men that Alexander had ordered trained in Persia while he was away in India. Among the troops from Macedonia, the hypaspists must have carried dory and aspis that they might counter the large opposing mercenary contingent. Both these and their sarissa-armed comrades likely stood eight-deep in the imperial phalanx.

We've no description of the battle in Cappadocia. However, it likely turned on success by Perdiccas on his right using some combination of his elite troops (hetairoi and hypaspists). In the collapse that followed, 4,000 of the insurgents died, probably hoplites from the bested left wing for the most part. Like their kind along the rest of the line, these had arrayed thinly (files of four to six) in front of the local spearmen and proved too slow to escape from the envelopment. Ariarathes and another 5,000 of his men surrendered. Perdiccas tortured and impaled the satrap and his kin before turning Cappadocia over to Eumenes and heading back to Babylon with the king.

Craterus, meanwhile, had crossed over to Thessaly from his arsenal in Cilicia. He brought 6,000 Macedonian infantry (Diodorus 18.16.4), which were probably four taxeis of pikemen. He also had 1,000 Persian bowmen and slingers plus 1,500 horsemen, the last including perhaps 800 companion lancers. There were also 4,000 mercenary hoplites in his column that had joined during the march. Craterus delivered all these troops to Antipater. Having already taken on Leonnatos' men, Antipater now had more than 40,000 heavy infantry, 3,000 archers and slingers and 5,000 horsemen (Diodorus 18.16.5). His heavy footmen consisted of around 10,000 hoplites (both hypaspists and hired) and 30,000 phalangites. The horsemen might have been around 2,000 Macedonian hetairoi with the rest lighter, javelin-armed riders. In addition to the 3,000 specialist missilemen (including 2,000 inherited from Leonnatos) there were probably some 5,000–6,000 peltasts on hand as well. Opposing this huge host was a much smaller army under Antiphilus, who could call on no more than 25,000 footmen and 3,500 cavalry per Diodorus (18.17.2). His infantry likely broke down into about 80 percent hoplites and the rest mostly peltast foot skirmishers.

These forces camped near the Peneius River in the vicinity of the town of Crannon, where Antipater, seeing his numerical advantage, offered battle. His foes delayed for several days as they gathered up as many troops as they could before coming out to fight. Having some 20,000 hoplites, the Greeks must have set up their phalanx across as wide an expanse as was practical, perhaps filing at depths of four (mercenaries) and six (militia). This would have let them match lengths with an enemy array that might have stretched across the plain for some 3.75km at eight men deep. Clearly, the rebels' best chance for victory lay in a mounted battle and this is what they sought, sending their riders out front to start the action. And, indeed, the Thessalian-led Greek horsemen soon began to take charge. At this juncture, Antipater moved to head off the sort of defeat that a preliminary cavalry reverse had put on Leonnatos the previous year. He led his phalanx forward, flushing the horsemen flank-ward and initiating shock contact with the thinly arrayed enemy spearmen.

The advantage now shifted. Unable to penetrate the pike hedge on the Macedonian left and center, the insurgents had no real hope of withstanding the deeper files pushing into them along the rest of the line. They therefore withdrew. In an amazing display of discipline, their hoplites were able to disengage and pull back in good order. Where they faced pikemen, this was done at minimal cost, those foes being poorly equipped to pursue even a short distance. However, along the leftward third of the rebel front, it was somewhat more mobile spearmen who stood in opposition and the Greeks paid dearly to get clear (most of the 500 soldiers they lost that day going down there and then). Once onto high ground at the rear, Antiphilus and his men held off all enemy attempts to advance uphill as their cavalry fell back to join them. Antipater broke off the fight at this point, having chased the enemy from the field at a cost of only 130 (less than 1 percent) of his men (Diodorus 18.17.5).

The battle at Crannon served to bring down Athens despite its somewhat inconclusive results. Seeing no chance for victory in the long run, the Athenians gave up and Antipater installed a garrison in their city, replacing the democracy there with an oligarchy of the wealthy. All of the other rebels began falling away after this save for the Aetolians, who fled into their highlands and held out into the winter. They were thus able to gain better terms when the Macedonians had to bring the Lamian War to a quick end in order to deal with a new conflict in Asia.

Cyrene II–IV (322 B.C.) and Cyrene V (322/321 B.C.)

Even as events played out in the Lamian War, other battles were being fought on the North African coast. The Spartan adventurer Thibron had landed there with a force of mercenaries and some exiles from Cyrene with the intent of exploiting ongoing civil unrest in that distant Greek colony. His men were, in fact, refugees from the shake-up in Babylon that had followed Alexander's return from India, having at that time fled to Crete in the employ of the king's corrupt treasurer, Harpalus. Thibron, who was part of Harpalus' inner circle, had then murdered him. This let him take what remained of the slain man's stolen fortune as well as control of his mercenary band of perhaps 6,000 hoplites and 1,000 missilemen. (Arrian's report [17.108.6] of 6,000 men with Harpalus likely counted only the spearmen, while Diodorus' 7,000 [18.19.2] provides the total.) Considering likely Cyrenean manpower (see discussion for Cyrene I in 400 B.C.), Thibron could add maybe 1,500 exile hoplites, 500 local foot skirmishers (one for each three spearmen) and 400 horsemen (around one per four spearmen). About a quarter of the latter would have formed 30 three-man chariot teams while the rest rode on horseback. In opposition, the Cyrenean loyalists might have fielded round numbers to the tune of 6,000 hoplites, 2,000 light footmen and 1,000–1,500 mounted troops. The horsemen would have been some 100 chariot teams and 1,000 cavalry.

These forces met in battle (Cyrene II) on open ground outside of the city and Thibron carried the day. Based on the foregoing speculation on manpower, the Spartan's edge came in heavy foot troops at the cost of a distinct disadvantage in horsemen. This suggests that his riders with the aid of superior light infantry support from their professional skirmishers were able to keep opposition mounted forces at bay just long enough for his phalanx to win the battle. No doubt deployed eight shields deep versus only six, the mercenary spearmen rapidly bested their amateur hoplite opponents, "killing many and taking captive no small number" (Diodorus 18.19.3). In this we might see 5–10 percent losses for the Cyreneans against only 3–5 percent for their foes. Thibron and his men extorted a treaty and money from Cyrene in the engagement's aftermath, going on to pillage what they wanted from its harbor and plan wider conquests in neighboring Libya. However, there was a falling out of thieves and one of Thibron's subordinates,

Mnasicles (from Crete and possibly leader of his archers), deserted to the Cyreneans. He then led a successful attack against the harbor that scored a fair share of the Spartan's booty and military gear. Thibron lost some men and ships soon afterwards while trying to raid into Libya for food.

Thibron did not give up after these reverses, but arranged instead to hire better than 2,500 additional soldiers from Greece to more than replace his losses. The Cyreneans decided to attack before these men could arrive and sallied to fight another battle (Cyrene III). This time, with the enemy phalanx probably no larger than theirs (maybe 6,000 hoplites on each side), it was the men from Cyrene who defeated Thibron, "killing many of his soldiers" (Diodorus 17.21.2). We might imagine that with both phalanxes at eight shields deep and the locals better inspired, the infantry fight stalemated as a superior Cyrenean mounted force carried the action on at least one wing. Still, the Spartan marauder survived to regain something like his original strength once the new mercenaries came ashore. He then fought the Cyreneans again in what Diodorus described as "a great battle" (18.21.4).

It's hard to square Diodorus' claim for the city's manpower at Cyrene IV (30,000 including citizens, Libyans and Carthaginians) and what we know about the size of the force with Thibron (7,000 original soldiers plus 2,500 additions) with the Spartan taking the victory. It would seem more likely that the action involved only around 8,000 heavy infantrymen on each side with the Cyreneans having been reinforced by no more than a couple of thousand hoplite-style Liby-Phoenicians. If so, it was the professionalism of Thibron's men that gave them the winning edge in an otherwise closely matched contest. All the same, the idea that the victors visited "great slaughter" on their foes might still be accurate. Indeed, a hard pursuit could very well have run losses for the locals and their allies up to 30 percent or more. At any rate, Thibron was successful enough on the field to then begin a siege against Cyrene itself.

The Cyreneans came under so much duress that they turned on each other, the common folk depriving the wealthy of their goods and driving them from town. Some of these outcasts fled to Thibron, while others made their way to Egypt where they appealed to Ptolemy for help. The Macedonian saw an opportunity here and sent Ophellas with an army to restore the oligarchs to power. This set off a round of realignment. The exiles with Thibron tried to join up with their peers among the approaching column and the Spartan and his men cut them down. Meanwhile, Cyrene's democratic regime saw more to fear from its native oligarchs than from the Greek raiders and allied with Thibron to oppose the invasion from Egypt. The ensuing battle might thus have found Thibron and his newfound friends fielding some 12,000 hoplites, 4,000 foot skirmishers, 700 cavalrymen and 100 chariots. Ophellas could have had a strong strike force of 9,000 pikemen (mostly Egyptian pantodapoi) and 3,000 hypaspists plus 2,000 or so outcast hoplites and 4,000–5,000 in light infantry. His cavalry perhaps came to no more than 500 horsemen if we follow Diodorus' claim that aid from Egypt included only "infantry and naval" elements (18.21.7). However, this seems extremely improbable. It's much more credible that Ptolemy provided cavalry support of some sort as well, maybe on the order of 600–800 riders. As such, the combat most likely turned on the Ptolemaic phalanx gaining the upper hand on one wing (probably with its hypaspists on the right). Cyrene V was a solid victory for Ophellas, who captured Thibron and went on to deliver the entire region to Ptolemy.

An Empire Divided

With Alexander little more than a year dead, competition among his former officers started to seriously afflict his legacy. The first overt outbreak was a plot by Perdiccas. He had adjudicated the dispersal of titles at Babylon in 323, keeping control over the new kings for himself to become de facto ruler of the realm. Now he planned to marry Alexander's sister Cleopatra and create a royal blood line as the basis for a legitimate dynasty. Seeing Antipater as a rival and potential roadblock to this scheme, Perdiccas went after his supporters, particularly Antigonus. But Antigonus and his son Demetrius fled to Europe and exposed the plot. Antipater reacted by bringing his current campaign in Aetolia to an end and making plans to send an army into Asia against Perdiccas. The first war among the Successors thus began.

Hellespont, Aetolia and Thessaly (321 B.C)

Antipater put Polyperchon in charge of Europe with a substantial force that included 15,000 heavy infantry (out of around 41,000 on hand) and 2,000 horsemen (out of 5,000) of whom 800 were hetairoi. He and Craterus then marched off for Asia that spring with the rest of the army. An embassy had gone to Ptolemy and he enlisted against Perdiccas as well. Seeing these threats on two fronts, Perdiccas split his forces to address them. He had a close bond with Eumenes after fighting to secure that man's satrapy and sent him to contest the crossing from Europe while he himself marched against Egypt. To help ensure Eumenes' success, Perdiccas assigned him capable assistants in the form of his brother Alcetas, who took charge of the fleet, and Neoptolemus, who had led the hypaspists. However, the latter chose to cast his lot with the other side and tried along with some of the Macedonians in Eumenes' army to usurp command. A skirmish followed in which many of Neoptolemus' followers died and he barely escaped, fleeing with 300 horsemen. The forces from Europe had, meanwhile, come over into Asia unopposed. Gathering in Neoptolemus, Antipater divided his own efforts. Taking 6,000 phalangites, 2,000 Greek hoplites, 1,000 foot skirmishers and 1,000 cavalry (including 400 hetairoi), he moved to join Ptolemy while Craterus led the remaining troops against Eumenes in a battle near the Hellespont.

Craterus had 20,000 infantry (Diodorus 18.30.4); mostly Macedonians, these were probably 15,000 pikemen (3,000 of them hypaspists), 2,000 Greek hoplites and 3,000 foot skirmishers. His cavalry numbered 2,000, including perhaps 800 hetairoi. Eumenes had an equal number of foot soldiers, though less capable Asians made up their majority. We might suspect 12,000 pantodapoi with pikes, 3,000 Macedonian phalangites and 2,000 mercenary hoplites along with 3,000 Asian light infantry. Where Eumenes held an advantage was in horsemen. He had 5,000 of these on hand, probably all javelin-armed. Craterus likely laid out his phalanx 16 men deep with his hypaspists on the far right. He himself rode with the hetairoi and some of the other horsemen on the right flank. Neoptolemus led the remaining, javelin-armed cavalry on the left. The light infantry split to give support to their horsemen on either wing. Eumenes would have copied this deployment; however, it was his intention to withhold his phalanx and settle the issue with cavalry and light footmen. He thus took post with the best of his horsemen on the right, directly opposite the traitorous Neoptolemus.

The ensuing action saw cavalry charge out to initiate fighting off either flank at some distance in front of the infantry arrays. Craterus fell early on, either thrown from his horse and trampled (Diodorus 18.31.3) or cut from the saddle by a Thracian (Plutarch Vol. II *Eumenes*, 27). Either way, his riders were then defeated and fled to their phalanx. On the other end of the field, Eumenes engaged Neoptolemus in a duel amid the general combat, killing him while taking only light wounds. The mounted fight here was fairly even, but the slain Neoptolemus' horsemen eventually broke off once they realized that their comrades on the right had been beaten. With leaders gone and both flanks and rear exposed to mounted attack, the opposing phalanx men surrendered to Eumenes without a fight, pledging to take up Perdiccas' cause. But they soon betrayed him and escaped at night to link with Antipater's column on its way to Cilicia.

Perdiccas marched into Egypt with Eumenes' victory having secured his rear, but was to meet disaster. Reaching the Nile, he came up against a strong point known as the Fort of Camels and wasted a day plus some good soldiers in a failed assault. Perdiccas responded by breaking camp to execute a night march and then attempt another crossing of the river, this time near Memphis. Things went even worse here. Getting only a portion of his force over before retreating under attack, he lost 2,000 men and top officers. It was a fiasco that cost Perdiccas the respect of his remaining troops and the Macedonians under Pithon now led a revolt that killed him. And when the mutineers subsequently went over to Ptolemy with the kings in tow, the Egyptian ruler played his hand well, gaining acclaim by not taking over himself and giving command to Pithon and Arrhidaeus (one of the rebel leaders and not the king).

The effort against Perdiccas thus bore fruit despite its defeat against Eumenes. Yet all was not going well back in Greece. The Aetolians there had taken advantage of Antipater's absence to break their recent treaty and attack neighboring cities. The Macedonian general Polycles marched to confront them and was beaten. The size of this action is not cited in our source (Diodorus 18.38.2), but perhaps involved no more than a small imperial detachment. This was probably 3,000 pikemen, 1,000 mercenary hoplites, 1,000 light infantry and 400 horsemen. The Aetolians would have used their full, 7,000-man levy: maybe 4,000 hoplites, 2,500 light infantry and 500 riders. If so, the victory likely came as a result of cavalry backed by a superior force of foot skirmishers overwhelming Polycles' light-armed flank screens. This triggered a rout that killed him and "no small number of his soldiers" (perhaps 20–30 percent).

The Aetolians next invaded Thessaly, where they convinced many of the natives to join in an uprising against Macedonia. They were thus able to initially put together a large army of 25,000 infantry and 1,500 cavalry (Diodorus 18.38.3). However, when the Acarnanians began raiding into the Aetolians' territory, the latter went home. This left the insurgents with maybe 12,000 hoplites, 7,000 light infantrymen and 1,000 or so horsemen. These were under the command of Memnon of Pharsalus. Polyperchon in his role as Antipater's proxy came against Memnon "with a considerable army" (Diodorus 18.38.6). This was probably a force of 9,000 pikemen, 3,000 hypaspists, 3,000 Macedonian light infantry, 2,000 mercenary missilemen and 1,600 horsemen. By deploying his hypaspist as spearmen four-deep on his right and the phalangites in eight-man files elsewhere, Polyperchon could have matched heavy-armed fronts with an eight shield deep rebel array. It then must have been his horsemen (800 hetairoi) on the right that carried the day. Coming to grips behind a strong skirmisher screen, they cleared out the Thessalian riders there to make a flank attack. This allowed the hypaspists, who likely had been no more than holding things even up to that point, to break through the opposing hoplites on their end of the line. Wrapping around from the flank, they then routed the rest of the insurgent phalanx. Menon fell as his foes "cut most of his army to pieces" (i.e. losses probably in excess of 25 percent). Polyperchon thus subdued Thessaly with just a single engagement.

Back in Asia, Antipater took advantage of his control over the kings to make a fresh distribution of the satrapies and other appointments. Notable among these was the assignment of Babylon to Seleucus and Antigonus' posting as general of the royal army. Leaving the pursuit of affairs in Asia to Antigonus, Antipater returned to Macedonia. This let him restore the kings to their proper homeland.

Orcynii (320 B.C.) and Cretopolis (319 B.C)

Antigonus marched into Cappadocia to confront Eumenes near Orcynii and managed to repeat the trick that Pithon had used against the Upper Satrapies' rebels three years previous. He contacted Apollonides, Eumenes' commander of cavalry, and arranged for him to desert during battle. With this pact in hand, the royal general took position on high ground above the enemy camp, which sat on a broad plain suitable for horsemen. His forces included more than 10,000 foot soldiers per Diodorus (18.40.7). This was probably only the heavy infantry with 9,000 pikemen (6,000 Macedonian and the rest pantodapoi) and 3,000 hoplites. In addition, he could call on 2,000 horsemen and must have had around 3,000 light infantry as well. (There were also 30 elephants present, but they don't appear to have seen any action at this time.) Eumenes had 20,000 infantry and 5,000 cavalry, essentially the same force fielded at the Hellespont. His foot troops were 12,000 pantopoi pikemen, 3,000 Macedonian phalangites, 2,000 mercenary hoplites and 3,000 Asian skirmishers.

Eumenes would have arranged his heavy infantry eight ranks deep with the hoplites on the right. This forced the royals to deploy part of their line very thinly in order to match frontages. Antigonus likely did this by setting up his pikemen at a depth of eight, but stretching out the hoplites on his right wing in files of only four. Once engaged, the phalanxes stalled against each other. This was, in fact, a signature moment in Grecian warfare. It was the very first time that two pike phalanxes had ever clashed on the field of battle (the heavy arrays hadn't come to blows at the Hellespont).

On the right wings, hoplites faced deep hedges with overlapping sarissai of sufficient length (4.6m) that they couldn't penetrate. Eumenes' longer files for his spearmen here were utterly wasted, since othismos and other advantages of depth simply couldn't be brought to bear. In the center of the field, where pikeman dueled with pikeman, there was more potential for offensive success, since there the weapons of the leading ranks reached to foes that were not so well protected. Yet strike capability still remained lower than in a traditional hoplite action. And given the less draining nature of a pike fight versus the muscular demands put on a shield-pushing spearman, it would take a good deal longer for any mismatch in physicality to be decisive. As a result, the non-elite pikemen engaged in the center were no more likely to deliver a quick decision than the phalangites and spearmen stalled against each other on their wings. This shifted the focus onto mounted action. It was here where the well-timed desertion of Apollonides and his troopers won the day for Antigonus. Stripped of their cavalry screen, Eumenes' heavy footmen underwent flank and rear attacks from the imperial riders and light infantry to disastrous effect, suffering a double envelopment that ran their losses up to 8,000 (40 percent). Antigonus and his troops followed up by capturing Eumenes' supply train as well. Bereft of food, most of the beaten men changed sides and Eumenes fled with 600 followers into the fortress at Nora.

Antigonus set out the next spring to take care of Alcetas and Attalus. The latter had joined the former with what remained of Perdiccas' army after his murder in Egypt as well as with other defectors upset with Antipater's dominance. These two had resisted all attempts against them to date and were encamped near the city of Cretopolis in Pisidia above the southern coastal plain of Anatolia. Attalus had brought about 10,000 infantry (maybe 6,000 pikemen, 2,000 hoplites and 2,000 light footmen) and 800 cavalry with him. Alcetas chipped in some 6,000 infantry and 100 horsemen. Perhaps 4,000–5,000 of his foot troops might have been professional hoplites with the rest being javelineers provided by local Pisidian allies. Antigonus made a swift surprise march and took post on high ground above the rebel camp much as he had done against Eumenes at Orcynii. Now with a little over half of Eumenes' men and having added more troops during his march to the coast, he had better than 40,000 foot soldiers and 7,000 horsemen (Diodorus 18.45.1). The infantry probably broke down into 24,000 pikemen (maybe 9,000 of them Macedonian), 8,000 hoplites and 8,000 lights. Importantly, Antigonus' sudden arrival and position let him hide his actual manpower, since the elevation and placing of screening forces in front made it difficult for his foes to judge the true nature of his contingents and formation. In particular, most of his cavalry could keep out of sight. In contrast, he had no trouble in accurately gauging enemy strength and dispositions from his vantage point on high.

Alcetas didn't wait to be attacked; instead, he set up his phalanx and charged out in front of it with his horsemen. His immediate targets were 1,000 mounted troops that Antipater had spread along his front. However, these had much greater light infantry support than that available to Alcetas and his riders and, despite taking considerable damage in the ensuing fight, were able to use both this and their uphill stance to gain the upper hand. Antigonus then led out his remaining 6,000 horsemen from where they hid behind either flank, sweeping around and down to threaten the phalanx on the flat below. Seeing that he might be cut off from his infantry, Alcetas hurriedly rode back to his lines. In doing so, he left most of his cavalry behind to be savaged by the more numerous imperial troopers.

Antigonus now gave the signal for his phalanx to advance and it came down the slope in a broad array. This was likely 2km across with pikemen covering the left half at 16-deep and the hoplites over the rest in files of eight. The rebels, ignorant of true enemy strength, had set up their formation at a uniform depth of eight along its entirety. They thus spanned a width of only about 1,300m. Thinning their spearmen into files of four would now have let them match fronts, but the rapidity of the imperials' charge plus assaults from their elephants in front gave no time for proper realignment. Facing serious overlaps on either flank from the opposing infantry line and being struck at side and rear by Antigonus' cavalry with very few of their own horsemen left to counter, Alcetas' troops fell apart in an utter rout. The defeated men quickly surrendered to join Antigonus, turning over many of their leaders including Attalus. Alcidas escaped for the moment along with his Pisidian friends; however, he eventually committed suicide when some of these made to betray him.

Shortly after the battle at Cretopolis, word went out that Antipater had died of an illness after leaving Polyperchon in charge back in Macedonia. Cassander, the son of Antipater, had become second in command at his father's passing, but wanted the top post. He now allied with Ptolemy toward usurping power. Nor was Cassander alone in having higher ambitions. Indeed, Antigonus desired to become an emperor and had a huge military with which to pursue that end. His royal army in Asia now counted 60,000 foot soldiers (perhaps 36,000 phalangites, 12,000 hoplites and 12,000 light footmen) and 10,000 horsemen plus 30 elephants (Diodorus 18.50.3). He also had access to funds for hiring more men if needed.

Antigonus set out to take over the Asian satrapies and replace their governors with his own men. First on his list was Hellespontine Phrygia. The satrap there, Arrhidaeus, had recently attacked nearby Cyzicus and thus made himself a prominent (and popular) target. Sending a force to expel Arrhidaeus, Antigonus at the same time marched on Lydia to deal with that province's satrap, Cleitus. While Arrhidaeus sent an army to free Eumenes from Nora and enlist his aid, Cleitus strengthened his garrisons and went himself to Macedonia to inform Polyperchon of the situation in Asia. Meanwhile, Antigonus proceeded to capture cities throughout Asia Minor by either force or persuasion. He and Cassander formed a pact at this time, both hoping to use the other to their own advantage.

By winter of 319/18, Cassander in Europe, Antigonus in Asia and Ptolemy in Africa had joined in a loose alliance of convenience, each with his own private agenda. Against these stood Polyperchon in Macedonia and many of the Asian satraps with Eumenes, these last throwing in with the kings under Polyperchon's control. Eumenes had escaped Cappadocia ahead of a pursuing army with about 500 horsemen and more than 2,000 infantry. He had agreed to serve as imperial supreme commander in Asia with a force that included the storied hypaspists of the Silver Shields regiments. Under royal orders, these had come up from their post guarding a royal treasury to meet Eumenes as he arrived in Cilicia. (A majority of the 3,000 Silver Shields must have joined the ranks as replacements over the years; still, some of those over 40 years of age had served since the beginning of Alexander's career.) Flush now with royal funds, Eumenes sent out agents to hire mercenaries and soon had added more than 10,000 foot soldiers and 2,000 horsemen. He then headed for Phoenicia, where he intended to collect a fleet as well. Meanwhile, there was a great deal of maneuvering in Greece during the spring and into the summer of 318 between the forces of Cassander and Polyperchon. Though no significant battle was fought, the latter was able to gain an advantage by granting the Greek cities greater autonomy within the empire. The focus then shifted to the Bosporus. There, Polyperchon's forces fought a successful naval battle, but were caught ashore by Antigonus, who launched a night attack and followed it up at sea in the morning to gain a major victory.

The rest of that year saw Antigonus go into Phoenicia and flush Eumenes and his men, who fled eastward to avoid a fight. They then suffered attacks from hostile locals as well as from the forces of Seleucus, the Babylonian satrap. Slipping away, Eumenes made his way into Media to shelter for the winter. He had added another 800 horsemen to total around 15,000 infantry and 3,300 cavalry (Diodorus 18.72.4). Meanwhile, Eumenes' friends in Europe were in retreat. Lack of success in the field there had degraded Polyperchon's stock. This caused many of the Greek states to bolt and Cassander even found some support in Macedonia itself during a brief campaign into his foe's heartland. The following months would thus see Polyperchon fighting off intrigues by the wife of King Arrhidaeus in an attempt to align her husband with Cassander. However, Polyperchon soon reasserted control. He now favored Alexander's offspring, and Olympias, who had returned to Macedonia to aid the rule of her grandson, brought about Arrhidaeus' death.

Coprates and Paraetacene (317 B.C.)

Eumenes moved in early 317 to gain funds from the royal treasury at Susa as well as pull in troops from the Upper Satrapies. The latter had recently repulsed an attempt at conquest by the Median satrap Pithon and Eumenes' emissaries found their forces already in the field under Peucetes, governor of Persia and former bodyguard to Alexander. His command came to 18,700 infantry and 4,600 cavalry (Diodorus 19.14.8). Meanwhile, at Susa, Eumenes was able to collect a plentiful sum of money. It's also probable that it was here that he took on another 3,000 elite hypaspists who later appear in his army, these likely having been on guard over the treasury there much as per the Silver Shields' assignment in Cilicia. Eumenes now headed east to unite with the satrapal host.

Antigonus had done some more recruiting of his own on the coast and then marched landward to oppose Eumenes. Reaching Babylon, he received more troops from Seleucus and Pithon before setting out again, moving through Susa and into the desolate country beyond in the midst of summer. This forced march cost him a good many men due to the extreme heat, but he eventually reached the Coprates River and camped on the western bank. Eumenes had by this time come on the scene as well, his camp sitting only a short distance away on the east side of another stream, the Pasitigris (a tributary of the Tigris into which the Coprates flowed).

Antigonus began crossing the Coprates using local boats, sending a squadron of 400 horsemen along with two taxeis of Macedonian pikemen (3,000) to form a bridgehead. He then landed some 6,000 light infantry so that they could forage on the far bank. Eumenes suddenly came against these advance detachments with a flying column of 4,000 infantry (probably hoplites and possibly including at least 1,000 of the hypaspists from Susa) and 1,300 mounted troops. His horsemen fell upon the enemy foot skirmishers and cavalry, catching them completely disordered to initiate a rout. As for the phalangites, these managed to pull into a fighting formation; however, they ended up fleeing at first onset of Eumenes' phalanx, which was easily able to overlap them and had supporting cavalry to wrap around their flanks. The bested men fled to the river in a mob and tried to re-board, but only swamped their boats in an undisciplined rush to get away. A few swam across, many more drowned and the rest were either killed or captured as Antigonus watched, unable to help as he had no boats on his side of the river. Before it was over, Eumenes and his men had taken 4,000 prisoners and slain perhaps as many more at very little cost.

With all of his boats gone and the enemy alert, Antigonus could see no safe way across the Coprates and withdrew. He decided to march to Ecbatana in Media where he could establish a base and plan another approach to the Upper Satrapies. This proved a difficult trek. With hostile locals picking at his column along the way, Antigonus lost a bounty of men, warhorses and pack animals before reaching the more settled part of Media. Once at Ecbatana, however, he was able to gather 2,000 horsemen, 1,000 replacement mounts and enough beasts of burden to restore his losses. Then, when his army had briefly rested and regained its morale, Antigonus marched for Persia, having learned that his foes were now in its capital of Persepolis. Eumenes set out to meet this advance and the two armies crossed in Paraetacene, the border region of Persia northeast of Suza and adjoining Media.

Both sides having scouted the other, the contending forces arrayed for action behind protection from river-cut ravines, yet neither general was willing to risk a charge across such disadvantageous terrain. After some skirmishing and maneuvering, Eumenes got the jump on a withdrawal toward the city of Gabene (Gabiene), which offered a good source of supplies for whichever army got there first. Antigonus led a cavalry pursuit with his infantry trailing as best it could. Catching up with the rear of Eumenes' column, he and his horsemen paraded across some high ground, acting as if their entire army was present and preparing for battle. They thus gave Eumenes pause and gained a long enough delay for their foot soldiers to catch up and turn this fiction into reality when Antigonus led his full array down from the heights late in the day.

Eumenes had set up for battle, aligning his phalanx with more than 6,000 mercenary hoplites on the left and about 5,000 pantodapoi next in line. On the far right, he placed the 3,000 or so Silver Shields inside of the better than 3,000 hypaspists from Susa. Plutarch's description (Vol. II *Eumenes*, 33–34) of the Macedonian troops (Silver Shields and other hypaspists) makes it clear that they were armed with sarissai, as were the pantodapoi. Given their posting to the left, there is some reason to think that the mercenaries might also have been armed with pikes as was the Macedonian custom on that wing. However, it seems more probable that most (if not all) of them were traditional hoplites, which was clearly the norm for hired heavy infantry in this period. If so, the phalanx would have stretched across a front of around 2.4km in close order with files of eight for the pikemen and four for the spearmen. In front of this infantry array were 40 elephants, spread widely with light infantry between each beast. Off the left wing, Eumenes assigned 3,150 horsemen and put 150 Indian riders and 50 lancers outside of them to cover the space up to anchoring high ground on that flank. The entire left wing mounted array would have spanned nearly 850m at a depth of eight. In front of the cavalry on this side were 45 elephants set at 15m intervals with foot archers and slingers filling the interstices. Cavalry off the right wing consisted of 2,300 riders, including 900 hetairoi lancers. Spread eight-deep along some 600m, these horsemen were backed at their far end by a separate group of 300 picked riders and fronted by a body of 100 more horsemen. The latter along with another 200-rider squadron angled beyond the end of the main line were to serve as hedges against a potential sweep by the enemy around the unanchored right flank of Eumenes' formation. There were 40 elephants in front on that side of the field, spaced every 15m with light footmen in the intervals. In all, Eumenes' line must have stretched almost 4km onto the plain.

Antigonus observed these arrangements and adjusted his array accordingly as sundown drew near. Coming down at last onto the flat to fight, his phalanx had more than 9,000 mercenary hoplites on its left wing next to 3,000 Lycians and Pamphylians (hoplites with aspides and auxiliary javelins). On the right of the spearmen were more than 8,000 pantodapoi with pikes. His crack Macedonian phalangites held the right wing at nearly 8,000 strong. Antigonus' numerical advantage in heavy-armed troops would have let him set the hoplites six to eight-deep and file his phalangites at 16, yet still match fronts with the enemy's much thinner formation. Antigonus placed a majority of his cavalry alongside the left wing. This included 1,000 mounted archers and lancers plus 200 riders equipped in the "Tarantine" style (javelins and small shields) and other cavalry to reach a total of around 5,000. (Bennett and Roberts [2009, 63] provide a good discussion of Diodorus' exaggerated claim [19.29.2] that there were 2,200 Tarantines here.) Containing the lightest armed horsemen, this force was meant to wheel about and overwhelm the smaller mounted contingent deployed on the open end of Eumenes' line. On his right, Antigonus took station with the remaining 3,500 or so riders, including all of his heavier troopers. These counted 1,000 hetairoi under his son Demetrius and an agema of 300 companion lancers (with whom Antigonus himself rode), which had backing from 100 Tarantines. It was Antigonus' design to use these elite horsemen on the closed/right side of the field in conjunction with his Macedonian pikemen on that wing to win the battle. Further to this purpose, he placed the 30 finest of his elephants out in front on his right, spreading them like those of Eumenes with light footmen in between. Antigonus divided his other 35 pachyderms between fronting his phalanx and leading for the left-side cavalry.

As the formations closed into combat, the light horsemen on Antigonus' left quickly began to gain an advantage, their arrow fire doing a great deal of damage. Eumenes reacted by bringing lighter equipped riders over from the other side of the field to join his supporting foot skirmishers in a fierce counter-attack. With the elephants on that flank chipping in as well, Eumenes troops then managed to repulse the mounted archers, Tarantines and other riders, driving them toward the highlands behind. Meanwhile, the phalanxes had been battling for some time all along the line. Neither side had been able to gain much advantage in this duel, since spearmen were facing deep and difficult to pierce pike arrays on either wing whose phalangites had little penetrating potential of their own. It was a struggle in which the hypaspists, led by the Silver Shields, were particularly effective, successfully stalemating the very best of Antigonus' hoplites. Now, with the mounted force that had been protecting their flank in retreat, those mercenaries were dangerously exposed and gave way, withdrawing before they could be enveloped. Their defeat doomed the rest of Antigonus' phalanx as each division's troops had to pull back when the flight of comrades on the left bared that side. Antigonus soon had his entire infantry array rushing rearward with the enemy striking hard at its trailing ranks. It was at this crucial juncture that the wily old general saw a golden opportunity to make good on his objective of winning the day on the right, though certainly not in the way he'd originally planned.

Antigonus and his picked horsemen had held position along their portion of the line even as the enemy phalanx moved forward in pursuit off to their left. This created a gap behind the charging infantry array with the right end of its body of cavalry on that side of the field. Antigonus led his hetairoi into the opening and made a lateral attack on the opposing riders that sent them scurrying away. Therefore, as his foot soldiers regrouped upon reaching the foothills, he and his horsemen were now in command of half the ground and well positioned to threaten Eumenes' rear.

There was an attempt by both generals to reorder at this point for a second round. However, it was now late evening and, though the moon shown bright, their men were exhausted and wouldn't reengage. Over Eumenes wishes, his troops retired, leaving Antigonus to hold the battlefield, control the bodies of the fallen and lay claim to a formal victory. All the same, he had lost 3,700 infantry (13 percent if these were all heavy-armed) as well as 54 horsemen. Eumenes, despite having over 900 wounded, suffered only 540 infantry fatalities (3 percent of his heavy array) while "very few of his cavalry fell" (Diodorus 19.31.5). Thus, once his dead were cremated and buried the next day, Antigonus arranged for his foes to take up their fallen on the following morning and marched off to put as much distance as he could between his badly damaged force and further action. Eumenes and his men were too tired to give chase and both armies went into winter quarters.

Gabene (317/16 B.C.)

Antigonus was eager to take advantage of his still considerable edge in heavy manpower and, once he felt his troops were sufficiently recovered by late December, set out once more to engage Eumenes, marching via the shortest route toward his enemy's position in upper Media. Alerted to this threat, Eumenes sent out some men to delay his foe by posing as a confronting army. He then scrambled to gather up his real host from its widely scattered stations. When he had collected it, he rushed to meet Antigonus and his men on the open plain near Gabene. The armies involved were similar to those that had met at Paraetacene (minus the losses there plus a few recent recruits). Antigonus had 22,000 in heavy infantry (6,000 less than before) and 9,000 horsemen (a few more) and 65 elephants (Diodorus 19.40.1–4). Eumenes countered with 36,700 footmen (having added 1,700 local skirmishers), 7,000 in cavalry (versus 6,100 previously) and the same 114 elephants. His heavy infantry likely was no greater than the 17,000 he'd fielded just a few months earlier.

Antigonus set up as he had Paraetacene, placing his Macedonian pikemen on the right with the pantodapoi next, all these at 16-deep; he then spread out his spearmen at a depth of eight to complete the phalanx. Eumenes, however, took a different tack. Arraying all of his heavy infantry in files of eight, he moved his pike-armed hypaspists to the left wing this time (the 3,000 Silver Shields again inside of the other 3,000, who were in flank position), seeking to generate the sort of offensive force that he'd lacked at Paraetacene by having his best troops have at similarly armed pikemen rather than the hoplites they'd faced in that previous engagement. He then deployed the pantodapoi next in formation and had his mercenary spearmen take the right wing. Eumenes intended to carry the fight on his stronger left against the opposition's top troops, refusing his weaker wing much in the past fashion of Epaminondas. Further to this end, he took station with the best of his cavalry (including many from the Upper Satrapies under Peucestes) off the left flank while posting his lesser riders to the right. He instructed the latter (and presumably their entire wing) to avoid combat until he had won the day on the other side of the field, where Antigonus and his crack Macedonians (both mounted and afoot) were standing. Both generals lined their elephants in front, placing bodies of light infantry in the intervals.

The action opened with the elephants coming together all along the line, and then Eumenes left-wing horsemen engaged Antigonus and his elite riders. Seeing a dense cloud of dust going up from the dry earth as the mounted men moved about, Antigonus sent a detachment from his left wing to ride around the enemy line. These were his Median horsemen and some of those equipped in Tarantine style, who took advantage of the obscuring dust to skirt unobserved past Eumenes' right flank, racing on to capture his baggage train. Meanwhile, Antigonus and the hetairoi charged ahead off their own right with such élan that Peucestes and his squadron took flight, drawing 1,500 others from the Upper Satrapies along to seek safety at the rear. Eumenes with his few remaining horsemen and elephants on that side of the field continued to fight

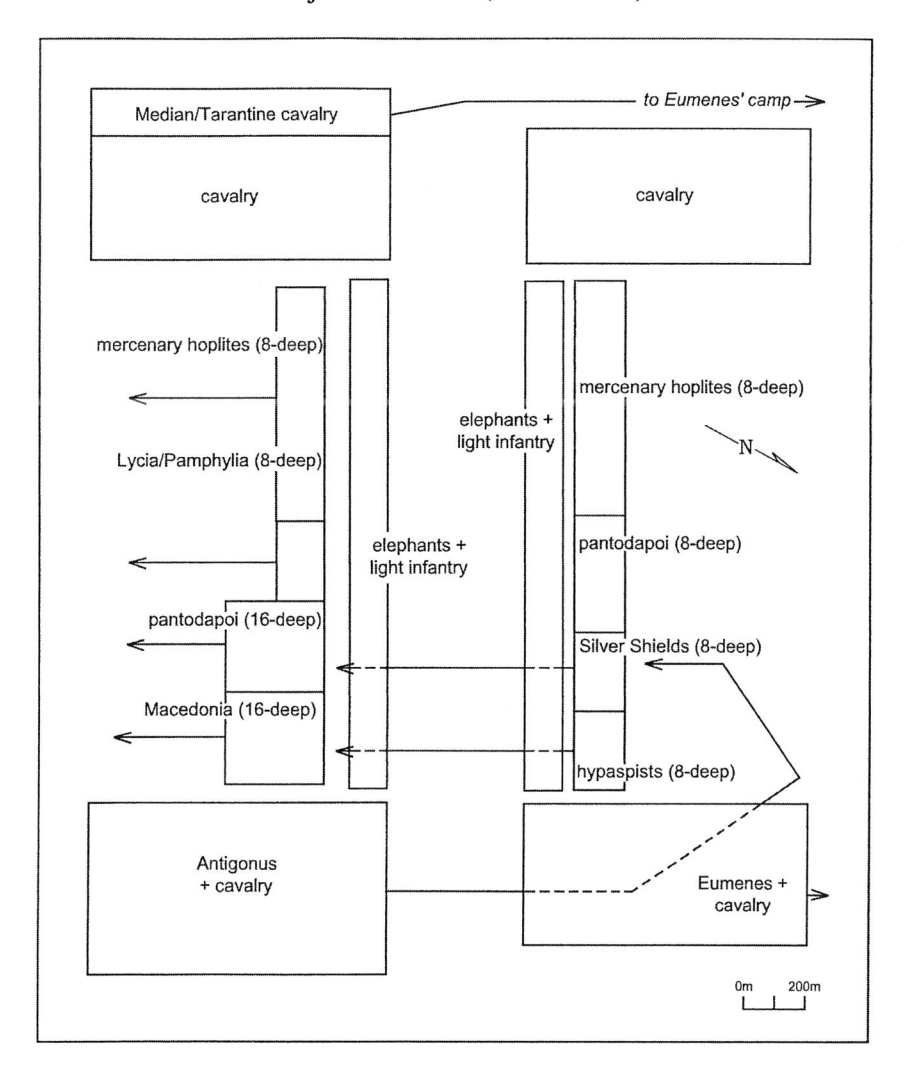

BATTLE OF GABENE (317/16 B.C.) (BOXES REPRESENTING FORCES ARE EXAGGERATED TO SHOW RELATIVE SIZES.)

valiantly, but it was hopeless and, when his best elephant went down, Eumenes rode back and around to join his still only lightly engaged cavalry on the other wing.

Yet, though Eumenes was suffering poorly in the mounted action, his phalanx was doing well. The leading elephants had somehow cleared out of the way (perhaps escaping to join the horsemen off either flank) and, just as planned, the elite hypaspists on Eumenes' left, led by the Silver Shields, were out-dueling their Macedonian counterparts, wounding and killing men in the leading ranks to move the opposing array back all along that wing. Antigonus' phalangites could eventually take it no more and withdrew, causing the rest of his heavy formation to give up the fight as well. Lunging at their retreating foes, Eumenes' pikemen and hoplites now took a heavy toll from those trying to get away. Diodorus put the retreating array's dead at more than 5,000 (19.43.1), a loss rate of over 20 percent reflecting particularly fierce and effective pursuit.

Antigonus reacted to this disastrous turn of events by holding back a portion of his victorious cavalry to counter Eumenes and his remaining horsemen while sending the rest to attack the enemy phalanx, which was giving chase without benefit of mounted protection. Realizing their peril, the hypaspists formed a square and, holding off the attacking cavalry, abandoned the field.

At this point, their pikeman and hoplite comrades must have paid a steep price. We've no figures, but Antigonus' riders probably cut down many that were fleeing in a manner nowhere near as effective as the ordered retreat of the hypaspists. Eumenes forces thus might have suffered 5–10 percent in fatalities here in addition to 2–3 percent taken along the line of battle

Eumenes, unable to rally Peucestes and his horsemen, joined his infantry as darkness fell. He wanted to renew the fight while his allies from the Upper Satrapies preferred a withdrawal to their homelands. However, it was the Macedonian foot soldiers that had the final say. The enemy was in possession of their families and goods with the captured baggage train and they entered into negotiations to get them back. The Macedonians ultimately agreed to join Antigonus and gave up Eumenes for execution, which sent his remaining satrapal allies running for their own safety. (After this bit of treachery, Antigonus would put no trust in the Silver Shields and arranged for the most contentious of them to be assigned a few at a time to hazardous missions from which they were not expected to return.) Antigonus went back to Persia and, claiming all of Asia, once more redistributed the satrapies of that part of Alexander's conquests. Seleucus escaped from Babylon at this time to join Ptolemy, and Antigonus had by year's end marched down with his army to winter in Cilicia, from where he could threaten Egypt in the spring. For his part, Ptolemy now made an alliance with Lysimachus and Cassander to prevent Antigonus from reuniting the empire under his rule and depriving everyone else of their domains.

The End of Alexander's Line

Back in Macedonia, Cassander had gained a superior position by the winter of 317/16. With Polyperchon invested in Thessaly and his son Alexander isolated with a last army in the Peloponnese, he besieged Olympias, Roxanne and the child king in Pella. Conditions in that city became so bad that some of its residents resorted to cannibalism and Olympias had to let many of her troops within the walls go out and surrender. Seeing all of their support evaporate, the royals tried to flee by sea, but were betrayed and had to come to terms. With the king now in hand, Cassander set out to reduce the last pockets of resistance to his control of Europe.

Amphipolis II (316 B.C.) and Aphrodisias (315 B.C.)

The only royal outpost refusing to submit in the north lay at Amphipolis. Aristonous was in command there and Cassander sent his general Cratevas to take the city. Aristonous didn't wait, but came out and fought Cratevas on open ground. It's likely that Cassander had sent a typical detachment of 4,000 heavy infantry (3,000 pikemen and 1,000 hoplites) along with a modest mounted contingent (maybe 400 horsemen) and some light infantry (perhaps 1,000 or so). As for his opponent, we don't know anything about the strength of Aristonous beyond Diodorus' claim that "he had many soldiers" (19.50.7). However, a strong garrison of at least 3,000 hoplites along with substantial light-armed support (hireling Thracian riders and peltasts) seems reasonable. At any rate, the resulting action cost Cratevas "most" of his troops and sent him into retreat with 2,000 men. (Note that this squares with the foregoing guess at his initial manpower in that the survivors represent a 40 percent minority of the estimated infantry.) Such extraordinary losses suggest a double envelopment, probably led by superior skirmishing on the part of the men from Amphipolis off both wings. Ultimately, though, Aristonous surrendered upon a request from the now captive Olympias acting on the king's behalf. It would prove one of her last acts. Cassander shortly thereafter had Olympias killed to leave Roxanne and her child alone in his custody.

The remainder of 316 saw Polyperchon flee Thessaly to join his son Alexander in the Peloponnese. Cassander then pushed past a force of Aetolians in the pass at Thermopylae and closed on the Isthmus of Corinth. When he found that narrow corridor sealed by an army under Alexander, he gathered boats and built barges at Megara to pass down the coast and land at Epidaurus. Alexander was then unwilling to engage and gave up his blocking position at the isthmus to withdraw into the interior. Faced with the approach of winter, Cassander returned to Macedonia, leaving his officer Molyccus behind with 2,000 men to insure future ease of entry into the Peloponnese. Polyperchon and his son would respond by allying with Antigonus in the coming year; however, after the subsequent assassination of Alexander, his father would become no more than a minor player in the succession game.

Asia was at this time the site of a duel for Cilicia and Caria, whose conquests were meant to serve as preliminaries for an invasion of Egypt by Antigonus. The first major action in this fight came in 315 when Ptolemy's subordinate Polycleitus gained a victory in a land/sea engagement along the Cilician coast at Aphrodisias. Ambushing a supporting force marching onshore (Diodorus 19.64.6), he had then routed Antigonus' fleet under the admiral Theodotus. We've no details on the onshore segment of this affair, but Polycleitus probably hit his foes' flank as they moved in column near the beach. The armies involved must have been fairly small. Polycleitus was perhaps able to deploy no more than 2,000 heavy infantrymen and 3,000 armed rowers (40 spearmen and one level of oarsmen from each of his 50 triremes). As for the force taken by surprise, it could well have consisted of 2,000–4,000 heavy infantry along with a few hundred each in foot skirmishers and horsemen. Antigonus paid back this reverse with his own surprise attack in Caria. His nephew Ptolemaeus caught Eupolemus (a general of Ptolemy's ally Cassander) and his 8,000 infantry and 200 horsemen in their beds near an otherwise unknown site called Caprima and captured the lot of them.

Hebrus River (314 B.C) and Epirus I–II, Callantia, Haemus Pass II (313 B.C.)

Back in mainland Greece, siege operations and shifting alignments dominated action over the next couple of years with the contending Macedonian warlords striving to bring or keep as many poleis as possible under their control. The few set battles that did take place during this period were all at the fringe of the Greek world. In the west, Cassander had campaigned in Acarnania to bring that region into his camp as a hedge against continued Aetolian resistance. Having succeeded there, he headed even farther northwest, taking Apollonia in modern day Albania and waging war into nearby Illyria. The latter led to a battle against the Illyrian Glaucias when that tribal king tried to contest a crossing of the river Hebrus in his homeland. Cassander drew up his army after getting over the stream and defeated the barbarian monarch and his men, forcing them to sign a treaty of submission. The scope of this engagement is unknown, but might have featured a Macedonian army of some 9,000–12,000 heavy foot (75 percent pikemen) and 400–800 hetairoi plus 2,000–3,000 foot skirmishers along with maybe 4,000–8,000 mercenaries (75 percent hoplites and the rest light infantry). These fought an Illyrian host that was maybe 6,000–10,000 strong in shielded spearmen with light support running around 10 percent of the total manpower. Like previous contests between these nationalities at Lyncus Plain (358), Grabaea (356) and Ardiaea (345), this action probably turned on success by the Macedonians' hetairoi and spearmen, who combined efforts to envelop the enemy left flank and break apart the Illyrian battle array.

Cassander's forces were again engaged in western Greece the next year when his brother Philip carried out a campaign against Aeacides, the king of Epirus. The Epirotes had cast their lot with a still hostile Aetolia and Philip set out to take them on before these allies could combine.

Perhaps commanding a force of 8,000 heavy infantry (6,000 pikemen and 2,000 hoplites), 2,000 foot skirmishers and 800 hetairoi, Philip fought a phalanx action against what must have been a somewhat smaller hoplite army (maybe some 4,000–6,000 local and mercenary spearmen with 1,000–2,000 light infantry and a few hundred horsemen) under Aeacides. Dealing out quite a few casualties (perhaps 10–15 percent) and taking some prisoners as well, Philip carried the day. Details on his victory are lacking, but it most likely featured his phalangites stalling the Epirotes on their right while his spearmen and cavalry overcame their left. However, Aeacides and most of his men got away and rallied to join Aetolian reinforcements. These might have been 3,000 or so troops such as that polis had put in the field a year earlier (Diodorus 19.68.1), maybe 1,000–1,500 spearmen and 500–1,000 foot skirmishers. Philip advanced to engage this force and repeated his previous success, killing Aeacides in the process. As a result of this loss, the Aetolians were so discouraged that they fled the cities to take refuge in the hills when the Macedonians dropped down into their country.

At about the same time as Philip gained his twin triumphs over Aeacides, Lysimachus went up against barbarian opposition on the eastern frontier of his Thracian satrapy. He was putting down a revolt there by Callantia, which lay on the west side of the Black Sea. The rebels were allied with neighboring Thracians and Scythians who had now arrived on the scene. Lysimachus was able to chase off the men from Thrace without a fight, but had to engage the Scythians in a pitched battle. We have very little data on this action. What we are told is that it was victory for Lysimachus in which he inflicted many casualties on the Scythians and pursued their survivors "beyond the frontiers" (Diodorus 19.73.5). We might suspect that he had nothing more than a garrison similar to that which he'd fielded at Odrysia back in 323. If so, there were something like 3,000 pikemen and 1,000 hoplites plus 2,000 horsemen and a thousand or so missilemen on foot. His barbarian foes, who were horse-archers and perhaps several thousand in number, might have fallen victim to tactics much like those Philip II had employed on the Dobruja Plain in 339. This called for Lysimachus' cavalry and light infantry to skirmish ahead of an anchoring phalanx, using the superior range of their bowmen and slingers to advantage while the heavy-armed formation spoiled the barbarians' usual circling tactics.

Having bested Callantia's allies, Lysimachus left some men behind to prosecute a siege (without success, as it would turn out) and headed home. This brought him up against Seuthes, the Thracian chief he'd met in battle at Odrysia a decade ago. Seuthes was now in league with Antigonus and had moved to block the pass over Mount Haemus. No doubt waged in a narrow space, this was a drawn-out affair in which "Lysimachus lost not a few of his own men, yet still destroyed a vast number of the enemy and overpowered the barbarians" (Diodorus 19.73.9). Just how Lysimachus did this isn't recorded, but he might have emulated Alexander's 335 triumph in this same pass, stacking his heavy-armed foot soldiers on one flank and covering the other with missile fire from his light infantry. Had the fight occupied an even more restricted portion of the passage than the crest forced by Alexander, Lysimachus could have pushed through with a deeply filed array fronted by his hoplites while supporting it with skirmisher volleys from behind. Regardless of such details, the poorly protected Thracians must have suffered mounting and unequal casualties during an extended exchange of missiles before yielding to pressure from the Macedonian's heavy footmen.

Despite his victories, Cassander ended the year 313 in distress. This was caused by Ptolemaeus, whom Antigonus sent out to aid a bid for freedom by the Greek poleis. Bringing 5,000 foot soldiers and 500 horsemen aboard 150 warships, Ptolemaeus had gathered another 2,200 infantry and 1,300 riders from Boeotians hostile to Cassander (Diodorus 19.77.2–4). He campaigned with this considerable force and, with help from a feint by Antigonus at the Hellespont, drove Cassander back into Macedonia while liberating Euboa, Phocis and all of Boeotia.

Gaza (312 B.C.)

Ptolemy went on the offensive in 312, marching with Seleucus into southern Syria/Palestine to engage Antigonus' son Demetrius. The latter was in place near Gaza with 10,000 mercenary footmen (8,000 hoplites and 2,000 foot skirmishers including some Persian archers), 2,000 Macedonians (pikemen), 1,000 Lycian and Pamphylian spearmen, 500 Persian slingers, 5,000 horsemen and 43 elephants (Diodorus 19.69.1, 19.82.1–4). Ptolemy moved on these with an army of 18,000 infantry and 4,000 cavalry (Diodorus 19.80.5). Most of his foot soldiers were Egyptian (perhaps 9,000 pantodapoi with pikes and 3,000 skirmishers). The rest were Macedonian (maybe 3,000 phalangites) and Greek (3,000 hired spearmen).

Demetrius was determined to win the battle with cavalry on his left wing. He thus took post there along with 3,500 horsemen, among which were all of his lancers (500 in his own squadron plus 800 hetairoi) and the shield-bearing Tarantine javelineers. In front of this mounted contingent, he placed 30 elephants, spreading them out with 1,500 of the light infantry between them (including the Persian slingers). His phalanx came next right. This probably had the Macedonians on the left with the Lycian/Pamphylian fighters and the mercenaries next in that order. All of these heavy footmen would have filed eight-deep. He put the remaining 13 elephants and 1,000 foot skirmishers out in front of the phalanx. Demetrius then deployed the rest of his horsemen (1,500) off the right wing with instructions to hold back until things were settled on the left. On the other side, Ptolemy had initially set up to favor his own left wing. He seems to have had the same design as Demetrius, replicating the past strategies of Epaminondas and Eumenes that sought to carry the day against the enemy's best men; however, once he saw that his foe was also favoring his left, he reordered to boost his right and again match strength against strength. This put Ptolemy, Seleucus and their 3,000 best riders on that flank with only 1,000 horsemen of lesser quality off the other end of the phalanx. We have no details of how his heavy formation was arranged. Most likely, it stood eight men deep with the Macedonian phalangites at the right, followed by the pantodapoi and then the mercenary hoplites on the far left. As a counter to the opposing elephants, Ptolemy and Seleucus sent men out front with spiked devices (caltrops) that would damage the beast's feet. They backed these with javelinmen and archers, who were under orders to target both the pachyderms and their mahouts.

The subsequent engagement turned on action between the two strongest mounted divisions. On that wing, the combination of caltrops and missile fire disabled Demetrius' elephants, and most of his horsemen then gave up after a lengthy and fairly even melee. Forced to withdraw with his fleeing riders, Demetrius was able to lead them off in good order. His phalanx, so far having been only lightly engaged at best with its counterpart, now broke apart as some of its men tossed spears and shields to run after their cavalry. Ptolemy's heavy troops closed about the enemy foot soldiers still on the field, killing a portion before the rest could surrender. (Diodorus cited only 500 lost on Demetrius' side [19.85.3], mostly horsemen. However, Plutarch [Vol. II *Demetrius*, 448] put the death toll at 5,000. If the claim by both historians of 8,000 captured is accurate and refers to phalanx men, then those killed more probably came to 2,000–3,000.) In all the confusion that followed the defeated army's flight, the victors found Gaza's gates still open and entered to seize the town with little effort.

Demetrius sent to Phyrgia for his father's help and retired to call up troops out of Cilicia and various garrisons. Seleucus headed to Babylon at this time with 800 infantry and 200 horsemen. Gathering more soldiers in route, he took over the city and recruited to bring his army to 3,000 footmen and 400 cavalry. He then ambushed Antigonus' general Nicanor at night along the Tigris and gained most of his 10,000 infantry and 7,000 riders as well. Having now collected a considerable army, he settled in to rule Babylonia. Ptolemy, in the meantime, sent the Macedonian general Cilles to engage Demetrius, who had moved into northern Syria. Demetrius learned of this and made a forced march to reach Cilles' camp before dawn. Striking that morning, he captured the Macedonian and 7,000 of his men without a fight. Having suffered this reverse and with Antigonus now marching down with an army to join his son, Ptolemy elected to abandon Syria and Phoenicia and retreat into Egypt. Antigonus and Demetrius spent the rest of the year carrying out an unsatisfactory campaign against Arab tribesmen in the vicinity of modern-day Jordan (as a preliminary step for the possible invasion of Egypt) and a more successful march to Babylon, which Seleucus' local general gave up rather than make a futile resistance against overwhelming odds.

Eurymenae I–II and Apollonia (312 B.C.)

Back in Greece, Antigonus' general Ptolemaeus was drawn from his campaign against Cassander by the revolt of his admiral, Telesphorus. The renegade commander had made a bid to take over and spoil Elis and its Olympic shrine on his own behalf. Ptolemaeus marched into the Peloponnese and resolved the situation without a battle, restoring Elean freedom and the shrine's wealth. Taking advantage of this distraction for his foe, Lyciscus, Cassander's general in Acarnania, took an army into Epirus to address a resurgence of resistance there. This involved the Epirotes new king, Alcetas, who had replaced the fallen Aeacides. Having a strong garrison contingent of perhaps 3,000 pikemen, 1,000 hoplites, 1,000 light infantry and 400 horsemen, Lyciscus moved to confront Alcetas, who had only a modest force and was awaiting help from his sons, Alexander and Teucer. When many of the Epirotes deserted rather than oppose the invasion, Alcetas fled to the city of Eurymenae and met Alexander, who brought a considerable reinforcement for his father.

Maybe fielding some 4,000 heavy-armed now, Alcetas engaged and defeated Lyciscus. We know little about this action beyond its general result; however, it's possible that Epirote spearmen might have overcome Macedonian hoplites on Lyciscus' right, these perhaps having filed at a depth of only four (half that of the foe and their own phalangites) to avoid an overlap. Lyciscus got away with much of his command, possibly due to effective screening of the retreat by his cavalry. Shortly thereafter, Deinias, another general of Cassander, arrived with more troops, and the Macedonians, maybe half as much stronger than before, gained a victory over Alexander and Teucer. In all likelihood, the second battle featured a point for point reversal of the previous engagement's particulars. Lyciscus took Eurymenae after Alcetas' sons and the other survivors had fled. Nonetheless, Cassander himself marched an army into Epirus in the end and established friendly relations with Alcetas.

Having calmed Epirus, Cassander took part of his army and moved on Apollonia. That city had revolted and cast out its garrison in the aftermath of Ptolemaeus' recent successes. Probably leading something like 6,000 phalangites, 2,000 hypaspists/hoplites, 2,000 foot skirmishers and 400 hetairoi, Cassander fought a battle before the city's walls against the townsmen and their allies (probably all Illyrian). Diodorus described the Apollonians as being "superior in number" (19.89.2), which suggests they might have had better than 10,000 Greek and barbarian spearmen along with several thousand in light infantry and 1,000 or so horsemen. Cassander, possibly beaten on his right and stalled elsewhere, took significant casualties (maybe 20 percent or more) and withdrew all the way to Macedonia. There, he would come to terms with Antigonus in the coming year, joining Lysimachus and Ptolemy in a pact that confirmed each in his realm. Cassander was to rule Macedonia and Greece under this agreement until such time that Roxanne's boy was old enough to assume his kingly duties as Alexander IV. Cassander then had the woman and her son murdered. This was readily accepted by the other Successors, since the youngster's demise removed an heir of Alexander who might have challenged the legitimacy of their own titles. In 309, Cassander would go on to precipitate the assassination of Heracles, Alexander's son by his mistress Barsine and the last of the great conqueror's direct blood-line.

Agathocles of Syracuse

Syracuse had fallen under less popular rule after the death of Timoleon and a much more restrictive oligarchic cabal known as the "Six Hundred" seized control c. 330. Opposition to this regime found a leader in Agathocles, a wealthy factory owner who had run afoul of the ruling party and fled to Italy. He rose to prominence there as a mercenary commander fighting against Syracusan expansion. Able to return home c. 319 during a brief interruption in the oligarchs' rule, Agathocles suffered banishment once more when they reclaimed power. He now waged war on Sicilian soil, leading a private army of exiles, Siculi and hirelings (Griffith 1935, 198) against the Six Hundred and their allies from Carthage. When a Carthaginian-mediated truce restored him again to Syracuse, he became the city's general (*strategos*) only then to instigate a coup in 316 and establish a mercenary-backed dictatorship. Harboring grand ambitions, this new tyrant set out to extend his sway across the rest of Sicily.

Galeria (312 B.C.) and Ecnomus Hill (311 B.C.)

Agathocles had by 314 brought all of the major Greek cities of Sicily under his nominal control. This arrangement was formalized in a treaty with Carthage that recognized Syracuse's mastery over the entire island save for the western portion (known as the "epicraty") that had long been subject to Punic rule. However, Agathocles wanted to eventually control Carthaginian Sicily as well and began building up his forces to that end. Able to call on something like 5,000 Syracusan citizens and a like number of allied Greeks, he also amassed mercenaries to the tune of 10,000 foot soldiers and 3,500 horsemen (Diodorus 19.72.2). As this was going on, there arose fresh resistance to his dictatorship at Acragas and Messana, the latter openly sheltering many that he had cast from Syracuse.

Agathocles set out in 312 to pacify the trouble-makers in his realm, opening with a march on Messana at the island's northeastern tip. Expelling its Syracusan exiles, that city submitted without a fight. The tyrant then headed down to Acragas on the southern coast, but found that a Carthaginian fleet had landed there to reinforce the town. With the Carthaginians having thus been first to breach the treaty of 314, Agathocles took the liberty of raiding into their territory to the west, subduing various sites by either force or negotiation. This spurred Deinocrates, leader of the exiles from Syracuse, to ask for help from Carthage and gather up an army of his fellow outcasts. Deinocrates and his co-commander Philonides had a force of 3,000 infantry (perhaps 75 percent hoplites) and 2,000 cavalry (Diodorus 19.104.1–2). They set up camp outside the otherwise unknown town of Galeria. Agathocles kept most of his army to meet any threat from Carthage while sending two of his officers, Pasiphilus and Demophilus, to deal with the exiles. Their command was the same size as that of the opposition (5,000 soldiers per Diodorus). Probably all mercenaries, these troops likely matched the ratio of footmen to cavalry among their foes.

The rebels deployed with Deinocrates in charge of one wing (the right?) and Philonides the other, cavalry and light infantry no doubt split off either flank. Their phalanx would have stood in files of eight. Agathocles' men must have arrayed in identical fashion to yield a matching heavy front across some 280m. Once engaged, the hoplites fought evenly, with both their strength and enthusiasm well matched. However, the dictator's phalanx eventually gained the victory (most likely on its stronger right), killing Philonides as it pushed back his wing and put it to flight. Deinocrates then had no choice but to withdraw as well lest his still resistant portion of the line be flanked. Pasiphilus commanded the successful Syracusan wing, which now slew many among its foes running from the fight. Losses among the exiles probably included better than 10 percent killed at a cost of less than 5 percent for the victors.

The Carthaginians had at this time taken a strong position on Ecnomus Hill in the vicinity of Gela. Agathocles brought the rest of his army up against them, but, being only a small force (maybe one or two 3,000-man divisions), they refused to come down and engage openly. Ravaging the surrounding area, the tyrant withdrew for the winter. In the spring, he came back with his entire host to once more offer battle; now, however, he had to face much more than the garrison that had previously held the hill, because Carthage's Hamilcar had arrived from Africa with a substantial fleet and army. He had sailed with 130 triremes that had 14,200 soldiers aboard. This indicates that most of his galleys must have been configured as troop-carriers, replacing two banks of oarsmen with passengers to allow for 120 of the latter. The remaining vessels (less than 20) acted as escorts with a full complement of rowers and only 40 marines aboard. Per Diodorus (19.106.2), his troops included 2,000 citizens, 10,000 Liby-Phoenician perioeci, 1,000 hired Greeks and 200 Etrurians — all of these using hoplite-style gear. He also had 1,000 expert slingers from the Balearic Islands to add to whatever light infantry he could gather once ashore. However, a storm had struck his heavily loaded fleet in route. This cost him 60 of the triremes and about half of his heavy infantry as well as 200 supply ships. Finally getting his battered armada to Sicily, he was able to restore his strength with local garrison troops, mercenaries and Sicilian allies so as to still deploy 40,000 foot soldiers and nearly 5,000 mounted men (Diodorus 19.106.5). Agathocles camped near Ecnomus Hill across the Himeras River (which was a saline estuary here) and a stand-off began with neither army willing to attack through the water. They settled instead for small raids and one of these forays then triggered a grand battle.

A contingent of Greeks crossed the Himeras and began to drive off cattle found outside the enemy fortifications. Seeing this, some of the Carthaginians came out to give chase, following the fleeing raiders over the river only to be ambushed on the far side by a picked team of Agathocles' mercenaries. The tyrant was ready to exploit this developing situation and, as the ambushers pursued their beaten foes, he brought his whole army behind them with the intent of taking the barbarians unprepared. Leading with a column of heavy infantry (perhaps 12,000 hoplites arrayed nearly 50-deep across 250m), he filled in an outer moat and pushed down the palisade beyond to gain access to the camp interior. Inside, he came up against only that part of the enemy force which could be accommodated within this single facility. We might suspect something like 4,000–7,000 heavy-armed men (the original garrison plus Hamilcar and 1,000 or so citizen soldiers from his fleet). Thrown into confusion by this sudden assault, the Carthaginians had no chance to get into a proper formation and could only fight like a mob.

The ensuing action was chaotic, swaying back and forth around the moat and point of penetration just inside the palisade. Had Agathocles gained such favorable circumstances on open ground, he would surely have notched a quick triumph; but with both sides packed into so small an area, the contest was slow and bloody going. Still, the better-ordered Greeks were making steady progress as they shoved from behind and speared ahead to force themselves ever farther within the camp perimeter. At this point, Hamilcar, who had his 1,000 Balearic slingers with him, brought those deadly missilemen into play. Able to fire from higher ground at the center of the hilltop camp, they wrought havoc among extremely long Greek files that made easy targets. Their shower of projectiles "wounded many and even killed a few," hitting with such force that "they shattered the defensive armor of most of them" (Diodorus 19.109.2). Taking fearsome damage, those in the Greek rear began to pull away, bringing their fore-rankers with them as Agathocles' array withdrew from the palisade breach. Yet his men remained game and came back to threaten the fortifications at several points. Just then, though, reinforcements arrived to rescue Hamilcar. These were Liby-Phoenician spearmen backed by allied Sicilian cavalry (each contingent around 5,000 strong), who hit the Greeks at flank and rear. (Diodorus improbably described the new arrivals as troops that had come over "from Libya ... by water" at just this key moment. However, these must have been the Libyans already on hand, marching to the sound of battle from nearby in company with the local cavalry.)

Under attack from all sides, the Greeks were routed and ran for their lives, but the level nature of the ground allowed Hamilcar's horsemen to ride down and savage them for a long distance. Just as bad, the fleeing men suffered dreadfully from thirst after their long and heated battle and many in desperation drank salty water from the Himeras as they tried to get away. The result was that just as many died from dehydration as fell to weapons in the pursuit. At day's end, 7,000 of Agathocles men (nearly 60 percent) lay dead on the field (Diodorus 19.109.5) while Carthage lost only 500 (7–12.5 percent of the heavy footmen upon Ecnomus). All the same, though much smaller than those of Agathocles, the African losses were high for a victor in this era, suggesting just how close the Greeks had come to success before Hamilcar's reinforcements turned the fight around.

Agathocles shut himself inside Gela. Then, when Hamilcar gave up on a siege, escaped with what was left of his army to Syracuse. All had gone wrong for the tyrant so far, but he now came up with a bold plan to salvage his cause: he would leave an adequate force with his brother Antander to defend Syracuse while he invaded Africa toward drawing the Carthaginians out of Sicily.

White Tunis I (310 B.C.) and Anapus Valley and White Tunis II (309 B.C.)

Agathocles used the arrival of some cargo vessels as a diversion and broke for the open sea with 60 triremes loaded with fighting men for the assault on Carthage. Aided by the fall of night and an eclipse the next day (August 15, 310), he raced around the upper shore of Sicily to then head for North Africa. The enemy galleys followed the entire way in a close chase, but Agathocles and his entire flotilla managed to make it onto the beach at Cape Bon (the tip of the peninsula containing Carthage) just as their pursuers pulled within bowshot. (The Greek tyrant clearly hadn't set up his triremes as troop-carriers with only one bank of oars, since he never could have won the long race had his rowers been at less than full strength.) Once on dry land, Agathocles burned his ships. This had two functions. First, as a purely practical matter, he didn't have enough men to guard a grounded fleet and carry out offensive operations at the same time. Second, by destroying their sole means of escape, he was stoking his men's enthusiasm to fight. Victory was now their only way home.

At about 240 per ship, Agathocles' triremes had carried around 14,400 passengers, sailors and oarsmen. In light of the scope of his campaign, he must have used mostly combatants for the latter in order to boost his military manpower. Still, his strength was low for so grand a project. Among Agathocles' troops, Diodorus (20.11.5) listed 5,500 hired spearmen (including 2,500 under his son Agatharchus), 3,500 Syracusan militiamen, 3,000 non–Greeks (Etruscans, Samnites and Celts, perhaps 1,000 each) and a personal bodyguard of 1,000 hoplites (picked mercenaries). All of these were heavier, shielded infantry for his main line of battle. He also had 500 archers and slingers as well as 900 unarmed crewmen. He outfitted the last with shield-covers stretched over sticks, which gave the appearance of being aspides so that the enemy might at a distance mistake them for hoplites.

Agathocles led his troops inland and took the Carthaginian city of Megalopolis. He then captured White Tunis (probably near the modern city of Tunis) and set up camp in the open nearby. The ruling council at Carthage appointed the fierce political foes Hanno and Bormilcar to lead a response that Diodorus put at 40,000 infantry, 1,000 cavalry and 2,000 chariots (20.10.5). Justin (22.6.5) claimed they had only 30,000 men, yet this might have been solely the heavy infantry (ten 3,000-man divisions) with an additional 10,000 light-armed troops making up Diodorus' number. However, while 1,000 in cavalry seems reasonable, 2,000 chariots do not. We might suspect an inflation here of times ten the actual count of these four-horse, three-man vehicles.

The Carthaginians advanced on Agathocles, who set up in a narrow place where he could prevent overlap by the opposing infantry line as well as preclude mounted flank attack. This might have let him file at eight or more shields across a front of 1.5km while placing his missilemen on the rough ground off either flank as a further hedge against envelopment. His formation had the mercenary spearmen under his son on the right, the Syracusans at center and the non–Greeks rearward on the left behind the dictator and his elite bodyguard, who held the foremost ranks on that wing. Hanno had the chief command on the other side and appears to have been confident (due to his edge in numbers) and accepted the unfavorable setting. With Bormilcar in charge of the left wing and taking the right himself, he "made his phalanx deep since the terrain prevented him from extending it on a broader front" (Diodorus 20.10.6). At 1.5km in width, his heavy array would have been twice normal depth with 20-man files. Hanno initially had his chariots and cavalry out front, but these, having charged in turn, retired with their supporting light footmen after proving both ineffective against the well-anchored Greeks and vulnerable to bow and sling fire. Hanno's formation then advanced against the opposing heavy front to initiate a brutal shock fight.

The battle was a long one in which the Carthaginians' greater depth didn't add enough advantage to push through the stubborn Greeks. Hanno, who was fighting at the fore on his right with the crack spearmen of the 3,000-man Sacred Band, was repeatedly wounded and, utterly played out, fell dead. Morale was an important factor in such an even melee and Hanno's loss began to swing it in favor of Agathocles and his select hoplites. Still, the Sacred Band kept on battling. However, on the other end of the field, Bormilcar decided to withdraw to high ground. Diodorus suggested that this had political motivations, with Bormilcar hoping to become tyrant by blaming his fallen rival for a defeat. Yet it might merely have been a case of frustration with having to fight in a disadvantaged venue, since Hanno had indeed been foolish to engage in such a tight place. Bormilcar therefore might have pulled out toward seeking a decision another time on fairer ground. Whatever the reason, the Carthaginian ordered the men on his wing to move back; however, trying to do this from the front with what seems to have been poorly drilled troops was a grave error and those at the back of his files panicked in the mistaken belief that their front-fighters had met defeat. This turned an orderly retreat into something more resembling a rout. Over on the Carthaginian right, the Sacred Band had been holding up well, but now had to give way as those beside them fled to expose that flank. Agathocles pursued only a short distance, no doubt wary of the enemy's still intact horsemen, whom he could not match.

Diodorus (20.13.1) claimed that Agathocles lost 500 men (4 percent) and Justin (22.6.6) put his losses at 2,000 (15 percent). Common figures for a hard-fought victory in this period favor the former. Diodorus set Carthage's dead at 1,000 (3 percent), but admitted that others listed the cost as high as 6,000 (20 percent). Here, Justin's figure of 3,000 (10 percent) looks the more likely in light of there having been little pursuit.

Though they retained a sizeable fighting force, the Carthaginians were nonetheless badly distressed by this reverse and called to Hamilcar on Sicily for help. After making a failed bid to intimidate Syracuse into surrender, he supplied 5,000 men (many of them Greek and including horsemen). Meanwhile, Agathocles, who lacked the manpower to assault Carthage itself, set about capturing lesser sites. The Carthaginians took this opportunity to make an attempt on Tunis, which the tyrant had fortified as a base. Learning of this, Agathocles made a show of marching to the city's aid and frightened away the Punic forces. Once the reinforcement from Hamilcar arrived, however, the Carthaginians again went after Tunis. This time, Agathocles marched back toward the town in secret and, camping without fires, struck at dawn to take the besiegers unaware, killing over 2,000 and gaining a number of captives as well. The tyrant then hit Libyan tribesmen who had joined in the attack on his base despite having recently pledged loyalty to him. In an action otherwise not described, he slew their king along with many others.

The people of Carthage thus ended the year in tough straits, shut up inside their walls with Agathocles overrunning their territory. And things got no better the next spring when a disaster in Sicily added to their woes. Hamilcar had been trying to take Syracuse by storm. In the course of the action, the defenders had occupied Euryelus, which sat at the western end of the broad, east-west elongated upland of Epipolae that stretched from the city's north side into the interior. They had stationed there some 3,000 infantry (with maybe 2,400 hoplites) and 400 horsemen. Thinking to take this strongpoint and then move across the plateau to threaten Syracuse from above, Hamilcar set out at night, marching with baggage train and all along the north bank of the Anapus River. This put him well south of Epipolae so as to avoid detection as he looped about and came up an access route on the northwest end of the highland for a sneak attack. The Carthaginian general had at least 4,000 African spearmen (from citizens that had sailed with him two years earlier and the troops that had been garrisoned at Ecnomus). He also had local allies and mercenaries to the tune of 16,000–20,000 hoplites as well as 10,000–12,000 mostly barbarian foot skirmishers and 4,000–4,500 horsemen.

The Carthaginian column had Hamilcar and some of his Africans (1,000 or so citizens?) in the lead, followed by the cavalry under the Syracusan exile Deinocrates, the remaining barbarian infantry and, finally, the Greek foot soldiers. Trying to pass along a slender path, the accompanying baggage train and camp followers created a great deal of crowding as they fought for room, the resulting tumult attracting the enemy's attention. Charging down from Euryelus, the Syracusans took the strung out Carthaginian host in the right flank to devastating effect. Under fierce attack in the dark and thinking that their assailants were much more numerous than was actually the case, Hamilcar's army thrashed about and, unable to tell friend from foe in the gloom, killed many of its own before breaking apart into terrified flight. When those about Hamilcar took to their heels, he was left to be overwhelmed and captured by the enemy. The Syracusans would execute him and send his head to Agathocles. Though the Carthaginians rallied and Hamilcar's subordinates took command, their campaign was in tatters. About all that they could do now against the Syracusans was blockade them by sea. Worse yet, Acragas now led most of the other Sicilians out of Punic alliance and began to wage war against both Syracuse *and* Carthage. Electing Xenodicus as general, the Acraganians captured Gela and added its resources to their own. They then set out to free the island from all foreign influences.

Back in North Africa, Agathocles was riding high, having sway over most of the countryside and able to taut those in the city with the head of their general. But trouble arose at this juncture within his own ranks when the dictator's son Agatharchus murdered a well-respected officer during a drunken argument. Calls for Agatharchus' death nearly led to his father paying that penalty in his place. Hearing of this problem within the enemy camp, the Carthaginians saw a chance to catch their foes in disorder and arrayed for battle in front of White Tunis. They were convinced that Agathocles had lost control and fully expected his army to desert to their side. But the tyrant put on a tremendous display of humility to win back his men and was able to lead them out united. Probably deploying some 12,000 spearmen in files of four, he charged into an opposing heavy force that stood 30,000 strong and ten-deep, yet was unprepared to fight. The attack threw the barbarians into confusion and they broke for the rear, not stopping until they had reached their base. There's no indication that Agathocles gave chase, so he probably didn't deal his beaten foes all that much physical harm; nevertheless, the psychological damage must have been great.

Zuphones Territory (308 B.C.) and Syracuse, Carthage/Midlands, Carthage/Interior and Acragas III (307 B.C.)

Agathocles left Agatharchus in charge at Tunis in early 308 and advanced to engage a Carthaginian army that had taken the field to punish and win back some of the local nomadic tribesmen that had broken away. His picked force included 8,000 infantry (maybe 7,500 hoplites and 500 light missilemen) and 800 horsemen. The latter were likely a mix of Libyan allies and riders that had come with him from Syracuse as foot soldiers and since secured mounts. He also fielded a squadron of 50 Libyan chariots of the three-man variety. Some nomadic warriors joined his column once he entered their realm, but these were to prove of little value save as guides. Agathocles followed the enemy into the territory of the Zuphones tribe. Some of those nomads had now reconciled with the Carthaginians and began to harass the Greek advance; however, Agathocles was able to counter using his archers and slingers

Crossing a stream, Agathocles' phalanx engaged foes likewise arrayed in close order. Manpower for Carthage in this action is unknown beyond being somewhat higher than for Agathocles. A reasonable guess would be 6,000 citizens and/or Liby-Phoenician spearmen (two divisions) plus 3,000 Greek hoplites, some light infantry (1,000 or so) and up to 1,000 horsemen (half of them Greek). The Grecian spearmen on both sides were probably filed at a depth of eight while the African heavy infantry stood ten-deep. Taking advantage of superior position on the far bank, the Punic forces inflicted a fair number of casualties on their enemies, who were fording across with some difficulty; yet, Agathocles' troops proved the better fighters, forcing their way up onto dry ground despite facing greater depth along much of the line.

Where Greek battled Greek at even odds (probably on Carthage's right) the action stalemated; however, Agathocles and his best men on his own right eventually routed the Africans there. And once these gave way, the rest of their formation withdrew to avoid being surrounded from its defeated flank. The Greek horsemen fighting for Carthage then put up hard resistance to delay Agathocles' contingent; still, his hoplites broke through and moved against the last enemy footmen, who had retired to their camp. Working across rough ground with equal losses on either side, the tyrant and his men were well on the way to taking this position when they had to break off to rescue their baggage train, which had come under attack from nomads (both those with Carthage as well as nominal allies). In the end, Agathocles probably lost about 5 percent of his heavy array while taking down maybe three times as many among the opposition. He also captured around 1,000 of the Greeks that fought for his foes, over 500 of them being exiles from his own city (Diodorus 20.39.5).

Returning to Tunis, Agathocles sought to gain strength for a direct attempt on Carthage by allying with Ophellas, whom Ptolemy had put in charge of the region around Cyrene. That ambitious fellow agreed to a pact that would give him all of Libya. For his share, the Greek tyrant would keep Sicily and Italy (to then be free of Punic interference). However, shortly after the Macedonian arrived, Agathocles killed him and took over his army. This let the tyrant increase his host by over 10,000 infantry (mercenary and Cyrenean hoplites plus skirmishers), 600 horsemen and 100 chariots. Even as his Greek foe was carrying out this bit of treachery, Bormilcar was attempting a tyranny at Carthage. This led to fighting in the streets, but ultimately failed and Bormilcar lost his life. The Carthaginians were in considerable disorder at this juncture, and Agathocles, though he was unaware of this, was able to campaign about the Libyan region with great success over the next few months. With all seemingly going well, he then decided in early 307 to personally address the situation back on Sicily. Leaving Agatharchus to command in Africa, he set out for Syracuse with 2,000 soldiers, using some ships built in the captured port of Hippu Acra.

Even as Agathocles set sail, Xenodicus was leading rebel forces against Syracuse in a bold bid to climax his campaign against the tyrant's rule. He had more than 10,000 foot soldiers (probably 8,000 hoplites and 2,000 skirmishers) and 1,000 horsemen (Diodorus 20.56.1–2). The tyrant's generals, Leptines and Demophilus, came out to meet him with 8,200 infantry (including maybe 6,000 spearmen) and 1,200 cavalry. The ensuing phalanx action was "a bitter fight" (Diodorus) in which the Syracusans prevailed. Given that the victors might have been only six shields deep versus eight for Xenodicus, it must have been their more skilled and seasoned mercenary hoplites that secured success, outlasting less capable militia spearmen in a grueling slug-fest on one wing (likely the losers' left) to break the entire enemy formation. Xenodicus retired to his base at Acragas, having lost 1,500 (nearly 20 percent) of his hoplites. Shortly thereafter, Agathocles landed on Sicily to lead marches about the island and add further to rebel woes. Deinocrates, the Syracusan exile, now took leadership of the rebellion. He collected 20,000 infantry and 1,500 cavalry (Diodorus 20.57.2) to renew the fight. But Agathocles, having fewer men, only followed behind him, picking away and badgering, but never submitting to open battle.

The new leadership in Carthage decided upon a different approach to their war with the Greeks. They split their strength into three armies, each with around 10,000 men (perhaps 6,000 heavy infantry plus 4,000 foot skirmishers and cavalry combined), sending one column into the coastal area, another against the nearby midlands and the third deeper into the interior. As these expeditions began to experience success in regaining those sectors for Carthage, Agatharchus tried to counter by dividing his own men among three counter-forces.

The general Aeschrion led the first Greek contingent to see action, tangling with the Punic element operating in the midlands area. Under Hanno, the Carthaginians set up an ambush and fell on their enemies as they marched in column. The Greeks were taken in the flank by surprise and lost 4,000 foot soldiers (50 percent) plus 200 horsemen (25 percent) as well as Aeschrion. Disaster then struck Agatharchus' effort in the interior as well. Here, the Punic commander, Himilco, hid half of his army in a nearby city. He then advanced against the Greeks under Eumachus. Offering at first to fight, he turned about and retreated as if panicked, drawing his foes into a pursuit that passed near town. The division hidden there charged out at this point to utterly rout the Greeks. They fell back onto a hill poorly supplied with water and Himilco, after weakening them with thirst, overpowered their position. This episode cost all but 30 footmen and 40 riders from an initial Greek force of 8,000 infantry and 800 cavalry (Diodorus 20.60.8).

Agatharchus was badly beaten on multiple fronts and nearly all of his local allies bolted. He sent to his father for help. Agathocles turned over operations on Sicily to Leptines and gathered 17 warships in preparation to aid Agatharchus. Adding another 18 Etruscan ships that arrived at the last minute, he then ventured out and defeated the Carthaginian fleet blockading Syracuse's harbor to clear the way to Africa. While this was happening, Leptines was carrying out a plundering expedition against Acragas, where Xenodicus was still holding out. In political hot water ever since his defeat before Syracuse, Xenodicus chose to silence critics with an open engagement despite having an army of inferior quality. Leptines probably had a force much like the one he and Demophilus had deployed earlier in the year. This would have been 6,000 hoplites, 2,000 foot skirmishers and 1,000 cavalry in round numbers. Xenodicus' manpower "fell little short of that of his opponents" (Diodorus 20.62.4), maybe totaling about as many foot soldiers. but only 500 or so horsemen. However, as had been the case previously at Syracuse, "in morale [he] was far inferior since the citizen army had been formed amid indulgence and a sheltered way of life and the other had been trained in military service in the field in constant campaigns." The battle thus proved an easy one for Leptines' phalanx. Arrayed at the same depth as their foes (likely eight shields), the Syracusan hirelings quickly carried the fight to chase the Acraganians into their city, killing more than 500 hoplites (8–9 percent) and 50 horsemen at very little cost. Xenodicus survived, but fled to Gela a ruined man.

Carthage (307 B.C.) and Torgium (305 B.C.)

Once back in Africa, Agathocles sought to reverse his bad fortune with a march on Carthage. He arrayed his phalanx at a likely six men deep with (per Diodorus 20.64.2) 6,000 Greek hoplites and nearly as many Etruscans (perhaps approaching 4,000 including those who had just sailed in with the tyrant), Samnites and Celts (maybe around 1,000 each). There were also probably several thousand in light infantry on hand (armed rowers and nearly 500 archers and slingers). His mounted forces tallied 1,500 horsemen plus some chariots. (Diodorus claimed 6,000 chariots, but there is probably one digit too many here, making 600 the true count. And even then, only 100 from Cyrene might have been of actual use, since the others were Libyan and that nation's troops don't appear to have been willing to fight, including some 12,000 infantry nominally on Agathocles' side.) The Carthaginians must have had half again more heavy footmen (around 18,000) as well as 12,000 light infantry and horsemen; still, they stuck to high ground and were unwilling to come down to risk battle on the plain.

Agathocles decided to take the fight to his foes and advanced uphill to engage. This assault seems to have had little chance to succeed, with Agathocles' men being "hard pressed" (Diodorus 20.64.4) from the start and able to do no more than hold out for a time. Ultimately, the enemy's greater depth (probably ten) and elevation took its toll and they began to force the Greek mercenaries and others down the slope. Agathocles had no option but to disengage and withdraw into his camp. His losses came to 3,000 on the day (just over 25 percent), indicative of both a disadvantaged fight and fiercely disputed retreat that had likely cost his opponents less than 5 percent killed.

If we are to believe Diodorus (20.65–67) the night after this battle was witness to some truly extraordinary events. These fantastic happenings began with the celebratory burning of captives in the Carthaginian camp setting off a devastating blaze. Then, amid the confusion of this disaster, a large number of the Libyans who were allied to Agathocles (but had not participated in the fighting) approached in the dark trying to give up. Thinking that these soldiers were Greeks come to exploit the holocaust, those in the camp panicked and, in all the disorder and darkness, slaughter ensued in an orgy of "friendly fire" as men mistook comrades for foes. The entire army took fright and fled for Carthage with many falling to their death from cliffs in the rush. While this tragedy was unfolding, the Libyans who had helped to precipitate it turned back toward the Greek lines. As they neared Agathocles' camp, people there reacted in terror, believing their victorious enemies were descending to finish them off. This set off a night-shrouded frenzy with friend fighting friend in a stunning repeat of what had happened to the Carthaginians. Diodorus claimed some 4,000 lives were lost amid the tumult, more than had died in the preceding battle. Morning thus saw both sides in great disarray, having been defeated by their own fears.

With his army now nearly destroyed, Agathocles decided to escape back to Syracuse, but was betrayed by his youngest son, Heracleides, whom he had planned to abandon. Seized at first by his troops, they eventually let him go and he managed to sneak off and sail home. In doing this, he left behind not only Heracleides but Agatharchus as well and both were killed in revenge for his escape. The Greeks still in Africa then made peace with Carthage, most going into its service right there and the rest settling on Sicily in Punic territory.

Back at Syracuse, Agathocles resumed his civil war with a still powerful rebel faction. The tyrant was plagued by desertions and became so despondent over his lack of success that he offered in 306 to come to favorable terms with Deinocrates. That exile, however, rejected the offer, aspiring now to claim Agathocles' entire empire for himself. The result was that these two met in battle the next year to settle things. This took place near Torgium, which is otherwise unknown, but must have lain some distance from the sea in eastern Sicily (Freeman 1894, 466). Agathocles was at this time down to only 5,000 foot soldiers (maybe 4,000 spearmen and 1,000 skirmishers) and 800 cavalry (Diodorus (20.89.1–2). Deinocrates, on the other hand, fielded a large force of 25,000 infantry (perhaps 16,000–20,000 hoplites) and 3,000 horsemen.

It's hard to believe that the tyrant would risk engagement at such long odds on open ground, thus it seems overwhelmingly probable that the fight took place in some confined terrain where he was able to ward his flanks and engage with his array filed at least four shields deep (if not deeper) against a phalanx that must have had 16 or more per file. Even so, he could never have realistically expected the "stubborn battle" described by Diodorus to go his way if allowed to play out fully. However, he had a surprise in store for Deinocrates, as he had arranged for 2,000 of the exile's spearmen to change sides. The fight had gone on for only "a short time" when the traitors turned against those beside them, throwing the rebel formation into chaos. Convinced that these turncoats were more numerous than was actually true, Deinocrates and his men fled. Most of the horsemen got clear, but between 4,000 and 7,000 of the defeated spearmen took up a hilltop position close by and surrendered that night to Agathocles. The tyrant collected their arms and then had them all shot down to crush the uprising for good. Still, he was a practical man, and would later fend off further trouble by taking in many of the exiles who had escaped, including Deinocrates. Indeed, the latter would become a trusted lieutenant in the remaining years of the tyrant's rule.

Empire's End

In the Successor Wars, Antigonus' son Demetrius had landed in Greece during 307 to strike a blow against Cassander. He began then to gain his reputation as a master besieger by taking fortifications on the hill of Munychia and liberating Athens before next doing the same for Megara with another successful investment. Under orders from his father, he left the comfort of Athens the next year and sailed against Ptolemy. He put into shore on the Egyptian ruler's territory at Carpasia on the northeast tip of Cyprus. Securing the immediate vicinity, Demetrius marched down to threaten Salamis, where Ptolemy's brother Menelaus, who commanded on the island, was waiting for him with an army gathered from all of his outposts.

Cyprian Salamis III (306 B.C.)

Demetrius led a force of 15,000 foot soldiers (likely 3,000 hoplites, 9,000 pikemen and 3,000 skirmishers) and 400 horsemen (Diodorus 20.47.1–3). Arraying his phalanx on the plain just west of Salamis, he would have filed the entire heavy division eight men deep to cover a front of around 1,125m in close order while dividing his light-armed men (both mounted and afoot) off either wing. His spearmen no doubt stood on the right side of their phalanx. Emerging from the city, Menelaus fielded an army of 12,000 infantry (likely 9,000 hoplites and 3,000 light skirmishers) plus 800 cavalry. He must have lined up eight shields deep to match the enemy front and, like his opponent, spread all the horsemen and foot skirmishers outboard on either side. The battle that then took place was a victory for Demetrius in which the spearmen on his right wing perhaps overpowered troops of lesser quality on the enemy left. With his array flanked on one side, Menelaus was forced to pull back behind his walls, having lost 1,000 (8 percent) of his men in the fight. Worse still, 3,000 more had been taken prisoner. It's possible that those captured had stood on the enveloped wing (where most of the casualties would have been taken as well) and gave up in mass when cut off from the city. Demetrius' losses were probably less than 3 percent.

Ptolemy sailed for Cyprus with a large fleet to recover this defeat, but was then himself bested in a naval action and returned to Egypt. With no hope now for relief from the siege, Menelaus gave up and turned his army over to Demetrius. (Plutarch put the surrendered force at 12,000 infantry and 1,200 cavalry [Vol. II *Demetrius,* 454]. If we are to reconcile these figures with those of Diodorus, Menelaus must have received reinforcement at some point after his defeat.) Gathering up men from across Cyprus, Demetrius went on to add another 16,000 infantry and 600 horsemen to his host. Both Antigonus and his son took the title of king in the aftermath of this triumph, and Ptolemy, Lysimachus and Seleucus would eventually follow suit. The Successor warlords thus all became self-made royalty save for Cassander, though others began to refer to him as a monarch as well.

The fracturing of Alexander's empire into separate kingdoms was now well advanced, yet Antigonus still sought to reassemble the entire realm for himself. He therefore called Demetrius back from Cyprus and, putting him in charge of his fleet, set out to conquer Egypt. He had for this task a huge army of more than 80,000 foot soldiers, 8,000 horsemen and 83 elephants (Diodorus 22.73.2). But this grand campaign came to naught when Antigonus found Ptolemy's defenses too stout and, running short on supplies, returned to Syria. He had to content himself with sending Demetrius to Rhodes the next year (305), where he embarked on a siege to add that island to his father's domain. This concentration of effort in Asia left an opening for Cassander to attack Athens. However, the Athenian general Olympiodoros sailed to Phocis and brought its second largest city, Elatea, into revolt. Along with the Aetolians, he then broke an investment there, somehow besting a contingent of Cassander's army (Pausanius 1.26.3, 10.34.2). With this threat of a force at his rear, Cassander gave up on his effort in Attica and went home.

Demetrius' assault on Rhodes turned into an epic operation, which only ended in 304 when the Rhodians came to terms, agreeing to ally with Antigonus in return for remaining free of a garrison. Demetrius next turned his efforts back to Greece, where he sailed to deprive Cassander first of Chalcis on Euboa and then all of Boeotia. He followed this by making an alliance with the Aetolians and moving into the Peloponnese in 303. There, he took Sicyon, Corinth and Arcadian Orchomenos. By 302, Cassander was becoming desperate and tried to come to terms with Antigonus. The aging king refused, being intent on a total victory that would deliver Greece into his hands alone. Cassander then pulled Lysimachus, Seleucus and Ptolemy into alliance so that they might save their kingdoms by putting an end to Antigonus' imperial ambitions.

Cassander sent his general Prepelaus to reinforce Lysimachus and the latter crossed the Hellespont. His invasion force might have numbered around 21,000 foot soldiers with 12,000 Macedonian pikemen, 6,000 hoplites (at least half of them mercenaries) and 3,000 Thracian peltasts. He also likely had a modest cavalry contingent of maybe 2,000 horsemen, perhaps all

Thracian. Prepelaus split off with a third of the army to campaign as far down as Ephesos in Ionia while Lysimachus himself took the main force into the northern interior. In the course of his operations, Lysimachus captured both Synnada (where Antigonus' treasury sat in Phrygia) and Sardis in Lydia, their garrison commanders deserting to add more troops to his effort (perhaps 12,000 pantodapoi pikemen, 4,000 hoplite mercenaries and 3,000 foot skirmishes along with a few horsemen). Meanwhile, Seleucus was on his way to bring further reinforcement from the Upper Satrapies.

Antigonus, though now 80 years old and in semi-retirement, reacted to the incursion into his territory by leading out what manpower he had on hand. This might have come to 18,000 pantodapoi with pikes, 6,000 mercenary hoplites, 10,000 light missilemen and 10,000 in cavalry. Seriously short of mounted support, Lysimachus was unwilling to engage until Seleucus could arrive with more horsemen; he therefore maneuvered to avoid a pitched battle. Eventually, Antigonus gave up the chase as winter approached. He had by now learned of the new threat from Seleucus and sent for his son from abroad so that they could combine strengths for a final showdown. Demetrius was in Thessaly facing Cassander's remaining 29,000 infantry and 2,000 cavalry with his own host of 56,000 foot soldiers (8,000 Macedonians, 15,000 hired hoplites, 25,000 allied Greeks and 8,000 light-armed mercenaries) and 1,500 horsemen (Diodorus 20.110.4). But when he received the order to join his father, he made a hurried truce with Cassander and withdrew to Asia with his Macedonians and mercenaries.

Demetrius landed at Ephesos and recovered that site. He then went on to take back the coastal region up as far as the Hellespont to block further entry from Europe. The Lycians and Pamphylians, who had joined against Antigonus, now switched sides and 2,000 Illyrian spearmen that Cassander had settled on the Thracian frontier also went over to the Asian monarch. Furthermore, when Cassander sent his brother Pleistarchus with more troops (12,000 infantry and 500 horsemen [Diodorus 22.112.1]), they couldn't cross at the Hellespont and had to sail along the Black Sea coast instead, doing so in three tranches due to a shortage of boats. The first of these sailings got through, but the second was captured and the third was almost completely lost in a storm (Pleistarchus himself barely surviving). Thus, only a third of this reinforcement ever reached Lysimachus (maybe 3,000 pikemen and 1,000 spearmen). Adding to allied woes, Ptolemy, who was coming with an army as well, didn't make it. After reaching Phoenicia, the Egyptian ruler heard a false report that Lysimachus was already defeated and returned to Africa. Things were beginning to look rather bleak for the Thracian king at this point; just then, however, he finally got some good news. Seleucus had arrived from the Upper Satrapies at last, bringing with him 20,000 infantry (maybe 1,000–2,000 mercenary spearmen and the rest light-armed), 12,000 cavalry (all javelineers and archers), 480 elephants and more than 100 scythed chariots (Diodorus 20.113.4). As each side's forces now went into camp to ride out the winter, it was becoming clear that an epic confrontation would take place in the spring.

Ipsus (301 B.C.)

The various contingents came together early in the next campaigning season to form two huge armies. These then closed on each other to array for battle near Ipsus, which lay just north of Synnada on the broad Phrygian plain. Antigonus and Demetrius set up their phalanx across a front around 4km wide with their pikemen likely 16-deep and the hoplites and barbarian spearmen filed at eight shields. Based upon past deployments, the 8,000 Macedonian phalangites would have been at the tip of the right wing. Antigonus, too aged to ride with the cavalry, took his post there among his countrymen. Next in line were 18,000 pantodapoi phalangites, followed by the Lycian and Pamphylian spearmen (maybe 3,000) along with the Illyrians (2,000) and, finally, Greek mercenary hoplites (some 19,000) filling out the left wing. The mercenaries were those brought from Greece less about 2,000 left as part of garrisons (Diodorus 22.111.3) plus 6,000 that had been with Antigonus.

Intending to carry the fight with cavalry off the right wing, Demetrius was there along with the hetairoi and the best of his lighter horsemen, maybe 6,000 mounted troops in all out of 10,000 on hand. The remaining riders sat off the left flank with orders to hold back until Demetrius was victorious on the other end. The Antigonids had 75 elephants, enough to front (at 15m separation) the cavalry standing eight-deep and 2m wide per rider on the left flank. With light infantry between each beast, these would help defend that end of the line from opposing elephants. Demetrius would not need such aid for his attack from the right flank, while the phalanx in the center was no doubt equipped with caltrops to impede any enemy pachyderms that might come that way.

Across the field, Seleucus seems to have held supreme command. He set up his phalanx to match fronts with that of the opposition by filing his pikemen at eight and the spearmen at six. In all likelihood, he placed his 15,000 Macedonian phalangites on the right and 12,000 pantodapoi with pikes in the center while his hypaspists (3,000 spearmen) and Greek hoplites (8,000) took the left wing. The cavalry was divided evenly with 7,000 riders taking post off each side of the heavy footmen. (Plutarch [Vol. II *Demetrius*, 462] put the allied horsemen at 10,500, but Diodorus indicated 12,000 with Seleucus alone. Lysimachus must have added a couple of thousand more including some heavier lancers.) Elephants were arrayed across the front of the entire formation, with around 40 leading the horsemen on each flank and 400 or so in place before the phalanx. As usual, these creatures stood 12–15m apart with foot skirmishers stationed in between. All of this looked to be very much in line with the tactics that Successor armies had been using for a couple of decades, emulating Alexander the Great by attacking with a strong right (though even more cavalry-dominant than in Alexander's day) and refusing the left. In fact, however, subsequent events would show that Seleucus was actually planning something quite a bit different.

The action opened with the mobile forces off the wings going at it. This phase saw a fierce struggle between very evenly matched elephant contingents on the Antigonid left, where Lysimachus was in command on the allied side. On the right, though, Demetrius and his men swung wide around the advancing enemy pachyderms and, leaving light infantry behind to deal with the bypassed creatures, struck hard at the cavalry beyond. These were light horsemen from the Upper Satrapies who rode under Antiochus, the son of Seleucus. Demetrius' heavy lancers easily carried the fight here as Antiochus and his riders gave way and retired rearward in fairly good order. Seeing their foes retreating but still in sound fighting form, Demetrius led his troopers in pursuit that he might render them unable to rally before he turned against the opposing phalanx's rear and exposed left flank. It was at this crucial juncture that Seleucus sprang a major tactical surprise.

Though Seleucus had arrayed the bulk of his elephants across the front of his phalanx, he never intended to have them mount an attack from there. He was well aware of how caltrops could neutralize such an assault (after all, it had been he and Ptolemy who had introduced Demetrius to that trick at Gaza in 312) and wasn't going to waste his time on such a doomed effort. Instead, he gave a signal and all the unengaged mahouts in advance of his phalanx turned their great beasts to the left and led them off with supporting light infantry squads running fore and aft of each animal. Once all were beyond the wing of their heavy array, the mahouts wheeled to the left as the foot skirmishers came up alongside and advanced toward where Demetrius was chasing Antiochus' men. It seems that they were actually drawing him away as part of a deliberate maneuver. In consequence, when Antigonus' son did eventually reverse course toward the allied phalanx, he unexpectedly found his way back hopelessly barred by hundreds of elephants and thousands of missilemen.

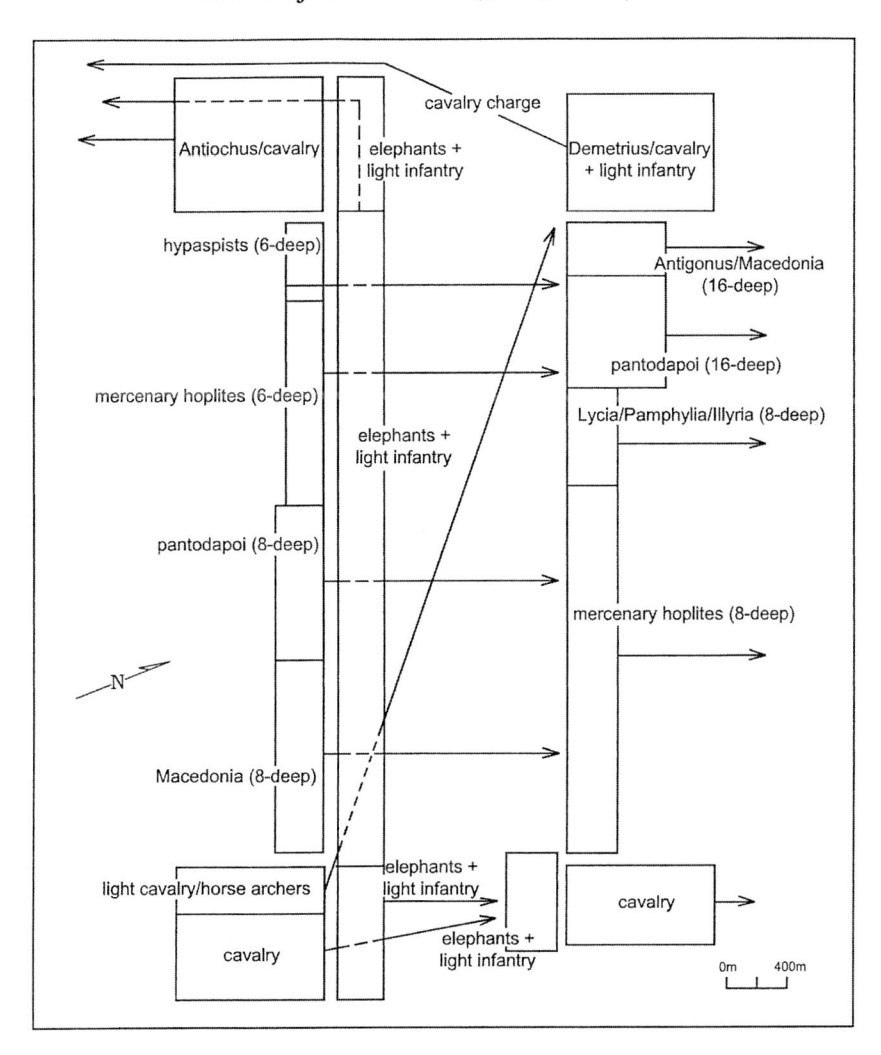

BATTLE OF IPSUS (301 B.C.) (BOXES REPRESENTING FORCES ARE EXAGGERATED TO SHOW RELATIVE SIZES.)

Seleucus now triggered the next phase of his tactical plan, pulling mounted javelinmen and horse-archers from his right flank to send them against the Antigonid phalanx where Demetrius' charge and subsequent isolation had deprived it of any sort of cavalry screen. Riding all around the enemy heavy infantrymen, these Asian riders savaged them with missiles from a safe distance. Helpless to fight back, phalangites and hoplites alike began to fall into disorder, a few breaking away to flee and entire units lowering their weapons in surrender. Finally, when the allied phalanx began closing across the field to attack, Antigonus' army fell apart completely, with those of its men who didn't give up throwing away their weapons and shields to run. As for Antigonus, the old king gallantly stood fast as his bodyguard joined the flight, going down to his death amid a hail of javelins. There was nothing that Demetrius could do and he escaped with 500 of his horsemen, picking up a few foot soldiers in route as he made his way to Ephesos and took ship for Greece.

MANPOWER, CHARIOTS AND ELEPHANTS • Ipsus is not well documented due to the loss of our best source for this period (Diodorus' account survives only in fragments). This leaves most of what we know to come from Plutarch (Vol. II. *Demetrius*, 462–463). Unfortunately, his account is short, deficient in hard data and concentrates on Demetrius to the exclusion of much of what was happening elsewhere on the field. As a result, reconstruction of this battle in any depth requires a great deal of speculation. Fortunately, we have gross figures on the infantry and mounted contingents for both armies and can use data from previous related deployments to backfill likely details on the content and form of the contending formations. The general course of the action is then reasonably described; still, there remains tremendous uncertainty in two particular areas: What happened to the chariots and what was really going on with the elephants that stopped Demetrius from returning to the battle? The first of these questions seems best answered by proposing that the chariots never saw action. While every other arm (infantry, cavalry and elephants) gets its due in Plutarch's account of the engagement, the chariots receive no mention at all. Thus, they either didn't participate or their role was so peripheral as to be unworthy of note.

As for the deployment of elephants against Demetrius, this is a vexing and crucial issue. The tack taken here is one proposed long ago by Tarn (1930, 68–69) that Seleucus had his son retreat to draw Demetrius and his horseman rearward so that a planned maneuver by the bulk of the allied elephant corps could cut him off. This seems entirely reasonable in that it's unlikely such a major evolution as that described for the elephants in this battle was improvised "on the fly." It must have been a carefully thought out and practiced exercise. If so, the elephants stationed in front of the allied phalanx were a tactical reserve and, when Demetrius fell for the false retreat, they carried out a well-drilled evolution to near perfection. Objections (see Bennett and Roberts [2009, 111]) that elephants had never before been employed as a reserve and that chancing such a stunt was unconscionable are rather weak.

Since use of elephants in reserve is documented in later years, such an approach at Ipsus wouldn't be impractical, but rather simply something new. Moreover, our record of this tactic was by Alexander the Great's cousin, Pyrrhus of Epirus, and it's a trick that he might very well have learned at Ipsus. After all, he rode there beside his brother-in-law Demetrius as a youth and saw the maneuver's effectiveness first hand. The only innovation he then added was to place his own much smaller team of pachyderms in the rear, rather than out front. Nor should we discount Seleucus' willingness to gamble. He needed some kind of trick like this if he was to better his odds against a phalanx twice as deep as his own. He also had plenty of light infantry to screen his exposed flank should the ploy have gone wrong.

Demetrius tried to take refuge in Athens, but the Athenians, to his great surprise and bitter disappointment, denied him a landing out of fear of reprisal from the victors at Ipsus. He then headed toward the Thraceward region to initiate a sea-borne campaign there. Back in Asia, Lysimachus and Seleucus were carving up the Antigonid territories and the latter laid claim to lower Syria. Nominally part of Antigonus' holdings, this region was, in fact, disputed with Ptolemy, whose garrisons held much of the land. As long as they lived, Seleucus and Ptolemy would refrain from dueling over this prize, but their descendents would end up waging war for its possession. For his part, Lysimachus now held nominal control of Anatolia up to the Taurus Mountains. Yet there were disputes here as well. Many of the coastal cities still harbored hostile garrisons that were supporting Demetrius as he began to prey on Lysimachus' holdings in Thrace. And in rugged portions of the interior, there were local chieftains holding sway that would have to be subdued. Thus, in the end, this latest distribution of the remains of Alexander's empire didn't finally settle the succession, but merely acted as a spur for another round of fighting in the next century.

Tactical Discussion 323–301 B.C.

Dominant tactics applied by the Successor generals at the very dawn of the Hellenistic period varied according to their background. Therefore, we see Antipater, who had not participated in the Persian conquest, approaching battle much as Philip II might have, with cavalry and infantry leading in tandem. In contrast, an Asian campaigner like Leonnatos fought with his horsemen in the lead more in the manner of Alexander. Yet with either approach, heavy footmen usually played a key role. This reflected that challenges facing these generals came from hoplite armies well enough equipped with horsemen and foot skirmishers so as to offset opposition light-armed forces and compel a decision by shock combat between phalanxes. Moreover, some actions in this interval saw the Macedonians relying just as much if not more on contingents of mercenary spearmen as they did on their own troops. Sometimes waged across restrictive Greek battlegrounds, these fights were, in fact, little different from those between polis armies in the mid-century's Third Sacred War.

Once combat began to take place *between* the Successors, there was an immediate shift toward more cavalry-oriented tactics by commanders that had fought under Alexander and were strongly influenced by his methods. This made "all mounted" decisions, which had earlier been anomalies, into common occurrences. In fact, it wasn't until Orcynii in 320 that phalanxes equipped with pikes on both sides actually came to blows. This was followed by another such action at Paraetacene (317). While both battles ended up with cavalry being decisive, there was some dueling between the heavy infantry arrays, especially in the later action. What we see in these engagements is that, despite lofty claims for Eumenes' elite, pike-armed hypaspists at Paraetacene, fighting between phalangites and spearmen was generally inconclusive. The hoplites couldn't usually get close enough to inflict any real harm nor could the pikemen normally deal out sufficient damage to take the battle ground for their side. This was the ancient equivalent of trench warfare, with defensive potential so much greater than offensive capability that a stalemate is virtually certain.

The solution to this gridlock came swiftly thereafter at Gabene (317/16). By placing phalangites opposite their own kind, Eumenes gave back to his phalanx its ability to carry a battle. With both armies' long weapons now able to reach and more effectively inflict wounds upon foes that lacked protection from large, closely arrayed shields, his superior hypaspist pikemen led the way to seize the field. And though these men would in the end yield to a cavalry maneuver (proving that Philip's combined-arms approach was just as valid as ever), their initial success pointed the way for a new phase of Hellenistic infantry tactics. (Gaza in 312 was an example of this evolving style. *Both* armies there initially sought to line their phalangites on the left per Eumenes' precedent, with Ptolemy then exchanging his wings to pit pike against pike.) Mounted forces might still rule the day, as they ultimately did at Gabene (and subsequently at Gaza and Ipsus), but a phalanx *could* be decisive. All it needed to do was secure its flanks in some way and thus negate mounted attacks while its pikemen thrust to victory against like-armed foes. For this, if nothing else, Eumenes deserves recognition as the most influential warlord of his era.

* * *

As the 4th century came to a close, the death of Antigonus and his dream of ruling a reunited Macedonian Empire marked permanent fragmentation of the Hellenistic world into a scatter of separate realms. Macedonia, Babylonia and Egypt would go on to spawn their own separate dynasties. These proved vibrant, continuing to wage war and spread Greek culture over the next 170 years. Yet never again was a Grecian monarch destined to approach Alexander's vision of world conquest. Future struggles were to start out with a focus on much more petty territorial interests and then descend into a desperate fight for survival as, one by one, the Successor kingdoms fell prey to Rome, a growing new power that had ambitions to match even those of Alexander.

Conclusions

"All military laws and military theories which are in the nature of principles are the experience of past wars.... We should seriously study these lessons.... We should put these conclusions to the test of our own experience, assimilating what is useful, rejecting what is useless, and adding what is specifically our own."
                                                                                                        Mao Tse-tung

There is a general evolutionary sequence that carries through Greek and Macedonian land battles of the 4th century B.C. This starts with dominance of the Doric phalanx as executed by the Spartan army. Refined over a period of two centuries, Sparta's approach depended on its best hoplites stationed on the right (offensive) wing to either overlap and envelop or otherwise fight their way through and break the opposing left as a preliminary to turning that flank and defeating the entire enemy array. Sometimes final victory might then require a second, reformed attack should the opposition have had similar success on its own right. Grand examples of this routine at its height can be seen at Nemea River and Coronea II in 394. Supplementary components of the technique were the left wing of the phalanx and light-armed troops (mounted and afoot) on post off either flank. The role of the spearmen on the left (defensive) wing was to engage and hold their facing foes long enough for the attack wing to carry the battle on the right. As for the light-armed men, they occasionally took direct part in envelopment, but most often played a more defensive role. This called for neutralizing their opposite numbers to keep them out of the hoplite fight.

Primary advancement of the foregoing tactics through the period 400–387 involved better use of cavalry along the edges of the phalanx. This was a trend that continued to develop 386–360. Horsemen began playing an even larger part at that time, especially for Theban armies under Pelopidas and Epaminondas. Their riders were very active and sometimes came off the flanks to fight out front between the heavy arrays as documented at Tegyra (375) and Leuctra (371). Yet they still weren't meant to be decisive. Instead, they strove to give greater aid to their hoplites by hiding deployments crafted to counter traditional Spartan tactics. Such arrangements called for very deep files on an attack wing to the left. This tack saw action at Leuctra and Mantinea II (362), maybe having debuted at Tegyra or even earlier. The other new element in the Thebans' tool chest was to hold back (refuse) their defensive wing, which now stood on the right. This was designed to deny the enemy a chance for victory there that might then necessitate reforming for a second attack. While such approaches worked well at Leuctra, they showed serious weaknesses at Mantinea II. Pammenes and other Thebans perhaps used overloaded files on a few occasions afterward, but this otherwise became an evolutionary dead end.

The period 359–336 saw Macedonia's Philip II move things forward by drawing upon prototypes developed by Iphicrates of Athens to put pikemen (phalangites) on the left and center of his phalanx. This produced a superior technique to Theban refusal of the defensive wing. He then combined highly trained hoplites with Macedonia's unique, shock-capable cavalry to create an attack wing of exceptional prowess on his right. There seems to have been some adjustment after a pair of defeats against Onomarchos in 353, perhaps lengthening pikes (sarissai) for greater defensive capability; all the same, this approach was highly effective and forever changed the trajectory of Grecian tactical evolution. Close partnership between horsemen and infantry was decisive in most of Philip's battles and furthered the trend of more active cavalry use.

Unlike Philip, Alexander III (336–323) rarely faced opponents who intended to carry the day with heavy infantry. He thus often had to adapt the Macedonian formation, which was derived from and at its best against Doric phalanxes, to combat lighter-armed foes unusually strong in cavalry. This led him to come up with unique infantry arrays for lesser actions as well as the concept of a second phalanx standing in reserve. Along with these innovations for his foot soldiers, he began to use horsemen in an extremely aggressive manner, leading them to open and turn the tide of battles before bringing his hoplites and pikemen up to finish the job. Granicus River (334) and Gaugemela (331) are prime demonstrations of this method. While Philip had operated in a somewhat similar mode against a few cavalry-rich barbarian armies in the past, Alexander was clearly pioneering methods far beyond any routines inherited from his father. So successful was he in this approach that later Macedonian generals were heavily influenced to fight whenever possible in the same way.

The challenge facing those that followed Alexander in early Hellenistic times (323–301) was that, unlike foes of their late king and role model, most of their opponents had plenty of heavy infantry. These included not only Greek hoplites, but also fellow Macedonians once the Successor Wars got underway. The influence of Alexander and his methods was nevertheless powerful enough to prevent a complete reversion to Philip's techniques; rather, there remained a strong emphasis on cavalry action at the fore. To be sure, heavy footmen sometimes played significant parts in engagements during this era as per Paraetacene (317) and Gabene (317/16). Yet, to a large extent, the roles of predominant attack arm and defensive arm were reversed in these battles at century's wane from what they had been at its start. It was now heavy infantrymen that more often than not gave support by neutralizing their counterparts while horsemen served as the tools of decision.

And just as the tactics of Grecian warfare evolved, so too did the dominant nature of the men who used them. There had been three Greek armies in the field at the dawn of the 4th century with the two that clashed at Cyrene being composed of amateur soldiers. Mostly small farmers, these men took up arms only by necessity to defend or regain their homes and local government. And their leaders were no different, having temporarily donned the mantel of command in anticipation of returning to a civilian trade when the current crisis was over. But the third army fighting at this time was very different. This was the band of mercenaries who had backed Cyrus at Cunaxa, now transformed into a roving instrument for hire. These men never lost their sense of nationality, always being proudly Greek, yet making war was their only profession and their allegiances were no longer intimately tied to native soil. Grecian hosts of the future were destined to more closely resemble this team of paid warriors than the people's militias that did battle at Cyrene. This was a trend that really took off with rise of the full-time Macedonian army and Phocis' dependence on pro fighters in the 350s, growing ever stronger until it became rare to see amateurs in the ranks by century's end. Moreover, what was true for the rankers was equally so for their leaders.

With the exception of Pelopidas and Epaminondas of Thebes, this century's preeminent commanders were no longer part-time soldiers, but truly men of battle, whether they led mercenary corps or were warlord rulers. And they came from many different Grecian states: Athens (Xenophon and Iphicrates), Sparta (Agesilaos), Phocis (Onomarchos), Macedonia (Philip and Alexander) and even Cardia in Thrace (Eumenes). Much as Mao advised, all of these fighting men drew on past practices for their tactics, yet often made clever and significant modifications to them as well, abandoning weak elements and sometimes adding entirely fresh ones borrowed from far afield or created in their own fervent minds. Taking advantage of the better-trained professional talent in their armies, these mortal gods of war produced an astounding cumulative effect over the course of the 4th century, evolving a highly potent military system that let them conquer much of the known world.

Appendices:
Pitched Battles 400–301 B.C.

1: Combat Factors

Symbol	Explanation
W	Factor was an advantage to *winner* of the battle
L	Factor was an advantage to *loser* of the battle
D	Engagement was *drawn* with no clear winner
HI	Superior performance by heavy infantry with small or no numerical advantage*
HS	Significant advantage (a third up to two times greater) in heavy infantry manpower*
HO	Overwhelming advantage (two times or more) in heavy infantry manpower*
CV	Superior performance by cavalry with small or no numerical advantage
CS	Significant advantage (a third up to two times greater) in cavalry manpower
CO	Overwhelming advantage (two times or more) in cavalry manpower
LI	Superior performance by light infantry with small or no numerical advantage
LS	Significant advantage (a third up to two times greater) in light infantry manpower
LO	Overwhelming advantage (two times or more) in light infantry manpower
SA	Surprise attack (assault/ambush not anticipated by its target)
SM	Surprise mobilization (force's arrival in area not anticipated by its opposition)
MV	Maneuver on the battlefield (tactical movement of troops in the midst of combat)
FM	Exceptional formation design (non-traditional ordering of troops prior to combat)
TR	Use of terrain elements (natural or manmade) to advantage on the battlefield
HM	Fighting on or near 'home ground' (action in direct defense of one's homeland)
N	Engagement took place on neutral ground

		Manpower Factors									Other Factors					
Date	Battle	HI	HS	HO	CV	CS	CO	LI	LS	LO	SA	SM	MV	FM	TR	HM
400	Cyrene	W	-	-	-	W	-	-	-	-	-	-	-	-	-	N
400	Colchis	-	W	-	-	-	-	W	-	-	-	-	W	L	L
400	Metropolis	-	W	-	-	-	-	W	-	-	-	-	-	-	L	L
400	Calpe H. I	-	-	L	-	-	W	-	-	W	-	-	-	-	-	W
400	Calpe H. II	-	-	L	-	-	W	-	-	W	-	-	-	-	-	W
400	Calpe H. III	-	L	-	-	-	L	-	-	L	-	-	-	-	-	L
399	Bithynia	-	-	L	-	-	W	-	-	W	-	-	-	-	-	W
398	Cyllene	W	-	-	-	L	-	-	W	-	-	-	-	-	-	N
395	Pactolos River	-	-	W	-	-	L	-	-	-	-	-	-	-	-	L
395	Sardis I	-	-	L	W	-	L	W	-	L	W	-	-	-	-	L
395	Dascyleium	-	-	L	-	-	W	-	W	-	-	-	-	W	-	W
395	Haliartus	W	-	-	-	-	-	-	-	-	W	-	-	-	-	W
395	Naryx I	-	W	-	-	-	W	-	-	W	-	-	-	-	-	L
394	Nemea R.	W	-	-	-	L	-	-	L	-	-	-	W	-	-	W
394	Coronea II	W	-	-	-	-	-	-	-	-	-	-	W	-	-	L
394	Messana II	W	-	-	-	-	-	-	-	-	-	-	-	-	-	W
394	Taruomenium	-	-	L	-	-	-	-	W	-	-	-	-	-	W	W

213

Appendix 1

Date	Battle	HI	HS	HO	CV	CS	CO	LI	LS	LO	SA	SM	MV	FM	TR	HM
393	Abacaene	W	-	-	-	-	-	-	-	-	-	-	-	-	-	W
392	L.W. Corinth	-	L	-	-	-	-	-	-	-	-	-	-	-	W	N
390	Lechaion	-	W	-	-	-	L	-	-	W	-	W	-	-	-	N
390	Methymna	W	-	-	-	-	-	-	-	-	-	-	-	-	-	L
389	Laus River	-	-	W	-	-	-	-	-	-	W	-	-	-	W	W
389	Elleporus River	-	L	-	W	-	-	-	-	-	W	-	-	-	-	L
389	Acarnania	-	-	W	-	-	W	-	-	L	-	-	-	-	L	L
389	Cremaste	-	-	L	-	-	-	-	-	W	W	-	-	-	W	N
388	Tripyrgia	-	L	-	-	-	-	-	W	-	W	-	-	-	-	L
386	Citium	W	-	-	-	-	-	-	-	-	-	-	-	-	-	W
385	Mantinean Plain	-	W	-	-	-	-	-	-	-	-	-	-	-	-	L
384	Pyrgi	W	-	-	-	-	-	-	-	-	-	-	-	-	-	L
382	Olynthus I	-	W	-	W	-	-	-	-	-	-	-	L	-	-	L
381	Olynthus II	-	L	-	-	-	-	-	-	-	-	-	-	-	W	W
379	Plat.-Thebes Rd	-	-	L	-	-	W	-	-	-	-	W	-	-	-	N
378	Cithaeron Pass	-	-	L	-	-	W	-	-	-	-	W	-	-	L	N
378	Thespiae	-	W	-	-	W	-	-	-	-	-	-	-	-	-	L
377	Cabala	W	-	-	-	-	-	-	-	L	-	-	-	-	-	W
377	Graos Stethos	W	-	-	W	-	-	-	-	-	-	-	-	-	L	L
376	Cronium	W	-	-	-	-	-	-	-	W	-	-	-	-	-	L
376	Tanagra III	-	W	-	-	-	W	-	L	-	-	-	-	-	-	L
375	Tegyra	-	-	L	-	-	L	-	L	-	-	-	-	W	L	W
374	Phlius	W	-	-	-	-	-	-	-	-	-	-	-	-	-	N
373	Mendesian M.	-	-	-	-	-	W	W	-	-	-	-	W	-	-	L
373	Corcyra Cem.	-	W	-	-	-	-	-	-	-	-	-	L	-	-	W
371	Leuctra	-	L	-	-	L	-	-	L	-	-	-	W	W	-	W
371	Tegea II	W	-	-	-	-	-	-	-	-	-	-	-	-	-	W
371	Elymia	-	-	W	-	-	L	-	-	L	-	-	-	-	-	W
370	Deum	-	-	W	-	-	-	-	-	W	-	-	-	-	L	L
370	Tegeatis Pass	-	-	W	-	-	-	-	-	W	-	-	-	-	L	L
369	Amyclae	-	-	W	-	-	L	-	-	L	L	-	-	-	-	L
369	Corinth	-	-	L	-	-	-	-	-	W	-	-	-	-	-	N
369	Sicyon Plain	-	-	-	W	-	-	-	W	-	-	-	-	-	-	L
368	Phlius Crossing	-	-	L	-	-	W	-	-	-	-	-	-	-	-	W
368	Tearless Battle	-	L	-	-	-	L	-	-	-	-	-	-	-	-	N
368	Pherae Road	-	-	W	-	W	L	W	-	L	-	-	-	W	-	L
367	Cappadocian N.	-	-	L	-	-	L	-	-	L	-	-	-	-	W	W
366	Corinthian Gate	-	L	-	-	-	W	-	-	W	-	-	-	-	-	W
365	Lasion	-	-	W	-	-	-	W	-	-	-	-	-	-	-	L
365	Ellis-Cyllene	-	-	W	-	-	-	-	-	W	-	-	-	-	-	L
365	Cromnus	-	L	-	-	-	L	-	-	L	W	-	-	-	-	N
364	Cynoscephalae I	W	-	-	W	L	-	-	-	-	-	-	-	-	L	L
364	Olympus	-	L	-	-	-	L	-	-	-	-	-	W	-	-	W
362	Mantinea II	-	-	-	-	-	-	-	-	-	-	-	-	-	-	D
361	Cilician Gate	-	-	L	-	-	L	-	-	L	-	-	-	-	W	W
360	Egyptian Canals	-	-	L	-	-	L	-	-	L	-	-	-	-	W	N
359	Methone	-	-	L	-	-	W	-	-	W	W	-	-	-	-	W
358	Paeonia	-	-	W	-	-	L	-	-	L	-	-	-	-	-	L
358	Lyncus Plain	W	-	-	-	-	W	-	-	-	-	-	-	-	-	L
357	Ortygia	-	L	-	-	-	W	-	-	-	-	-	W	-	W	W
357	Chios	W	-	-	-	-	-	-	W	-	-	-	-	-	-	W
357	Pherae I	-	W	-	W	-	-	-	-	-	-	-	-	-	-	L
356	Crenides	-	-	W	-	-	L	-	-	L	-	-	-	-	-	L
356	Grabaea	W	-	-	-	-	W	-	-	-	-	-	-	-	-	L
356	Odrysia I	-	-	W	-	-	L	-	-	L	-	-	-	-	-	L

Combat Factors in Greek and Macedonian Pitched Battles (400–301 B.C.)

Date	Battle	HI	HS	HO	CV	CS	CO	LI	LS	LO	SA	SM	MV	FM	TR	HM
356	Phaedriades	-	W	-	-	W	-	-	W	-	-	-	-	-	-	N
356	Amphissa I	W	-	-	-	-	-	-	-	-	W	-	-	-	-	W
356	Amphissa II	W	-	-	-	-	-	-	-	-	L	-	-	-	-	L
355	Argolas	-	-	W	-	-	-	-	-	W	-	-	-	-	-	N
355	Neon	W	-	-	-	-	W	-	-	W	-	-	-	-	W	-	L
355	Phyrgia I	-	L	-	-	L	-	-	W	-	-	-	-	-	-	W
355	Sardis II	-	-	-	-	W	-	-	W	-	-	-	-	-	-	L
355	Tmolos Camp	-	L	-	W	L	-	-	W	-	W	-	-	-	-	W
354	Pherae II	-	W	-	-	W	-	-	-	-	-	-	-	-	-	L
354	Pherae III	W	-	-	-	L	-	-	-	-	-	-	-	-	-	W
354	Crescent Hills	W	-	-	-	L	-	-	-	-	W	-	-	-	-	W
354	Hermeum	-	W	-	-	W	-	-	W	-	-	-	-	-	-	L
354	Phrygia II	W	-	L	-	-	L	-	-	L	-	-	-	-	-	W
354	Phrygia III	W	L	-	W	-	L	-	-	L	-	-	W	-	-	W
353	Crocus Plain	W	-	-	-	-	W	-	W	-	-	W	-	-	L	N
353	Pagasae	-	W	-	-	-	-	-	-	-	-	-	-	-	-	N
352	Orchomenos	W	-	-	-	-	-	-	-	-	-	-	W	-	-	W
352	Cephissus River	W	-	-	-	-	-	-	-	-	-	-	W	-	-	W
352	Coronea III	-	-	W	-	-	-	-	-	W	-	-	-	-	-	W
352	Naryx II	W	-	-	-	-	-	-	-	-	W	-	-	-	-	N
352	Orneai I	-	W	-	-	-	W	-	-	L	-	-	-	-	-	N
352	Orneai II	W	-	L	-	-	W	-	-	L	-	-	-	-	-	L
352	Telphusa	-	-	W	-	-	W	-	-	W	-	-	-	-	-	N
352	Messenia I	-	-	W	-	-	W	-	-	W	-	-	-	-	-	N
352	Messenia II	-	-	W	-	-	W	-	-	W	-	-	-	-	-	N
352	Messenia III	W	-	-	-	-	W	-	-	-	-	-	-	-	-	L
348	Olynthus III	-	-	W	-	-	-	-	L	-	-	-	-	-	-	L
348	Olynthus IV	-	-	W	-	-	-	-	L	-	-	-	-	-	-	L
348	Tamynae	W	-	-	-	-	-	-	-	-	-	-	-	-	-	N
347	Hyampolis	-	-	-	-	W	-	-	-	-	-	-	-	-	-	L
347	Coronea IV	W	-	-	-	L	-	-	-	-	-	-	-	-	-	L
347	W. Boeotia	W	-	-	-	L	-	-	-	-	-	-	-	-	-	L
345	Sidon	W	-	-	-	L	-	-	-	-	-	-	-	-	-	W
345	Ardiaea	-	-	W	-	-	W	-	-	-	-	-	-	-	-	L
344	Pelusium	W	-	-	-	-	-	-	-	-	-	-	-	-	-	N
344	Nile W. Bank	-	-	-	-	-	-	-	-	W	-	-	-	-	-	N
344	Syracuse-Leon.	W	-	-	W	-	-	-	W	-	-	-	-	-	-	W
341	Crimisus River	W	-	-	L	-	W	-	-	-	W	-	-	-	W	W
341	Odrysia II	-	-	W	-	-	L	-	-	L	-	-	-	-	-	L
341	Odrysia III	-	-	W	-	-	L	-	-	L	-	-	-	-	-	L
340	Strymon Valley	-	-	W	-	-	L	-	-	L	-	-	-	-	-	L
339	Hierae	-	-	W	-	-	-	-	-	-	W	-	-	-	-	N
339	Dobruja Plain	-	-	W	W	-	L	-	-	W	-	-	-	W	-	L
339	Hister Valley	-	-	L	-	-	W	-	-	W	-	-	L	-	-	W
338	Damyrias River	W	L	-	-	-	-	-	-	-	-	-	-	-	L	N
338	Abolus River	-	-	-	W	-	-	W	-	-	-	-	-	-	-	W
338	Chaeronea	W	-	-	-	-	-	-	-	L	-	-	W	-	-	L
335	Haemus Pass I	-	-	W	-	-	-	-	L	-	-	-	-	-	-	L
335	Lyginus River	-	-	W	-	-	W	-	L	-	-	-	-	-	-	L
335	Hister River	-	-	W	W	-	L	-	-	L	-	-	-	W	W	L
335	Pelion	W	-	-	-	-	W	-	W	-	-	-	-	-	-	L
334	Granicus River	-	W	-	W	-	L	-	-	L	-	-	-	-	L	L
334	Sagalassos	-	-	W	-	-	-	-	-	L	-	-	-	-	L	L
333	Issus	W	-	L	W	-	L	-	-	L	-	-	-	-	W	L
333	Memphis	W	-	-	-	-	-	-	-	-	-	-	-	-	-	L

Appendix 1

Date	Battle	HI	HS	HO	CV	CS	CO	LI	LS	LO	SA	SM	MV	FM	TR	HM
331	Gaugamela	W	-	-	W	-	L	-	-	L	-	-	-	-	-	L
331	Vs Corrhagus	-	W	-	-	-	-	L	-	-	-	-	-	-	-	N
331	Megalopolis	-	W	-	-	W	-	-	-	W	-	-	-	-	-	N
330	Aria	-	-	-	W	-	-	-	-	-	-	-	L	-	-	L
329	Jaxartes	-	-	L	-	-	W	-	-	W	-	-	-	-	W	W
329	Alexandria Esc.	-	-	-	W	-	L	-	-	W	-	-	-	W	-	L
329	Polytimetos R.	-	-	L	-	-	W	-	-	L	-	-	-	-	-	W
328	Xenippa	-	-	W	W	-	-	-	-	-	-	-	-	-	-	L
328	Gabai	-	-	W	W	-	-	-	-	-	-	-	-	-	-	L
327	Pareitakene	-	-	W	W	-	-	-	-	L	-	-	-	-	-	L
327	Aspasia	-	-	W	-	-	W	-	-	L	-	-	-	W	L	L
327	Massaka	-	-	W	-	-	W	-	-	L	-	-	-	-	-	L
327	Bazira	-	-	W	-	-	L	-	-	L	-	-	-	-	-	L
327	Ora	-	-	W	W	L	-	-	-	L	-	-	-	-	-	L
326	Hydaspes River	-	-	W	-	W	-	-	-	L	-	-	-	-	-	L
323	Upper Satrapies	-	L	-	-	-	W	-	-	L	-	-	W	-	-	L
323	Plataea II	-	W	-	-	W	-	-	W	-	-	W	-	-	-	L
323	Therm.-Lamia	-	W	-	-	-	W	-	-	W	-	-	-	-	-	W
323	Odrysia IV	-	-	-	-	-	-	-	-	-	-	-	-	-	-	D
322	Lamia	-	-	-	-	-	W	-	-	-	-	-	-	-	-	W
322	Rhamnus	W	-	-	-	-	W	-	W	-	-	-	-	-	-	W
322	Cappadocia	W	-	-	-	-	-	-	-	-	W	-	-	-	-	L
322	Crannon	-	-	W	-	W	-	-	W	-	-	-	-	-	-	L
322	Cyrene II	W	-	-	-	-	L	-	-	L	-	-	-	-	-	N
322	Cyrene III	W	-	-	-	-	W	-	-	W	-	-	-	-	-	W
322	Cyrene IV	W	-	-	-	-	L	-	-	L	-	-	-	-	-	L
322	Cyrene V	W	-	-	-	L	-	-	-	W	-	-	-	-	-	N
321	Hellespont	-	-	-	-	-	W	-	-	-	-	-	-	-	-	W
321	Aetolia	-	-	-	W	-	-	-	-	W	-	-	-	-	-	W
321	Thessaly	-	-	-	-	-	W	-	L	-	-	-	-	-	-	L
320	Orcynii	-	L	-	W	-	L	-	-	-	-	-	W	-	-	L
319	Cretopolis	-	-	W	-	-	W	-	-	W	-	-	-	-	W	L
317	Coprates	-	W	-	-	-	W	-	-	L	W	-	-	-	-	W
317	Paraetacene	-	W	-	-	W	-	-	-	-	-	-	-	-	-	L
316	Gabene	-	W	-	-	W	-	-	-	-	-	-	-	-	-	L
316	Amphipolis II	-	L	-	-	-	W	-	-	W	-	-	-	-	-	W
315	Aphrodisias	W	L	-	-	-	L	-	-	W	W	-	-	-	-	L
314	Hebrus River	-	W	-	-	-	W	-	-	W	-	-	-	-	-	L
313	Epirus I	-	W	-	-	W	-	-	W	-	-	-	-	-	-	L
313	Epirus II	-	W	-	-	W	-	-	-	-	-	-	-	-	-	L
313	Callantia	-	-	W	-	-	L	-	-	W	-	-	-	W	-	W
313	Haemus Pass II	-	-	W	-	-	L	-	-	L	-	-	-	-	W	L
312	Gaza	-	W	-	W	-	-	W	-	-	-	-	-	-	-	L
312	Eurymenae I	W	-	-	L	-	-	-	-	-	-	-	-	-	-	W
312	Eurymenae II	-	W	-	-	-	-	-	-	-	-	-	-	-	-	L
312	Apollonia	W	-	-	-	-	W	-	-	-	-	-	-	-	-	W
312	Galeria	W	-	-	-	-	-	-	-	-	-	-	-	-	-	N
311	Ecnomus Hill	-	W	-	-	-	W	-	-	W	W	-	-	-	-	L
310	White Tunis I	W	-	L	-	-	L	-	-	L	-	-	L	-	-	L
309	Anapus Valley	W	-	L	-	-	L	-	-	L	W	L	-	-	-	W
309	White Tunis II	W	-	L	-	-	L	-	-	L	-	-	-	-	-	L
308	Zuphones Ter.	W	-	-	-	-	-	-	-	L	-	-	-	-	L	N
307	Syracuse	W	L	-	-	-	-	-	-	L	-	-	-	-	-	W
307	Carthage/Mid.	W	-	-	-	-	-	-	W	-	W	-	-	-	-	W
307	Carthage/Inter.	W	-	-	-	-	-	-	W	-	W	-	-	-	-	W

Date	Battle	HI	HS	HO	CV	CS	CO	LI	LS	LO	SA	SM	MV	FM	TR	HM
307	Acragas III	W	-	-	-	-	W	-	-	-	-	-	-	-	-	L
307	Carthage	-	-	W	-	-	W	-	-	W	-	-	-	-	W	W
306	Cyp. Salamis III	-	W	-	-	-	L	-	-	-	-	-	-	-	-	L
305	Torgium	W	-	L	-	-	L	-	-	L	W	-	W	-	W	L
301	Ipsus	W	-	-	W	-	-	-	-	-	-	-	W	-	-	L

2: Decisive Factors*

Symbols	Explanation
SZ	Size/scale of battle based on the number of heavy infantrymen involved
SK	Skirmish (involving less than 1,000 heavy infantrymen)
MN	Minor battle (involving at least 1,000 but less than 5,000 heavy infantrymen)
MJ	Major battle (involving at least 5,000 but less than 10,000 heavy infantrymen)
GD	Grand battle (involving 10,000 or more heavy infantrymen)
*	Indicates a drawn battle with no clear-cut winner
Heavy infantry	Armored foot soldiers (hoplites or equivalents (can include light-armed men if in single, integrated formation as per Persian kardakes)
Light infantry	Light (unarmored) foot soldiers (primarily missile troops)
Cavalry	Mounted troops (includes chariots and elephants)
MA	Surprise mobilization: arrival of an army that is unanticipated by its enemy
SA	Surprise attack: an assault that is unanticipated by its target
Maneuver	A tactical movement of troops in the midst of a battle, (includes planned desertions)
Formation	Use of an exceptional design for troop arrangement
Terrain	Use of topography (natural or manmade) to advantage on the battlefield
XXX	Nationality of combatants, example: SPR=Sparta
(XXX)	Nationality employing mercenaries, example: (MAC) = Macedonia

Combatant Key

A: ABY=Abydos, ACA=Acarnia, ACH=Achaean, ACR=Acragas, AEN=Aenis, AEO=Aetolia, AIG=Aigina, AIT=Aitolia, ARC=Arcadia, ARG=Argos, ASN=Asian, ATH=Athens
B: BAR=barbarian, BEE=Boeotian exiles, BOE=Boeotia, BYZ=Byzantium
C: CAP=Cappadocia, CAR=Carthage, CEL=Celts, CHA=Chalcidian, CHI=Chios, COE=Corinthian exiles, COL=Colchians, COR=Corinth, COY=Corcyra, CRE=Crenides, CRN=Carian, CYG=Greek Cypriot, CYP=Punic Cypriot, CYE=Cyrenean exiles, CYR=Cyrene
E: EGY=Egypt (undifferentiated), ELI=Elis, ELO=Elis oligarchs, ELP=Elis popular party, EPR=Epiris, ETR=Etruscan, EUB=Euboa
G: GRK=Greek
H: HRC=Heraclea
I: IBR=Iberians, ILY=Illyrians, IND=Indian, ION=Ionian, ITG=Italian Greeks
L: LEO=Leontini, LOZ=Ozolian Locris, LSE=Lesbos exiles, LUC=Lucanians
O: ORC=Orchomenos
M: MAN= Mantinea, MAC=Macedonia, MES=Messenians, MET=Methymna, MOS=Mossynoecians, MRC=mercenaries, MRG=mercenary Greeks, MSA=Messana, MYE=Mytilene exiles, MYT=Mytilene
P: PAO=Paeonians, PEL=Peloponnesian, PER=Persian, PHE=Phlius exiles, PHL=Phlius, PHO=Phocis, PHN=Phoenician, PHR=Pherae, PIS=Pisidians, PLA=Plataea, PRR=Persian rebels
R: RHG=Rhegion
S: SCG=Sicilian Greeks, SCL=Siculi, SCY=Sicyon, SPR=Sparta, SYH=Scythia, SYE=Syracusan exiles, SYR=Syracuse
T: TAN=Tanagra, TEE=Tegean exiles, TEG=Tegea, TEU=Tegea unionists, THB=Thebes, THR=Thrace, THS=Thespiae, THY=Thessaly, TSL=Thessalian League

*A Decisive Factor is a Combat Factor judged critical in the winner's avoiding a defeat or draw. Decisive Factor(s) for each battle must include at least one Manpower Factor and may include one or more Other Factors (those vitally complementary to the decisive manpower group[s] success).

Appendix 2

Date	Battle	SZ	Winner(s)	Loser(s)	Decisive Factor(s)
400	Cyrene	GD	CYL	CYR, MES	heavy infantry
400	Colchis	GD	MRG	COL	heavy infantry, formation
400	Metropolis	GD	MRG	MOS	heavy infantry
400	Calpe Harb. I	SK	THR	MRG	light infantry
400	Calpe Harb. II	SK	MRU (ATH)	MRG	light infantry
400	Calpe Harb. III	GD	MRG	PER, THR	heavy infantry
399	Bithynia	SK	THR	MRG	Light infantry, cavalry
398	Cyllene	SK	ELP	ELO	heavy infantry
395	Pactolos River	GD	SPR, PEL, ION	PER	heavy & light infantry
395	Sardis I	GD	SPR, PEL, ION	PER	Light inf., cavalry, SA
395	Dascyleium	SK	PER	GRK	cavalry, formation
395	Haliartus	MG	THB	ORC, HRC, PHO	heavy infantry, SA
395	Naryx I	MG	BOE	PHO	heavy infantry
394	Nemea R.	GD	SPR, ELI, PEL	ATH, BOE, COR	heavy infantry, maneuver
394	Coronea II	GD	SPR, ORC, MRG	BOE, ATH, MRG	heavy infantry, maneuver
394	Messana II	MG	MSN, MRG	RHG	heavy infantry
394	Taruomenium	MG	SCL	SYR, MRG	light infantry, terrain
393	Abacaene	GD	SYR, MRG	CAR	heavy infantry
392	L.W. Corinth	MG	SPR, SCY, COE	ARG, COR, MRU	heavy infantry, terrain
390	Lechaion	MN	ATH, MRC	SPR	light infantry
390	Methymna	MN	ATH, MYT, LSE	PEL, MET, MYE	heavy infantry
389	Laus River	GD	LUC	ITG	heavy infantry, terrain
389	Elleporus Riv.	GD	SYR, MRG	ITG	heavy infantry
389	Acarnania	MG	SPR, ACH, PEL	ACA	heavy infantry
389	Cremaste	SK	ATH, MRC	SPR, MRG, ABY	light infantry, terrain
388	Tripyrgia	MN	ATH, MRC	PEL, AIG	light & heavy infantry
386	Citium	MG	CYG, MRG	PER	heavy infantry
385	Mantinean Pl.	MG	SPR, THB, TEG	MAN	heavy infantry
384	Pyrgi	MN	SYR, MRG	ETR	heavy infantry
382	Olynthus I	GD	SPR, PEL, THB	CHA	cavalry, heavy infantry
381	Olynthus II	GD	CHA	SPR, PEL, THB	heavy infantry
379	Plat-Thebes R.	SK	THB	PLA	cavalry, mobilization
378	Cithaeron Pass	SK	MRC	THB	light infantry
378	Thespiae	GD	THB, BOE	PEL, THS	heavy infantry
377	Cabala	GD	SYR, MRG	CAR	heavy infantry
377	Graos Stethos	SK	SPR	THB	heavy infantry, cavalry
376	Cronium	GD	CAR	SYR, MRG	heavy infantry
376	Tanagra III	GD	THB, BOE	PEL, TAN	heavy infantry
375	Tegyra	MN	THB	SPR	heavy infantry, formation
374	Phlius	MN	PHE, MRG	PHL	heavy infantry
373	Mendesian M.	MN	MRG	EGY	light infantry, maneuver
373	Corcyra Cem.	MN	COR	SPR, MRG	heavy infantry
371	Leuctra	GD	THB, BOE	SPR, PEL	heavy infantry, form., man.
371	Tegea II	MN	TEG	TEU	heavy infantry
371	Elymia	MN	MAN	MRG	heavy infantry
370	Deum	MG	ARC	TEE, SPR	light infantry
370	Tegeatis Pass	MG	ARG, ELI	BEE, SPR	heavy infantry
369	Amyclae	GD	THB, BOE	SPR, BEE, TEE	heavy infantry
369	Corinth	SK	MRC (SPR)	THB	light infantry
369	Sicyon Plain	MN	IBR, CEL	SCY	light infantry, cavalry
368	Phlius Crossing	MN	PHL	ARC, ARG	cavalry
368	Tearless Battle	GD	SPR, IBR, CEL	ARC, ARG	heavy infantry
368	Pherae Road	MG	THB, BOE, MRG	THS	cavalry, light inf., form.
367	Cappadoc. Nw.	GD	PRR	PER	heavy infantry, terrain
366	Corinthian G.	SK	PHL	SYC, PEL	heavy infantry

Decisive Factors in Greek and Macedonian Pitched Battles (400–301 B.C.) 219

Date	Battle	SZ	Winner(s)	Loser(s)	Decisive Factor(s)
365	Lasion	MG	ARC	ELI	heavy infantry
365	Ellis-Cyllene	MG	ARC	ELI	heavy infantry
365	Cromnus	MG	ARC	SPR	heavy infantry, SA
364	Cynosceph. I	GD	THB, BOE, MRG	THB, MRG	heavy infantry, cavalry
364	Olympus	GD	ELI, ACH	ARC, ARG, ATH	heavy inf., SM
362	Mantinea II	GD	THB, PEL, MRG*	SPR, ATH, PEL*	heavy infantry, cavalry*
361	Cilician Gate	GD	PRR	PER	heavy infantry, terrain
360	Egyptian Can.	GD	MRG (EGY)	PER	heavy infantry, terrain
359	Methone	MN	MAC	MRG	light infantry, surprise
358	Paeonia	MG	MAC, MRG	PAO	cavalry, heavy infantry
358	Lyncus Plain	GD	MAC, MRG	ILY	cavalry, heavy infantry
357	Ortygia	MG	SYR, SCG	MRU	heavy infantry, maneuver
357	Chios	MG	CHI, BYZ, CRA	ATH	heavy infantry
357	Pherae I	GD	MAC, MRG	PHR, MRG	heavy infantry, cavalry
356	Crenides	MG	MAC, MRG, CRE	THR	cavalry, heavy infantry
356	Grabaea	MG	MAC, MRG,	ILY	cavalry, heavy infantry
356	Odrysia I	MG	MAC, MRG	THR	cavalry, heavy infantry
356	Phaedriades	MN	PHO, MRG	LOZ	heavy infantry
356	Amphissa I	SK	LOZ	PHO	heavy infantry, SA
356	Amphissa II	SK	MRG (PHO)	LOZ	heavy infantry
355	Argolas	GD	PHO, MRG	THY, MRG	heavy infantry
355	Neon	GD	THB, BOE, MRG	PHO, MRG, ACH	heavy infantry, formation
355	Phyrgia I	GD	PRR, MRG	PER	heavy infantry
355	Sardis II	GD	PER	PRR, MRG	cavalry
355	Tmolos Camp	GD	PRR, MRG	PER	cavalry, SA
354	Pherae II	GD	MAC, MRG, THL	PHO, MRG, PHR	heavy infantry
354	Pherae III	GD	PHO, MRG, PHR	MAC, MRG, THL	heavy infantry
354	Crescent Hills	GD	PHO, MRG, PHR	MAC, MRG, THL	heavy infantry, SA
354	Hermeum	GD	PHO, MRG, ACH	THB, BOE	heavy infantry
354	Phrygia II	GD	PRR, MRG	PER	heavy infantry
354	Phrygia III	GD	PRR, MRG	PER	cavalry, hvy inf., maneuver
353	Crocus Plain	GD	MAC, MRG, THL	PHO, MRG	cavalry, SM
353	Pagasae	MG	MRG (ATH)	MRG (MAC)	heavy infantry
352	Orchomenos	GD	THB, BOE	PHO, MRG, THY	heavy infantry, formation
352	Cephissus R.	GD	THB, BOE	PHO, MRG, THY	heavy infantry, formation
352	Coronea III	MN	BOE	PHO, MRG	heavy infantry
352	Naryx II	GD	PHO, MRG, THY	THB, BOE	heavy infantry, SA
352	Orneai I	GD	SPR, MRG, PHR	ARG	heavy infantry
352	Orneai II	GD	SPR, MRG, PHR	THB, ARG, SIC	heavy infantry
352	Telphusa	MN	BOE	MRG (SPR)	cavalry, heavy infantry
352	Messenia I	MN	BOE	MRG (SPR)	cavalry, heavy infantry
352	Messenia II	MN	BOE	MRG (SPR)	cavalry, heavy infantry
352	Messenia III	GD	SPR, MRG, THY	THB, MES	heavy infantry
348	Olynthus III	GD	MAC, MRG	CHA, MRG, ATH	heavy infantry
348	Olynthus IV	GD	MAC, MRG	CHA, MRG, ATH	heavy infantry
348	Tamynae	MG	ATH, EUB, MRG	EUB, MRG	heavy infantry
347	Hyampolis	MN	BOE	PHO	cavalry
347	Coronea IV	MN	BOE	PHO	heavy infantry
347	W. Boeotia	MN	PHO	BOE	heavy infantry
345	Sidon	GD	PHN, MRG	PER	heavy infantry
345	Ardiaea	GD	MAC	ILY	cavalry, heavy infantry
344	Pelusium	MN	MRG (EGY)	MRG (PER)	heavy infantry
344	Nile W. Bank	GD	MRG (PER)	MRG (EGY)	light infantry
344	Syracuse-Leon.	GD	SYR, MRG	MRG	heavy infantry, cavalry
341	Crimisus River	GD	SYR, MRG	CAR	hvy inf., surprise, terrain

Appendix 2

Date	Battle	SZ	Winner(s)	Loser(s)	Decisive Factor(s)
341	Odrysia II	GD	MAC, MRG	THR	cavalry, heavy infantry
341	Odrysia III	GD	MAC, MRG	THR	cavalry, heavy infantry
340	Strymon Valley	MG	MAC	PAO	cavalry, heavy infantry
339	Hierae	MN	MRG (CAR)	MRG (SYR)	heavy infantry, SA
339	Dobruja Plain	GD	MAC, MRG	SYH	cav., light inf., formation
339	Hister Valley	GD	THR	MAC, MRG	light infantry
338	Damyrias R.	MG	SYR	MRG	heavy infantry
338	Abolus River	GD	SYR	MRG	cavalry, light infantry
338	Chaeronea	GD	MAC, MRG	ATH, THB, BOE	heavy infantry, maneuver
335	Haemus Pass I	MG	MAC, MRG	THR	heavy infantry
335	Lyginus River	GD	MAC, MRG	THR	heavy infantry
335	Hister River	MN	MAC	THR	cav., hvy. Inf., form., ter.
335	Pelion	GD	MAC, MRG	ILY	heavy infantry
334	Granicus River	GD	MAC	PER, MRG	cavalry
334	Sagalassos	GD	MAC	PIS	heavy infantry
333	Issus	GD	MAC	PER, MRG	heavy inf., cavalry, terrain
333	Memphis	MG	MRG	EGY	heavy infantry
331	Gaugamela	GD	MAC	PER, MRG	cavalry, heavy infantry
331	Vs Corrhagus	GD	MRG (SPR)	MRG (MAC)	heavy infantry
331	Megalopolis	GD	MAC, BOE, MRG	SPR, MRG, PEL	heavy infantry
330	Aria	SK	MAC, GRK, THR	PER	cavalry
329	Jaxartes	MN	BAR	MAC	light infantry, terrain
329	Alexandria Es.	SK	MAC, MRG	SCY	cavalry, formation
329	Polytimetos R.	MN	PER	MAC, MRG	cavalry
328	Xenippa	MN	MAC, MRG	PER	cavalry
328	Gabai	MN	MAC, MRG	PER	cavalry
327	Pareitakene	MG	MAC	PER	cavalry
327	Aspasia	GD	MAC, MRG	IND	heavy infantry, formation
327	Massaka	GD	MAC	IND	cavalry
327	Bazira	MN	MRG (MAC)	IND	heavy infantry
327	Ora	MN	MAC	IND	cavalry, heavy infantry
326	Hydaspes R.	MG	MAC	IND	cavalry
323	Up. Satrapies	GD	MAC, MRG	GRK	cavalry, maneuver
323	Plataea II	GD	ATH, MRG	BOE	heavy inf., SM
323	Therm.-Lamia	GD	ATH, MRG	MAC	heavy infantry
323	Odrysia IV	MN	MAC, MRG*	THR*	heavy infantry, terrain*
322	Lamia	GD	GRK, MRG	MAC	cavalry
322	Rhamnus	MG	ATH	MAC, MRG	heavy infantry, cavalry
322	Cappadocia	GD	MAC	MRG, CAP	heavy infantry
322	Crannon	GD	MAC, MRG	GRK	heavy infantry
322	Cyrene II	GD	MRG, CYE	CYR	heavy infantry
322	Cyrene III	GD	CYR, MRG	MRG, CYE	cavalry
322	Cyrene IV	GD	MRG, CYE	CYR, MRG, CAR	heavy infantry
322	Cyrene V	GD	MAC, CYE	MRG, CYR	heavy infantry
321	Hellespont	GD	MAC, MRG, ASN	MAC, MRG	cavalry
321	Aetolia	MG	AEO	MAC, MRG	light infantry, cavalry
321	Thessaly	GD	MAC	GRK, MRG	cavalry
320	Orcynii	GD	MAC	MAC, MRG, ASN	cavalry, maneuver
319	Cretopolis	GD	MAC, MRG	MAC, MRG	cavalry, hvy inf., terrain
317	Coprates	MG	MAC, MRG	MAC	heavy infantry, cavalry
317	Paraetacene	GD	MAC, MRG, ASN	MAC, MRG	cavalry
316	Gabene	GD	MAC, MRG, ASN	MAC, MRG	cavalry
316	Amphipolis II	MG	MRG	MAC, MRG	light infantry, cavalry
315	Aphrodisias	MG	MRG	MRG	heavy infantry
314	Hebrus River	GD	MAC, MRG	ILY	cavalry, heavy infantry

Date	Battle	SZ	Winner(s)	Loser(s)	Decisive Factor(s)
313	Epirus I	GD	MAC	EPR	heavy infantry
313	Epirus II	GD	MAC	EPR, AET	heavy infantry, cavalry
313	Callantia	MN	MAC, MRG	SCY	light inf., cavalry, form.
313	Haemus P. II	MN	MAC, MRG	THR	heavy infantry, terrain
312	Gaza	GD	MAC, EGY, MRG	MAC, MRG	cavalry
312	Eurymenae I	MG	EPR	MAC, MRG	heavy infantry
312	Eurymenae II	GD	MAC, MRG	EPR	heavy infantry
312	Apollonia	GD	GRK, ILY	MAC, MRG	heavy infantry
312	Galeria	MN	MRG	SYL, SCG	heavy infantry
311	Ecnomus Hill	GD	CAR	SYR, MRG	hvy inf., cavalry, SA
310	White Tunis I	GD	SYR, MRG	CAR	heavy infantry
309	Anapus Valley	GD	MRG (SYR)	CAR	heavy infantry, SA
309	White Tunis II	GD	SYR, MRG	CAR	heavy infantry
308	Zuphones Ter.	GD	SYR, MRG	CAR, SYE	heavy infantry
307	Syracuse	GD	SYR, MRG	SCG	heavy infantry
307	Carthage/Mid.	GD	CAR	SYR, MRG	heavy infantry, SA
307	Carthage/Inter.	GD	CAR	SYR, MRG	heavy infantry, SA
307	Acragas III	GD	SYR, MRG	SCG	heavy infantry
307	Carthage	GD	CAR	SYR, MRG	heavy infantry, terrain
306	C. Salamis III	GD	MAC, MRG	MRG	heavy infantry
305	Torgium	GD	SYR, MRG	SCG	hvy inf., man., SA, ter.
301	Ipsus	GD	MAC, MRG, ASN	MAC, MRG, ASN	cavalry, heavy infantry

3: Heavy Infantry Losses and Point/Cause of Formation Failure*

Symbols   Explanation

PF	Point of failure within the losing formation
RW	Failure on the right wing
LW	Failure on the left wing
SW	Failure on a single, undesignated wing
BW	Failure on both wings
CT	Failure in formation center
FR	Failure among the front ranks
RR	Failure among the rear ranks
MR	Failure among the middle ranks
SR	Failure at both sides and rear
CF	Failure on flank of a column

***PF** (point of failure) is that area of a battle formation that first decisively gives way to the enemy. **Cause of Failure** is the primary method used by the victors in overcoming their enemy at the Point of Failure. Figures for **HL/HT** (heavy infantry losses/heavy infantry total) are either derived from historical reports or represent the author's estimates (with mean averages for ranges). HL/HT are usually stated in round numbers and include no auxiliaries (those not ranked in the main formation), whether mounted or on foot. Note that light-armed men are included if they were part of an integrated main battle formation such as that used by the Persian kardakes. Front fighting is shock (hand-to-hand)/missile combat along the leading edge of the battlefront. Othismos is pushing by a formation file to apply forward pressure at the leading edge of the battlefront. Envelopment is the act of defeating a wing of an opposing linear battle array (or both wings in the case of a double envelopment), either turning around its end or the adjacent interior when the end is defeated. Offsetting envelopments occur when opposing armies each are successful on one wing and the battle is not subsequently resolved decisively.

Appendix 3

DR   Drawn result
HL/HT   Heavy infantry losses (deaths)/total heavy infantry manpower (includes light-armed men when in single, integrated formation as per Persian kardakes)
<50   Less than 50 killed (i.e. 0–49)
<100   Less than 100 killed (i.e. 50–99)
*   Number includes at least some quantitative input from historical source(s)
**   Losing side also carried out a turn/envelopment on one wing

Date	Battle	PF	HL/HT Winner	HL/HT Loser	Cause of Failure
400	Cyrene I	RW	250/5,000*	2,500/5,000*	front fighting
400	Colchis	CT	<50/8,000*	250/5,000	front fighting
400	Metropolis	FR	<50/8,000*	500/5,000	front fighting
400	Calpe Har. I	SR	0/0	400*/400*	double envelopment
400	Calpe Har. II	SR	0/0	392*/400*	double envelopment
400	Calpe Har. III	FR	<50/4,500*	600/6,000	front fighting
399	Bithynia	BW	0/0	185*/200*	double envelopment
398	Cyllene	FR	<50/400	<50/500	front fighting
395	Pactolos R.	FR	<50/11.000*	0/0	front fighting
395	Sardis I	RR	<100/11,000*	5,000*/24,000	surprise attack
395	Dascyleium	FR	0/0	100*/500*	front fighting
395	Haliartus	FR	200/4,000	200/4,000	surprise attack
395	Naryx I	LW	500*/3,000*	1,000*/2,000	envelopment
394	Nemea R.	LW	1,100*/18,500*	2,800*/24.000*	envelopment **
394	Coronea II	LW	600/15,000*	1,750/15,000*	envelopment **
394	Messana II	LW	200/4,500	500*/4,500	envelopment
394	Taruomenium	FR	0/0	600*/7,500	front fighting
393	Abacaene	FR	150/8,000	800*/8,000	front fighting
392	L.W. Corinth	LW	430/3,150*	1,000*/5,000*	envelopment **
390	Lechaion	FR	<50/1,000	250*/600*	front fighting
390	Methymna	FR	<50/1,350	100/1,100	front fighting
389	Laus River	SR	200/27,000	7,000/10,000	surprise attack
389	Elleporus Riv.	FR	400/15,000*	5.000/20,000	surprise attack
389	Acarnania	FR	<100/6,500*	300*/2,500	front fighting
389	Cremaste	CF	0/0	280*/900*	surprise attack
388	Tripyrgia	CF	<50/800*	350*/1,000	surprise attack
386	Citium	LW	150/8,000	600/8,000	envelopment
385	Mantinean Pl.	LW	200/4,000	250/2,500	othismos, envelopment
384	Pyrgi	FR	<100/2,000	150/2,000	front fighting
382	Olynthus I	RW	150/12,000	150/8,000	envelopment
381	Olynthus II	LW	300/8,000	1,200/12,000	front fighting
379	Plat-Thebes R.	FR	0/0	20*/500	front fighting
378	Cithaeron Pass	BW	0/0	100/120*	double envelopment
378	Thespiae	LW	200/7,000	500/5,000	envelopment
377	Cabala	LW	750/15,000	1,500/15,000	envelopment
377	Graos Stethos	FR	100/2,100	150/2,000	front fighting
376	Cronium	LW	750/15,000	2,800/14,000	front fighting
376	Tanag. III	RW	100/7,000	900/4,000	othismos, envelopment
375	Tegyra	RW	<50/500	100/1,000	othismos, envelopment
374	Phlius	FR	100/2.000	300*/2,000	front fighting
373	Mendes. M.	BW	100/2,225	750/2,500	double envelopment
373	Corcyra Cem.	LW	100/2,000	225/1,500	envelopment
371	Leuctra	RW	300*/6,000	1,000*/8,000	othismos, envelopment
371	Tegea II	FR	<50/1,500	100/1,700	front fighting
371	Elymia	FR	<50/1,000	0/0	front fighting
370	Deum	SR	150/4,000*	1,100*/1,100*	double envelopment
370	Tegeatis Pass	RW	<100/6,000	200*/1,000	othismos, envelopment
369	Amyclae	BW	600*/13,000	200/4,700	double envelopment

Date	Battle	PF	HL/HT Winner	HL/HT Loser	Cause of Failure
369	Corinth	FR	0/0	<100/300*	front fighting
369	Sicyon Plain	SW	<50/1,500	70*/1,500	envelopment
368	Phlius Crossing	FR	<50/450	<100/900	front fighting
368	Tearless Battle	LW	0*/4,000	2,000/7,000	front fighting
368	Pherae Road	FR	100/8,000	0/0	front fighting
367	Cappadoc. Nw.	FR	1,000*/15,000*	4,000/32,000	front fighting
366	Corinthian G.	FR	<50/350	100/500	front fighting
365	Lasion	FR	<50/5,000	200/700*	front fighting
365	Ellis-Cyllene	FR	<100/5,000	125/2,500	othismos
365	Cromnus	FR	<50/2,500	<50/3,500	othismos
364	Cynosceph. I	FR	500/10,000	3,000/10,000	front fighting
364	Olympus	LW	250/5,000	700/7,000	othismos, envelopment
362	Mantinea II	BW	1,500/20,000* (DR)	1,800/18,000* (DR)	offsetting envelopments
361	Cilician Gate	FR	750/15,000	4,000/32,000	front fighting
360	Egyptian Can.	FR	100/8,000	2,000/16,000	othismos
359	Methone	CF	0/0	225/3,000	surprise attack
358	Paeonia	BW	<50/8,000	0/0	front fighting
358	Lyncus Plain	LW	200/8,000	2,000/7,000	envelopment
357	Ortygia	SW	74*/4,000	800*/6,000	envelopment
357	Chios	FR	100/4,000	100/4,000	front fighting
357	Pherae I	LW	200/10,000	500/4,000	envelopment
356	Crenides	BW	<100/9,000	0/0	front fighting
356	Grabaea	LW	200/8,000	1,900/6.500	envelopment
356	Odrysia I	BW	<100/11,000	0/0	front fighting
356	Phaedriades	LW	<50/2,000	400/1,500	envelopment
356	Amphissa I	CF	<50/450	20*/450	surprise attack
356	Amphissa II	FR	<50/450	<50/450	front fighting
355	Argolas	FR	100/8,000	250/4,000	othismos
355	Neon	RW	250/10,000	2,400/8,000	othismos, envelopment
355	Phyrgia I	FR	750/15,000	1,800/16,000	othismos
355	Sardis II	SW	650/16,000	2,500/12,500	envelopment
355	Tmolos Camp	RR	200/10,000	2,000/14,000	surprise attack
354	Pherae II	FR	300/14,000	800/8,000*	front fighting
354	Pherae III	FR	300/15,000	300/13,000	front fighting
354	Crescent Hills	BW	100/14,000	3,000/12,000	surprise attack
354	Hermeum	LW	200/10,000	500/7,000	othismos, envelopment
354	Phrygia II	FR	200/15,000	3,000/32,000	othismos
354	Phrygia III	LW	<50/8,000	6,500/26,000	othismos, envelopment
353	Crocus Plain	LW	500/20,000*	6,000*/16,000*	envelopment
353	Pagasae	FR	100/4,000	250/3,000	othismos
352	Orchomenos	RW	150/7,000	900/7,500	envelopment
352	Cephissus R.	RW	150/6,000	600/2,000	envelopment
352	Coronea III	BW	<50/1,000	<100/400	double envelopment
352	Naryx II	FR	<100/5,000	500/6,000	surprise attack
352	Orneai I	FR	100/7,000*	200*/4,000	othismos
352	Orneai II	FR	300/7,000*	350/14,000	front fighting
352	Telphusa	FR	<50/1,000	100/450	front fighting
352	Messenia I	FR	<50/1,000	100/450	front fighting
352	Messenia II	FR	<50/1,000	100/450	front fighting
352	Messenia III	FR	300/6,500	400/6,500	front fighting
348	Olynthus III	LW	200/20,000	500/10,000	othismos, envelopment
348	Olynthus IV	LW	200/19,000	2,500/9,000	othismos, envelopment
348	Tamynae	FR	200/4,000	400/4,000	front fighting
347	Hyampolis	SW	<50/1,000	<100/1,000	envelopment
347	Coronea IV	FR	<50/1,000	100/1,000	front fighting

Appendix 3

Date Battle	PF	HL/HT Winner	HL/HT Loser	Cause of Failure
347 W. Boeotia	FR	<50/1,000	<100/1,000	front fighting
345 Sidon	LW	200/16,000	650/16,000	othismos, envelopment
345 Ardiaea	LW	300/16,000	1,000/8,000	envelopment
344 Pelusium	FR	<50/1,000	<50/1,000	front fighting
344 Nile W. Bank	BW	100/5,000	3,000/5,500	double envelopment
344 Syracuse-Leon.	FR	300/7,000	3,000/6,250	front fighting
341 Crimisus River	FR	200/11,000*	10,000/24,000	surprise attack
341 Odrysia II	BW	200/20,000	0/0	front fighting
341 Odrysia III	BW	200/19,000	0/0	front fighting
340 Strymon Valley	BW	<100/5,000	0/0	front fighting
339 Hierae	SR	<50/1,000	400/400	surprise attack
339 Dobruja Plain	FR	<50/18,000	0/0	front fighting
339 Hister Valley	FR	0/0	<50/18,000	front fighting
338 Damyrias R.	FR	<100/3,000	800/4,000	front fighting
338 Abolus River	SW	150/6,000	2,500*/6,000	envelopment
338 Chaeronea	LW	750/30,000*	2,000/28,000*	envelopment
335 Haemus Pass I	RW	<50/5,500*	0/0	envelopment
335 Lyginus River	FR	40*/11,500*	0/0	front fighting
335 Hister River	FR	<50/4,000*	0/0	front fighting
335 Pelion	FR	350/11,500*	700/8,000	front fighting
334 Granicus River	BW	<100/12,000*	4,000*/8,000*	double envelopment
334 Sagalassos	FR	<50/12,000	0/0	front fighting
333 Issus	LW	450/15,000*	10,000/32,000	envelopment
333 Memphis	FR	<100/4,000	400/5,000	othismos
331 Gaugamela	LW	1,200*/15,000*	4,000/15,000*	envelopment
331 Vs Corrhagus	LW	250,6,000	1,000/4,000	othismos, envelopment
331 Megalopolis	LW	3,500*/27,000*	5,300*/16,000*	othismos, envelopment
330 Aria	FR	0/0	0/0	front fighting
329 Jaxartes	FR	0/0	<50/3,000*	front fighting
329 Alexandria Es.	BW	0/0	0/0	double envelopment
329 Polytimetos R.	SR	0/0	1,200/1,200	double envelopment
328 Xenippa	FR	<50/3,000*	0/0	front fighting
328 Gabai	FR	<50/3,000*	0/0	front fighting
327 Pareitakene	SW	<50/6,000*	0/0	front fighting
327 Aspasia	SW	<50/23,000*	0/0	front fighting
327 Massaka	FR	<50/15,000*	0/0	front fighting
327 Bazira	FR	<50/2,500	0/0	front fighting
327 Ora	FR	<50/3,000	0/0	front fighting
326 Hydaspes R.	BW	500*/6,000*	0/0	double envelopment
323 Up. Satrapies	BW	400/9,000*	1,500/15,500	double envelopment
323 Plataea II	FR	100/13,000	350/7,000	othismos
323 Therm.-Lamia	SW	300/21,500	3,000/13,000*	othismos, envelopment
323 Odrysia IV	FR	<100/4,000	0/0	front fighting
322 Lamia	RW	400/15,000	400/16,500*	front fighting
322 Rhamnus	RW	100/5,000	1,200/4,500	othismos, envelopment
322 Cappadocia	LW	200.21,000	4,000/10,000	othismos
322 Crannon	FR	130*/40,000*	500*/20,000*	front fighting
322 Cyrene II	SW	<100/7,500*	500/6,000	othismos, envelopment
322 Cyrene III	SW	<100/6,000	500/6,000	envelopment
322 Cyrene IV	FR	250/8,000	2,500/8,000	front fighting
322 Cyrene V	LW	300/14,000	1,200/12,000	front fighting
321 Hellespont	RW	0/17,000	0/17,000	double envelopment
321 Aetolia	SW	100/4,000	1,000/4,000	envelopment
321 Thessaly	LW	200/12,000	3,000/12,000	envelopment
320 Orcynii	BW	300/12,000*	8,000*/17,000	double envelopment

Heavy Infantry Losses and Point/Cause of Formation Failure

Date	Battle	PF	HL/HT Winner	HL/HT Loser	Cause of Failure
319	Cretopolis	BW	0/32,000*	0/12,500	double envelopment
317	Coprates	BW	<100/4,000	2,500/3,000*	double envelopment
317	Paraetacene	LW	3,700*/28,000*	540*/7,000*	envelopment
316	Gabene	LW	5,000*/22,000*	1,200/6,000*	envelopment
316	Amphipolis II	BW	100/3,000	2,400/4,000	double envelopment
315	Aphrodisias	CF	<50/2,000	900/3,000	surprise attack
314	Hebrus River	LW	300/15,000	2,000/8,000	othismos, envelopment
313	Epirus I	LW	100/8,000	250/5,000	othismos, envelopment
313	Epirus II	LW	100/8,000	250/5,000	othismos, envelopment
313	Callantia	FR	<50/4,000	0/0	front fighting
313	Haemus P. II	FR	<50/4,000	0/0	front fighting
312	Gaza	LW	<50/15,000*	2,500/11,000*	envelopment
312	Eurymenae I	RW	100/4,000	500/4,000	othismos, envelopment
312	Eurymenae II	LW	150/6,000	500/4,000	othismos, envelop.
312	Apollonia	LW	250/10,000	1,600/8,000	envelopment
312	Galeria	LW	100/2,250	250/2,250	envelopment
311	Ecnomus Hill	SW	500*/15,500	7,000*/12,000*	surprise attack
310	White Tunis I	LW	500*/13,000*	3,000*/30,000*	envelopment
309	Anapus Valley	CF	<50/2,400*	1,500/15,000	surprise attack
309	White Tunis II	FR	250/12,000	3,000/30,000	front fighting
308	Zuphones Ter.	LW	350/7,500	1,000/9,000	envelopment
307	Syracuse	LW	300/6,000*	1,500/8,000*	envelopment
307	Carthage/Mid.	CF	150/6,000*	3,000/6,000	surprise attack
307	Carthage/Inter.	SW	500/6,000*	6,000*/6,000*	surprise attack
307	Acragas III	FR	250/6,000	500/6,000	front fighting
307	Carthage	FR	500/18,000	8,000*/12,000	othismos
306	C. Salamis III	LW	300/12,000	1,000*/9,000	front fighting
305	Torgium	SW	300/6,000	3,000/16,000	envelopment
301	Ipsus	RW	<50/50,000	500/38,000	cavalry, heavy infantry

Bibliography

Ancient Sources

Aelian. (c. A.D. 165–235): Eclectic Roman writer whose works include historical anecdotes relevant to 4th century B.C. Greek warfare. (*Historical Miscellany [Varia Historia]*, Cambridge, MA: Harvard University Press, 1997).

Aeneas Tacticus. (early-mid 4th century B.C.): likely Aeneas of Stymphalus, a general of the Arcadian League in the Peloponnese. A writer of several military studies relevant to the 4th century B.C. his only surviving work deals with sieges. ("Aeneas on the Defense of Fortified Positions" in *Aeneas Tacticus, Asclepiodotus, Onasander*, Cambridge, MA: Harvard University Press; 1928, p. 26–228).

Aeschines. (390–314 B.C.): Athenian orator, statesman and soldier whose surviving speeches shed light on 4th century events. (*The Speeches of Aeschines*, 1919, Cambridge, MA: Harvard University Press).

Anaximenes. (c. 380–320 B.C.): Historian from Lampsacus who composed works now lost on the history of Greece, Philip II and Alexander III.

Aristobulus. (late 4th-early 3rd century B.C.): Historian who served with Alexander and wrote of his reign, a major influence on Arrian.

Aristotle. (384–322 B.C.): Greek philosopher and tutor of Alexander the Great whose works provide details relevant to warfare in 4th century B.C. Greece. ("The Athenian Constitution" in *Aristotle: Athenian Constitution, Eudemian Ethics, Virtues and Vices*, Loeb Classical Library, Cambridge, MA: Harvard University Press, 1952, p. 2–186; *Politics*, New York: Oxford University Press, 1995).

Arrian. (late 1st-early 2nd century A.D.): Lucius Flavius Arrianus, Greek-born Roman soldier and historian and author of an account of the career of Alexander the Great. (*Arrian, The Campaigns of Alexander*, New York: Penguin Books, 1971 [A. Selincourt trans]; *The Landmark Arrian, The Campaigns of Alexander*, New York: Pantheon Books, 2010 [P. Mensch trans]).

Asclepiodotus. (late 2nd-late 1st century B.C.): Philosopher and writer of an academic work on military affairs relevant to the 4th century B.C. ("Tactics" in *Aeneas Tacticus, Asclepiodotus, Onasander*, Cambridge, MA: Harvard University Press; 1928, p. 244–341).

Callisthenes. (d. c. 327 B.C.): Greek historian whose works are now lost, but provided some information on 4th century B.C. events to surviving histories, including that of Diodorus.

Curtius. (early 1st century A.D.): Quintus Curtius Rufus, Roman soldier and historian and author of a history of Alexander the Great in Latin. (*Quintus Curtius Rufus, The History of Alexander*, New York: Penguin Books, 1984).

Demosthenes. (c. 384–322 B.C.): Greek orator, statesman and soldier whose speeches yield details on 4th century B.C. events. (*Demosthenes, Vol. I–III*, Cambridge, MA: Harvard University Press, 1926-1930).

Didymus. (1st century B.C.): Prolific compiler of ancient writings whose works contributed important details on 4th century B.C. history via scholiasts.

Diodorus Siculus. (c. 90–20 B.C.): Sicilian historian whose surviving works include coverage of events in the 4th century B.C. Greek world. (*Library of World History*, Vol. I–XII, Cambridge, MA: Harvard University Press, 1933-1967).

Dionysius of Halicarnassus. (late 1st century B.C.): Greek historian whose surviving works detail early Roman history and shed light on events in Grecian Italy. (*Roman Antiquities*, Vol. I–VII, Cambridge, MA: Harvard University Press, 1937-1950).

Ephorus of Cyme. (c. 405–330 B.C.): Greek historian whose work is now lost, but was used as a source on 4th century B.C. events in the surviving works of others, including Diodorus and Plutarch.

Frontinus. (c. A.D. 35–103): Roman writer whose collection of military stratagems includes many from 4th century B.C. Greek warfare. (*Stratagems*, Cambridge, MA: Harvard University Press, 1925).

Herodotus. (480s-420s B.C.): Greek historian often referred to as the 'father of history' whose work culminates at the end of the Persian invasion of 480-79 and offers insights on military affairs relevant to the 4th century B.C. (*The Landmark Herodotus, The Histories*, New York: Pantheon Books, 2007).

Hyperides. (389–322 B.C.): Athenian statesman and orator whose surviving speeches contribute details on 4th century B.C. events.

Isocrates. (436–338 B.C.): Greek orator whose speeches provide detail on 4th century B.C. events. (*Isocrates, Vol. I–III*, Cambridge, MA: Harvard University Press, 1928-1945).

Justin. (late 2nd century A.D.): Likely M. Iunianius Iustinus, a Roman writer who summarized the now lost work of Pompeius Trogus, which came largely from Greek sources and included coverage of 4th century B.C. (*Justin, Epitome of the Philippic History of Pompeius Trogus*, Atlanta, GA: Scholars Press, 1994)

Livy. (59 B.C.– A.D. 17): Roman historian whose works include useful detail on the warfare among the Italians relevant to the 4th century B.C. (*Livy, Rome and Italy, Books VI–X of The History of Rome from its Foundation*, New York: Penguin Books, 1982).

Lysias. (c. 458–380 B.C.): Athenian speech writer whose surviving works shed light on events in the early 4th century B.C. (*Lysias*, Cambridge, MA: Harvard University Press, 1930).

Nepos, Cornelius. (c. 110–24 B.C.): Roman writer whose works included biographies of a number of 4th century B.C. Greek generals. (*Cornelius Nepos*, Cambridge, MA: Harvard University Press, 1984).

Onasander. (1st century A.D.): Greek philosopher who wrote a treatise on generalship that includes information relevant to 4th century B.C. warfare. (*Aeneas Tacticus, Asclepiodotus, Onasander*, Cambridge, MA: Harvard University Press, 1928, p. 368–527).

Oxyrhynchus Historian. (late 5th-early 4th century B.C.): Greek writer known from fragments found in Oxyrhynchus (in Egypt) whose work includes coverage of the early 4th century B.C. (*Hellenica Oxyrhynchia*, London: Aris and Phillips, 1988).

Pausanias. (2nd century A.D.): Greek travel writer whose works include numerous historical details relevant to the 4th century B.C. (*Description of Greece, Vol. I–V*, Cambridge, MA: Harvard University Press, 1918–1955).

Philistus. (c. 430–356 B.C.): Sicilian historian whose work is now lost, but provided source material to Timaeus and, hence, to Diodorus on events in Sicily during the 4th century B.C.

Philochoros. (c. 340–261 B.C.): Greek historian whose works survive only in fragments, specialized in the history of Attica and was a major source for other Hellenistic chronographers.

Plato. (c. 429–347 B.C.): Greek philosopher and student of Socrates whose works contain information regarding 5th and 4th century B.C. military matters. (*Laches and Charmides*, Cambridge, MA: Hackett, 1973).

Plutarch. (c. A.D. 45–120): Greek philosopher and writer whose works include biographies of Greek military figures of the 4th century B.C. (*Plutarch's Lives, Vol. I and II*, New York: Modern Library, 2001).

Polyaenus. (2nd century A.D.): Macedonian rhetorician whose collection of stratagems include many from the 4th century B.C. Greeks. (*Polyaenus, Stratagems of War, Vol. I and II*, Chicago: Ares, 1994).

Polybios. (c. 208–124 B.C.): Greek historian whose works on the 3rd and 2nd centuries B.C. also shed some light on 4th century B.C. military practices. (*The Histories, Vol. I–VI*, Cambridge, MA: Harvard University Press, 1922–1927).

Ptolemy. (367/66–282 B.C.): Macedonian general and Hellenistic ruler of Egypt (as Ptolemy I) whose lost history of Alexander heavily influenced other historians.

Strabo. (c. 64 B.C.–post A.D. 21): Most important geographer of ancient times, whose works supply numerous details about places and events in the 4th century B.C. (*Geography*, 8 vol. Cambridge, MA: Harvard University Press, 1917–1932).

Theopompus. (1st century B.C.): Roman historian whose work relevant to the 4th century B.C. drew from earlier Greek sources and is lost save for summarization in Justin.

Thucydides. (c. 460–c. 400 B.C.): Greek historian and Athenian general whose work on the Peloponnesian Wars of the 5th century B.C. has relevance for 4th century B.C. military affairs as well. (*The Landmark Thucydides, A Comprehensive Guide to the Peloponnesian War*, New York: Pantheon Books, 1996)

Timaeus. (c. 350–260 B.C.): Greek historian whose work, now lost, sourced the surviving works of others, including Diodorus and Plutarch.

Xenophon. (c. 430–350 B.C.): Greek general and historian whose works include coverage of Greek wars down to 362 B.C. (*Hellenica, Vol. I and II*, Cambridge, MA: Harvard University Press, 1918–1921; *The Landmark Xenophon's Hellenika*, New York: Pantheon Books, 2009; *Anabasis*, Cambridge, MA: Harvard University Press, 1922; *Agesilaus* in *Scripta Minora*, Cambridge, MA: Harvard University Press, 1925).

Modern References

Adcock, F.E. 1957: *The Greek and Macedonian Art of War*. Berkeley: University of California Press.

Akurgal, E. 1985: *Ancient Civilizations and Ruins of Turkey*. Ankara, Turkey: Haset Kitabevi.

Allen, L 2005: *The Persian Empire*. Chicago: University of Chicago Press.

Anderson, J.K. 1970: *Military Theory and Practice in the Age of Xenophon*. Berkeley: University of California Press.

_____. 1974: *Xenophon*. New York: Charles Scribner's Sons.

Anson, E.M. 2010: "The Asthetairoi: Macedonia's Hoplites" in E. Carney and D. Ogden (eds.), *Philip II and Alexander the Great, Father and Son, Lives and Afterlives*. Oxford: Oxford University Press.

Ashley, J.R. 1998: *The Macedonian Empire, The Era of Warfare Under Philip II and Alexander the Great 359–323 BC*. Jefferson, NC: McFarland.

Austin, M. 2006: *The Hellenistic World from Alexander to the Roman Conquest, A Selection of Ancient Sources in Translation, 2d Ed*. Cambridge: Cambridge University Press.

Balfour, D. 2010: "Boeotian Crack Troops, The Theban Sacred Band," in *Ancient Warfare* Vol. 4, Issue 3 (June 2010).

Barber, R. 1990: *Blue Guide Greece*. New York: W.W. Norton.

Bardunias, P. 2011: "Storm of Spears and Press of Shields, the Mechanics of Hoplite Battle," in *Ancient Warfare, Special Issue 2011: The Battle of Marathon*.

Bar-Kochva, B. 1976: *The Seleucid Army, Organization and Tactics in the Great Campaigns*. Cambridge: Cambridge University Press.

Bennet, M., ed. 1998: *Dictionary of Ancient and Medieval Warfare*. Mechanicsburg, PA: Stackpole Books.

Bennett, B., and Roberts, M. 2008: *The Wars of Alexander's Successors 323–281 BC, Volume I: Commanders*

& Campaigns. Barnsley, South Yorkshire: Pen & Sword Military.

Best, J.G.P. 1969: *Thracian Peltasts and their Influence on Greek Warfare.* Groningen, Netherlands: Wolters-Noordhoff.

Billows, R.A. 1990: *Antigonos the One-Eyed and the Creation of the Hellenistic State.* Berkeley: University of California Press.

Bosworth, A.B. 2002: *The Legacy of Alexander; Politics, Warfare, and Propaganda under the Successors.* Oxford: Oxford University Press.

_____. 2010: "The Argeads and the Phalanx," in E. Carney and D. Ogden (eds.), *Philip II and Alexander the Great, Father and Son, Lives and Afterlives.* Oxford: Oxford University Press.

Bradford, A.S. 2001: *With Arrow, Sword and Spear, A History of Warfare in the Ancient World.* New York: Barnes and Noble.

Bruce, I.A.F. 1967: *An Historical Commentary on the Hellenica Oxyrhynchia.* Cambridge: Cambridge University Press.

Buckley, T. 1996: *Aspects of Greek History, 750–323 b.c. A Source Book Approach.* London: Routledge.

Burn, A.R. 1968: *The Warring States of Greece.* New York: McGraw-Hill.

Bury, J.B. 1900: *A History of Greece to the Death of Alexander.* London: MacMillan.

Carey, B.T., J.B. Allfree and J. Cairns. 2005: *Warfare in the Ancient World.* Barnsley, South Yorkshire: Pen & Sword Military.

Cartledge, P. 1987: *Agesilaos and the Crisis of Sparta.* Baltimore: Johns Hopkins University Press.

_____. 1989: "Hellenistic Sparta," in P. Cartledge and A. Spawforth, *Hellenistic and Roman Sparta: A Tale of Two Cities.* London: Routledge.

_____. 2002: *Sparta and Lakonia, A Regional History 1300 to 362 BC,* 2d ed. London: Routledge.

_____. 2003: *The Spartans–The World of the Warrior-Heroes of Ancient Greece.* New York: Overlook Press.

Caven, B. 1990: *Dionysius I, War-Lord of Sicily.* New Haven, CT: Yale University Press.

Cawkwell, G.L. 2002: "The Decline of Sparta," in M. Whitby (ed.), *Sparta.* London: Routledge.

_____. 2005: *The Greek Wars: The Failure of Persia.* New York: Oxford University Press.

Cernenko, E.V., A. McBride, and M.V. Gorelik. 1983: *The Scythians 700–300 BC.* Oxford: Osprey.

Champion, J. 2009: *Pyrrhus of Epirus.* Barnsley, South Yorkshire: Pen & Sword Military.

_____. 2010: *The Tyrants of Syracuse, War in Ancient Sicily, Volume I: 480–367 BC.* Barnsley, South Yorkshire: Pen & Sword Military.

Chaniotis, A. 2005: *War in the Hellenistic World.* Malden, MD: Blackwell.

Chrimes, K.M.T. 1949: *Ancient Sparta: A Re-examination of the Evidence.* Manchester: Manchester University Press.

Cole, P.J. 1981: "The Catapult Bolts of 'IG' 22 1422," in *Phoenix* Vol. 35, No. 3 (Autumn, 1981):216–219.

Connolly, P. 1981: *Greece and Rome at War.* London: Macdonald Phoebus.

Cook, J.M. 1983: *The Persian Empire.* New York: Barnes and Noble.

Cornell, T.J. 1995: *The Beginnings of Rome–Italy and Rome from the Bronze Age to the Punic Wars (c. 1000–264 BC).* London: Routledge.

Cummings, L.V. 1940: *Alexander the Great.* New York: Grove.

Daly, G. 2002: *Cannae, The experience of battle in the Second Punic War.* London: Routledge.

Delbruck, H. 1990: *Warfare in Antiquity: History of the Art of War, Vol. I.* Lincoln: University of Nebraska Press.

Dodge, T.H. 1890: *Alexander: A History of the Origin and Growth of War from the Earliest Times to the Battle of Ipsus, Vol. I and II.* London: Greenhill Books.

Ducrey, P. 1986: *Warfare in Ancient Greece.* New York: Schocken Books.

Engels, D.W. 1978: *Alexander the Great and the Logistics of the Macedonian Army.* Berkeley: University of California Press.

English, S. 2008: "Hoplite or Peltast? Macedonian 'Heavy' Infantry," in *Ancient Warfare* Vol. 2, Issue 1 (Feb.–Mar. 2008): 32–35.

_____. 2011: *The Field Campaigns of Alexander the Great.* Barnsley, South Yorkshire: Pen & Sword Military.

Errington, R.M. 1993: *A History of Macedonia.* New York: Barnes and Noble.

Farrokh, K. 2007: *Shadows in the Desert, Ancient Persia at War.* Oxford: Osprey.

Ferrill, A. 1992: "Alexander in India" in Cowley, R. (ed.), *Experience of War.* New York: W.W. Norton.

Fields, N. 2008: *Tarentine Horsemen of Magna Graecia 430–190 BC.* Oxford: Osprey.

Fine, J.V.A. 1983: *The Ancient Greeks, A Critical History.* Cambridge, MA: Harvard University Press.

Fitzhardinge, L.F. 1985: *The Spartans.* London: Thames and Hudson.

Forrest, W.G. 1969: *A History of Sparta 950–192 BC.* New York: W.W. Norton.

Freeman, E.A. 1894: *The History of Sicily from the Earliest Times, Vol. IV.* Oxford: Clarendon Press.

Fuller, J.F.C. 1987: *A Military History of the Western World: Volume I, From the Earliest Times to the Battle of Lepanto.* New York: Da Capo.

_____. 1989: *The Generalship of Alexander the Great.* New York: Da Capo.

Gabriel, R.A. 2010: *Philip II of Macedonia, Greater than Alexander.* Washington, DC: Potomac Books.

_____, and Boose, D.W. 1994: *The Great Battles of Antiquity, A Strategic and Tactical Guide to Great Battles that Shaped the Development of War.* Westport, CT: Greenwood.

_____, and Metz, K.S. 1991: *From Sumer to Rome–The Military Capabilities of Ancient Armies.* New York: Greenwood.

Gaebel, R.E. 2002: *Cavalry Operations in the Ancient Greek World.* Norman: University of Oklahoma Press.

Garlan, Y. 1995: "War and Peace," in J. Vernant (ed.), *The Greeks.* Chicago: University of Chicago Press.

Goldsworthy, A.K. 1996: *The Roman Army at War, 100 BC–AD 200.* Oxford: Clarendon.

Grainger, J.D. 2007: *Alexander the Great Failure, The Collapse of the Macedonian Empire.* London: Hambledon Continuum.

Grant, M. 1987: *The Rise of the Greeks*. New York: Collier Books.

Green, P. 1990: *Alexander to Actium: The Historical Evolution of the Hellenistic Age*. Berkeley: University of California Press.

_____. 1991: *Alexander of Macedon, 356–323 b.c.: A Historical Biography*. Berkeley: University of California Press.

Griffith, G.T. 1984: *The Mercenaries of the Hellenistic World*. Chicago: Ares.

Hamilton, C.D. 1979: *Sparta's Bitter Victories, Politics and Diplomacy in the Corinthian War*. Ithaca, NY: Cornell University. Press.

Hammes, T.X. 2004: *The Sling and the Stone, On War in the 21st Century*. St. Paul, MN: Zenith.

Hammond, N.G.L. 1994: *Philip of Macedon*. Baltimore: Johns Hopkins University Press.

_____. 1997: *Alexander the Great*. Chapel Hill: University of North Carolina Press.

Hanson, V.D. 1989: *The Western Way of War: Infantry Battle in Ancient Greece*. New York: Alfred A. Knopf.

_____. 1999: *The Soul of Battle, From Ancient Times to the Present Day, How Three Great Liberators Vanquished Tyranny*. New York: The Free Press.

_____. 2008: "New Light on Ancient Battles," in *Military History Quarterly* Vol. 20, No.2: 28–35.

_____, ed. 1993: *Hoplites: The Classical Greek Battle Experience*. London: Routledge.

Harding, P. 1985: *Translated Documents of Greece & Rome, Vol. 2, From the End of the Peloponnesian War to the Battle of Ipsus*. Cambridge: Cambridge University Press.

Head, D. 1982: *Armies of the Macedonian and Punic Wars 359–148 BC*. Goring-by-Sea, UK: Wargames Research Group.

_____. 1992: *The Achaemenid Persian Army*. Stockport, UK: Montvert.

Heckel, W. 1992: *The Marshals of Alexander's Empire*. London: Routledge.

_____. 2002: *The Wars of Alexander the Great 336–323 BC*. Oxford: Osprey.

_____. 2006: "Callisthenes and the Alexander Sarcophagus," in *Historia* Band 55/4: 385–396.

_____, C. Willekes, and G. G. Wrightson. 2010: "Scythed Chariots at Gaugamela: A Case Study," in E. Carney and D. Ogden (ed.), *Philip II and Alexander the Great, Father and Son, Lives and Afterlives*. Oxford: Oxford University Press.

_____, and R. Jones. 2006: *Macedonian Warrior, Alexander's Elite Infantryman*. Oxford: Osprey.

Higgins, M.D., and R.A. Higgins. 1996: *A Geological Companion to Greece and the Aegean*. London: Gerald Duckworth & Co.

Hodkinson, S. 1993: "Warfare, Wealth, and the Crisis of Spartiate Society," in J. Rich and G. Shipley (eds.), *War and Society in the Greek World*. London: Routledge.

Holt, F.L. 2005: *Into the Land of Bones, Alexander the Great in Afghanistan*. Berkeley: University of California Press.

Hornblower, S. 1991: *The Greek World, 479–323 b.c.* (rev. ed.). London: Routledge.

_____, and A. Spawforth (eds.). 1996: *The Oxford Classical Dictionary*. New York: Oxford University Press.

Howatson, M.C. (ed.) 1991: *The Oxford Companion to Classical Literature*. New York: Oxford University Press.

Hutchinson, G. 2000: *Xenophon and the Art of Command*. London: Greenhill Books.

Jones, A.H.M. 1967: *Sparta*. Oxford: Blackwell.

Koepfer, C. 2009: "The Sarissa," in *Ancient Warfare*. Vol. 3, Issue 2 (Apr.–May 2009).

Lazenby, J. 1990: "Hoplite Warfare," in J.W. Hackett ed., *Warfare in the Ancient World*. New York: Facts on File.

Lee, J.W.I. 2007: *A Greek Army on the March, Soldiers and Survival in Xenophon's Anabasis*. Cambridge, MA: Cambridge University Press.

Liddell, H.G., and R. Scott. 1996: *Greek-English Lexicon–With a Revised Supplement*. New York: Oxford University Press.

Lonsdale, D.J. 2004: *Alexander the Great, Killer of Men, History's Greatest Conqueror and the Macedonian Art of War*. New York: Carroll and Graf.

Macadam, A. 1993: *Blue Guide, Sicily*. New York: W.W. Norton.

Marsden, E.W. 1969: *Greek and Roman Artillery, Historical Development*. New York: Oxford University Press.

McCartney, E.S. 1923: *(Greek and Roman) Warfare by Land and Sea*. Boston: Marshall Jones Company.

McGregor, M.F. 1987: *The Athenians and Their Empire*. Vancouver: University of British Columbia Press.

McInerney, J. 1999: *The Folds of Parnassos, Land and Ethnicity in Ancient Phokis*. Austin: University of Texas Press.

Meiggs, R. 1992: *The Athenian Empire*. Oxford: Clarendon.

Mitchell, S. 1996: "Hoplite Warfare in Ancient Greece," in A.B. Lloyd ed., *Battle in Antiquity*. London: Gerald Duckworth & Co.

Montagu, J.D. 2000: *Battles of the Greek and Roman Worlds: A Chronological Compendium of 667 Battles to 31 BC, from the Historians of the Ancient World*. London: Greenhill Books.

Munn, M.H. 1993: *The Defense of Attica, The Dema Wall and the Boiotian War of 378–375 b.c.* Berkeley: University of California Press.

Ober, J. 1991: "Fortress Attica," in *Journal of Military History* Vol. 3, No. 2: 26–35.

Oldfather, W.A. 1928: "Notes on the Translations," in *Aeneas Tacticus, Asclepiodotus, Onasander*. Cambridge, MA: Harvard University Press.

Olmstead, A.T. 1948: *History of the Persian Empire*. Chicago: University of Chicago Press.

Park, M. 2007: "The Silver Shields, Philip's and Alexander's Hypaspists," in *Ancient Warfare* Vol. 1, Issue 3 (Oct.–Nov. 2007): 25–28.

_____. 2009: "The Fight for Asia, the Battle of Gabiene," in *Ancient Warfare* Vol. 3, Issue 2 (Apr.–May 2009): 29–36.

_____. 2012: "Doomed Men of Distinction, the Battle of Gaza, 312 B.C.," in *Ancient Warfare* Vol. 5, Issue 6 (Feb. 2012): 26–33.

Parke, H.W. 1933: *Greek Mercenary Soldiers: From the Earliest Times to the Battle of Ipsus*. Chicago: Ares.

Penrose, J. (ed.), 2005: *Rome and Her Enemies, an Empire Created and Destroyed by War.* Oxford: Osprey.

Pietrykowski, J. 2009a: *Great Battles of the Hellenistic World.* Barnsley, South Yorkshire: Pen & Sword Military.

_____. 2009b: "In the School of Alexander, Armies and Tactics in the Age of the Successors," in *Ancient Warfare* Vol. 3, Issue 2 (Apr.–May 2009): 21–28.

Powell, A. 1991: *Athens and Sparta: Constructing Greek Political and Social History from 478 BC.* London: Routledge.

Prevas, J. 2002: *Xenophon's March into the Lair of the Persian Lion.* Cambridge, MA: Da Capo.

_____. 2004: *Envy of the Gods: Alexander the Great's Ill-fated Journey Across Asia.* Cambridge, MA: Da Capo.

Pritchett, W.K. 1965: "The Battle of Leuktra," in *Studies in Ancient Greek Topography, Part I.* Berkeley: University of California Press.

_____. 1969: *Studies in Ancient Greek Topography, Part II (Battlefields).* Berkeley: University of California Press.

_____. 1971–1991: *The Greek State at War*, 5 vols. Berkeley: University of California Press.

_____. 1982: "Battle of Tegyra in 375 B.C,". in *Studies in Ancient Greek Topography, Part IV (Passes)*. Berkeley: University of California Press.

Rahe, P.A. 1981: "The Annihilation of the Sacred Band at Chaeronea," in *American Journal of Archaeology*, Vol. 85, No. 1 (Jan. 1981): 84–87.

Ray, F.E. 2009: *Land Battles in 5th Century B.C. Greece: A History and Analysis of 173 Engagements.* Jefferson, NC: McFarland.

Rodgers, W.L. 1937: *Greek and Roman Naval Warfare: A Study of Strategy, Tactics, and Ship Design from Salamis (480 BC) to Actium (31 BC).* Anapolis, MD: Naval Institute Press.

Roy, J. 2004: "The Ambitions of a Mercenary," in Fox, R.L. (ed.), *The Long March, Xenophon and the Ten Thousand.* New Haven, CT: Yale University Press.

Rusch, S.M. 2011: *Sparta at War; Strategy, Tactics, and Campaigns 550–362 BC.* London: Frontline Books.

Sabin, P. 2007: *Lost Battles, Reconstructing the Great Clashes of the Ancient World.* London: Hambledon Continuum.

Sage, M.M. 1996: *Warfare in Ancient Greece, A Sourcebook.* London: Routledge.

Santosuosso, A. 1997: *Soldiers Citizens and the Symbols of War–From Classical Greece to Republican Rome 500–167 b.c.* Boulder, CO: Westview Press.

Schmitz, M. 2011: "Skill at Arms, Professionalism in the Army of Alexander the Great," in *Ancient Warfare* Vol. 5, Issue 1 (Feb. 2011): 42–41.

Schwartz, A. 2009: *Reinstating the Hoplite; Arms, Armour and Phalanx Fighting in Archaic and Classical Greece.* Stuttgart, Germany: Franz Steiner Verlag.

Sekunda, N. 1987: *The Ancient Greeks: Armies of Classical Greece, 5th and 4th Centuries BC.* Oxford: Osprey.

_____. 1989: "The Persians," in J.W. Hackett (ed.), *Warfare in the Ancient World.* New York: Facts on File.

_____. 1998: *The Spartans.* Oxford: Osprey.

_____. 2006: *Hellenistic Infantry Reforms in the 160's BC.* Gdansk, Poland: Foundation for the Development of Gdansk University.

_____, and S. Chew, 1992: *The Persian Army 560–330 BC.* Oxford: Osprey.

_____, and R. Hook, 2000: *Greek Hoplite 480–323 BC.* Oxford: Osprey.

_____, and A. McBride, 1984: *The Army of Alexander the Great.* Oxford: Osprey.

_____, and J. Warry, 1998: *Alexander the Great, His Armies and Campaigns 334–323 BC.* Oxford: Osprey.

Shipley, D.R. 1997: *A Commentary on Plutarch's Life of Agesilaos, Response to Sources in the Presentation of Character.* Oxford: Clarendon.

Shipley, G. 2000: *The Greek World after Alexander 323–30 BC.* London: Routledge.

Smith, A., IV. 2011: "The Anatomy of Battle, Testing Polybios' Formations," in *Ancient Warfare* Vol. 5, Issue 5 (2011): 41–45.

Snodgrass, A.M. 1967: *Arms and Armour of the Greeks.* Ithaca, NY: Cornell University Press.

Souza, P. de, W. Heckel and L. Liewellyn-Jones. 2004: *The Greeks at War, From Athens to Alexander.* Oxford: Osprey

Spence, I.G. 1993: *The Cavalry of Classical Greece, a Social and Military History with Particular Reference to Athens.* Oxford: Clarendon.

Stylianou, P.J. 1998: *A Historical Commentary on Diodorus Siculus Book 15.* New York: Oxford University Press.

Strauss, B.S. and J. Ober, 1990: *The Anatomy of Error: Ancient Military Disasters and Their Lessons for Modern Strategists.* New York: St. Martins Press.

Talbert, J.A. (ed.). 1991: *Atlas of Classical History.* London: Routledge.

Tarn, W.W. 1984: *Hellenistic Military and Naval Developments.* Chicago: Ares.

Thompson, M. 2007: *Granicus, 334 b.c.: Alexander's First Persian Victory.* Oxford: Osprey.

Tomlinson, R.A. 1972: *Argos and the Argolid from the End of the Bronze Age to the Roman Occupation.* Ithaca, NY: Cornell University Press.

Tritle, L.A. (ed.). 1997: *The Greek World in the Fourth Century: From the Fall of the Athenian Empire to the Successors of Alexander.* London: Routledge.

Trundle, M. 2004: *Greek Mercenaries, from the Late Archaic Period to Alexander.* Routledge, London.

Tuplin, C. 2004: "The Persian Empire," in Fox, R.L. (ed.), *The Long March, Xenophon and the Ten Thousand.* New Haven, CT: Yale University Press.

Ueda-Sarson, L. 2001a: "Macedonian Unit Organization," in *Slingshot* 214: 35–38 and 216: 16–19.

_____. 2001b: "Ariian 4.4.6–7 and Macedonian Combined-arms Tactics Against the Skythians," in *Slingshot* 219: 26–28.

_____. 2002a: "The Evolution of Hellenistic Infantry, Part 1: The Reforms of Iphikrates," in *Slingshot* 222: 30–36.

_____. 2002b: "The Evolution of Hellenistic Infantry, Part 2: Infantry of the Successors," in *Slingshot* 223: 23–28.

_____. 2003: "Alexander's Elephants" in *Slingshot* 227: 19–22.

_____. 2004: "Tarantine Cavalry," in *Slingshot* 236: 21–25.
Warmington, B.H. 1960: *Carthage*. London: Robert Hale.
Warry, J. 1980: *Warfare in the Classical World*. London: Salamander Books.
_____. 1991: *Alexander 334–323 BC: Conquest of the Persian Empire*. Oxford: Osprey.
Waterfield, R. 2006: *Xenophon's Retreat: Greece, Persia and the End of the Golden Age*. Cambridge, MA: Belknap Press.
_____. 2011: *Dividing the Spoils: The War for Alexander the Great's Empire*. Oxford: Oxford University Press.
Webber, C. 2001: *The Thracians 700 BC–AD 46*. Oxford: Osprey.
Wees, H. 1995: "Politics and the Battlefield," in A. Powell (ed.), *The Greek World*. London: Routledge.
Whitby, M. 2004: "Xenophon's Ten Thousand as a Fighting Force," in Fox, R.L. (ed.), *The Long March, Xenophon and the Ten Thousand*. New Haven, CT: Yale University Press.
Wilcken, U. 1967: *Alexander the Great*. New York: W.W. Norton.
Worley, L.J. 1994: *Hippeis, the Cavalry of Ancient Greece*. Boulder, CO: Westview Press.
Worthington, I. 2008: *Philip II of Macedonia*. New Haven, CT: Yale University Press.
Yalichev, S. 1997: *Mercenaries of the Ancient World*. London: Constable.

Index

Abrocomas 144
Abydos 35, 72, 143
Acarnania 22, 34–35, 37, 43, 52, 55, 131, 135, 138, 182, 191, 194
Achradina 125
Acragas 195, 199–201
Adaios 113–114
Adranum (Hadranum) 124–125
Aeacides 191–192, 194
Aemilius Paullus 90
Aeschrion 201
Aetna 97
Aetolia 34, 143, 175, 181–182, 191
Agatharchus 197, 199–201, 203
Agathocles 195–203
agema 142, 145–147, 153, 165, 187
Agesilaos II 18–20, 22, 24–26, 32–38, 51–52, 54–55, 61, 65, 67–68, 70, 81, 83, 118, 156, 172, 212
Agesipolis 36, 41–42, 46
Agios Athanasios Tomb 90
Agis II 17–18
Agis III 150–151, 156–158
Agrianians 93, 140–142, 145–146, 148, 153, 158–160, 165–169
Albania 128, 191
Alcetas (brother of Perdiccas) 181, 183–184
Alcetas (exile) 40
Aleisthenes 21
Alexander (of Epirus) 194
Alexander (of Pherae) 73–74, 79–80
Alexander (of Sparta) 69
Alexander (son of Polyperchon) 190–191
Alexander II 73, 87–88
Alexander III (The Great) 3, 37, 89–90, 93, 96, 103, 129–175, 177–181, 185, 192, 195, 204, 206, 208–209, 211–212
Alexander IV 194
Alexander Mosaic 76, 89, 150, 155
Alexandria (Egypt) 151
Alexandria (India) 159
Alexandria Eschate 101
Amanic Gate 147
Ambracia 138
Amphipolis 100, 102, 129, 139–140, 190
Amphissa 104–105, 131
Amyntas (mercenary) 150–151
Amyntas (satrap) 163, 165
Amyntas III 43

Anabasis 11
Anapus River 199
anastrophe 60, 68
Anaxibius 15, 35
Antalcidas 5, 31, 36–38, 41, 50, 61, 67
Antander 197
Antigonus 174, 181–194, 203–209
antilabe 8, 90
Antiochus 206
Antipater 129, 139, 143, 151, 156–158, 162, 171, 174, 176–179, 181–187, 208
Antiphilus 177–179
Aornos Rock 167
Apollonides 182–183
Arabian Peninsula 171
Arcadian League 68, 73
Ardiaei 128, 129
Argaios 86–87
Ariarathes 177–178
Ariston 6
Aristonous 190
Aroandus (Orontes) 115–117
Arrhabaeus 89
Arrhidaeus (Macedonian officer/satrap) 182, 184
Arrhidaeus (Philip III) 164, 174, 177, 185
Arsaces 100
Artabazus (Persian commander) 77
Artabazus (satrap) 110, 114–117
Artaxerxes II 11, 19, 36, 60, 72, 75, 77, 143
Artaxerxes III (Ochus) 114, 117, 122–124, 143
Artaxerxes IV (Arses) 143
Aspasii 166
aspis 8–10, 76, 89–91, 93
Assakanians 166, 167
Assyria 39, 147, 172
asthetairoi 163–164
Atheas 130
Athenian League/Confederation, Second 50, 99, 135
Attica 35, 51, 204
Attinas 162
Autariates 141
Autocles 73

Babylon 11, 171, 174, 178–179, 181–182, 185, 190, 193–194, 209
Babylonian spearmen 153
Bactria/Bactrians 154–155, 159, 162–166, 168

baivarabam 16
Balearic Islands 196
Bardylis 95–96, 102, 141
Barsine 195
Belesys 123
Bessos 159, 161
Boeotian League 51, 55, 62, 135
Boeotian War 21
Boibeis, Lake 109
Bormilcar 198, 201
Bosporus 15, 36, 185
Boumelos River 151
Byzantium 13–15, 99, 129, 140

Cadmea 43, 49, 53, 138, 142
caetrati 72
Calibius 67
Callantia 192
Callias (of Athens) 33
Callias (of Chalcis) 121
caltrops 193, 206
camels 152
Campanians 97
Cape Bon 197
Cappadocia 76–77, 144, 172, 177–178, 182, 184
Cappadocian infantry 178
Caprima 191
Cardia 212
Caria/Carians 16–18, 39, 76, 99, 115, 144, 146, 191
Carystus 122
Cassander 184–185, 190–192, 194–195, 203–205
Catana 123
Celts 72–73, 126, 141, 147, 202
Centriporis 102–104
Cephision 119
Cephissus River/Valley 106, 117, 131–132, 135
Cersobleptes 102–103, 129
Chabrias 35, 49–52, 54–55, 71, 99–100
Chaereas 61
Chalcidian League 42–44, 103, 119–121
Chalcidice 38, 42–43, 102, 120, 128
Chalcis 121, 204
Charidemus 120
The Charioteers 52
chariots (Carthaginian/Libyan) 126, 127, 180, 198, 200, 202
chariots (Cyprian) 8
chariots (Cyrenean) 8–9, 201–202
chariots (Indian) 168–169

Index

chariots (Persian) 19–20, 152–153, 155, 205, 208
Cheirisophus 11–14
Chersonese 116, 120
Chios 99
Cilicia 39, 123, 147, 151, 155, 174, 178, 181, 185–185, 190–191, 193
Cilician Gate 77–78, 147
Cilles 194
Cissidas 73
Cithaeron, Mount 50, 54
Cleander 14–15
Cleandridas 84
Cleinius 124
Cleitus (of Illyria) 141
Cleitus (satrap) 184
Cleombrotus 49–51, 54–55, 61–64, 66–67
Cleopatra 181
Coenus 163, 167, 169
Colchians 11–12
Copais, Lake 20, 34, 56, 117
Corcyra 60–61, 131
Corrhagus 156–157
Cos 99
Craterus 164, 168–171, 174, 178, 181
Cratevas 190
Crenides 102–103, 111, 129
Crete/Cretans 22, 151, 156, 165, 179, 180
Ctesicles 60
Cunaxa 11, 15, 17, 152, 211
cyclosis 36, 63, 82, 84, 136
Cyme 116
Cyreans 16–18
Cyrene/Cyrenaica 6, 8–10, 179–180, 200–202, 211
Cyrus (The Younger) 11, 15, 211
Cyrus I (The Great) 75
Cythera 31
Cyzicus 143, 184

Dahae 165, 168
Dardanians 86, 95, 103, 141
Darius I 165
Darius III 75, 143–144, 147–148, 150–156, 158–159, 172
Dascyleium 18–19, 152
Datames 76–78, 88, 114
dathabam 17
Deinias 194
Deinocrates 195–196, 199, 201, 201
dekka 94
Delian League 50
Delium 56, 63, 66, 84
Delphi 61, 90, 104–105, 107, 111, 114, 117, 130, 137
Delphic Amphictyony 104, 131
Dema Wall 51
Demetrius 181, 187, 193–194, 203–208
Demophilus 195–201–202
Demophon 49
Dercyllidas 16–17
Derdas 43–45
Diodochi *see* Successors
Dion 97–99
Dionysius I (The Great) 26–30, 38, 40–41, 46–48, 72, 137–138
Dionysius II 48, 96–99, 124–125, 138

doratismos 7
Dorians 6
dory 7
doryphoroi 89
dunasteia 43

Ecbatana 159, 188
Egypt 6, 12, 39, 51, 58–59, 76–77, 83–84, 88, 93, 122–124, 151, 171, 174, 180–183, 190–191, 194, 204, 209
Egyptian spearmen 59
elephants 152, 164, 166, 168–170, 183–184, 186–189, 193, 204–208
Entella 125
envelopment 9–10
Epaminondas 3, 38, 42, 48, 51, 53, 57, 62–65, 67–68, 70–72, 74, 76, 81–85, 88, 90, 92, 107, 117, 130, 188, 193, 210–211
eparitoi 69, 73, 78–79
Ephesos 16, 18, 116, 146, 205, 207
epibatai 34–36
epicraty 195
Epidaurus 71, 191
epilektoi 6
Epipolae 97, 125, 199
Epirus 40, 96, 191, 191, 194, 208
epomides 8
Erigyius 160
Eritrea 121
Etruscans (Tyrrhenians) 41, 97, 202
Euboa 22, 81, 104, 121, 131, 192, 204
Eudamidas 42–44
Eumachus 201
Eumenes 174, 177–178, 181–190, 193, 209, 212
Euphron 74
Eupolemus 191
Euryelus 199
Eurymedon River 34, 147
Euthymus 127
Euxine (Black) Sea 11, 13, 30, 36, 100, 130, 192, 205
Evagoras I 38–40
exeligmos Lakonikos 76
exeligmos Makedonikos 76
exeligmos Persikos 76

falcata 97
field work(s) 31–32, 36, 50, 71, 98, 147
Fort of Camels 182
The Four Hundred 167

Gela 196–197, 199, 202
Getae 140–141, 162–163
Glaucias (of Illyria) 191
Glaucias (of the Taulantians) 141–142
Gordian 147
Gorgidas 52
Gorgopas 36
Grabus 102, 104
Gylis 26

Haemus, Mount 139–140, 192
Hamilcar (opponent of Agathocles) 196–197, 199

Hamilcar (opponent of Timoleon) 125
hamippoi 101, 106, 108, 110–112
Hanno (commander Carthage/Midlands) 201
Hanno (commander White Tunis I) 198
harnmost 14
Harpalus 171, 179
Hasdrubal 125
hazarabam 17, 75
hegemon 137
Helisson 119
Hellespont 16, 24, 35, 129, 143, 181, 183–184, 192, 204–205
Hellespontine Phrygia 184
Heloris 28, 30
helots 6, 15, 22, 23, 42, 70
Hephaestion 165
Heracleides (mercenary) 97
Heracleides (son of Agathocles) 203
Heracles 195
hetairoi (companions) 89
Hicetas 124–128
Himeras River 196–197
Himilco (Carthaginian commander 396) 7
Himilco (commander at Carthage/Interior) 201
Himilco (son of Magon) 47–48
hippakontistai 163
hippeis 8
Hister (Danube) River 130, 139–142
hopla 7
hoplite (Greek) 6–8
hoplite (Persian) *see* kardakes
hypaspists 89–90
hyperaspizantes 89,
Hyperides 135
Hypermenes 61
Hyrkania/Hyrkanian (Caspian) Sea 159

Iberians 73, 97, 126
Illyrians 40, 43, 96, 102–103, 128, 130, 139, 141–142, 205
Indian Caucasus (Hindu Kush) 159, 165
Indian Ocean 170
Indus River 165, 167, 169–171
Ionia 15–18, 20, 24, 26, 31, 34, 36, 83, 137, 146, 205
Iphicrateans 88
Iphicrates 3, 31–33, 35, 37, 58–61, 71, 76–77, 85, 88, 91, 136–137, 211–212
iphicratides 59
Ischolaus 69
Ismenias 21–22
Italian League 29–30

Jason 67, 96, 101
javelin 8
Jordan 194

Kachales River 106–107
Kallidromon, Mount 106
kardakes 76–77, 83, 114–116, 123, 148–150, 152–153, 171

King's Peace *see* Peace of Antalcidas
knemides 8

Lacedaemon (Laconia) 5
Laches 134
Lacrates 123–124
Lamia/Lamian War 176–177, 179
Langaros 141
League of Corinth 137, 139, 142, 156
Leonidas 77, 134
Leonnatos 165–166, 176–178, 209
Leontiades 43
Leontini 97, 124–125
Leosthenes 175–176
Leptines (brother of Dionysius I) 30, 48
Leptines (general of Agathocles) 201–202
Lesbos 34, 99, 147
Letodorus 175
Leucadia 127
Leucas 131
Liby-Phoenicians 46
Lilybaeum 125, 127
lochos 11
Locris (Italian) 29
Locris (Opuntian/eastern) 20–21, 25, 81, 106–107, 117
Locris (Ozolian/western) 22, 43, 56, 69, 105, 117, 131
Lucanians 29–30
Lycians/Pamphylians 163, 187, 193, 205, 207
Lyciscus 194
Lycurgus 38
Lydia 15, 115–116, 146, 184, 205
Lyppeius 102–104
Lysander 18, 20–21
Lysanoridas 49
Lysimachus 174, 176, 190, 192, 194, 204–206, 208

Macedonian Shield Monument 90
machaira/kopis 8, 97
Maedi 129
Magon 28, -29, 46–47
mahouts 169, 193, 206
Malea 21–22, 24
Malians 73
Mamercus 128
Mantias 87
Marakanda 161
Marathon 115
Mardia/Mardians 159
Massagetae 162–163
Mausolus 99
Mazaeus 123
Media 159, 174, 185–186, 188
Megalopolis 71, 118, 119, 156–158, 198
Megara 32, 43, 71, 131, 139, 191, 203
Memnon (of Pharsalus) 182
Memnon (of Rhodes) 143–144, 146–147, 172
Memnon (Thracian governor) 156
Memphis 124, 151
Menelaus 203–204
Mentor 123–124
Messenians 6, 9–10, 71, 73, 118–119

Methone 87–88, 104, 136, 151, 172
Micion 177
Miletus 146
Mnaseas 118
Mnasicles 180
Mnasippis 60–61
Molossians 40, 96
mora 21, 55–56, 65
Mossynoecians 12
Myriandros 147
Mysia 114–115
Mytilene 34, 147

Nectanebos 59, 123–124
Neon (of Sparta) 13–14
Neoptolemus 181
Nicanor 193
Nicostratus 123–124
Nora 183–184

oblique order 65, 90
Old Mercenaries 153
Olpae 37
Olympias 76, 185, 190
Olympiodoros 204
Onomarchos 107–114, 117–118, 136, 211–212
Ophellas 180, 200
Ortygia 97–99, 125
Oscans 29, 97
othismos 8–9, 11, 31, 36, 59, 63–64, 66, 90–91, 95, 98, 106, 151, 183
Ouxioi 158

Paeonians 93–95, 103, 129, 145, 150, 153, 155
Pammenes 88, 106, 110, 116–117, 210
Pandionis 121
panoply 8
Panthoedas 54–55
pantodapoi 178, 180–181, 183, 186–188, 193, 205–206
Paphlagonians 144, 147
Parmenio 102–103, 129, 139–140, 142–143, 155–156, 160
Parnassos, Mount 104, 106
Pasiphilus 195–196
Pasitigris River 185
Peace of Antalcidas 5, 36–38, 41, 50, 61, 67
pectorales 29
Peithon 174
Pelion, Mount 110
Pelopidas 38, 41–42, 48–49, 51, 55–57, 63, 65, 68, 73–74, 79, 80, 84–85, 210–211
Peloponnese 6, 9, 13, 17, 20, 22, 31, 34, 38, 41, 50–51, 53–54, 56, 58, 67, 69, 71–72, 74–75, 78, 80–81, 85, 118–119, 122, 143, 156–157, 175, 190–191, 194, 204
Peloponnesian League 5–6, 43
peltasts 8
pelte 8, 87, 94
Pelusium 123, 151, 182
Peneius River 178
Perdiccas (Macedonian general) 165, 174–175, 177–178, 180–183
Perdiccas III 86, 92

Perinthus 129
perioeci (Spartan) 6, 41–43, 46, 60, 66, 69, 70
Persepolis 159, 186
Persian Gate 159
petrobolous mechane/mechanical bow 26, 110, 142, 144, 151
Peuce (Pine) Island 140
Peucetes 185
pezhetairoi (foot companions) 89, 146
Phalaeccus 118, 122
phalangite 91
phalanx (Doric) 9, 76, 101, 136, 140, 210–211
phalanx (Macedonian) 9, 76, 89, 91, 93, 108–109, 136, 210–211
Pharnabazus (Persian general) 147
Pharnabazus (satrap) 14–17, 19, 20, 59, 60
Pharsalus 182
Phayllos 108, 114, 117–118
Philine 164
Philip (brother of Cassander) 191–192
Philip II 3, 59, 86–96, 100–104, 106–111, 113–114, 117, 120, 122, 128–139, 141, 143, 145, 157, 160, 162, 164, 171, 172, 174, 192, 209, 210–212
Philiscus 72
Philistus 97
Philomelus 104–107
Philon 175
Philonides 195–196
Philotas 140, 160
Phocion 121–123, 177
Phoebidas 42–43, 53, 56
Phoenicia 58, 123, 150–151, 185, 194, 205
Phrataphernes 160
Phyrgia 14, 114, 144, 146–147, 193
pikeman (Iphicratean) 58–59
pikeman (Macedonian) *see* phalangite
Pinaros River/valley 147–149
Pisidians 146, 183–184
Pitane 143
Pithon 175, 182, 185
Plataea (479) 134
Pleistarchus 205
Plutarch (of Eritrea) 121
polis 5
polje 42
Polybiades 46
Polycleitus 191
Polycles 182
Polyperchon 181–182, 184–185, 190–191
Polytropus 68
ponor 42
porpax 8, 90
Porus 168–170, 172
Praxitas 31–32
Prepelaus 204–205
Propontis (Sea of Marmara) 143
Proxenus 67
pteruges 8
Ptolemaeus 191
Ptolemy (general/satrap/king) 143,

146, 159, 165–166, 174, 180–182, 184, 190–191, 193–194, 200, 205–206, 208–209
Ptolemy (usurper) 73
Pydna 90, 100
Pyrrhus (of Epirus) 208

rafts 141
Rhizon Gulf 128
Rhodes 99, 143, 204
Roxanne 164, 174, 190, 194

Sabaces 151
Sacred Band (Carthage) 126–127, 198
Sacred Band (Thebes) 52, 55, 63, 66, 71, 82, 84, 131–135
salpinx 9
Sardinia 46
Sardis 18–19, 37, 114–115, 146, 205
sarissa 88, 90–91, 109, 112, 130, 163–164
sarissophoroi/prodromoi 139
Satibarzanes 159–160
satrap/satrapy 15
sauroter/styrax 7
scutum 29
Scythians 130, 155, 161–162, 192
Seleucus 174, 182, 185, 190, 193–194, 204–208
Selymbia 129
Seuthes II 15–16
Seuthes III 176, 192
Shipka Pass 139
Sibyna spear 95
Sicans 26, 48
Siculi 26, 28–29, 195
Silver Shields 164, 184–190
Sippas 176
The Six Hundred 195
Smicres 13
Social War 99–100, 106, 114–115
Socrates 134
Sogdian Rock 164

Sogdiana 159–164
Spaectaria 37
spartiates 5, 66
Sparto-Boeotian War 75, 78
Sphodrias 50–51
Spitamenes 161–163
Stageira 120
Stasenor 160
Stasippus 67
strategos 195
Stratocles 133
Struthus 33
Strymon Valley 129
Successors 174
Susa 158, 185–186
Synnada 205
Syria/Palestine 93, 123, 162, 193–194, 204, 208
Syrian Gate 147
Syrmus 140

Tachos 83
taka 75–76
Tarantine 187–188, 193
Taulantians 141–142
Taxila 165, 167
taxis 33, 92
Telesphorus 194
Tempe 139
The Ten Thousand 73
Teres 129
Termessos 146
Teucer 194
Theodotus 191
Therimachus 34
Thermopylae 20, 77, 114, 134, 175–176, 191
Thessalian League 96, 100, 106–107, 111–112
Thessaly 20–21, 24, 46, 72–73, 78–79, 81–82, 88, 92–93, 96, 100–101, 103, 106–108, 110–111, 114, 119–120, 144, 157, 176, 178, 182, 190–191, 205

Thibron (mercenary) 179–180
Thibron (Spartan general) 15, 33
thorax 8
Thrace 13, 15–16, 24, 58, 86–88, 92–93, 102–103, 129–130, 139, 143–144, 147, 156–157, 174–176, 192, 208, 212
Thrasybulus 34
The Three Hundred 78, 80, 157
Thuria/Thurians 29, 84
Tigris River 152, 185, 193
Timoleon 124–128, 195
Tissaphernes 15–19
Tithraustes 19–20
Tomb of Judgment 90
toxeuma 104
toxon 8
toxotai 8
transport/carrier (horse) 40–41, 72, 125
transport/carrier (troop) 41, 72, 99, 196–197
Triballi 130, 140–141
trireme 35, 39–40, 60, 62, 72, 85, 99–100, 111, 124, 126, 177, 191, 196–197
Trojan Pass 139
Tyre 39, 151

Ukraine 5, 130
Upper Satrapies 174–175, 182, 185–186, 188, 190, 205–206

Xenodicus 199, 201–202
Xenophon 3, 11–19, 21–22, 24–25, 32–35, 37, 212
Xerxes 77
xiphos 8
Xyston 92

Zacynthus 97
Zuphones 200